D1176036

A Spirit Capable

A Spirit

The Story of Commonwealth Edison

Capable

John Hogan

THE MOBIUM PRESS/Chicago 1986

Library of Congress Catalog Card Number: 86-061287

ISBN: 0-916371-04-2

Designed by Mobium Corporation for Design and Communication,
Chicago, Illinois.

Printed and bound at R. R. Donnelley & Sons Company,
Crawfordsville, Indiana.

For Mike and Kath

Commonwealth Edison provides electricity to 3.0 million customers (8 million people) in Chicago and northern Illinois. Extending into 25 counties, Edison's 11,525 square mile service area covers about one-fifth of Illinois but includes 70 percent of its population.

Contents

Illustrations

Preface

When George Travers, whose memory of people and events in the history of Commonwealth Edison is one of the wonders of the modern corporate world, asked me on behalf of the company to write its 100-year history, I didn't need to think it over. Responding in a proposed treatment, I said that such a project would be "exciting, challenging—even a bit awesome." The task proved every bit of that, but also richly rewarding and one hell of a lot of fun.

For nearly two-and-a-half years, writing this book gave me something to do between phone calls from reporters as well as an alternative in the evening and on weekends to the ball park, racetrack, or favorite watering holes. There is no telling how much money I saved. Poring over the company archives, old photographs, reams of news clippings, virtually every issue of the employe publications, along with related books and pamphlets, and talking with veteran employes heightened my feeling of kinship with the Edison men and women who have gone before, not only the giants of the company, but the rank-and-file as well—the people who read the meters, strung the cable, tended the generating stations, kept the accounts, and performed the countless other tasks associated with supplying the service territory with electricity. I empathized with one William A. Durgin of the Testing Department, who, after undertaking the 25-year history of the company entirely on his own time, declined to continue for fear of 'breaking down in health.' The History Committee subsequently proposed that Durgin work on the project full time at the corporate office while continuing to do as much as possible on his own.

The company never placed me in Durgin's position; George made it clear from the outset that there would be no leave of absence or even work reduction. No matter. Somehow the project inched its way toward completion and probably would not look very much different if I had worked on it exclusively. So my deepest thanks go to George—friend; mentor; executive assistant, office of Edison Chairman and President James O'Connor; and chairman of Edison's Centennial Committee—for his confidence and encouragement. Thanks, too, to Jim O'Connor and my immediate boss, Don Petkus, not only for their confidence but also for allowing me to pursue the project with a free hand. Their only instructions were to do the best job possible.

Rebecca Grill, my colleague in the Communications Services Department, provided invaluable assistance, particularly in researching the role of women in Edison history and selecting the photographs used in the book. The editing of Molly DeSchryver, who spent the summer of 1985 as an intern in our department, greatly improved the first draft and reminded me that even a quarter-century in the news business does not make one immune to misplaced modifiers and other grammatical pitfalls.

Additional thanks go to Rosemary Dolowy of Communications Services, who used the magic of the word processor to transform the seemingly indecipherable pages from my Royal manual, with their countless additions, deletions, and corrections, into readable copy; to Manager of Nuclear Safety Frank Palmer, who reviewed the book for technical accuracy; to Edison Librarian Barbara Kelly and Assistant Librarian Grace Pertell, whom I was never able to stump with a question about a historical fact, a source, or a quotation; to Mike Duba and his staff, keepers of the Edison archives, who guided Rebecca and me through that labyrinth; to Dr. Harold Platt, professor of urban history at Loyola University of Chicago, for his advice and encouragement; and finally to Judy Brady, for sharing the hopes and frustrations of the project from Day One—and for being herself.

J. H.
Chicago, Illinois
January 2, 1986

I believe that man will not merely endure: he will prevail.

He is immortal, not because he alone among creatures has an inexhaustible voice, but because he has a soul, a spirit capable of compassion and sacrifice and endurance.

William Faulkner,
    Speech upon receiving
    the Nobel Prize for
    Literature, Dec. 10, 1950.

I

One

Metropolis
On
The
Prairie

I n November 1878, 11 months before Thomas A. Edison
would finally develop the first practical incandescent electric light bulb, a slender 18-year-old waited for a train on a
dingy platform of London's Metropolitan Underground
Railroad, better known to the locals as "The Sewer."
Looking for something to pass the time while traveling to his job
as a two-dollar-a-week clerk to a London newspaper editor, the
young man bought a copy of an American magazine that contained an article about Edison. He was enthralled, both by the
dawning world of electricity and by the shaggy American genius
who was its foremost developer. It was the sort of otherwise
mundane occurrence, like young George Gershwin at Coney
Island hearing a player piano for the first time, that sets the
course of an individual's life. It was the beginning of a longtime
hero worship—including 12 years as chief assistant to Edison
himself. He would spend another 40 years transforming the
Wizard's principles into an electrical network that functions to
this day as the foundation of modern industry and contemporary
life.

The young man was Samuel L. Insull, the first chairman
of what is now Commonwealth Edison Company, whose Horatio
Alger-like ascent to become the most powerful utility magnate
the world would ever know, and whose ultimate humiliation
and exile would become one of the Greek tragedies of American
business.

Insull's parents were lower-middle-class Victorians. His
father, perennially unsuccessful in the business world, operated
a small dairy in London during Sam's early years, then shuffled
through a succession of jobs, including secretary to a branch of a
national temperance league. Both of Insull's parents were fervent
temperance crusaders, as well as religious zealots and all-around

3

activists, always ready to defend the underdog or espouse an unpopular cause. For many years Insull's mother conducted a shelter for alcoholics. His father was said to be happiest on the platform, saving souls and denouncing Demon Rum. This opposition to drinking rubbed off on Sam—a lifelong teetotaler. He also inherited his father's love of the stump, but instead of preaching temperance, he spent his life extolling the virtues of central station electric power.

Recalling his introduction to the world of Thomas Edison years later, Insull remarked, "At that time, we hardly knew of the existence of the telephone. But few in the world knew anything about electric lighting experiments."

Insull would learn a good deal more about electricity in very short order. Three months after his awakening in the London underground, he lost his job to another young man, a rich man's son who was willing to work for nothing to gain experience. It turned out to be the biggest break of Insull's young life. He answered an ad in the newspaper, and two days later he found himself working as secretary to none other than the London representative of the Thomas A. Edison Company, Colonel George Gouraud, who was in the city to establish an Edison telephone company. When Gouraud set up his first telephone exchange, young Sam manned the switchboard and became the first telephone operator in Europe. Attending the batteries was another young man the world would hear from— George Bernard Shaw.

Insull labored day and night for Gouraud and his associates, and confided his ambition to serve as secretary to Edison himself. He even turned down an attractive offer to join a prominent international banking house in New York.

Edison's man in London was pleased with Insull's work and, in turn, recommended him to the Wizard himself, who was in need of a confidential secretary to assist him in the mammoth task of revolutionizing the world's lighting methods. In December 1879, scarcely two months after he had perfected the light bulb, Edison offered the position to Insull, who, needless to say, leaped at it.

Insull didn't arrive in New York until February 28, 1881. The personal chemistry between the two was evident from the moment Insull was ushered into Edison's office, about 8 p.m.

More than anything else, the two had in common an insatiable appetite for hard work. They immediately plunged into Edison's concerns of the moment—a new lamp factory, new dynamo shops, an underground distribution system. They worked without interruption until past four the next morning.

Samuel L. Insull, company leader from 1892-1932, at the height of his career.

If Insull had worshiped Edison since that day in "The Sewer," their first meeting placed him even more under the spell of the American inventor, as the Englishman later admitted.

"He spoke with very great enthusiasm of the work before him," Insull recalled, "namely, the development of his electric lighting system, and his one idea seemed to be to raise all the money he could with the object of pouring it into the manufacturing side of the lighting business. I remember how extraordinarily I was impressed with him on this account, as I had just come from a circle of people in London who not only questioned the possibility of the success of Edison's invention, but often expressed doubt as to whether the work he had done could be called an invention at all."

Insull confessed that he had no idea what his duties with Edison would be. "I did whatever he told me," he noted, such as buying the Wizard's clothes, answering his correspondence, writing his checks, fetching his umbrella, and generally serving as Edison's Man Friday.

But Edison soon realized that his young assistant was ready for headier stuff. Insull quickly became the operating chief of the Edison system with full charge of the Wizard's business affairs. He held Edison's power of attorney and handled the financing. Though almost totally deaf and a man of few words, Edison did not lack character perception. He quickly saw in Insull many of his own traits, particularly the desire and ability to work longer and harder than even he himself did, and an unflagging sense of personal devotion. At the same time, however, Insull managed to compensate—brilliantly—for one major shortcoming of the Edison persona, a lack of organizational skills. Insull was a genius of order and efficiency.

Insull soon became caught up in the project which at that time commanded the full energies of Edison and the men around him—construction of the world's first central station generating plant. On September 4, 1882, Edison threw the switch at the Pearl Street generating station in New York, and the world's first electric light and power system was energized. Although only one generator could be used because of speed and control problems, it was sufficient to light 400 lamps belonging to 85 customers. The idea of central station power, whose gospel Insull would preach for the next 50 years, had begun, though it would be slow in taking off.

Edison had intended the Pearl Street Station to be a showpiece that would encourage additional central stations everywhere. The startup of the station was widely publicized, but not soon imitated. In this regard it failed. A marvelous achievement, everyone agreed, but investors held onto their money. Chicago would not see its first central station until 1888. Edison returned to electrical manufacturing and dispatched Insull upstate to Schenectady to build a plant. As general manager, Insull oversaw expansion from an operation employing 250 workers to one with 6,000. This plant would later become the nucleus of the General Electric Company.

Pearl Street Station went into service less than a year before the opening of an internationally famous neighbor, the Brooklyn Bridge, one of the grandest engineering achievements of the 19th century. Edison's company submitted a bid to install incandescent lighting on the bridge, but the contract went to an arc light manufacturer who offered to supply 70 lamps at a lower cost than Edison proposed. That turn of events notwithstanding, Edison, like many thousands of others, "was enormously fascinated by the bridge and spent hours watching its progress," according to *The Great Bridge* by David McCullough. The author says Edison took "some extraordinary movies of the bridge, among the first he ever made, of the final weeks of construction."

The night before the official opening of the Brooklyn Bridge, the arc lights were tested for the first time. People aboard ferry boats in the East River "were suddenly astonished to behold overhead a great display of light across the bridge from (New York to Brooklyn)," McCullough related. "Whether they knew it or not, they were looking up at the future—steel and electricity."

Soon after Insull had arrived in this country, a friend in London cabled him and suggested that he "had been in America just about long enough to be able to draw the long-bow as well as any of those Yankees with whom [he] had been associating." If Insull's friend facetiously thought that Easterners ran around with bows and arrows, what must he have thought of Midwesterners?

Chicago, where Sam Insull would settle a little more than a decade later, had been incorporated for only half a century. In the early 1830s, Chicago was a frontier outpost. Its residents numbered only about 50, living in a few dwellings clustered around the second Ft. Dearborn. The original fort had been burned and plundered by Indians during the War of 1812, the culmination of a massacre that claimed the lives of 39 men, 2 women, and 12 children, and which left 20 wounded. Four years later, the Indians ceded to the United States a large strip of land that included Chicago and settled elsewhere.

Lake Michigan, the principal reason for Chicago's location, logically provided an impetus to early growth. With the opening of the Erie Canal in 1825, a new route became available to Easterners looking to migrate West. The Canal linked the Hudson with the Great Lakes and opened an avenue of water to Buffalo, Cleveland, Detroit—and Chicago. Steam navigation on the Great Lakes began in 1833, the year of Chicago's incorporation as a town. Four lake steamers entered Chicago's harbor that year; three years later the number had risen to 400 and would continue to climb until the harbor became a virtual forest of masts. In *Chicago: Growth of a Metropolis*, Harold M. Mayer and Richard C. Wade observe: "Lumber from northern Wisconsin and Michigan, iron from the northern Great Lakes area, men and goods from the East, all moved across the water to the crowded wharves of the (Chicago) river while other vessels carried the grain of the new country to mills in New York and New England. Tonnage entering the harbor jumped from 440,000 in 1844 to over 3 million in 1869. As many as 300 vessels arrived in a single 12-hour period, passing through the drawbridges at a rate of two a minute at peak hours."

Still another body of water was key to the development of the future metropolis on the prairie. The Illinois and Michigan Canal, envisioned by Marquette and Joliet a century and a half earlier, was begun in 1836, and Chicago became a center of construction activity. Additionally, the I&M Canal led to the establishment of 13 permanent communities, including Lemont, Romeoville, Lockport and Joliet, along its 97-mile course which linked Chicago to the Des Plaines, Illinois and, ultimately, Mississippi rivers. Along this narrow, shallow waterway—punctuated by limestone locks, many of which survive today—floated tow boats laden with wheat, corn, pork, lumber and coal on their way to northern and eastern consumers.

Of even greater importance to the development of Chicago, the railroad came in 1848, coincidentally, the year the canal opened. Its beginnings, however, were inauspicious.

The city's first mayor, a real estate speculator and all-around wheeler-dealer named William B. Ogden, 12 years earlier had conceived the idea of a rail line linking Chicago with the wealthy lead-mining town of Galena, Illinois, some 150 miles west. Ogden and his partners laid out the route on paper, but many years elapsed before any track was laid. Ogden soon learned how much more easily he could sell real estate than shares in a proposed railroad. Moreover, the depression of 1837 chilled expansion in general; virtually every leading business person was either wiped out or severely harmed.

8

As the depression slowly lifted, growth resumed, as did plans for the rail line. Finally, on an autumn day in 1848, a third-hand, 11-year-old locomotive named the Pioneer chugged into the city—not from western Illinois, but from the western suburb of Oak Park. The 10-ton Pioneer was the standard bearer of the Galena and Chicago Union Railroad, whose directors made a ceremonial trip from Chicago to Oak Park and back. Nevertheless, it was a triumph for Ogden. A month later, the Pioneer brought in a load of wheat from the Des Plaines River, foretelling the day when Chicago would become the rail and aviation center of the nation. By 1852, four more rail lines had joined the Galena and Chicago Union—two connecting with the East, one with the South, and another with the West. By the time another four years had passed, Chicago was the hub of 10 lines, spanning nearly 3,000 miles of track that brought 38 freight and 58 passenger trains into and out of the city each day.

As rail and water connections multiplied, so, too, did overland routes, strengthening Chicago's ties with the East and West and carrying their share of the flood of people and goods swelling the young metropolis. The newly-invented telegraph provided unprecedented speed of communication with the rest of the country. Gas lighting appeared in the city in 1850; in Quincy, Rock Island, and Springfield in 1854; and in Galena, Ottawa, and Peoria in 1855. The first telephone exchanges arrived in the late 1870s.

The population leaped from about 50 in 1830 to 4,170 in 1837, the year the town became a city. By 1850, the number had grown to nearly 30,000—still not a lot, considering the population would soar to 300,000 in another two decades—but as Mayer and Wade point out, ". . . as the twig was bent, so the tree would grow. Nearly all the elements that characterize the city today were already present. Chicago had become the hub of the major transportation routes, presaging its destiny as the nation's busiest rail and air center. Clybourne's meat-packing plant foreshadowed the day when the town would be called the 'hog butcher to the world.' McCormick's reaper had been on the market just a few years, but farmers already looked for a Chicago trademark on industrial goods. And grain elevators and bulging warehouses signaled a unique connection between the urban merchant and the rich farmlands of the Middle West."

But this, too, would pass away—much of it, anyway—during three incredible days in October 1871. In a bit of understandable hyperbole, *Chicago Tribune* publisher Joseph Medill, in an editorial, called the Great Fire "...a calamity without parallel in the world's history..." More accurate was Medill's observation that Chicagoans had resolved that their city would rise again. Another civic booster, John Stephen Wright, was even more emphatic in the fire's aftermath: "Chicago will have more men, more money, more business within five years than she would have had without the fire."

More than 100 years later, Chicago's recovery from the Great Fire stands as a remarkable, almost unbelievable achievement. The image of the phoenix, rising from its own ashes, has been invoked time and time again. With nearly $200 million in property damage, 100,000 homeless, four square miles gutted, the central business district obliterated, at least 250 dead, the task of rebuilding must have seemed impossible at first to all but the Medills, Wrights and a few others.

But Medill had been correct; before the smoke had barely cleared away, individual business entrepreneurs were setting up shop, thousands of temporary dwellings were erected, and construction of some 200 permanent structures was under way. In retrospect, Chicago learned that it had probably grown too fast for its own good, much of the growth wooden and shoddy. The City Council passed an ordinance banning wooden construction in the downtown area. Aside from minimizing the chances of another catastrophic fire, the new law had at least one side benefit that its authors probably hadn't considered: it brought in a flood of architects, eager to rebuild an entire city in the shape of the future.

Reconstruction of the city proceeded rapidly throughout 1872, but the following year, an economic depression gripped the entire nation, lasting until 1879. Nonetheless, Chicago, now established as a rail, manufacturing and meat packing center, fared better than most sections of the country. Rebuilding slowed but by no means halted.

By 1880, prosperity returned, and a new cycle of building and expansion proceeded, highlighted by the appearance of structures that put a new word in the dictionary: Skyscraper. The first steel-frame skyscraper was the 10-story Home Insurance Building, erected in 1883–84 on the northeast corner of LaSalle and Adams Streets. Architect William LeBaron Jenney utilized a revolutionary concept: instead of relying on heavy masonry, he designed a cage of wrought iron and steel beams to support much of the weight of the building, whose exterior amounted to no more than a "skin" pulled over this rib cage. Razed in 1931 to make way for the present Field Building, the Home Insurance Building is recognized as the forerunner of such feats as the Sears Tower and the John Hancock Center.

Though six stories taller than the Home Insurance Building, the Monadnock Building, which still stands at 53 W. Jackson Blvd., relies on a 72-inch masonry wall at the base to support its weight. Designed by Daniel Burnham and John Wellborn Root and completed in two sections, in 1892 and 1893, the Monadnock Building is regarded as one of the finest examples of the Chicago school of architecture and is a National Historic Landmark.

Development of the skyscraper allowed the city to expand upward as well as outward, and other historic buildings, such as the Chicago Stock Exchange, Auditorium Theatre Building, and the Rookery, took their places on the skyline. Outward expansion also continued. Between 1880 and 1893 (the year of the World Columbian Exposition), the city gained 120 square miles and 200,000 in population.

An expanding cityscape demanded better transportation. Horse-drawn street cars first appeared in 1859, followed by an import from San Fransisco—cable cars—in 1882. By 1894, Chicago had 86 miles of cable tracks and more than 450 cars. However, another urban innovation, the electric trolley car, was already making its appearance and soon would send the horse car and cable car to oblivion. The new trolleys zipped along at speeds of nine to 12 miles an hour, carrying some 200 million passengers in 1893 on more than 500 miles of track that crisscrossed the city. In this same benchmark year in the city's history, the first elevated line began service, followed in 1897 by the circle of L tracks that would make downtown Chicago known the world over as "The Loop."

Electric lighting, first demonstrated publicly in Chicago in April 1878, did not start with Thomas Edison, contrary to popular belief. Edison gave the world a practical light bulb that worked anywhere. As early as 1844, however, arc lighting, in which light is produced by an arc created by current passing between two electrodes, was used in a production of the Paris Opera and actually lit the streets of the French capital in 1877. One year later a night soccer match played under arc lights in Sheffield, England, drew 30,000 fans. In this country, the arc lamp was displayed at the Philadelphia Centennial Exposition in 1876. Thus the concept was hardly new when John P. Barrett, Superintendent of the Chicago Fire Alarm Telegraphs (chief electrician), mounted two battery-operated arc lamps atop the famed Water Tower and turned them on for a crowd that had learned of the demonstration from newspapers. The following morning, the *Chicago Tribune* reported: "The gleam slowly gathered into a ray, which slanted through the darkness, and succeeded in bringing into unpleasant prominence a cow shed in the vicinity. The ray at its brightest was about a foot broad at the start, and widened to perhaps twenty feet at the base on the ground. The flickering seems to be caused by the disproportion of the wire and battery." The first private use of arc lighting occurred a year and a half later to mark former President Grant's arrival in the city after an around-the-world trip. Perhaps in acknowledgement of the general's reputation, the lamps were mounted outside the front and rear of a saloon on Madison Street.

The following year, 1880, the redoubtable Potter Palmer installed a pair of arc light fixtures in the Palmer House for the Republican National Convention that nominated James A. Garfield for President. Two downtown stores also installed arc lighting systems that year. The flickering notwithstanding, arc lights with their wide beams were simply too powerful for practical use inside the home.

The city obtained its first commercial arc lighting plant in 1881, located in the basement of the Central YMCA building. Organized by two Chicago men, S. S. Badger and A. C. Badger, the company operated about 50 arc lamps for several different customers in the neighborhood. Two years later, the Badger Company built a small plant in Joliet and began supplying arc lighting to that community.

In the early '80s, small electric lighting companies popped up like crocuses in spring—not only in the Chicago area but throughout the country. The Chicago telephone directory of 1880 lists no fewer than 10 firms under the heading "Electrical Instruments," and the number grew rapidly in succeeding years. Many of them didn't last long, though, as more substantial companies gobbled them up by consolidating their lighting systems. Arc light plants gradually enlarged, equipment became more efficient, electric construction methods improved, and the lamps themselves were made better, burned better, and looked better. Equally important, the rates were reduced.

In New York, Edison continued to find his dream of central station power a tough sell in the marketplace. His financial backers wanted to collect patent royalties, not invest huge new capital expenditures in generating stations. Instead of large central power stations that would distribute electricity to all manner of customers, as the Wizard envisioned, the investors favored the sale of small, isolated plants that would provide power for large buildings, factories, and those few residences which could afford it.

Isolated plants sold well. The Edison Company for Isolated Lighting sold more than 300 of them by early 1883, while another subsidiary of the Edison Electric Light Company manufactured lamps and still another made dynamos. On the other hand, only two cities had central station power—Boston and Great Barrington, Massachusetts. Banks wouldn't lend money for central station construction.

The Edison Company for Isolated Lighting entered the Chicago market in early 1881 through the efforts of a long-time Edison associate named George H. Bliss. Like Edison, Bliss had been a railroad telegrapher and one of the earliest pioneers in the electrical business in Chicago. Bliss, with two partners, became the agent for the Isolated Lighting Company in Illinois, Wisconsin and Iowa. The agency opened offices at 143 LaSalle Street and took over the first Edison plant in Chicago, located in the factory of the United States Rolling Stock Company. The plant contained the originally designed Edison generator and furnished electricity for 130 lamps. The company soon added a second plant that powered 60 lamps in the basement salesroom of a wholesale warehouse. Over the next few months, still more installations came on line, supplying lighting to the Palmer House dining room and two floors of the McCormick Reaper

Works, as well as the National Life Building, the first office building in Chicago wired for incandescent electric lighting.

Installing electrical service in the early days required a certain degree of savvy, not to mention muscle, on the part of the street crews. One of the early crewmen was Henry Jampolis, a 250-pounder who would spend 45 years with Commonwealth Edison. Jampolis, who first went to work for an early arc lighting firm, recalled an incident at the House of David, a restaurant and bar near Monroe and Clark streets, that illustrates the time's widely held apprehension, if not downright fear, of electricity and electric lighting. The saloon's proprietor wanted an arc light strung inside. However, when Jampolis and his crew arrived to do the wiring, the landlord greeted them by saying that if any man put wires under the sidewalk there would be some shooting. Jampolis may have weighed 250 pounds, but he was nobody's fool. He and his men departed and returned that evening. "I invited the owner to the bar room," Jampolis explained, "sat down and talked to him, and when I got through with him he was asleep." Jampolis failed to explain whether "when I got through with him" meant that he leveled the man, drank him under the table, or just talked him to sleep. In any event, the arc lighting crew took the landlord's gun and put it behind the bar. Then, as Jampolis continued, "(We) placed the ceiling boards and inside wiring, ran the cable under the sidewalk, and when he awakened the light was burning in place. There was quite an argument, but he was afraid to cut the wires. No shooting occurred."

Ironically, the confrontation Jampolis described represents a 180-degree turn from situations that present day utility crews sometimes encounter. Nowadays, some people threaten violence when faced with the prospect of their electricity being shut *off*.

Jampolis found himself in another dicey situation when he and his co-workers were running cable under the sidewalks on the Near North Side. He said, "The owner of three buildings in one block objected and, as we had no conduit in the street, the only way we could get the cable run in was to drop in the coal hole and run it on the curb wall. When we got to his second building he appeared with two sons, armed with shovels and hatchets and defied us to go further. Our men were anxious to complete the job, and they threw one of the sons down the coal hole." During the battle that followed, someone reported a riot to the police, and the arriving officers attempted to arrest Jampolis. Before they arrived, however, Jampolis had filled out a blank letterhead from the city electrical department, giving his crew the authority to run cable in that block and forging the name of the city's chief electrician (John Barrett, who had demonstrated the arc lights at the Water Tower several years earlier). "I read it to [the police sergeant]", Jampolis continued,

Laying underground cable in the early days. Permits were difficult to obtain due to strict city building codes after the Great Chicago Fire of 1871.

"and he took it and looked at it and said, 'Officer, you stay here and protect Mr. Jampolis and let the men run that cable,' but I saw to it that the 'permit' was destroyed as soon as I left the job."

The reason Jampolis and his men ran cable underground was that the Chicago City Council had passed an ordinance in 1881, requiring all electric wires to be placed in that manner. The ordinance was to have gone into effect two years later, but the city allowed it to slide for several more years. Finally, the city actually began arresting utility employes who were caught stringing wire from poles. Although overhead lines were an eyesore, the principal reason the city ordered them placed under-

15

ground was that they obstructed the use of fire-fighting equipment. Chicago didn't need any lessons in fire safety.

While the Bliss agency continued to sell Edison's isolated lighting plants and the arc lighting companies pursued their narrow speciality, at least one prominent Chicagoan, General Anson Stager, followed the developments with keen interest. A district vice president of Western Union and president of Western Electric, Stager was acquainted with both Edison and Bliss. He came to support Edison's view that the future of electricity generation lay in large central stations that would transmit power for incandescent lighting and other needs across wide areas. The General sold his belief to a number of well-off acquaintances who had the wherewithal to transform the vision into reality, although the transformation would take several more years.

Consequently, Stager went to New York to negotiate with the parent Edison company, the Edison Electric Light Company, for the authority to establish a Chicago firm that would not only take over the Bliss agency and sell Edison equipment, but would also develop the city's first central station. On May 2, 1882, the Western Edison Light Company, forerunner of Commonwealth Edison Company, was incorporated by General Stager, Normal Williams, and John M. Clark. The stated objective of the new company was "to acquire, purchase, own, sell, lease and dispose of any and all rights and uses under letters patent, or otherwise, for the production and distribution of electricity for light, heat and power;" to produce and sell electricity; "and to manufacture, sell, purchase and lease engines, machinery and all apparatus necessary therefore. . ." The backers of the company invested $500,000 in 5,000 shares of $100 each.

One of those first stockholders was John W. Doane, a wholesale grocer, importer of coffee and tea, and Prairie Avenue socialite. The 1800 block of Prairie was the silk stocking district of the times, lined with the mansions of millionaires, many of whom had made their fortunes in the rebuilding of the city after the Great Fire. Several of these homes stand today as the showpieces of the Prairie Avenue Historic District.

On Nov. 10, 1882, Mr. and Mrs. Doane celebrated their silver wedding anniversary with a gala party for some 400 people in their home at 1827 Prairie. The guest list read like a Who's

16

Who of Chicago, including names such as Mr. and Mrs. Marshall Field, Mr. and Mrs. George M. Pullman, and John Crerar. While the main reason for the celebration was the Doanes' 25th wedding anniversary, the guests undoubtedly sensed that a more significant story was being written. The Doane home was the first Chicago residence to be wired with incandescent electric lighting, and the anniversary gala marked its debut.

The next morning the *Chicago Tribune* ran a lengthy story about the "brilliant social event," describing the Doane home as "probably the finest house west of New York. . . . The interior of the house is as exquisitely rich as taste and art can make it, and last night it presented a scene of grandeur and beauty rarely witnessed.

"Mr. Doane has illuminated his house with 250 of the Edison electric incandescent lights, and they made the house brilliant in the extreme and brought out the elegant toilets in all their rich colors." The article continued with a detailed description of the home, the floral designs, and the attire worn by the Doane women.

A small isolated plant in the basement of Doane's coach house supplied the electric current. The plant consisted of a high-speed engine and a belted Edison bipolar generator. The wires ran through underground tubes from the coach house to the home, where they were concealed under the floorboards. Shortly after the Doanes' anniversary party, the adjacent residences of Thomas Dent, Marshall Field, Edson Keith, and Joseph Sears were wired and supplied by the plant in the basement of Doane's coach house, which could supply electricity for 550 lamps. Again, underground tubes carried the wiring.*

Doane had contracted the isolated plant three months earlier, laying out the princely sum of $7,197 to the fledgling Western Edison Company. The wiring of Dent's home cost $971, Field's $876, Keith's $1,264, and Sears' $1,092. The cost of each job illustrated the limitations of the market for isolated installations to Stager and colleagues. It would be no easy task to sell incandescent electric light anywhere but in the homes of the rich or in the downtown business district. So they continued to

---

*Fire destroyed the Doane home in 1927, 28 years after it had been sold. The plot where it stood is part of the Historic District.

go hunting where the ducks were, selling isolated plants that consisted of an engine, a dynamo, wiring, and lamps, while awaiting the time when they could launch a full-scale central station.

They took a small step in that direction with the startup of what they considered a miniature central station in the basement of their headquarters at 51–43 Wabash Ave., a four-story structure owned by none other than John Doane. After they had wired their own building, the company's managers ended up with some surplus capacity, so they also supplied a few neighboring buildings in much the same way that Doane's residential plant had supplied its neighbors. The plant in the Doane building was operated by only one man, who worked from 2 p.m. until midnight on weekdays and till 1 a.m. on Saturdays. At his 40-year company anniversary gathering years later, this one-man crew confessed that he was rarely overburdened.

By the end of 1882 the Western Edison Light Company had sold 27 isolated plants, including the installation of the world's first hydro incandescent lighting station for the Appleton Edison Light Company in Wisconsin. Western's equipment sales totaled more than $57,000. The company could power nearly 4,500 lamps. Over four years, the company's tally was 24,880 lamps, $359,900 in equipment sales, and wiring contracts worth $10,415.

When General Stager died in 1885, John M. Clark became president of Western Edison. That year also saw the arrival in Chicago of Robert Todd Lincoln, the only surviving member of the president's family. After a stint as U.S. Secretary of War in two administrations, Lincoln joined with Edward S. Isham, one of the leaders of the Chicago bar, to form the law firm of Isham and Lincoln, later Isham, Lincoln and Beale. The firm has been the general counsel of Commonwealth Edison and its predecessors ever since.

Shortly before his death, Stager prepared to establish a new organization to replace Western Electric. In 1885 he and Lincoln went to New York together to see Edison about forming a new company. Lincoln had inherited his father's love of jokes and tall tales, so the meeting with Edison developed into a bull session. The three men had such a good time, the story goes, that the hour got away from them. Lincoln and Stager suddenly realized that they had to catch a train back to Chicago and hastily said goodby to Edison. Not until they were well on their way did they realize that they had forgotten the primary purpose of the visit.

In spite of their whimsical meeting with Edison, Stager, Lincoln, and their colleagues shrewdly moved ahead with their plan to establish a new electric utility. In March 1887, after months of laying legal groundwork, a group spearheaded by Lincoln, Clark, and John B. Drake persuaded the Chicago City Council to pass an ordinance granting Western Edison the right to use underground wires and conductors to transmit electricity in an area bounded by North Avenue, 39th Street, Lake Michigan, and Ashland Avenue, roughly 2 1/2 miles by 7 miles. Step two was now ready for execution. With the franchise in hand, Lincoln, Clark, Drake, and 36 other stockholders formed the Chicago Edison Company and petitioned the Illinois Secretary of State for a charter. The language of the petition was similar to that of Western Edison's—to produce, supply, and sell electric light and power, plus the machinery to produce power, and "to acquire, purchase, own, sell, lease and dispose of any and all rights and uses under letters patent, or otherwise; for the production and distribution of electricity for furnishing light, heat and power . . ." Then, according to the plan, Chicago Edison acquired Western Edison's newly granted franchise. The transaction was a formality, unmarked by any of the machinations of some of today's corporate takeovers, since many of the directors of Western Edison and Chicago Edison were one and the same. For step three, Western Edison sold back to Edison Electric Light Company of New York its rights as exclusive agent to sell Edison electrical equipment in Illinois, Wisconsin, and Iowa. At the same time, Chicago Edison contracted for those rights, although the franchise initially covered Cook County only.

The last transition business left before Lincoln, Clark, and the others was the dissolution of the Western Edison Light Company, which they achieved in June. The state officially recognized the demise of the five-year-old company on July 2, 1887. Chicago Edison, immediate predecessor of the present Commonwealth Edison, stood in its place.

Two

Mr.
Sargent
Builds
A
Plant

Thomas Edison's central station engineers in New York, in 1887 the recognized experts in the field, were flabbergasted. These were the same men who had brought Pearl Street on line and had added half a dozen years of experience to that achievement. The events in Chicago presented an affront to their reputation. Who did this 28-year-old upstart think he was? His company was paying the Edison Electric Light Company for, among other things, the benefit of its experience and advice on plans for the city's first central station. Adopting the plans of its youthful chief engineer—unheard of, as far as New York was concerned. In retrospect, Chicago Edison's action represents one small, early blow against the Second City syndrome.

The man who rankled Edison's New York people was Frederick Sargent, who had become chief engineer of Western Edison in 1884 and continued in that position with the new company. Interestingly, Sargent was born in England on the same day, November 11, 1859, as Samuel Insull, with whom he would work closely for most of his life.

Initially, Chicago Edison had asked the engineering department of Edison Electric Light in New York to design and lay out a central station at 139 (later 120) W. Adams St., opposite the Rookery Building, then under construction, and less than a block from the present Edison Building at 72 W. Adams. The Wizard's men prepared the plans and submitted them to the Chicago firm, where Sargent reviewed them, found them to be unnecessarily complicated and unsuited to conditions in Chicago, and recommended that they be turned down. Chicago Edison officials heeded Sargent's advice. They had him draw up plans of his own, liked what they saw, and adopted them. A New York Edison lieutenant fired off a huffy letter to Sargent asking him to justify his temerity, not so that New York could learn anything, but in the author's words, "in order to reinforce the position which *I* take" (my emphasis). The writer then posed 13 technical questions to Sargent and asked him to fill in the blanks after each one. The Chicago engineer did so, clearly and concisely. The New Yorker's degree of enlightenment, if any, is not recorded.

Before Chicago Edison decided on Sargent's plans, the company had canvassed the probable lighting load in the downtown area, then chose the location of the plant and laid out the street mains and distribution system. The boundaries decided upon were Harrison, Market (now north-south Wacker Drive), and Water Streets (now east-west Wacker Drive), and Michigan Avenue, an area about two-thirds of a mile east and west and five-sixths of a mile north and south. The planners anticipated an ultimate demand of 150,000 lamps, plus a small number of electric motors. As things turned out, the planners greatly underestimated the growth of the city's business center. The anticipated demand was exceeded within six years, partly because of the increasing use of elevators and electric motors.

Frederick Sargent served as a consulting engineer for the Chicago Edison Company and its successor, the Commonwealth Edison Company. Prior to holding these posts, he was chief engineer and general superintendent of the Chicago Edison Company and chief engineer of the Western Edison Light Company.

The Chicago Edison planners wanted to locate the power plant near the center of load, so they purchased a building at 180–182 Monroe St., west of LaSalle Street, and moved in steam boilers, a 50-horsepower engine, and an Edison bi-polar generator. However, they soon decided to construct a new building, totally tailored to the company's requirements, rather than a remodeled structure. In June of 1887, work began at the 139 W.

Adams site. The plant on Monroe Street provided power to a small number of customers for less than a year.

The site of Chicago's first central station hardly afforded a pleasant view: a long, narrow vacant lot, filled with debris and muddy water. Under the personal supervision of Frederick Sargent, the project took shape, but according to Commonwealth

The original Edison Building decorated in celebration of the end of the Spanish-American War in 1898.

Edison historian H. A. Seymour, the structure wasn't any more aesthetically pleasing than the vacant lot upon which it rose. Seymour wrote that "the Adams Street site was mysterious if not forbidding in outward appearance. It was evidently built more for solidity than ornament, and its facade seemed to suggest that of an armory. The walls were very thick. The foundation under the entire structure was a solid bed consisting of several transverse layers of iron rails, reinforcing a mass of concrete three feet thick. From this foundation massive pillars rose to support the two floors on which rested the engines and dynamos, these floors being carried independently of the sidewalls to avoid transmitting excessive vibration from the machinery to offices and other portions of the structure."

The three-story structure was finished in August 1888, and after only a few days of tests, the plant began service to customers. The building itself housed virtually the entire Chicago Edison organization. The ground floor contained the general offices and storerooms. A small electric lighting salesroom was added the following year, as well as the engine room and lower boiler room. Immediately above the engine room, the second floor supported another boiler room and the dynamos. Belts from each of the engines passed through the floor to two of the generators. The Meter Department was located above the offices. The switchboard and bus-bars were also on the second floor; coal bunkers with a capacity of 1,200 tons were on the third floor, above the boiler rooms.

At first the station had four 200-horsepower engines tied to eight Edison bipolar dynamos on the floor above. One year later, the company added two more 200-horsepower engines belted to four additional Edison bipolars as the connected load soared from approximately 6,000 to 15,000 lamps. Maximum load had increased to 618 kilowatts, double that of the first year. In fact, the Adams Street Station, running 24 hours a day, operated in a chronic overload condition almost from day one, finally carrying then-incredible loads of up to 3,200 kilowatts in its last years.

According to another early company historian, Ernest Edkins, "During the period of unusually heavy load, the appearance of the Adams Street Station suggested a glimpse of Dante's Inferno. The engines were constantly pushed to their utmost capacity under the heavy overload. In the roaring dynamo room, the smell of shellac and varnish from the hot armatures told the same story. Switches and bus-bars were frequently too hot for the bare hand, while in the boiler room the half-naked firemen, shoveling coal with feverish energy, made one feel as if an explosion might furnish a climax at any moment."

The early days of the station were, indeed, marked by at least two minor off-site explosions and two fires. In one instance, a serious short circuit developed, but no one could locate the source. The Underground Department went to look for the trouble. After a day or two of scouring the service territory, a crew came across an unusual sight on LaSalle Street, outside City Hall, the scene of many an unusual sight over the years—a manhole plugged by a beer keg. Checking with a policeman on duty, they got the story: a strong explosion had blown away the original manhole cover, which barely missed a streetcar. Faced with an open manhole and a broken cover, the resourceful officer requisitioned the beer keg, empty, no doubt, and put it in the hole. However, the iron bands on the keg caused another short, which blew out the keg and burned off the lower bands. The determined cop retrieved the keg and put it back into the manhole. With the metal bands burned away, there was nothing left to cause another short circuit, so the keg stayed put, good temporary protection, as the officer explained, for the slow-moving traffic on LaSalle Street.

About the same time, Adams Street Station experienced its first fire. While Frederick Sargent and his aides held their regular post-supper meeting in a first floor office, a workman's torch set off a blaze in the basement joists, near the cables, directly below the office. Sargent and another man put out the blaze with fire extinguishers, but in the meantime, someone called the Fire Department. With visions dancing in his head of firemen spraying water on the cables, Sargent ducked outside, locked the front door, and awaited their arrival. When the firefighters showed up, Sargent explained that the blaze was out. But the firemen would have none of that. According to an anonymous eyewitness, they "grabbed him by the throat, tore off his shirt-front and collar and threw him into the gutter. Chief Sweeney arrived in time to prevent any damage being done to the station."

Conscientious employe that he was, Sargent felt obligated to report the fire immediately to one of the company's directors. The only one he could find was John Drake, who was playing host to a dinner party at a downtown hotel. Sargent must have provided quite a sight as he strode into the hotel ballroom in his torn and soiled clothes to relay the message to Director Drake. Drake gallantly invited Sargent to join the party, but Sargent declined.

In late 1889 Adams Street Station fell victim to a more serious fire that shut down the plant for six hours. After firemen extinguished the blaze, employes worked feverishly to bring the

25

station back on line as quickly as possible. One crew, armed with pickaxes, dug up the cement floors to replace cable. When the plant was ready for startup, about 5 p.m., the company realized that virtually every switch of every light served by the station would be "on," forcing the dynamos to start up under full load. The company attempted to instruct the largest customers to open their main switches to reduce the load, but grave doubts still existed as to whether or not the plant could come back under such conditions. The superintendent decided that there was one way to find out. With boiler steam at full pressure and engines running smoothly, he positioned a man at each of the eight switches, and, handkerchief in hand to signal transmission, waited for the generators to reach top speed. Then he waved the handkerchief. "For an instant there was a terrific groaning which made us all gasp," according to a worker who was present, "then the entire circuit started up as perfectly as under ordinary conditions." Young Chicago Edison had averted a lengthy blackout.

It is an unwritten precept of journalism and history that good news is no news. Newspapers and history books record floods, not that the Mississippi River stayed within its banks on most days; they tell of traffic accidents, not of the thousands of motorists who made it to work and back home safely. So it is with utilities. Much of what is remembered concerns fires or explosions, debilitating storms, or other calamities. Accomplishments are taken for granted and little remembered, if not forgotten altogether. What is worth remembering about Adams Street Station is that from the day it opened in 1888 until the day it shut down in 1894, replaced by newer and better technology, it ran on a 24-hour schedule, chronically overloaded, and still provided exceptionally good service in an era when electric service was brand-new. In an August 1889 issue, the magazine *Western Electrician* called the Adams Street plant "one of the largest and most complete central station incandescent electric lighting plants in America."

After the generating station ceased operating in August 1894, a distribution center serving downtown used some of its space, while offices of the rapidly growing young company utilized the rest. At the turn of the century, 120 W. Adams was entirely rebuilt and enlarged to six stories with a French Renaissance facade—quite a transformation for the building Seymour called "mysterious, if not forbidding." The building continued to hold many Edison offices until 1914–15, when the company moved up the street to its new headquarters at 72 W. Adams, acquired from the Continental and Commercial National Bank. "Old 120" still served the company in a variety of ways, housing a meeting place, employment agency, and basement rifle range. It was sold in 1922.

Even as the incandescent lighting demand on Adams Street Station rapidly multiplied in the late '80s and early '90s, the arc lighting companies proved to be stubborn competitors. People who had bought arc lamps were slow to discard them in favor of incandescent lighting, which had a nicer look but cost more per candlepower hour. Improvements in arc lighting technology, combined with the lower cost, made these lamps popular for theater marquees and other outdoor uses in which economy was more important than appearance. Also, the lower rates and better service that came about as arc lighting companies became larger in size but fewer in number made arc lights popular. Edison's answer to this competition was, "If you can't lick 'em, join 'em." At least for awhile, anyway. The company regarded arc lighting as an unavoidable side issue that would go away eventually, but in the meantime, it would introduce arc lighting service in 1890 to the customers of the central station, waiting for the day when they would dispose of their arcs and replace them with incandescent bulbs.

A furniture store and lunch counter became the first Edison arc lighting customers. The following year the company had 218 arc lamps connected; by the end of 1892, nearly 1,000 were in service. In 1892 Edison sold incandescent lamps to customers for 65 cents apiece. The company exchanged new for burned-out lamps free of charge for its lighting customers.

Then, as now, getting some people to pay their electric bills posed a bit of a problem. Frederick Sargent himself discovered this fact early on, but also concocted a novel means of collecting from at least one reluctant customer. The target of Sargent's scheme was a saloonkeeper who hadn't paid for several months and who drove off the bill collectors with a club whenever they appeared. Sargent and a colleague named John Henry Goehst went to the saloon, poked around outside, and found a rear window which would permit a man to drop into the basement. Then they returned one evening when the bar was crowded. The two of them agreed that Goehst would go into the basement, while Sargent would go into the tavern and attempt to collect the bill. If he succeeded, he was to come out and help Goehst back out of the basement window. If not, he was to stamp his foot three times on the floor above. That would be the signal to Goehst to cut off the power.

The Chicago Edison Street Department in the early 1900s. Fourth from the right, with the boy, is believed to be J.H. Goehst.

Sargent maneuvered the saloonkeeper to the rear and tried to persuade him to settle his bill, but true to form, the man rushed for his club. At that, Sargent stamped his foot three times and the lights went out. The anonymous narrator of this vignette leaves us hanging as to what happened after that, but we can imagine the surprise of the saloonkeeper, who thought perhaps that Sargent possessed some magical powers—not unlike the quick-thinking protagonists in *King Solomon's Mines* or *A Connecticut Yankee in King Arthur's Court*, who saved their skins by ''causing'' an eclipse of the sun moments before they knew it would occur. If so, we can further assume that the bill got paid. We do know that Goehst got out of the basement because his name turns up many more times in early Edison history.

In 1889 Sargent left Chicago Edison for New York to join the company that would soon take the name Edison General Electric. Insull was a vice president of the firm. In 1891 Sargent was back in Chicago and, with Ayres Lundy, launched the engineering consulting firm of Sargent & Lundy. Sargent served as consulting engineer for Commonwealth Edison until his death in 1919. To this day, Sargent & Lundy remains Edison's architect/engineer for major construction projects.

Back in New York, things were not going well for Thomas Edison. The parade, at least the march of central station power, was passing him by. For one thing, the Thompson-Houston Electric Company of Lynn, Massachusetts, which had already infringed on Edison's patents, was outperforming him in central station construction. For another, he never pursued the development of electric railroads, even though he had pioneered the concept. Others took up the torch, so that by 1889 more than 150 street railways ran in the United States. In short order, electric rail demand for power exceeded that of electric lighting —a particular blow to Edison because he was one of the first to realize that the success of central stations vitally depended on power load. Embarrassing as these developments were, the most galling turn of events centered on the development of alternating current.

A former Edison employe named Nikola Tesla, once fired by the Wizard, discovered the concept of the alternating current (AC) motor. Westinghouse Electric seized the idea and in 1886, George Westinghouse and William Stanley perfected a transformer that made it possible to transmit AC power for hundreds of miles. Edison's direct current system, on the other hand, could transmit electricity only about two miles. The Westinghouse people envisioned large, centrally located generating stations, transmitting high voltage electricity for miles and miles, then reducing the voltage for distribution. Edison could be stubborn, particularly in matters of pride, and in this instance, his pride had received quite a blow. He not only opposed alternating current, but he set out to prove its alleged dangers.

For one, he brought in a man named Harold P. Brown and gave him the run of his laboratory. The name Harold P. Brown rates only an aside in the story of electricity's development: to prove the supposed dangers of AC, he developed the electric chair. Various promotions came about and original terms, one more macabre than the next, were suggested for this new method of execution—electromort, dynamort, electrocide. Since Brown's electric chair operated on alternating current, Edison himself thought AC's champion should be duly recognized: someone who went to the chair would be "Westinghoused."

New York State adopted this form of execution in 1888. Others in the state had better uses for AC. In 1893, a group planning to electrify Buffalo with hydroelectric power from Niagara Falls opted for AC instead of DC. One of the project's engineers called the coming of AC the greatest step in the development of electricity since 1878, the year that Edison perfected the incandescent light bulb. Competition between AC and DC, the so-called "battle of the currents," was waged in a number of cities. When Edison finally agreed to join the AC business at the urging of Insull and others, his people turned out equipment inferior to that of Westinghouse.

In *America's Electric Utilities: Past, Present and Future*, Leonard S. Hyman writes, "In a little more than a decade, Edison put more than a half century of research into practical application, conceived and invented an entire industry, and then became a reactionary who hampered the industry's progress and threatened to fossilize it at a primitive stage of development." While that may be true, the legacy of Thomas Alva Edison speaks for itself. In addition to the incandescent electric light bulb, the man left behind the electronic stock exchange ticker, the phonograph, the motion picture, the modern research laboratory, and a total of 1,093 patents. If he hadn't built and demonstrated the Pearl Street Station, the light bulb might have remained just an unusual toy with no system to bring it into homes, offices, and factories. His total contribution was a better life for his contemporaries and countless generations to come. In 1979, commenting on the 100th anniversary of the invention of the incandescent bulb, the president of the International Brotherhood of Electrical Workers, Charles Pillard, estimated that Edison's inventions directly or indirectly account for about one of every five jobs in the United States. But less than 10 years after the invention of the bulb, Edison's business colleagues were asking, "What have you done for me lately?"

The Wizard, in fact, would do plenty, but his future achievements, such as the phonograph and the motion picture, would fall outside the domain of electric power generation. "Having pursued the electric arts with demonic energy until he had worked out a complete system and satiated his own curiosity," Insull's biographer Forrest McDonald observes, "Edison was, after 1884, simply no longer interested in electrical inventions. . . . Though he was in charge of research and development for Edison General Electric and did considerable research for the company, particularly in traction, this work was singularly fruitless." The year 1884 also brought personal tragedy to Edison with the death of his wife, Mary. According to those close to him, he was never the same.

One of Edison's earliest backers who sought new conquests was Henry Villard, a German-American transportation executive and financial speculator who had had Edison install an incandescent lighting plant on his yacht as early as 1880. Villard was wiped out in the financial panic of 1883–84, returned to Germany for two years, then suddenly reappeared on the scene with the backing of powerful German bankers. Villard concocted a scheme to form an international cartel, starting with Edison's manufacturing ventures, to control the electric business worldwide. To that end, he prepared a plan to consolidate all of the Edison companies and the traction firm of Sprague Electric Railway and Motor Company. A group of American bankers, headed by financier J. P. Morgan, gave their blessing after assuring themselves of favorable treatment. The Morgan group had financed Edison's early experiments, held his patents, loaned money to his company, and owned a sizeable minority bloc of shares. Edison and his operating boss, Sam Insull, realized they were approaching shark-infested waters. A few years earlier Morgan and his friends had attempted to seize control of the Edison manufacturing companies, only to be defeated by Insull, who rallied enough minority shareholders to beat back the challenge.

Nevertheless in late 1888 and early 1889, chronically short of cash to meet their payroll and other obligations, Edison and Insull agreed to go along with the plan. Edison would receive about $1.75 million in cash and stocks, his associates about $1 million (of which $75,000 would go to Insull) and the Edison manufacturing companies an infusion of fresh capital. It would be a refreshing change for Edison and Insull, who in effect had been borrowing money for years. In explaining the acceptance of Morgan's and Villard's terms, Edison wrote, "Mr. Insull and I were afraid we might get into trouble for lack of money. ... Therefore ... we concluded it was better to be sure than to be sorry."

The Edison General Electric Company was formed in January of 1889 with Villard as president and four of his men as directors. Edison, Insull and two of their colleagues completed the nine-man board. Insull became second vice president, in charge of manufacturing and sales. Villard left the actual management of the company to a caretaker while he searched for other mergers. Insull, on the other hand, set out to improve the efficiency of the manufacturing companies, slashing prices, boosting profits and establishing a national sales force—a concept virtually unknown in the corporate world of the 1880s. But the price of expanding the organization was high. Insull, on behalf of Edison GE, tapped Morgan and his crowd for a loan of $3.5 million which the bankers could call in whenever they saw fit.

In addition to Westinghouse, Edison GE's principal rival was the Thompson-Houston Company, whose policy, according to McDonald, "was scarcely distinguishable from theft. Thompson-Houston expanded into every line of electrical manufacturing that promised profit, and it did so by a special means. It spent no money on developing new products, leaving that to the more foolhardy. If the research left the inventor financially strapped, Thompson-Houston would buy up the patents for a minimal sum. If the invention could not be acquired by that means, Thompson-Houston simply infringed on the patent."

In his search for further mergers, Villard opted to pursue Westinghouse. He gladly would have cut a deal with Thompson-Houston, but he based his choice on the practical fact that Westinghouse at the time was the smaller company and therefore more likely to be a quiescent partner. Villard also realized that Edison GE needed Westinghouse's AC knowledge and equipment. So even as the "battle of the currents" raged and

Thomas Edison vilified the competition, Villard and George Westinghouse held private meetings and moved toward consolidation.

A string of judicial victories for Edison GE, beginning in late 1889, caused Villard to reverse his field. The decisions confirmed Edison's lamp patents and invalidated those of others, paving the way for Edison GE to force its competitors out of the electric light business. Villard figured, "If you can lick 'em, why join 'em?" He broke off the negotiations with Westinghouse and went after the larger Thompson-Houston Company. The decision placed him in the ring with two of the shrewdest operators of the late 19th Century—J. P. Morgan and Charles A. Coffin, president of Thompson-Houston. Villard needed Morgan's approval of any merger because his banking group was a large minority stockholder in Edison GE, and any corporation of the proposed size would need to rely on the big banks controlled by Morgan.

Negotiations between Villard and Coffin proceeded smoothly, but just as the merger was about to be consummated, with GE as the dominant partner, Coffin balked. Villard had played a game of one-upmanship, and had won. When Morgan was informed of what had taken place, he summoned Coffin, which is precisely what the Thompson-Houston chief had intended. He walked Morgan through a series of figures crafted to show the superior efficiency and profitability of Thompson-Houston over Edison GE. The persuasive Coffin made his point: Morgan decided to have Thompson-Houston acquire Edison, instead of the other way around. At Coffin's suggestion, nonetheless, the transaction would be a consolidation rather than an acquisition. However, Thompson-Houston would carry the higher value and its people would consequently assume control of the newly-formed company.

Morgan suddenly informed Villard that he was through. Villard, stunned, wanted to fight, but Morgan held the trump card—the $3.5 million loan which he could use to crush the Edison Company. Edison was also out of the business—the very business he had created, although he wound up with about $5 million as a result of the consolidation. Insull was the only Edisonian who was given a top position with the new company —a $50 million colossus to be known as the General Electric

Company. He was made second vice president under Coffin and another man at a salary of $36,000 a year. Villard had a holding company to fall back on, and a little later he offered the presidency to Insull.

At age 32, Sam Insull had some hard thinking to do.

Three

Criticizing
The
Teachings
Of
Moses

I t was as if the paths of Sam Insull and Chicago Edison were predestined to meet—and remain linked for 40 years. In 1892 both were young, vigorous, full of potential, brimming with ideas, optimistic about the future of electricity, and searching for the right vehicle to utilize these attributes. They found each other.

Edison President E. T. Watkins had resigned the year before, leaving the company's directors with a rapidly expanding operation and no immediate inkling as to who should run it. Between 1888 and 1892, Chicago Edison's peak load had jumped from 313 kilowatts (kw) to 3,200, the exact size of its generating capacity. Connected load had zoomed from 1,100 kw in 1889 to 7,800 kw and annual output from 169,000 kilowatthours to 5,827,000 in the same four years. The urgent need for new capacity, the imminent 1893 World Columbian Exposition with its possible opportunities, increasing financial burdens, and a welter of other challenges required aggressive new leadership.

Even though they needed a strong executive, the Edison directors did not rush to appoint a successor to Watkins. About the time Insull told Coffin that he would stay on just long enough to assist with the General Electric Company merger, Chicago Edison directors Edward L. Brewster and Byron L. Smith wrote to Insull, asking him to recommend the best person for the Chicago Edison job. Over the years, Insull would rarely be accused of having a small ego, but in this instance, propriety overcame self-opinion and prevented him from volunteering immediately. Despite the fact that the Chicago job would mean a salary drop, to $12,000 from $36,000 annually with GE, and the lowered prestige of moving from a $50 million corporation to an $885,000 one, Insull perceived advantages to the shift. He had been interested in the city ever since Edison had spoken of it as

"one of the best cities in the world for our line of business."
More important, Brewster and Smith were offering the opportunity to run the whole show. If he stayed in the electricity
business in the East, he would remain subordinate to Villard or
Coffin.

While Insull cast about for a delicate way to propose his
own credentials, his mother, who was visiting him in New York,
stepped forward with a bit of practical advice. Since the Chicagoans had asked him who he thought was the best man, he
should tell them the truth—Samuel L. Insull. He acted upon the
maternal suggestion and submitted his application, stating that
"it is the best opportunity that I know of in the United States to
develop the business of the production and distribution of electrical energy."

The Chicago Edison directors, aware of Insull's handsome
salary at GE, soon overcame their surprise at his willingness to
take a two-thirds pay cut, and eagerly accepted his offer. Insull
imposed two conditions: that the directors, not he, would assure
the constant availability of sufficient working capital and that
the company would immediately begin construction of a new
generating station. The issuance of $250,000 in new stock, all of
it sold to him, would finance the plant. Insull borrowed the
entire amount from Marshall Field, who in his old age saw this
32-year-old British transplant as a man with a future.

Chicago Edison's board of directors elected Insull president at a meeting held on May 26, 1892. He took charge of the
company on July 1. At his own insistence, Insull received a
three-year contract—not to prevent an early dismissal, but to
force himself to remain in a city whose amenities hardly impressed him. He recalled earlier trips to Chicago during which he
would pass evenings sitting on the porch of the Sherman House,
betting with fellow guests on the number of rats that would
crawl out of the sewers in the street. The contract was a hedge
against any sudden impulse he might have to pull up stakes and
return to New York or London. That was how distasteful he
found physical conditions in Chicago, business opportunities
notwithstanding.

When Insull arrived, he found Chicago Edison only one
of more than 20 small electric lighting companies, and not even
the largest at that. Between 1882 and 1905 the Chicago City

Council granted 29 electric franchises, only three of them city-wide. The City Council, which would continue to lose members to the federal penitentiary as late as the 1970s and 1980s, reached its zenith of corruption during the late 19th century. Electric franchises, like other civic plums, fell to the highest bidder. Insull hated this sort of arrangement, not necessarily because of moral principles—he would soon become one of the most skilled political operators the city would ever know—but because it ran completely counter to his belief that a utility had to be a regulated monopoly to succeed. "While it is not supposed to be popular to speak of exclusive franchises," Insull told an industry group early in his tenure, "it should be recognized that the best service at the lowest possible price can only be obtained . . . by exclusive control of a given territory being placed in the hands of one undertaking . . . In order to protect the public, exclusive franchises should be coupled with the conditions of public control, requiring all charges for services fixed by public bodies to be based on cost plus a reasonable profit. . . . the central station company that works toward this end will, in my opinion, show a far greater return on the money invested by its stockholders and be able to quote a lower price to its customers than the company which undertakes to do the purely retail electric light and industrial power business of the community, as the latter forms but a small portion of the possible business offering."

It would be a number of years before state government would appreciate the logic of Insull's proposal and establish a system of granting exclusive territorial rights to utilities in exchange for the state's right to regulate service and establish the price charged by the utility. Though slowly adopted, however, the regulated monopoly form of utility service continues to this date in Illinois and most other states. The concept of best possible service at lowest possible price remains the basic philosophy of Commonwealth Edison.

In addition to a utility's need to enjoy monopoly status in its own territory and to charge the lowest possible rates, three other fundamental principles would guide Insull as he led Chicago Edison: the company must maintain a highly efficient physical plant of adequate capacity, operate an aggressive marketing program to obtain a large base load, and ensure continuous mass production with a high load factor. Not everyone in the

1890s electricity business understood or appreciated these revolutionary ideas. But Insull obtained the complete backing of his board of directors and moved into action. As biographer McDonald notes, "with every major step he blazed a trail that other central station operators were to follow."

First, he bought out a competitor, the Fort Wayne Electric Company, and moved several bipolar generators from its plant to Chicago Edison's new 27th Street Station at 2640 S. Wabash Ave., built to serve the growing South Side. The Edison board approved this action less than three weeks after Insull had taken over. No fewer than 27 additional acquisitions, costing more than $3.1 million, would follow over the next decade. Acquired about the same time as Fort Wayne Electric, the Chicago Arc Light and Power Company added a substantial load of series arc and incandescent lamps on alternating current to the Edison system. The company took over Chicago Arc's power plant and two additional buildings at Washington Street and the Chicago River. In addition to the plant, the structures housed offices, shops, and laboratories over four decades.

In those days, electrical manufacturers usually gave their franchises the exclusive right to use the manufacturer's equipment in the service territory of the company holding the franchise. Thus, with the purchase of Fort Wayne and Chicago Arc, Insull obtained exclusive rights to use every major kind of electrical equipment except that of Westinghouse. With Insull holding most of the cards, six of the small central station companies in Chicago sold out to him in 1894–95. Westinghouse established a lighting company in Evanston and granted it an exclusive license for Cook County, but Insull bought up that company, too, creating a complete monopoly.

Another early move, far bolder, was aimed at relieving the overworked machinery and overcrowded conditions at 120 W. Adams St. First, Insull bought a little time, not to mention a little more capacity, by renting space in the basement of a building on Monroe Street, across the alley from the Adams Street Station. Here the company moved in four additional dynamos and two small steam engines supplied by the boilers across the way. Insull then instructed his fellow Britisher, Fred Sargent, to design a revolutionary new generating station, with an initial capacity of 6,400 kw, twice the size of the original Adams Street operation. What's more, the new station would stand some two-thirds of a mile from the center of the company's load, on a large tract of inexpensive land along the west bank of the Chicago River at Harrison Street, adjacent to the tracks of a coal-hauling railroad. The river would allow Sargent and his colleagues, Chicago Edison Electrical Engineer Louis A. Ferguson and Drafting Engineer C. G. Y. King, to use condensing generators. This enabled the company to slash in half the amount of coal needed to produce a kilowatthour, more than offsetting the increased investment in distribution lines necessitated by the plant's outlying location.

"But the plans for the station were drawn on such a grand scale," recalled its chief engineer, W. L. Abbott, "that after they were finished and estimates of cost were made, the engineers stood aghast, wondering whether after all it would be wise for the company to risk millions on the venture, which, to be profitable, should have a load far in excess of what the wildest optimist could expect within a reasonable amortization period."

But Insull was proved right, which was usually the case when second-guessed by engineers. As McDonald observes, "The engineering achievement was widely heralded, but the engineering aspect was second to a subtle economic consideration. At Insull's instructions, Sargent made the plant not only a huge one for the day (1,250-horsepower engines and two 400-kilowatt generators) but expandable to several times its initial capacity. This was Insull's first step toward mastering the complexities of central station economics. As a manufacturer he had learned that the bigger the generating equipment the lower the unit cost of capacity, and as a central station operator he realized that an ever-larger generating plant was the key if investment costs were to be kept within reasonable limits."

Abbott's concerns about overbuilding were allayed within a few years of Harrison Street Station's official startup in August of 1894, when the Adams Street plant was shut down because of obsolescence. The following year, the Harrison plant reached its original planned capacity of 6,400 kw. The load continued to grow "by leaps and bounds," according to Abbott. The station's capacity hit 8,900 kw by 1901, then nearly doubled to 16,200 kw over the next two years.

"The station men adopted a rule that each successive high load record should be fittingly celebrated by smoking a box of cigars bought at the chief engineer's (his own) expense," Abbott recalled, "and during the latter part of each year, when the system load was increasing, the chief would be kept busy borrowing money to pay for those celebrations."

He also remembered that the growing loads provided the station hands with an interesting diversion—betting on the day's peak. According to Abbott, the wagering continued until somebody noticed that one of the electrical switchboard operators usually won the pool. The rest of the work force found out "that those skillful electricians ... could vary the reading of the switchboard instruments several thousand amperes by varying the amount of cold air admitted from the windows on the switchboard gallery to the back of the switchboard and to the shunt of the switchboard instrument."

Harrison Street Station was the largest and most economical power plant in the country, but a scant six years after it went into service, the company again had to face a prospective shortage of capacity. As Abbott put it, ". . . within 10 years from the time the first shovel of mud was dredged from the bank of the drydock, the station was completed, fully loaded, enlarged, obsolete, and the construction of its rival and successor, the Fisk Street Station, was well underway."

The company eagerly wanted Harrison Street to be ready for the World Columbian Exposition of 1893. So accurately did the engineers plan their work, according to Abbott, that the first engine was ready for its initial run on New Year's Eve, 1892. Plant engineers fired it up, no doubt in anticipation of a dual celebration. The engine made half of a revolution, then quit, emulating a sister unit owned by GE nicknamed "The White Elephant." The first Harrison Street engine didn't complete its first revolution until October 1893, after it had been almost entirely rebuilt. It did run that fall and winter, but only to provide peak service when Adams Street was overloaded. In spite of its lumbering start, Engine No. 1 and the others that joined it finally went into full-time service in August 1894, and performed with few interruptions over the years.

The World's Fair would, indeed, become a milestone in electrical development, providing a dazzling spectacle of illumination and a showcase for the most advanced equipment. Chicago Edison, however, was not to supply power to the Fair. The Fair's site in Jackson Park, on the South Side, fell at least four miles beyond the company's central business district service territory and therefore beyond the reach of its direct current transmission. The Fair would operate a power plant of its own. Westinghouse and two other firms were the principal contractors for the installations.

According to the public's perception of electricity, the highlight of the Exposition was, as Seymour states, "the magnificent effect of the 66,000 incandescent electric lamps and 533 Helios arc lamps which banished night there, outlining the splendid white buildings and illuminating the beautiful fountains and lagoons. If electric lighting needed a stimulant it received it there. Beautiful photographs of the effects went all over the world." General Electric displayed a 100-foot Tower of Light which contained 10,000 lamps in various colors. That company also exhibited a display of 2,500 lamps of various sizes, shapes and colors—no two alike.

While these lavish displays captured the public's imagination, more mundane electrical devices appealed to the practical nature of Main Street America. Thousands of fairgoers, the large majority of them without electric service, would for the first time witness electric appliances such as flatirons, heating pads, water heaters, and coffee pots, all of which made life easier. It must have been quite an education, because electricity in those days was used almost exclusively for lighting or for small industrial motors, and even those uses were not yet widespread. In 1892 more than one million people lived in Chicago, but only about 5,000 of them used electric lighting. The city was an enormous market just waiting to be tapped, and Sam Insull intended to tap it. But first he and his colleagues needed to master the fundamentals of pricing and marketing electricity, something no one in the U.S. electric industry had accomplished.

The product itself presented the fundamental difficulty. For all practical purposes, a large amount of electricity, unlike shoes or ships or sealing wax, cannot be stored; it has to be manufactured, sold, and delivered simultaneously. The production line can't slow down when inventories build up. Furthermore, a utility must have sufficient plant to meet the peak demand of its customers on a given time of day or year when the maximum amount of electricity is being used. When the demand isn't there, a portion of plant capacity remains unused—clearly not the most economic of situations. The obvious solution is to fill in the valleys that exist between the peaks by enticing customers to use electricity during off-peak periods. Thomas Edison himself first identified this problem, which would plague utilities through the present time. Since nighttime lighting used the most electricity in Edison's day, he tried to increase daytime usage by encouraging office and department store lighting and the use of small motors, as in elevators. Edison failed because those who did get the message turned to isolated plants of their own rather than to the central station. Future "load management" problems would center on nearly the opposite: the public's apparently unshakable habit of demanding the greatest amounts of electricity daily between 9 a.m. and 10 p.m. and seasonally on hot summer days.

Insull began tinkering with price structures soon after he arrived in Chicago. The Edison Company had been charging about 20 cents a kilowatthour (kwh), but the new president scrapped that arrangement in favor of a declining rate that started at 12 cents per kwh and dropped in increments to 5.4 cents, using lower rates to reward customers as they used more and more electricity. Insull found that this schedule worked fine for increasing the consumption of existing users but did little to encourage new business. So Insull adopted the most flexible approach possible toward prospective customers: charge whatever it takes to get their business, just as long as you get their business.

It worked. Between 1892 and 1895 Chicago Edison quadrupled its connected load, while annual sales rocketed from 2.8 to 13.7 million kwh. Yet Insull and his people still did not understand their manufacturing costs. He would remark later that "there was not a man in the central station business prior to 1890 who understood anything about the principles controlling the proper disposal of the product that he manufactured."

The Edison chief stumbled upon the answer by accident. He returned to England in 1894 to spend the Christmas holidays, a "postman's holiday," as it turned out. He was spending a few days in the southern coastal town of Brighton when he noticed a curious circumstance: every shop in town seemed to burn electric lights with no apparent regard for the amount or cost of the energy consumed. Puzzled, Insull sought out the local official who managed the municipal generating station, a young man named Arthur Wright, who gladly explained an invention of his that made the abundant use of electricity economical to the shopkeepers and profitable to the municipality. Wright called his invention a demand meter. It operated on the proposition that the cost of producing electric light is really two costs, fixed and operating, which vary from customer to customer. According to Insull's account of the meeting, Wright told him to suppose "that you have a customer who owns a vacation cottage wired for 20 lamps, but he burns them only three or four weekends a year. Because you have to invest so much money in equipment to be ready to serve him any time he flicks his switches, it costs more than half as much to serve him those few weekends as it would to serve him day and night throughout the year. Now suppose . . . that you have another customer who has the same number of lamps but uses them for several hours every night. To charge these two customers the same rate would be absurd; you make more money out of the second customer at a nickel a kilowatt-hour than you do out of the first at four times that rate."

Consequently, Wright divided the cost into components, one to determine how much equipment was needed to serve the customer and the other to see how much he used the equipment. The charge was a combination of the two, a principle later known as the declining bloc rate. The customer paid the maximum charge for the first few hours of service, to cover his demand on the central station, then saw his charges decline in steps as he used more and more electricity. Insull had already implemented the second half of the equation, charging the lowest price to obtain the maximum number of customers, so he returned to Chicago armed with a new rate structure.

He also returned to grapple with the bugaboo that had stymied Thomas Edison and which Wright apparently had not considered—load factor, the ratio between a generating station's capability and its actual amount of use. He reached three conclusions: first, that service should be extended to as many customers as possible, because they used electricity only a fraction of the time but not all at the same time and therefore could be served by the same central station; second, that isolated plants were economically unsound, since one central station could serve many customers; and third, that competition was ridiculous because of the size of the investments required and resulting duplication of service.

Insull related these principles to one of his crack young engineers, Louis A. Ferguson, then sent him to Brighton to study Wright's system in detail and adapt it to Chicago Edison's operations. Ferguson made his study and returned to Chicago, convinced that Wright's theory was sound. In September 1896, the company bought and installed 14 Wright demand meters for a test period. The system proved itself within a year, after which the company placed the meters in general use.

Ferguson then turned his attention to another growing pain: how to serve the rapidly expanding service territory with the limitations of direct current transmission. The obvious solution of switching to AC wasn't practical because Chicago Edison had too much invested in DC. Besides, as good as AC was for transmission, it didn't work well for distribution; at the higher frequencies required for electric lighting, AC caused incandescent lamps to flicker constantly. Ferguson obtained two machines called rotary converters that combined the best of both worlds. He installed one of the machines at the Harrison Street Station and had someone wind it backward, so that it took DC from the plant, converted it to AC, stepped up the voltage, and sent it across town to the 27th Street Station and the other converter. The second machine reconverted the AC to DC and stepped down the voltage for distribution to customers. A single generating station could now serve all of Chicago.

Sam Insull was, above all, the consummate salesman. With Wright's demand meter under one arm and Ferguson's rotary converter under the other, he could push the company's sales effort as never before. The company certainly did not lack enthusiasm. "Even those who were responsible for the engineering development were keenly interested in selling the product," according to Edison historian J. F. Rice.

Edison's new business overtures were placed under one roof in 1895 with formation of the Contract Department, whose activities included the sale of power, heat, wiring, industrial equipment, and household appliances, in addition to lighting.

44

Under the leadership of the hard-driving John F. Gilchrist, the department expanded from five to 25 salesmen in 1898. "Gilchrist and his men, armed with precise knowledge of costs, could calculate the exact amount any prospective customer was paying for gas lighting or isolated electric lighting and offer the service for less," McDonald observed. "Even more important, they could now bid for a power market as well as a lighting market."

Gilchrist's salesmen, the "general contract agents," not only used low rates to attract new business, but "evolved a long series of ingenious and attractive special offers of one kind and another to assist the solicitors in getting new customers on the lines," Seymour reported. Gilchrist would, for instance, send out his solicitors on hot summer days and have them sell electric fans from their buggies. Some of the men would peddle several buggy loads to the sweltering populace. Another ploy was to offer for a limited time the free installation of six outlets in unwired homes if the homeowner would sign a one-year contract for electric lighting. The offer was so popular that many homeowners, having accepted the six free outlets, paid to have the rest of the home wired. Gilchrist also initiated regular monthly after-hours sales meetings at which the men exchanged experiences and techniques that proved successful.

Another tool of even greater value to Edison's all-out quest for new business arose. Insull summed it up in a speech some years later when he quoted a newspaper friend as advising, "Early to bed, and early to rise; work like Hades, and advertise." In those days, the Edison marketer went from door-to-door, canvassing wiring customers. Potential customers appeared most receptive to the visits if they had seen an Edison ad in the papers. In fact, many of these householders requested the visits. "We do not have to send our canvassers today to visit eight or ten houses before they can discover a possible customer," Insull boasted. "Daily newspaper advertising, properly written and persistently presented to the public, has had the result of so increasing the demand for our product that in the downtown district and the thickly settled residence districts our business is obtained from people who first invite us to call on them."

When the Advertising Department began in 1901, the company was selling about $2,000 worth of appliances daily. The department sent postcards, letters and brochures to customers, touting the advantage of fans, motors, signs and other electric appliances. The Advertising Department also maintained about 2,000 large electric signs throughout Chicago which carried messages such as, "Particular People Prefer Clean Air, That's Why Their Homes Use Electric Lights," and, "When Conversation Lags, Talk About Electricity." In 1904, the company signed a $40,000 contract with Bates Advertising of New York to create a direct-mail ad campaign which, according to Seymour, "was a bold and successful stroke. It was probably the first move of such magnitude on the part of any utility in the direction of advertising its service."

One of the longer-running marketing and ad campaigns was aimed at overcoming the competition of the Humphrey gas arc lamp, sold by the Peoples Gas Company. The Humphrey lamp emitted a great amount of light, but it also produced a great amount of heat, an obvious disadvantage in Chicago summers. Nevertheless, the Humphrey lamp remained popular, particularly among small shopkeepers, with thousands in place throughout the city. Dana Howard, Edison's first advertising director, launched a vigorous ad campaign to replace the Humphrey lamp with electric arc lamps. At first the campaign did not seem to catch on, but with favorable rates and the improved technology of electric arc lamps, the company finally succeeded. But according to Rice, "It was not until 1907, when the tungsten lamp of 60-watt size was perfected, that the displacement of both electric and gas arcs began on a large scale. The company devised a fixture containing four 60-watt lamps which was either sold or rented to customers, and a very active campaign was begun which resulted in the installation of 50,000 of these units inside of five years. It was only a few years after this that gas arc disappeared as a serious competitor."

Edison's advertising department also built a traveling exhibit called "The Electric Cottage" and produced ads that promoted the 80 different appliances it housed. Another campaign featured a stage celebrity of the day, Trixie Friganza, with ads in which she used an electric iron to press petticoats.

In 1903 Gilchrist put a new wrinkle in the advertising program when he launched the publication of *Electric City* magazine, a monthly distributed free to the public, usually at drug stores where people could help themselves from display cabinets placed there by the company under a rental agreement with the proprietor. *Electric City* would depict the joys and benefits of electric service. To reduce its overall cost to the company, the magazine carried paid advertising, typically placed

Stage celebrity Trixie Friganza presses a petticoat with an electric iron in an Edison advertisement.

by electrical manufacturers and suppliers. The first edition of the magazine numbered eight pages and 5,000 copies. By the time it ceased publication in 1917, due to high printing costs associated with World War I, *Electric City* averaged 36 pages and 40,000 copies a run.

Chicago Edison got into the retail sales business in 1909 with the opening of the Electric Shop at Michigan Avenue and Jackson Boulevard in downtown Chicago. As early as 1889, the company had a small salesroom in its headquarters at 139 W. Adams Street, but the opening of the Electric Shop represented a major effort to market electrical appliances and equipment to the public. The company opened a branch store in South Chicago two years later and subsequently located other branches in neighborhoods throughout the city.

The ground floor of the shop at Michigan and Jackson featured household appliances. The basement housed an Industrial Power Room that displayed lathes, drills, punch presses, and other motor-driven equipment. The Electric Shop did business at that corner until 1915, when its functions were moved to the newly acquired Edison Building at 72 W. Adams St.

In operating the shops, the company had three goals in mind: to make certain that customers used safe and efficient equipment, to increase the use of electricity and encourage further sales, and to improve the company's load factor, leading to lower average rates for the customers. In keeping with the first goal, Edison submitted new appliances to its Testing Department for comprehensive inspections that covered design, safety and efficiency before selling them to the public.

Additionally, the company promoted the sale of electric appliances by contractors and dealers by helping them finance installment sales. Chicago Edison even got into the automobile sales business by promoting electric cars in the early 1900s. The company advertised the Stanhope electric auto as a silent, clean, economical alternative to the early gasoline car. One ad showed a young man and woman in a Stanhope, along with the caption: "Too pleasant quite to count the miles, for in a Stanhope, miles are smiles."

The last Electric Shop operated by Edison closed in early 1963. The shops, once popular with the public, at one time had totalled about 40, but the proliferation of retail hardware and appliance stores made them unnecessary to encourage appliance sales. The popularity of the Electric Shops is illustrated by some early sales figures for the downtown location. In 1916, the Edison Building shop sold less than $500,000 worth of merchandise. Two years later, the total had increased to $840,000 and the following year, 1919, the shop chalked up nearly $2 million in sales.

On the other hand, Edison's popular light bulb service continued. In the late 1880s the company began supplying customers with standard incandescent lamps marked with the corporate logo. For many years Edison servicemen installed lamps for new customers. When the lamps burned out, the customer could either exchange them for new ones at agencies located throughout the city or have them delivered to the door by Edison truck. Though the days of home-delivered light bulbs have long passed, Edison remains the only electric utility in the country with a light bulb program for customers.

The early days of door-to-door canvassing produced their share of vignettes. When Louis Ferguson, the engineer Insull would dispatch to Brighton, England a few years later, called on a lighting customer, he noticed that the lights were becoming progressively dimmer. In fact, all of the lights in the neighborhood were the same way. Ferguson started to run to the old Adams Street Station about two blocks away, figuring, according to a 1923 article in *The American Magazine*, that "there must have been a simultaneous burning out of a number of 'safety catches' (fuses), crippling the entire system. It was evident to him, knowing thoroughly the equipment of his company, that a tremendous current was being carried on the neutral conductor of the big Adams Street trunk line, and it was only a question of minutes until very extensive and serious damage would be done." The trunk line was a three-wire system with two principal legs having about four times the capacity as the neutral.

Ferguson burst into the generating station, pushed his way through the crowd that had gathered, and flew into the switchboard room. As he pulled the largest switch, there was a blinding flash, and the city was plunged into darkness. "Even the red glow of the wires in the lamps vanished," the magazine article continued. "There was no current at all for an hour or so, until the burned-out fuses could be replaced, the generators started up again, and the equilibrium of the system restored. But if he had not pulled the switch when he did, the damage to the underground trunk line would have been so great that the company might not have been able to furnish service to its customers for many weeks."

The blinding flash cost Ferguson some of his hair, most of his mustache, and all of his eyebrows. The magazine story maintained that if Ferguson had not injured his right hand in a bicycle accident the previous weekend, he might have been blinded; if he had grabbed the switch with his right hand instead of his left, he could not have averted his head. The article continued, somewhat melodramatically, that "The next day there would have been a piece in the papers, just a short note probably, telling how a young electrical engineer of promise had been blinded when he pulled a switch through which passed a current of *10,000 amperes.*"

Because of this incident, Ferguson invented a copper fuse that bore his name and became the standard of the industry. "We had lead composition fuses on the (Adams Street) switchboard," Ferguson recalled years later. "The whole negative side was blown out ... I hit on the idea that perhaps copper fuses could be made, designed so that they would not blow out with an overload of 25 percent ... This (Ferguson) fuse will not burn out unless it has 100 percent overload on it."

The results of Chicago Edison's aggressive marketing program began to appear almost immediately after Insull assumed the presidency in 1892. Production quadrupled during Insull's first three years, then doubled again during the next three years to 26 million kwh in 1898. Shortly after the turn of the century, output neared the 100-million kwh plateau, so that Insull could go after a market that would make sales skyrocket like never before—the electric railway. But first the Edison chief would have to endure what McDonald described as his "initial bath of fire in Chicago's political inferno."

The streetcar lines and elevated railways in Chicago were controlled by Charles Tyson Yerkes, a transplant from Philadelphia who greased the City Council and state legislature as easily —and apparently as regularly—as his workers greased the streetcars. Under Illinois law, city councils held the power to issue franchises to public utilities, but only for a maximum of 20 years. Since he had fashioned his empire by buying up a number of small companies over a period of time, Yerkes found himself having to renew one franchise or another every few years, and that meant having to pay off the City Council each time.

By late 1896, however, Yerkes thought the time was opportune to get the politicians' hands out of his pockets once and for all. For one, his nemesis, Democratic Governor John Peter Altgeld, had been defeated in the November election by Republican John R. Tanner. Altgeld would automatically veto any bill that had Yerkes' fingerprints on it; Tanner, at least, was expected to have an open mind. Moreover, Yerkes' most important franchises would expire in only six years. Not only would the politicians undoubtedly demand the moon with a fence around it for renewal of the pacts, but also the coming deadline hampered Yerkes' ability to raise the capital needed to finance his expanding business. It would be difficult, if not impossible, to market long-term bonds of a company that could be disenfranchised, or effectively put out of business, within a few years.

So in the legislative session of 1897, Yerkes had legislation introduced that would have revolutionized utility regulation in Illinois. One of the key provisions of this package of bills would remove control of local transportation companies from corrupt city councils and place them instead under the regulation of a fair and impartial state commission. The bills also would have extended the franchises of all streetcar and elevated railway companies by 50 years. In return, the companies would pay the municipalities they served a one-time fee of $2,000 a mile and a percentage of gross revenues after that.

"Having framed such legislation," McDonald observed, "Yerkes now cheerfully set about the business of bribing the legislators to pass it. He reckoned that the price would be high; after all he was bribing politicians to pass laws that would make it unnecessary for him to bribe them again. Even so, he grossly underestimated the cost, for he was shortly buried in a public furor headed by as bizarre a collection of political bedfellows as Chicago had ever seen."

The furor apparently started when the *Tribune* reported that Yerkes had set aside a $500,000 slush fund to buy the votes of state senators and representatives. Ironically, posturing politicians, good government groups, reformers, business leaders, and Yerkes' numerous enemies banded together to scuttle the bills. Though crafted by a notorious political fixer and introduced by one of his bagmen, the legislation would have cleaned up utility regulation, catapulted Illinois into the 20th century, and established a model for the rest of the nation to follow. As it was, Wisconsin would create the pioneer utility commission—but not for another ten years.

Yerkes did salvage one minor victory from the legislative slaughter: passage of the Allen Law, which gave city councils the power to grant utility franchises for up to 50 years. The Allen Law didn't do Yerkes any good—he was politically dead after the slush fund scandal—but it was seized upon by a group of corrupt Chicago aldermen known as the Gray Wolves. With the ink barely dry on the Allen Law, the Gray Wolves figured out a scheme to profit from it. Their victim was to be Sam Insull, whose thoughts were not entirely on business at that time. He was courting actress Gladys Wallis, who would become his wife.

The same scheme had worked before. In 1895 a group of political figures that included Mayor John P. Hopkins and Democratic power broker Roger Sullivan set up a dummy corporation known as the Ogden Gas Company. Then they had a city ordinance passed which granted a liberal franchise to the corporation, much to the chagrin of the existing gas monopoly, People's Gas. The Hopkins-Sullivan combine then generously offered to sell out for $7.33 million. Peoples Gas, with its corporate eye as much on the carrot of the attractive franchise as on the stick of a rival company, accepted the offer. Sullivan, Hopkins, and their pals split the proceeds into 11 equal shares without so much as having delivered one therm of gas.

Now came Insull's turn. While not nearly as large or well-fixed as the gas company, Chicago Edison could be touched, the politicians calculated, for several hundred thousand or even a million dollars, to prevent the creation of a competitor with a 50-year franchise that covered the entire city. When the Gray Wolves approached Insull, though, he turned them down. So the Wolves moved on to step two, the creation of a dummy corporation called Commonwealth Electric Company and City Council passage of a 50-year franchise for the firm. Insull still said no. The Wolves then moved to transform the dummy corporation into an active competitor, figuring this would clinch the deal. But Insull held the final card. Chicago Edison held exclusive rights to buy the electrical equipment of every American manufacturer. The Wolves might have a long-term franchise, but franchises by themselves don't turn on any lights. Insull had won, and the Wolves knew it. Four months later, he bought Commonwealth, and a brand-new half-century franchise, for a paltry $50,000. The Allen Law was repealed the following year, so there Chicago Edison sat, the only electric utility in Illinois with a pact for more than 20 years.

The maneuvering earned Insull the grudging respect of Chicago's rough and tumble political operators. To head off future clashes, the Edison chief now moved to earn their friendship—and succeeded. He forged a particularly close friendship with Roger Sullivan which lasted until Sullivan's death nearly two decades later.

In 1899, the year after his battle with the Gray Wolves and the Hopkins-Sullivan faction, Insull proposed that state agencies should regulate utilities by setting rates and determining standards of service. His forum was the National Electric Light Association (NELA), of which he was president. He urged the membership to push for legislation that would provide for "exclusive franchises ... coupled with the conditions of public control, requiring all charges for services fixed by public bodies to be based on cost plus a reasonable profit. It will be found that this cost will be reduced in direct proportion to the protection afforded the industry. The more certain this protection is made, the lower the total cost of operation will be, and, consequently, the lower the price of the service to public and private users." "Protection" was the key word. Competition among utilities was anathema to Insull.

"It is supposed by many who discuss municipal affairs," he told NELA, "that the granting of competitive franchises for public service work is the true means of obtaining for users the lowest possible price for the service rendered, where, as a matter of fact, the exact opposite is the ultimate result. . .Acute competition necessarily frightens the investor, and compels corporations to pay a very high price for capital. The competing companies invariably come together, and the interest cost on their product (which is by far the most important part of their cost) is rendered abnormally high, owing partly to duplication of investment and partly to the high price paid for money borrowed during the period of competition." Insull's proposal was a bit too bold for his colleagues, however. They set up a committee to study the idea, and it languished.

Meanwhile, Chicago Edison quickly capitalized on the opportunity that the acquisition of Commonwealth Electric had provided. An 1898 operating contract between the two companies gave Commonwealth the right to call upon Chicago Edison for as much power as necessary to serve its considerably larger territory. The combined territory of the two companies, 33 miles long and eight miles wide, extended from the northern border of Chicago to the Indiana state line on the east. At the same time, Chicago Edison continued to absorb the small electric lighting companies that had sprung up in various outlying parts of the city, with six such acquisitions in 1897–98 alone.

This vastly expanded service territory didn't necessitate immediate expansion of the generating system, however, because of an improved load factor. Since most residential use of electricity was for lighting, the demand of the outlying neighborhoods during the day was negligible, freeing capacity for commerce and industry in the central business district. When stores, offices and factories closed for the day, customers went home and turned on the lights. Nevertheless, the number of Edison's customers still shot up from 7,300 in 1897 to more than 16,000 in 1900.

In 1901 the prize that Chicago Edison had coveted, the traction load, dropped into its corporate lap through a totally unexpected development—Yerkes' departure from the city. Surrounded by rumors of criminal indictment and pressured by his stockholders, Yerkes sold everything and left for London. The newspapers and reformers wouldn't have C. T. Yerkes to kick around anymore. Insull happily saw him go because Yerkes' leaving promised to make politics easier for all utilities. But while the Edison leader savored this development, he was beaten to the punch for one of the few times in his life. An entrepreneur named Charles A. Munroe, who had acquired a small hydroelectric plant on the Illinois River near Joliet, sat on the edge of a major coup. As Munroe sized up the situation, the streetcar companies and elevated railways in Chicago, as elsewhere, generated their own power. What made Chicago different was the fact that Yerkes was playing both ends against the middle: he not only owned streetcar and elevated companies, but a power equipment company as well. Thus, the crafty Yerkes had a captive market for his power company. Munroe surmised that Yerkes was probably jacking up the price of power to the streetcar and elevated lines, but with Yerkes out of the picture, the managers of these companies might appreciate a better offer. He was right. His first call, on the president of the Lake Street elevated, resulted in an agreement to buy all the power Munroe could deliver.

When Insull found out about Munroe's plans, he was thunderstruck. If this upstart could line up the rest of the transportation companies, he would become the leading supplier of electric power in Chicago almost overnight. Insull didn't realize that Munroe had little more ability to supply the amounts of power needed than the Gray Wolves when they tried to fleece him four years earlier. Munroe, a shrewd operator in his own right, certainly wouldn't enlighten Insull on this score. He sold his business to Insull. The Edison chief received two things in the bargain: a green light to take up the traction load and an insight into the character of a man whom McDonald describes as a "miniature Insull." The Edison chief brought Munroe into the organization, where he served as a top lieutenant for many years.

Insull then pursued the transportation companies, armed with statistics to prove that Chicago Edison could supply their power needs much more cheaply than the companies themselves could. He landed every one, doubling sales and improving the load factor. Mass transit passengers now used Edison electricity as they left home in the morning and as they returned in the evening, to contribute to the daily peak demand.

The message drawn from booming sales and an expanded service territory was clear: the company again urgently needed new capacity. In fact, the company required a new generating station from the inking of the first traction contract. Insull had some definite, though revolutionary, ideas about the type of plant he wanted. However, his own engineers emphatically told him that his ideas were not feasible. The situation was reminiscent of a story about an elderly professor of Biblical History who, year after year, asked the same single question on the final exam: "List, in order, the kings of Judea." Year after year students came to the final exam with their heads crammed with kings of Judea and not much else. Then one year, without warning, the old man changed the rules of the game. As usual, there was only one question on the exam, but it read: "Criticize the teachings of Moses." The class went into a quiet panic. Some tried to bluff their way through. One perplexed student, in a burst of imagination or lack thereof, finally scribbled: "Who am I to criticize the teachings of Moses?"

Who were mere engineers to criticize the teachings of Insull?

Four

"I Will Blow Up With It"

I f you drive the Dan Ryan Expressway in Chicago, chances are you've passed it many times, perhaps thousands, and have never given it a second glance. That's understandable. It's really not very eye-catching; it just sort of stands there, blending in with the aging industrial and residential skyline of the near Southwest Side. Few of the most knowledgeable Chicagoans are aware of the historical role played by this red brick building with three stacks, one taller than the other two.

Heading south out of the Loop, you drive through the interchange with the Eisenhower Expressway; pass the University of Illinois Chicago Circle campus, just out of view on the right, where the city's old Italian-American neighborhood used to stand; cross under Roosevelt Road; then begin a gentle climb, usually in heavy traffic, merging with cars and trucks from the Eisenhower. You pass Providence of God Catholic Church on the right, focal point of the Mexican-American Pilsen community, only the top half of the church visible from the expressway bridge in its front yard. You make a lazy curve to the right, then left as some of the traffic peels off toward the Stevenson Expressway to the west and Lake Shore Drive to the east.

Now you have a good look at it—Commonwealth Edison's Fisk Generating Station. Historic Fisk, revolutionary in its day, still very much a part of the Edison system, generating electricity to customers just as it first did in October 1903, two months before the Wright Brothers made another kind of history at Kitty Hawk and seven years before its infinitely better known neighbor, Comiskey Park, Charles A. Comiskey's "Base Ball Palace of the World," opened its gates to fans.

Yes, Fisk was there before the ball park, the college, the expressways, looking much the same now as it did when it went into service. It never would have gone into service without Sam Insull's determination, even stubbornness, and the unanimous support of Edison's board of directors in the face of outcries from technical experts who said it couldn't be done. Insull once sneered that the engineers at General Electric carried slide rules which they used to prove that anything was impossible. In this instance, however, even the imaginative Fred Sargent told the boss it couldn't be done. Insull had proposed to build nothing less than the world's largest central generating station, using a technology never before demonstrated on that scale.

Insull wanted to build three 5,000-kilowatt units at Fisk. The reciprocating steam engines in use at Harrison Street Station could handle only 4,000 kw, and were near the limit of size and stress. Even without the stress problems, a future plant with 50,000-kilowatt units would require an area the size of Chicago's Loop. Besides, Harrison Street was already overloaded, and expansion of that plant would have provided only a short-term solution to the mounting demand on the system. Insull and his engineers began looking to the steam turbine as a possible answer to the problem.

The steam turbine had existed for a number of years. The earliest type of steam machine, it served as a generating drive as early as 1884. Its problem was size. Before 1900, GE had turned out 600-kilowatt experimental turbines. In that year, the Hartford Electric Light Company installed a 1,500-kilowatt Westinghouse turbine. The most ambitious turbine work was being done in Europe, a fact that did not go unnoticed by Insull, but even there the largest turbines could provide no more than 1,000 kw. Again he dispatched Louis Ferguson to Europe in 1901, now to inspect turbine installations and bring back some innovations. This time, Sargent accompanied Ferguson. The two men checked turbine installations in Germany, Italy, and Switzerland and liked what they saw, convinced that Europe, according to Ferguson, "was tending very definitely to the turbo-generator unit with its low space requirement, comparatively simple mechanism and moderate cost."

GE president Charles Coffin balked at building 5,000-kilowatt turbines for Edison, offering instead to supply smaller units. Insull persisted, threatening to take his business to England. The threat of foreign competition adequately convinced

Coffin: he and Insull struck a compromise under which GE would assume the manufacturing risk and Chicago Edison pay for installation. If the unit didn't work, Insull told Coffin, "I will make no claim against you. . .all you have to do is take the apparatus out and throw it in the junk pile."

The installation would take place on the north bank of the Chicago River at Fisk Street, where it could easily draw a large volume of condensing water. Originally called Fisk Street Station, the company dropped the word Street in 1937 when the city changed the road's name to Carpenter Street. Edison formally placed an order with GE in December 1901 for the first 5,000-kilowatt Curtis turbo-generator. According to Seymour, "The engineering world could hardly believe its ears. It was not too much to say that other companies in the power business were well satisfied to mark time on their own plans and await the outcome of the Chicago company's great experiment."

The Fisk Street Station in late 1904—one year after it went into service.

Ground was broken on June 28, 1902, and Unit 1 went into service on October 2, 1903, a scant seven months after the foundations went down. Although the station could accommodate 14 such units, only three more went up from 1903 to 1906. All four were replaced within a few years by larger units with improved design and higher efficiency.

The startup of Fisk Unit 1, with attendant pomp and ceremonies, had its share of problems. According to Insull, a "terrific rumbling" occurred when the unit was first fired. The dignitaries were quickly hustled out of the area and the turbine shut down. The cause of the problem was discovered and fixed, but as Sargent got ready to start the unit again, he noticed Insull standing at his side. The engineer made it plain to his boss that he wanted everyone out of the area, Insull included. When the Edison chief asked why, Sargent replied that what he was doing was dangerous, and that he didn't know what might happen.

"Then why don't you leave?" Insull asked.

"Look, Mr. Insull. It's my job to stay here. I have to. But you don't. Don't you understand? This damned thing might blow up."

"If it blows up I will blow up with it anyway, in more ways than one, so I might just as well remain here."

Both men stayed, but there was no explosion, only history made as a new age of power dawned. At a civic luncheon at the station on Oct. 3, 1978, commemorating Fisk's 75th anniversary, Edison Chairman and President Thomas G. Ayers stated, "The electricity produced by Fisk Station through the years has contributed greatly to the city's growth and progress. Indeed, without Fisk and without the continued advances made in the development of central station power since that historic October day 75 years ago, Chicago would not have evolved into the great commercial/industrial center it is today."

Ten units, nearly two-and-one-half times the size of those that drew gasps from the industry a few years earlier, were installed at Fisk between 1906 and 1910. Insull later admitted that only the fourth unit had finally performed economically. In fact, equipment failures and operating problems cropped up aplenty in the early days, according to logs that provide a virtual day-to-day history. In a 1984 interview, Vern Stone, who had retired as the company's power production manager in 1966, remembered fishing one such log out of a wastebasket at Fisk in 1924, soon after he started work for the company. Stone concluded that the early station hands "didn't throw in the towel," in spite of their troubles, and the 64-page report "may serve as some solace to those who are presently confronted with equipment failures and have the responsibility of keeping the power flowing."

Condensation presented at least one of the recurring problems in the early days of Fisk Unit 1. "If the machine developed any peculiarity which the engineers did not understand," the report stated, "it was immediately shut down and frantic instructions were issued to the boiler room force to draw fires, but before this could be accomplished, the safety valves had commenced discharging volumes of steam—not being connected at this period with atmosphere, and, in consequence, after a few minutes, everybody was enveloped in clouds of steam, which when condensed on the boiler room ceiling, descended in a miniature tropical shower. Water tenders were provided with torches for these emergencies to look after their pressure and water gauges."

Stone also remembered a rivalry among the electrical, boiler, and turbine hands, with each group keeping largely to itself.

"One morning, an electrical operator who worked with me and I wanted to stay over (after the night shift) and go over to the boiler room to see how they met the load as it came up. The boiler room had 96 stoker-fired boilers—16 rows with six to a row. But...we had to get an OK from the chief engineer of the plant to permit us, after we'd finished work as operators, to go over to the boiler room to see how they brought up those boilers. I guess every outfit thought they were the only ones that operated the plant.

"Speaking of class distinction," Stone continued, "I spent a few months on the exciter floor, and they had Corliss engines for each of those vertical turbine generators. I asked the watch engineer, who was in charge of the plant at night, what the Corliss engines did with regard to the turbines. He said, 'You're on the electrical end, aren't you?' I told him yes. He said, 'Then get over there and mind your own damned business.' I don't think he *knew* what those engines were for."

In 1914 the station pioneered the development of horizontal turbine generator shafts to replace the former vertical design. As units grew in size, the increased speed of the shafts and the added weight of the larger units required the horizontal design to achieve maximum support of the station floor. Fisk Station also pioneered the use of separate buildings for the switching and power house equipment. The boilers and turbines were in one building, the switch gear in a smaller building about 50 feet away.

Even Tom Edison himself visited Fisk in January 1912. The guest register that the Wizard signed remains on display at the station. Fisk remained the largest generating station on the Edison system until 1959. In 1975 the American Society of Mechanical Engineers designated its first unit a National Historic Mechanical Engineering Landmark. It is enshrined at GE headquarters in Schenectady, New York. One of the histories of Fisk Station declares that the plant "has ever been since its inception a proving ground, not only for equipment and radical changes in methods of operation, but it has been the crucible in which many of the more efficient operating men now manning the great generating stations of the company have been developed."

During the decade after Fisk began generating power, Edison added two more large coal-fired stations—Quarry Street, on nine acres across the river from Fisk; and Northwest, on part of a 105-acre tract on the city's Northwest Side, bounded by Roscoe Street on the south, Addison Street on the north, Kimball Avenue on the west, and the north branch of the Chicago River on the east. Quarry Street Station began operating in 1908 and by 1910 had six 14,000-kilowatt turbo-generators. Northwest, which started up in 1912, boasted a pair of 20,000-kilowatt Curtis steam turbines, the largest individual units to date. In 1914 Northwest received a 30,000-kilowatt GE turbo-generator, again the largest in the world at that time.

While Edison had planted grass and flowers around Fisk —the first such treatment at one of its power plants—the landscape paled alongside that of Northwest, whose grounds the *Round Table* described as "a park-like estate of which any owner might be proud." The company retained most of the large trees that had graced the site when it was purchased, then added a number of smaller ones. Workers graded the low spots, planting lawns, flowering shrubs and hardy bushes. They laid out macadam driveways and cement walks, lining them with flower beds. The grounds proved functional as well as beautiful. For several summers, employes from throughout the company flocked to Northwest for a day's outing that included foot races, baseball games, and pole climbing contests—even archery and trap shooting—and of course, plenty of refreshments. Downtown employes concluded their normal six-day work week about noon on the Saturday of the annual picnic and rode special trains to the site.

In 1913 Commonwealth Edison absorbed the Cosmopolitan Electric Company and its 14,000-kilowatt Grove Street Station. Harrison Street Station, eclipsed by Fisk, Quarry Street, and Northwest, was demolished in 1916 to make way for the terminals and freight houses of the proposed Union Station. One memento of the old workhorse remains, a silent witness to nearly a century of Commonwealth Edison history: a handsome 1,200-pound clock, whose journey parallels the progress of the company itself and has come to symbolize Edison's durability and reliability.

The historic Edison clock has had several locations. Operating Engineer Don Boyd (left) and Unit Operator Stan Bednarczyk prepare it for shipment from Ridgeland Station to a display window at the Edison Building in 1982.

The Chicago Edison Clock, crafted by E. Howard & Company of Boston, originally ticked atop Harrison Street's main electrical switchboard when the station opened in 1894. It stands more than five feet high and has a face over three feet in diameter. Metal scrollwork around the face joins a broad foundation piece 11 feet long. According to Clarence Hall, retired division manager of fossil stations, the clock almost failed to survive Harrison Street's demolition. "When Harrison Street Station was closed down," Hall stated, "Alex Bailey, a young engineer at Harrison, saved the clock from being junked, along with the rest of the station." The clock went to the new Edison

Building at 72 W. Adams St., which had been purchased and turned into company headquarters the year before. The massive timepiece found a home on the third level of Customers Hall, a cavernous three-story room where the company's cashiers, tellers, and clerks worked. Before it was installed in that setting, the clock received a new interior—the original mechanical movement was replaced by an electrical one that regulated all other company clocks in the building.

The clock stood as a mute observer of cashier and customer service operations until 1947, when the company renovated Customers Hall, and the timepiece didn't fit into the new scheme of things. Again, according to Clarence Hall, Alex Bailey, now an assistant vice president, stepped in and "prevailed upon management to put it in storage. At the time Ridgeland (Station) was built in 1950, Bailey was head of the Production Department and requested the clock be incorporated as a part of the new station's design." Indeed it was, so when Ridgeland went on line as the showpiece of the Edison generating system, the company resurrected the clock and moved it to its new home at 4300 S. Ridgeland Ave. in southwest suburban Stickney. There it remained until Ridgeland was retired in 1982.

Repeating history, the clock then traveled from a retired generating station back to the Edison Building. It was formally unveiled and rededicated Nov. 9, 1982, in ceremonies conducted by Chairman and President James J. O'Connor. "It adds a thread of continuity to our company's history for those of us who like to hear about Edison people ... those who worked through the engineering and marketing brilliance of the Insull years, the spectacular advances in power engineering of the '30s, '40s, and '50s, and of course, the age of nuclear power." The clock now faces Adams Street from the center window of the ground level Customer Service Plaza, where thousands of passersby view it every day. It remains the oldest piece of operating equipment on the Edison system. "I only wish this clock could talk," O'Connor mused at the rededication ceremonies. "It has seen so many things."

After the 27th Street Station, Chicago Edison added nine substations, so that by 1903, 10 operated and 11 more went under construction. These substations received current from Fisk, Quarry, and Harrison Street Stations. Different types of substations supplied the incandescent lighting, industrial, and traction loads. For example, transformer substations reduced current to usable voltages for large industrial motors; rotary converter substations received high voltage and transformed it into direct current at the voltage needed by the streetcars and elevated trains; while the remaining substations stepped down to the low voltage required for lighting. Twenty-seventh Street was discontinued as a central station, but served as a substation beginning in 1907.

The load dispatcher, a job created in 1903, formed the center of this increasingly complex power system. One of his early responsibilities was to coordinate between Fisk and Quarry Street so that each would carry an appropriate share of the varying load. In front of him sat an operating board that showed all generating units, frequency changes, and transformers, as well as prints of the transmission and distribution networks. Indicators displayed the condition of all switches, while measuring instruments provided continuous readings of output and load across the system. The dispatcher maintained direct-line telephone contact with the generating stations and other key points on the system to deal with the complex control problems that included a number of simultaneous variables.

Edison's rapid assimilation of the electric railway and streetcar load sent sales soaring to staggering heights. By 1905, only three years after the company had signed up its first traction customer, production had doubled for the seventh time in 13 years. In another five years it quintupled to more than the combined output of New York Edison, Brooklyn Edison, and Boston Edison. In 1907, the year Chicago Edison and Commonwealth Electric joined to form the Commonwealth Edison Company, the company had grown 60 times larger than when Insull took over in 1892. By 1909, the traction load consumed approximately 65 percent of the company's output. And as the company added traction customers, it reduced rates to attract all other types of customers.

According to McDonald, "To win customers, Insull sold electricity at rates so low they appalled other central station men. His traction rates started at less than a cent a kilowatthour and scaled down to as little as four-tenths of a cent. To get power and light customers he used the same formula he used in getting traction customers: one part quality service, two parts hard selling, and three parts rate cuts. He continued to sell to large power customers by offering special contracts at whatever price was necessary to get the business. For commercial and residential customers he used uniform rate schedules and cut them as fast as possible."

The first rate cuts occurred in 1898. Another round followed in 1905, continuing every year thereafter for the next ten years. There would be 26 altogether before the company received its first rate increase in 1954. When Insull took over the company in 1892, rates for all classes of customers averaged about 20 cents per kwh. The average rate had dropped to 10 cents per kwh by 1897 and fell steadily to 2.5 cents by 1909. Edison's rates fell far below those of most other large cities. And as the rates swooped, the number of customers soared. The company added its 10,000th customer in 1898, its 50,000th in 1906, its 100,000th in 1909, and its 200,000th in 1913.

In spite of Edison's continuing rate reductions, Chicago politicians couldn't resist the temptation to posture a bit. A movement to bring about municipal ownership of electric utilities had been underway throughout the country almost since the beginning of electric utilities themselves. This movement reached a peak in the early years of the century, particularly in Illinois, which enacted a law authorizing the City of Chicago to set rates for all of its utility services. At the same time, a second law authorized the city to expand its small street lighting plant into a full-scale electric utility to rival Chicago Edison. On the political front, Edward F. Dunne got himself elected mayor by waging a one-issue campaign—immediate municipal acquisition of all transportation companies, a popular concept, considering all of the high jinks of the traction firms and the resulting bad publicity over the years. Insull counterattacked with something equally popular: a rate cut. He then negotiated a secret verbal contract to supply the city's largest streetcar company with all of its future power needs. While the city officials considered their strategy for acquiring the transportation companies, Insull continued to negotiate in secret, cutting deals to supply the power requirements of nearly all of the remaining transit lines. These deals would be binding regardless of whether the city acquired the companies.

This strategy immediately preceded the merger of Chicago Edison and Commonwealth Electric. Insull offered to cut rates still further if the City Council would approve the merger. Legally, Insull didn't need council approval, but he still wanted the blessing of a body dominated by anti-utility politicians. The aldermen, preoccupied with the traction companies and satisfied to have a hand in cutting rates, approved. Mayor Dunne, however, viewed the action as a personal rebuke and promptly vetoed it. Quite an act of political courage, or folly, for here was a mayor vetoing a measure to lower utility rates. But Insull remained undaunted. He loudly proclaimed that he would implement the rate cut anyway. In a face-saving effort, Dunne called in accountants from New York in an attempt to prove that Edison should reduce rates even further. The ploy failed miserably. The accountants told the mayor that Edison's books were in order and, if anything, the company's rates were probably the lowest in the world. Dunne never went public with the report, choosing to drop the matter entirely.

In 1907 Fred Busse became mayor, and a long period of tranquility followed. On Sept. 16 of that year, stockholders of both Chicago Edison and Commonwealth Electric approved the merger, and the two companies consolidated to become Commonwealth Edison Company. For the first time, Chicago had a unified power supply.

Five

An Anniversary And An Experiment

A crowd filled Orchestra Hall, longtime home of the Chicago Symphony Orchestra, on the night of April 29, 1912, but they had not come to hear a concert. They came to celebrate the 25th Anniversary of Commonwealth Edison and its predecessor companies. The Edison chapter of the National Electric Light Association sponsored the event. The star of the evening, of course, was Sam Insull, who had crafted the company from virtually nothing 20 years earlier into the foremost electrical utility in the world and who stood before the assembly at age 52 as the unrivaled leader of the industry. He had assumed the presidency of a company whose generating stations had a rating of about 5,000 horsepower and had increased it to some 400,000 horsepower. Additionally, companies that Insull controlled now had a combined capital of $175 million.

Insull began his remarks with a slide show, tracing the birth and development of the industry. He displayed a telegram from Thomas Edison, congratulating Commonwealth Edison employes "on the abnormally progressive spirit and work that has led to the wonderful degree of success you have attained in a quarter of a century." Then Insull recounted his own days with the Wizard at Menlo Park and talked about Pearl Street, the old 139 Adams building, Harrison Street, Fisk, Quarry Street, Northwest, the huge amounts of coal consumed by the company. He even predicted the eventual coming of electric heat. The crowd heard vintage Insull—windy, flowery, sentimental; plugging regulated monopoly, critical of demagogues, and lavish in praise of the Edison employe.

"But just imagine what would happen to a community like Chicago if our service stopped!" the Edison chief declared. "The wheels of industry would cease. The majority of newspapers would cease to be printed. The Post Office and the Federal Courts would have to shut down. In fact most of those things which contribute to the comfort of modern civilization would have to come to a standstill."

The first airplane delivery of a Federal washing machine took place on March 11, 1919. The plane took off from Grant Park and flew to Evanston customer Rufus C. Dawes.

Had he chosen to expand upon his review of the company's first quarter-century, Insull could have mentioned that Commonwealth Edison now spanned a city covering more than 200 square miles, with electricity available in virtually unlimited quantities for any purpose. The system boasted three principal generating stations and 41 substations, joined together by thousands of miles of overhead and underground lines.

The system served most of the big stores, office buildings, hotels, and industrial plants from which isolated generating plants had been removed. With the popularity of the electric car and truck, garages where the vehicles could be recharged enjoyed a brisk business. The 60-watt tungsten lamp went into use in 1906, marking the beginning of the end of the Humphrey gas arc lamp.

Guests at the Silver Anniversary celebration traveled to Orchestra Hall on streets which incandescent lights had illuminated for several years. The lights shone even brighter in shopping districts where local business groups had had their own street lighting systems installed and serviced by Edison under long-term contracts. The first of these had been installed along Milwaukee Avenue in 1908.

The ready availability of electric power fostered the invention of a number of labor-saving appliances in the early years of the century. The first modern electric washing machine and the electric toaster appeared in 1907. The same year saw the company's Contract Department launch a campaign that placed 10,000 electric flatirons in Chicago homes. Then came a portable lamp campaign, one for coffee percolators, and still another for home wiring. Edison's marketers were on a roll.

An Edison electric van delivering washing machines about 1910-1918.

In 1908, a Chicago janitor invented the first portable electric vacuum cleaner. Two years later came the first motor-driven, electrically heated ironing machine and the first practical electric range. At the same time, electric refrigeration made strides with Chicago butcher and floral shops, and electricity was now being used to make commercial ice on a large scale. At the opposite end of the thermometer, electric power was first used in Chicago for the reduction of steel casings, soon followed by the melting of large amounts of brass.

71

The 25th anniversary of the company also marked the expiration of the 25-year franchise obtained by Western Edison in 1887 and acquired two weeks later by the newly organized Chicago Edison Company. The expiration did not concern the company, however, because it still could operate under Commonwealth Electric's 50-year franchise obtained in the hectic year 1897. A rate-regulating ordinance which the Chicago City Council had adopted in 1908 also expired in 1912. The ordinance had placed a declining ceiling on rates. The Council ordered an investigation of the company's rates and passed a new ordinance in late 1913. It proved to be the city's last foray into the rate-setting business, for the Illinois Public Utility Commission, later the Illinois Commerce Commission, superseded it the following year. Nonetheless, Edison went along with the new ordinance, correctly figuring that it could not only live within the rate limits but voluntarily reduce rates faster than the schedule provided.

"So well did it succeed," Seymour writes, "that the peculiar and unforeseen restrictions of plant improvement during the war period notwithstanding, every important energy requirement of that feverish period was completely met, the staggering increases in costs of labor, fuel and all kinds of material and supplies were assimilated, and still the rate-reducing schedule was observed. This was an accomplishment of which Samuel Insull and all of his associates were justly proud, especially as other utility concerns of various kinds throughout the country had been forced to sue for rate increases to avoid bankruptcy, although their rates were comparatively higher than those of our company in most cases."

At the Orchestra Hall celebration, Insull did not mention one of his most recent, and most profound, accomplishments: the organization of the Public Service Company of Northern Illinois the previous August. He probably had concluded that a ceremony honoring a city utility was not the forum for suburban operations. Had Insull chosen to mention his expansion beyond the city limits, he might have begun with the Charles Munroe episode.

One of Insull's friends, Chicago attorney Frank J. Baker, had dogged him for years to develop electric service in the suburbs, but it was Munroe's attempt to snatch the traction load that actually prodded him into protecting his flanks. Consequently, Insull and Baker formed a small firm called the North Shore Electric Company in 1902. The purpose, Insull facetiously remarked, was "to get rid of Mr. Baker when he importuned me again and again to buy the old Highland Park plant." Buy the plant he did that year, along with the Waukegan Electric Light Company. North Shore Electric would also buy up and reorganize other small, financially strapped utilities operating in that area and put them on a sound footing. After Highland Park and Waukegan, North Shore acquired 11 additional companies by 1911, including operations in Evanston, Kenilworth, and Park Ridge.

What was good for one flank of Commonwealth Edison was also good for the others, Insull reasoned, so he added properties in Maywood, Elmhurst, LaGrange, and other communities to North Shore Electric. Using Munroe as his prinicipal negotiator, Insull organized four other small companies to form a ring around Chicago. These were the Economy Light and Power Company of Joliet, the Illinois Valley Gas and Electric Company (Streator), the Kankakee Gas and Electric Company, and the Chicago Suburban Light and Power Company (Oak Park). These five newly created companies had acquired 44 isolated gas and electric utilities by the time Public Service of Northern Illinois was formed. The isolated plants stretched from Antioch, near the Wisconsin state line, to Chillicothe, in downstate Marshall County, and served more than 100 communities outside Chicago.

For a time, there appeared to be no master plan to integrate these far-flung operations. McDonald offers an interesting theory about how they became one interconnected company and, in turn, how that undertaking paved the way for the far-flung transmission line networks that would bring electricity to virtually every corner of America. The theory centers on Insull's purchase of a new car in 1908.

The year before, Insull had bought a 160-acre farm with a large house outside Libertyville, in Lake County, 38 miles northwest of Chicago. He called the place Hawthorn Farm, moved his family in, and subsequently bought up all of the surrounding farms, increasing his holdings to 4,000 acres. He also built a mansion on the grounds. Like most rural locations at the time, the place ironically didn't have electric service. In fact, the town of Libertyville had only dusk-to-midnight electric lighting on its main street.

An isolated generating plant would have served the Insull family's needs very nicely, but Insull had always striven to get rid of such plants, not build them. So the Edison chief ran a six-mile line from the farm to Lake Bluff, to draw power from the North Shore Electric plant there. The line served Insull and a handful of other customers, and that was that for awhile.

In the summer of 1908, with his wife and young son away in Europe, Insull bought the new car, and in the little spare time he had, went on drives in the countryside. You can picture it happening. Quiet country roads. Practically no traffic. Plenty of time to think. A mind as quick and a nature as relentless as Insull's. The idea took shape over time: Why not electric service for rural areas?

The Edison chief set out to answer the question. He began a thorough survey in 1909 and completed it the following year. Then he developed what came to be known as the Lake County Experiment, which would attempt to determine whether or not a single power source could serve an interconnected number of villages as with city neighborhoods. It would be the first experiment linking centralized production with long distance transmission. The conventional wisdom claimed that Insull was crazy, that the economics weren't there. Some members of the press and financial community weren't bashful about saying so. Recounting the project years later, Insull recalled, "We selected for this experiment in 1910, a group of 22 little towns (along with 125 farms) well back from the Lake Shore suburban area, with populations of 300 and up. It was probably the poorest prospect for centralized electrical operations in all of my subsequent experience. Ten of these towns had electric service of a sort, but only at night, locally supplied by little plants that were one jump ahead of the sheriff. The other twelve towns and the intervening farms had no electric service whatsoever. We bought the little plants of the ten night-service towns. We then built transmission lines, centralized the production of current for the territory in one plant near Lake Michigan, and shut down the little plants." The result was 24-hour service for approximately 23,000 people who had had night-only electric service or none at

74

all, plus lower rates for the existing customers and a profit for North Shore Electric.

Insull had correctly figured a steep initial cost for closing the ten small plants, centralizing production in one plant, and building substations and transmission lines. The investment cost per kwh of demand practically doubled previous costs. However, the diversity of demand, the efficiencies of centralized production, and the sharp increase in sales more than offset the initial investment. The load factor improved 100 percent, fuel costs per kwh fell 70 percent, other operating costs dropped 84 percent, and the overall cost per kwh lowered by nearly 60 percent.

The Franklin Institute in Philadelphia invited Insull to explain the success of the Lake County Experiment. The lesson, according to the Edison leader, was that the initial investment in transmission lines for a rural area would always be high, but each addition of customers and each increase in sales would continually reduce it. As this pattern continued, Insull said, profits would certainly rise and rates would fall. The experiment also demonstrated, he continued, that rural areas experienced their peak electrical demand of the year in midsummer, unlike urban areas that peaked in the winter. This phenomenon showed that the same generating plant investment could meet both loads.

The Lake County Experiment proved that it was technically and economically possible to provide central station service to rural and suburban areas, "an entirely new conception of electric light and power possibilities," as Insull put it. Once again, the skeptics in the industry tripped over themselves in an effort to follow Insull's lead, and soon transmission lines extended across the Midwestern countryside. The Edison leader followed up by launching a movement within the National Electric Light Association to extend electric service to rural districts across the nation. He met with some support, some apathy, and some opposition, but eventually the movement resulted in the electrification of virtually every farm in the Midwest and some 80 percent of all farms in the United States. This movement in the Midwest kept the generation and distribution of electricity in the hands of private enterprise and obviated the government's Rural Electrification Administration (REA) in the 1930s.

Two years before the Lake County Experiment, an historic fire destroyed North Shore Electric's Spring Street Station in Waukegan. The blaze apparently started on the roof of the plant at about 10:30 p.m. on April 22, 1908. By the time the lone stationman on duty discovered it, the flames had made considerable headway, setting the stage for a spectacular accident. The plant was operating at full power when the fire broke out, and it was believed that gravel from the burning roof fell onto the generating unit inside the plant, disabling the governor that controlled the engine. A huge flywheel, 12 feet in diameter and weighing 3,600 pounds, depended on the governor for speed regulation. With the governor out of action, the giant flywheel began to gather speed until its centrifugal force caused it to tear loose from the shaft and engine, and according to Public Service Company historian Imogene Whetstone, it "sped like a fiery meteor through the wall of the building—continuing northward, through the walls of the old Armory which stood adjacent— sweeping everything in its path. The fire, meantime, had gained such headway that the plant was completely destroyed." There was no report of injuries, although the city had its power knocked out.

Fortunately, a new generating station was nearing completion in Waukegan. Julius Hecht, superintendent of station construction, ordered every station hand at Waukegan to strip down a generating unit at Maywood and prepare it for immediate shipment back to Waukegan. Six hours later, on the morning of the 23rd, the unit sat atop a Chicago and North Western flatcar, ready for shipping and reassembly. About 108 hours after the unit came off line at Maywood, it carried load at Waukegan, then a record time for a job of that magnitude. Some service came back the evening of the 23rd, with everything except street lighting restored the day of the 24th.

Interestingly, the revolution in transmission and interconnections brought about by the Lake County Experiment would have made this pressure-packed solution of the problem unnecessary, had the accident occurred a few years later. Service could have been restored almost immediately, if it were lost at all, simply by transferring power to Waukegan from elsewhere on the interconnected grid. Still, the operating crews of North Shore Electric earned the well-deserved gratitude of the commu-

76

nity, just as their brethren in Commonwealth Edison and its predecessor companies have done in countless other emergencies over the years. Every operating man in the company volunteered for duty after the fire and accident at Spring Street Station.

Once Sam Insull saw that the Lake County Experiment would succeed, he began working on a system to supply power to every Illinois community within a 50- to 75-mile radius of Chicago. In 1911, he merged his five outlying companies—North Shore Electric, Economy Light and Power, Kankakee Gas and Electric, Chicago Suburban Light and Power, and Illinois Valley Gas and Electric—into the Public Service Company of Northern Illinois. Fifty-six years had passed since the establishment of Public Service Company's first predecessor gas company at Ottawa and 28 years since the first electric predecessor at Joliet. The population of the service territory had grown from 117,000 in 1850 to 758,000 in 1910. A total of 39 predecessors composed the new company. They had served 50 communities with 6,700 customers, primarily with part-time power. In its first four years, Public Service added 100 new communities, 65,000 new electricity customers, and 56,000 gas customers, while slashing rates nearly in half. In 1913, Public Service absorbed the Northwestern Gas Light and Coke Company, removing the last remaining obstacle to the company's undisputed control of gas and electric service in the Chicago suburbs. By 1930 Public Service spanned a territory of 6,000 square miles, including more than 300 communities with 438,000 electricity and gas customers. As the company expanded, it shut down 55 municipal or privately owned generating stations and replaced them with substations and 875 miles of transmission lines from four large, efficient central stations. To oversee the burgeoning operation, the company bought a twin-engine Sikorsky airplane. The craft, which held eight people, could land on ground or water. To oversee operations at ground level, Insull built the Public Service Building in Libertyville, a two-story structure which was listed in the National Register of Historic Places in 1983. The building, begun in May 1928 and completed seven months later, is a stunning mixture of slate, cut stone, wood, stucco, brick, and wrought iron. An illuminated clock and metal dome highlight one of the entrances. Street level rooms displayed electrical kitchen appliances for passersby. At night, the Public Service Building was illuminated by 12 floodlights mounted on a building across the street and six others on another nearby structure.

Public Service made money from the beginning. It paid regular common stock dividends and grew from a $23 million corporation to an organization worth more than double that in a little more than five years. The new company stimulated rural growth by introducing an electrification extension program under which the company installed the necessary transformer and distribution line at its own expense and the farmer agreed to pay minimum monthly bills. The new contract, offered to prospective customers by marketers who specialized in rural sales, increased the number of farms served by electricity to more than 4,800 by the end of 1929, an increase of 37 percent for the year. The Model Farm near Mundelein further stimulated sales. Opened in August 1928, the farm demonstrated the desirability of electric and gas service in rural life to more than 50,000 visitors in its first 18 months. The Model Farm also became a sort of community center. Farmers held a picnic there in June 1929, complete with a horse-pulling contest and other events, that attracted 3,500 people.

Rural electrification played only one part in the socioeconomic revolution that took place in the 1910s and 1920s. The spread of electricity brought radio into the home and high-speed interurban electric railroads onto various rights-of-way. Automobiles became much more affordable as their production became standardized, and as the number of cars on the road multiplied dramatically, the roads themselves improved and increased. The booming motion picture industry brought the glamour of Hollywood as close as the neighborhood or town theatre.

A post-World War I song asked, "How ya gonna keep 'em down on the farm, after they've seen Paree?" Historian Seymour offers a quaint and not totally convincing answer: "All these things (mentioned above) help to keep the boys and girls on the farms, and to make the small country town pleasant to live in, if not actually superior to the city in their eyes. They all helped to make the mature worker more satisfied to stay wherever he was instead of being drawn as by a magnet to the most congested neighborhoods of larger communities. Conversely, they helped to relieve the ever increasing pressure upon city life and its local transportation problems, and to spread the 'unearned increment' of urban land values more evenly throughout the whole country."

The early success of Public Service Company caused Sam Insull to extend his gaze to the rest of the Midwest. If he could bring 24-hour electric service to rural Illinois, why not to other large rural areas that had no electricity? He answered this rhetorical question by forming a holding company known as Middle West Utilities Company. The company attempted, in effect, to make the entire Midwest one large Lake County Experiment. Excluding some small properties Insull already owned in southern Indiana, his first acquisition for Middle West was the Central Illinois Public Service Company (CIPSCo) in 1912. CIPSCo didn't have much at the time of acquisition: a streetcar line in Mattoon, a short interurban railroad and three part-time central stations. Within five years, Insull, assisted by his younger brother, Martin, had boosted the number of electricity customers from 15,000 with part-time and unreliable service to 40,000 with generally reliable service. At the same time, the brothers increased sales from 15 million to 50 million kwh per year while slashing commercial and residential rates by one-third. During this same period, Middle West bought plants that served 20 villages. By extending transmission lines the company brought service to another 55 communities. In another dozen years, CIPSCo's lines extended into nearly 500 communities. Before Middle West was finished, it had bought up every small lighting plant in central and southern Illinois—a total of 56.

Sometimes Insull acquired far-flung properties in which he had little or no interest as part of a package deal in order to obtain a property he really wanted. For example, he found himself buying generating stations that served small towns in Missouri, Maine, New Hampshire, Vermont, and upstate New York, as well as a streetcar line and a gas operation, in order to acquire five key Illinois properties and one in Indiana. In addition, CIPSCo often found itself getting into the gas, water, streetcar or ice business by acquiring local electric plants that also provided these services. On the eve of World War I, Middle West served 131,000 electric and 43,000 gas customers in 400 communities in 13 states. "As a business," McDonald concludes, "Middle West was expanding and keeping afloat, meeting its interest payments, amortizing the discounts on its stocks, making the payments on its preferred stock, and occasionally paying modest dividends on its common stock. But though hopes for its financial future might be bright, it would have been clear to anyone less optimistic than Samuel Insull that Middle West would never be as strong as its subsidiaries and would always be better at building utilities than at making money."

In the years immediately surrounding Commonwealth Edison's 25th anniversary in 1912, Insull and his lieutenants appeared to be everywhere at once, selling kilowatthours in Chicago and Chillicothe, expanding to Maine and Missouri, extending transmission lines across the Midwest, and peddling ice in downstate hamlets. Given this intensity, it does not seem unusual that the Edison chief had two prizes practically fall into his lap: the ownership of his biggest customer and the chairmanship of his chief competitor.

Commonwealth Edison's biggest customers in 1914 were the elevated railroads. According to McDonald, Insull did more than make the trains run on time; he gave the straphangers reduced rates, universal transfers, clean stations, courteous conductors, and labor relations so harmonious "that labor newspapers would attack politicians who said unkind things about the company for which members of the unions worked."

Commonwealth Edison's takeover of the elevated lines came about some three-and-a-half years after the L companies decided to merge, climaxing years of political turmoil, financial sleight-of-hand, the maneuverings of Charles Tyson Yerkes, and the abortive municipal ownership movement. Cash presented the major roadblock to the merger; the L companies were short and their credit was poor. So they turned to Sam Insull, who not only had the money but a vested interest in the companies because of the huge amounts of electricity they consumed. He agreed to guarantee a $6 million loan in exchange for stock in a voluntary association of elevated companies. If, after three years, a proposed merger between the L and surface lines did not materialize, Edison would put up the cash and get the stock. Some suggested that Insull orchestrated the scenario from the outset, because that was exactly the way it turned out. Edison advanced a little more money to the companies to provide working capital and wound up owning more than 80 percent of the stock. Insull became Chicago's traction king, and as his crown prince he chose the 40-year-old president of one of the lines, Britton I. Budd, who had worked his way up from assistant storekeeper. Together, Insull and Budd gave Chicago some of the best transit service it had ever known, while acquiring and upgrading the interurban lines that served the city. After a fashion, Insull's transit empire foreshadowed the creation of the Regional Transportation Authority (RTA) nearly six decades later. Neither organization provided a panacea for the area's transit woes, but the Insull operation seemed to enjoy a honeymoon with the press and public that the RTA never experienced.

Insull got to be chairman of the rival Peoples Gas Light and Coke Company in much the same way that he took over the elevated railroads—business people in big trouble were looking for a messiah with big money, and the list of such people was short indeed. Actually, the gas company chieftains didn't want him to run the organization; they wanted to buy his finely tuned political antennae and well-known clout, to help them out of years of political and financial difficulties that had brought the company to the edge of ruin. They offered $50,000 a year, with no operating responsibilities attached. Insull turned them down —he wasn't for sale.

But the gas company didn't give up: someone suggested a bit of subterfuge. According to a McDonald interview with longtime Peoples Gas attorney Francis L. Daily, the company had its workers construct a model gas engine, put it on display in the company showrooms behind a guardrail to prevent close inspection, and announced with much publicity and fictious figures that they had developed a revolutionary new motor. Not just any gas motor, but one that might very well be cheaper and more efficient than an electric motor. The gas company executive who dreamed up the hoax had figured rightly; while they might not buy Insull for cash, they could reach him by threatening his supremacy as the city's foremost supplier of power. In short, the Edison leader went for the ploy, hook, line and sinker, even slipping into the gas company building to have a look, from behind the guardrail, like the rest of the gawkers. Thus in September 1913 Sam Insull became chairman of the board of Peoples Gas Company.

Insull's actions in this affair seem curious in at least two regards. First, it was strange that a shrewd businessman could be taken in by such a sophomoric stunt, and second, that he remained with the gas company at all after discovering the stunt. At least his move to preserve Edison's supremacy had a precedent. After all, he had neglected to call the bluff of pretender Charles Munroe when he threatened to sell nonexistent power to the elevated railroads, electing instead to buy him off, as he would other petty raiders over the years. In the gas company episode, one questions what advice, if any, Insull received from his technical people about this Rube Goldberg gas engine. But Insull did not always react logically when threatened. In fact, his desperate maneuvering to stave off a presumed takeover two decades later would bring about the collapse of his corporate empire and send him into exile and disgrace.

Why did Insull stay with the gas company, then? First, he brought with him to the board two trusted business colleagues, John J. Mitchell, President of the Illinois Trust & Savings Bank, and business leader James A. Patten, giving the latter control of the five-member panel. Second, Insull always relished a challenge, and the condition of the gas company provided every bit of that. He considered the company weak, if not moribund. Nevertheless, he proceeded to rehabilitate it—a feat that he considered one of his greatest business accomplishments.

In one of his greatest political accomplishments, he created the State Public Utility Commission of Illinois, later the Illinois Commerce Commission, which went into operation on January 1, 1914. Insull had proposed the creation of such a body years earlier but pursued the concept with renewed vigor after the success of the Lake County Experiment and his rapid acquisition of small outlying utility companies. By 1911 he served more than 100 suburban communities. That meant he had to deal with as many municipal governments, each one free to impose its own electricity rates or attach other conditions of service.

Aided by his friend Roger Sullivan, the political powerhouse who had originally made Insull's acquaintance by trying to shake him down, the Edison chief succeeded in having a joint legislative committee formed to study relations between the state and its utilities. Insull strove mightily behind the scenes to create a body modeled after the Wisconsin commission. He testified privately before the committee, and lobbied the politicians in favor of such a commission. Publicly, however, he remained non-committal, realizing that anything supported by a utility leader would automatically attract considerable opposition. While Insull never resorted to bribery, he remembered well the fate of the Yerkes-supported legislation once the backing of the streetcar baron had become known.

In 1913 the General Assembly approved legislation patterned after the Wisconsin law. The new commission had the power to set rates and regulate service, but the Illinois law lacked one other important provision of its Wisconsin counterpart: granting the utilities open-ended franchises that could be revoked only for cause and giving the municipalities the power to take over the utilities, if their voters approved. As a result, even though local governments could no longer set rates, they still retained control of the franchises. The new commission got off to a good start, and only city council grafters, who had lost a meal ticket, and so-called progressives, who favored local control of utilities as a matter of principle, grumbled about it. By 1916, 33 states had such agencies.

Six

Doing
Things
Right

"I am a great believer in publicity," Insull told the Illinois Gas Association in 1919—like Babe Ruth saying he believed in the home run, Ty Cobb in the stolen base, or Knute Rockne in the forward pass. In any case, Insull stated, "I believe it is our duty to the properties we manage, to the stockholders who own them, and to the communities they serve, that we should enlighten those communities on the situation. I believe in doing it not in any gumshoe way, but openly and boldly. I believe in presenting the facts to the employes, whose interest is just as vital as that of the managers, to the citizens of the state who are owners of the properties, to every customer of a gas company and electric light and power companies, or a street railway."

Insull had already delivered that sermon for about 20 years, and it remains the policy of Commonwealth Edison to this date. Providing quick and accurate information to the news media, employes, shareholders, and other members of the public forms a part of everyday business. In disseminating the information—through employe publications, an employe television news program, news releases, broadcast interviews, responses to inquiries, paid advertising, a speakers bureau, reports to shareholders and word of mouth—Edison continues to explain Insull's fundamental rule of utility PR, namely, to tell everyone that the primary job of the company is to provide the best possible service at the lowest practical cost. Or, as the Edison chief spelled it out to his public relations people soon after World War I: "Practically everything that a public utility company does, or that any of its employes do, directly or indirectly affecting customers and relations between the company and its customers...is an item in public relations. Hence, furnishing satisfactory service at satisfactory rates—the best possible service at lowest practicable rates—is the first objective in public relations work, because that is of the greatest interest to the public. This is in strict accord with the principle quoted earlier: 'If the rights of the public are properly taken care of in producing lower costs and in steadily improving the service, the rights of the stockholders will take care of themselves.'

"But the public is in no position to judge service and rates when it knows nothing about the multitude of details involved in furnishing service, and nothing about costs and other factors that determine rates. If to this lack of knowledge by the public you add an appearance of mystery or secrecy, or even extreme reticence, in the operations of the business, you inevitably breed suspicion that the service is poorer or the rates higher than they ought to be. Hence, the second objective in the public utility industry's public relations work is: a public well informed on the tangible details, as well as on the social and industrial significance of the industry in all its ramifications."

Edison has followed these fundamentals ever since, although a series of rate increases beginning in the early 1970s, accompanied by the OPEC oil embargo in 1973, a few recessions, high interest rates, unemployment, and the accident at Three Mile Island in 1979, made good PR a much more difficult challenge than it was in Insull's heyday, when vastly different conditions permitted successive rate reductions. Nevertheless, notice how the same basic themes run through a speech by Edison Vice President Donald Petkus to a 1983 company financial conference at which he unveiled the company's new "Doing Things Right. And Proud of It." advertising campaign:

"General attitudes toward us have deteriorated as a result of rising rates and poor economic conditions. We're basically a victim of circumstances—given better times or stable rates we'd be enjoying the reputation we deserve. . .Our work force is second to none. We have been doing things right and that must continue. We can't let up, we have to work to minimize errors. Especially those that are in the public domain—courtesy at all levels must be paramount, penalties and fines have to be avoided, reliability cannot be compromised—we work in a fish bowl and have to be as close to perfect as possible.

"The majority of the consumers we serve believe we're doing things right. Higher costs and criticisms have shaken that belief. So we decided we had to speak out. We will be increasing all types of communications with all of our constituencies—employes, stockholders, the public sector, customers...Many members of the public...agree with our conclusion that we have not done enough to alert people to the magnitude of the job we perform, day in, day out and the critical role of electric power...We will show the teamwork and dedication at the division level when service needs to be restored under emergency conditions—like during a storm in the middle of the night...

"If the whole is the sum of its parts, then we want our customers to know that there certainly are many parts to a modern electric utility. Just as importantly, we want them to know that many of the system's parts have human faces, so a recurring theme in the commercials will be the dedication and professionalism of our people. But I strongly believe that any communications program is only as good as the product behind it. If we allow service reliability to slip, if we aren't careful to prevent mistakes on the job, if we are less than courteous to our customers—then the best communications program in the world is doomed."

A period of declining popularity for Commonwealth Edison and other utilities after World War I caused Insull to redefine his public relations principles and vigorously move to restore the faded lustre. A good part of the company's loss of public esteem resulted from Mr. Public Relations' own absence from the store during America's participation in the conflict. Although Insull had become an American citizen in 1896, he retained close personal and philosophical ties to his native England. For one thing, he still had family living there, including his aged parents. From the very outset of the war, in August 1914, Insull worked behind the scenes for the Allied cause. His work had to be on the q.t. because the United States had adopted a policy of strict neutrality, and if his efforts on behalf of the Allies had become known, he technically could have gone to jail.

Insull used his public relations skills to develop and disseminate pro-British propaganda. According to his biographer, "The first aim of British propaganda was to appeal to the Anglo-American heritage and community of interest; the second was to paint the Germans as barbarians and to seek support for Britain through pleas to justice, mercy and similar sentiments. To paint the Germans black, Insull helped arrange for the regular distribution of strongly biased war information to 360 American newspapers which had no press service and contributed nearly $250,000 toward financing this effort."

An event in the spring of 1916 afforded Insull the opportunity to help pave the way for America's entry into the war without actually taking sides. With other business and civic leaders, but without government officials, Insull helped organize a massive "preparedness parade" patterned after a similar demonstration in New York three weeks earlier. The objective of the march was to urge Congress to adequately prepare for "the defense of national honor and national interests." Nearly 2,500 Edison employes, urged by Insull to "volunteer" and given time off the job, were among the more than 130,000 American flag-waving participants who stepped through downtown Chicago.

When the United States declared war on Germany in April 1917, Insull could discard any pretext of neutrality. At the request of his friend, Illinois Governor Frank Lowden, he went to work full-time as head of the State Council of Defense of Illinois. President Woodrow Wilson had asked the governors of each state to establish such councils, which would report to a National Council of Defense. As envisioned by Wilson, the various state councils would act as crypto-spy organizations to monitor the activities of suspect persons, particularly German-Americans. Insull frowned on the negativism, envisioning far greater possibilities for the Illinois Council. He turned it into a multifaceted home-front war machine, headed by some of the top business and political leaders in the state. The Council established a speakers bureau and a publicity department that cranked out copy tinged with patriotic appeals and distributed it to newspaper editors throughout the state.

Edison sent 1,376 men—and one woman, company nurse Esther Webb—off to war. Twenty-three died during the conflict, many of pneumonia. Stanley Hloupe, formerly of Northwest Station, was the first killed in action, during the Battle of Marne in the summer of 1918. The company established a financial assistance program for the wives and children of employes who enlisted. And employes who remained on the job actively supported the Liberty Loan program, subscribing for more than $250,000 in bonds during the first week of the campaign alone.

The number of employes participating passed 82 percent by the end of the conflict.

The war ended on Insull's 59th birthday—November 11, 1918—and in its aftermath came a virtual avalanche of accolades from President Wilson, foreign governments, U.S. governors, and others. Insull became perhaps the most honored civilian warrior outside the government. But while he had labored all-out in the war effort, his carefully woven fabric of good governmental and public relations had started to unravel.

Through a combination of events, a movement to restore "home rule" to municipalities for utility regulation began to gather steam in 1915. The partisans who led the movement consisted of Insull's old nemesis, Edward Dunne, the ex-Chicago mayor who now reposed in the governor's chair; a coalition of good government types, who felt that utility regulation belonged with "the people," not with a state commission; and the remaining Gray Wolves, who longed for a return to the good old days of shaking down utilities for bribes and other favors. These elements prevailed upon the Illinois House to appoint a committee to study home rule. In 1917 the committee came out in favor of the concept, just about the time that another legendary Chicago figure, William Hale "Big Bill" Thompson, was leaping onto the bandwagon with both feet.

Republican Mayor Thompson, who once threatened to punch the Prince of Wales in the nose if he came to Chicago, had scored additional points with the city's large Irish and German populations by standing firmly against America's entry into the war on the side of England and the Allies. With this country's declaration of war in 1917, however, Thompson had to find a new populist issue. He found it in alleged war profiteering—and characterized the utilities as the biggest culprits of all. He had picked a handy issue. All across the country, utilities saw a severe postwar round of inflation drive up their cost of doing business. Money was scarce. The war had had a voracious appetite for capital. In fact, the United States spent more on financing its comparatively brief participation in the conflict than all of its corporations had invested in the previous century. Interest rates that had stood at just over three percent on the eve of the war jumped to eight percent in the postwar period, and some utilities had trouble borrowing money at even nine and ten percent.

To make matters worse, electric and gas utilities, particularly in the Midwest, witnessed a dramatic upsurge in demand. The electrical output of Insull's Middle West holding company subsidiaries leaped from 200 million kwh before the start of the war to some one billion kwh half a dozen years later. To meet the unprecedented demand, utilities had to raise large amounts of capital at most unfavorable rates. That need, in turn, sent every major utility in the country—electric, gas, and even transportation—scurrying to their newly created state utility commissions for rate increases.

Commonwealth Edison, with a sizeable reserve margin, was the only exception. The transit lines, particularly vulnerable to rising labor costs, suffered even harder blows than the electric and gas utilities, so that dozens of them went into receivership. Chicago's elevated railway companies survived by not paying their electricity bills to Commonwealth Edison, their *de facto* parent. Edison itself had to resort to the money well only once during this period, proving itself the strongest of all the Insull companies by far. Insull borrowed on his personal credit wherever he could and continually shifted money from one company to another. To prop up Middle West, he personally borrowed and loaned the holding company more than $12 million, and carried the company's payroll with his own funds.

People's Gas had an especially rough time, and came within an ace of going under. Beset for years by poor management, the company came out of the war with no cash, no credit, and a $1-million local tax bill. It also badly needed a new plant to meet the skyrocketing demand for gas. Sorely in need of a rate hike, the company amazingly found itself in court against an anti-utility crusader bent on slashing the rates.

Insull could have cut and run; he didn't have that much tied up in Peoples. But he never was one to run from a fight, and in this instance his civic pride took hold of him; he wasn't about to let Chicago's gas utility go belly-up for all the world to see. So in January 1919, Insull dispatched Sargent,* Munroe, and two other trouble-shooters up Adams Street, from

---

*Sargent's assignment would be one of his last. He was stricken while traveling in Europe that summer and brought home. He died at his Glencoe residence on July 26 at age 59.

the Edison Building to the Peoples Gas Building, with orders to streamline the bureaucracy without letting anyone go and without cutting the payroll—except at the very top.

Insull had an additional agenda of his own. First, he solved a seemingly insoluble problem—to satisfy a $1 million tax bill with no money in the till—like a magician waving a wand. How? "Mr. Insull spoke to some of his political friends," Munroe explained, according to McDonald. Then Insull went on to cut operating expenses to the bone and won a couple of rate increases, but still couldn't offset inflation and the rising cost of labor and material. An Insull-Munroe brainstorm finally turned the situation around. The Chicago area was dotted with industrial plants, including the big steel mills, that produced coke oven gas. Since much of this gas was being burned off as waste, Insull and Munroe wondered, why not try to buy it at a favorable price? Why not, indeed? Recalling his shrewd dealings with the elevated railways, Munroe lined up enough "dump" gas at a reasonable price to meet a quarter of the company's needs and put it into the black to stay.

However, Peoples still needed a new gas manufacturing plant, and had no way to finance it. Insull had been negotiating with the president of the intended manufacturer of the plant, but they snagged on the problem of raising the money. The talks dragged on for a year. Finally, Insull's counterpart, H. B. Rust of the Koppers Company, went to see his boss, Andrew W. Mellon, one of the richest men in America. Insull's reputation having preceded him, Mellon agreed to meet with this man from Chicago. So Rust arranged a meeting between the two at Mellon's home in Pittsburgh. Mellon and Insull passed a pleasant three hours, speaking of politics, world affairs, and the like but not about financing a new gas plant for Peoples. As Insull was leaving, Mellon pulled Rust aside and spoke with him briefly. On the ride to the train station, Rust informed Insull that the financing was all set; Mellon would guarantee the securities of the new subsidiary that would operate the gas plant with his own personal securities. The plant paid for itself in six years. By the time it began operating, Insull proudly announced that Peoples would resume the payment of the dividends it had suspended some three years earlier.

Waist-deep in alligators, Insull continued to straighten out the affairs of the gas company and keep his own companies afloat in troubled economic waters while the anti-utility crowd roared for a return to home rule. Unaccustomed to rising utility rates, the public demanded action, taking primary aim at the newly created agency granting the increases—the Illinois Public Utility Commission. They vented their frustration by blaming the messenger for the message—an old story indeed. The public itself could do little or nothing to alleviate inflation, high interest rates, rising labor costs, or other increases in the cost of doing business. But it could howl for the scalp of the commission that nonetheless appreciated the potentially disastrous effects of these factors on utilities and tried to do justice to utility and ratepayer alike. History would repeat itself in the late 1970s and early 1980s, when many of the same adverse conditions would motivate the state commission to grant a number of utility rate increases—only to meet legislation and some public support for an elected panel, rather than one appointed by the governor. In the post-World War I era, the proposed panacea was home rule and abolition of the existing commission.

Once again Insull took out his magic wand. He called a summit meeting of Mayor Thompson, Democratic boss Sullivan, the leaders of both parties in Springfield and others. Being true public servants, they decided to give the public what it wanted and had legislation passed in 1920 to abolish the Public Utility Commission. Suitable fanfare and loud denunciations of the commission accompanied debate and passage of the measure. Later in the same session, however, the legislature—this time with no hype at all—created the Illinois Commerce Commission and gave it virtually the same powers as the panel it had abolished. This was all part of the agreement worked out by Insull, Sullivan, Thompson, and the others. Thompson had been mostly talk, anyway. His chief financial backer for years had been none other than Sam Insull, and the two men were further tied by mutual friendships and political alliances.

The flap over state regulation flashed one more signal to Insull that conditions, in this particular case public and governmental relations, had gotten out of hand while he was preoccupied with the war effort. But the war had also provided him with a tool to turn the adverse conditions around—the Committee on Public Information of the State Council of Defense. Headed by publicist and former newspaperman Bernard Mullaney, the Committee had found spectacular success in promoting the war effort through its press releases, a speakers bureau, and other activities. What worked in wartime should work just as well after the shooting stopped, Insull reasoned. Without making any organizational changes, he gave the committee a new name and a new assignment. It would now call itself the Committee on Public Utility Information and it would attempt to make patriotism synonymous with a favorable attitude toward utilities. Insull kicked off the campaign by widely circulating an address President Wilson had made in 1916, urging business to be totally candid with the public in order to avoid any suspicions of dishonorable doings. Wilson's admonition jibed with Insull's own principles of public relations, so the Edison chief happily wrapped himself in the flag and presented the President's remarks as an official sanction for the Edison PR campaign. Mullaney and his troops then began to distribute a weekly newsletter of utility information which most editors in the state gladly accepted.

Considered the forerunner of modern corporate public relations, the Illinois Public Utility Information Committee soon had numerous imitators among the nation's utilities. According to McDonald, "By 1923 these agencies were turning out a stream of utility publicity that almost matched the volume of patriotic publicity during the war; one could hardly go anywhere or read anything without encountering the fundamentals of utility economics."

Meanwhile, Insull launched a concurrent campaign to sell stock to as many employes and members of the public as possible. He figured that if a customer owned stock in Commonwealth Edison, he would perceive the company's interest as linked with his own. The twin public relations campaigns achieved so much, McDonald concludes, that "By the mid-twenties, hating utilities was, in Chicago, as rare as hating mother and flag."

As Commonwealth Edison's relations with the public rapidly evolved in the post-World War I era, so did its relations with its own employes. Prior to the war, Insull had remained aloof from all but his top lieutenants and would fire any employe who failed to recognize him and offer a "Good morning, Mr. Insull," or "Good afternoon, Mr. Insull." McDonald theorizes that since the day-to-day activities of the State Council of Defense were informal, shirtsleeves-rolled-up affairs, Insull gained closer contact with, and new respect for, those further down the ladder. Insull's biographer also suggests that as the Edison leader and his wife, Gladys, grew apart, Insull drew closer to his employes, coming to think of them more as brothers and sisters in the same big family rather than as subordinates. The thaw in the boss's personality had its limits, though. Raymond Maxson, former Edison and Public Service Vice President, remembered introducing himself to Insull at a Public Service social function in the early 1920s, when Maxson was a new employe. Insull responded with a grunt, Maxson recalled. Whatever the extent of Insull's moderation, he set out to create a new type of corporate employe, intensely loyal to the community as well as the company. "You represent your company and your community. Be a credit to both," Insull preached. *Esprit de corps* was what he was after, and *esprit de corps* was what he got —by using several approaches to win employes' hearts and minds.

First, Edison employes received constant reminders of their vital role as public servants who worked for the best public service organization in the world. Insull himself preached that message to the employes from virtually every pulpit in the company, and other Edison officers did the same. Regular corporate news bulletins and a lively company magazine called the *Edison Round Table* sought to instill loyalty to the company and pride in one's work. Founded in 1909, the *Edison Round Table* served as both the company house organ and a digest of employes' doings as individuals and groups.

As his second general strategy to recast the image of Edison employes, Insull increased their fringe benefits. Two of the major benefits, the Service Annuity System and scholarships for employes, had been introduced before World War I. The Service Annuity System, which went into effect Jan. 1, 1912, provided a pension for employes at age 55 with 30 years of service or at age 60 to 65 with 15 years. The company has always carried the entire cost of the pension program. Reaching employes two days before Christmas 1911, the written announcement of the plan by the Board of Directors concluded by saying, "The Company extends to all its employes the Compliments of the Season."

In those days, Edison traditionally distributed free turkeys at Christmastime. After the war, when the company sweetened the fringe benefits, someone in management concluded that they could offer life insurance policies ranging from $500 to $1,500, for little more than the cost of the turkeys. However, tradition often dies hard, and the employes let management know that they would prefer to continue receiving their turkeys, thank you. Management responded with an educational campaign which eventually convinced the employes that they were better off with the insurance policies.

The scholarship program began modestly in 1909 with the Board authorizing the purchase of 28 night school scholarships at a total cost of $420. "Worthy" employes would receive them to improve their own skills which, in turn, would better the company. The concept has greatly expanded over the years, with thousands of employes continuing their education, and many earning advanced degrees at little or no cost to themselves under the company's tuition reimbursement program.

Founded in 1912, a corollary of the scholarship program, the Chicago Central Station Institute served to select and prepare college graduates for commercial duties in the Insull companies. A sort of ROTC of the electric utility industry, the Institute gave college graduates a one-year course, combined with on-the-job training in various departments of Insull's central station companies. Participants in the program received a salary from which they paid a tuition fee to the Institute.

Edison organized its own branch of the National Electric Light Association in 1908 which employes could join by paying annual dues of two dollars. The NELA Branch, whose membership grew to 500 the first year, held regular meetings to discuss all phases of the industry, particularly Edison's activities. The written records of these meetings soon evolved into the *Edison Round Table* magazine.

Other employe welfare programs that existed before the war included medical care and disability compensation. In addition to life insurance, company fringes added after the war included cafeterias at the largest work locations and a host of programs designed to promote employe fraternization. The most ambitious of these undertakings was the purchase in 1923 of a large, picturesque summer resort area on Lake Delavan, Wisconsin, about 90 miles north of Chicago. Here, in rustic cottages or a hotel, shaded by tall trees, employes and their families could spend their vacations at a nominal cost. The resort featured an 18-hole golf course, swimming, fishing, boating, tennis, baseball, and other activities. Borrowing a page from the travel brochures, the *Edison Round Table* strongly promoted attendance each spring and summer with feature stories and photos of the grounds and employes at play.

Employes' children frolic at Lake Lawn, the company-owned resort on Lake Delavan, Wisconsin (1930).

As the depression ground on, Edison quietly sold the resort on Christmas Eve 1936, to a company which had just built a factory at Delavan and planned to use the spa as a summer colony for employes. That announcement rated only two sentences in the *Round Table*. Still known as Lake Lawn Lodge, the resort has been open to the public for a number of years and is a popular year-round weekend getaway and vacation spot for people in the Chicago area and throughout the Midwest. Edison's identification with Lake Lawn continued indirectly over the years: the company held its annual Engineering Conferences there. The three-day conclaves, which combined technical presentations with socializing and use of the recreational facilities, ended in the early 1980s as a measure of austerity.

96

At home, Edison offered a wide range of social and recreational activities—something for everyone—to promote team spirit and company loyalty even further, to round out the

A company baseball team of the early 1900s strikes a determined pose.

total Edison Man or Edison Woman. The umbrella organizations for many of these activities were the Edison Club, which reached a peak of 7,700 members in the early 1930s, and the Electra organization for women. The precedent for a woman's group had been set by Annebell Fraser, Edison's librarian, who formed Electra in 1911. It merged with the Edison Club in October 1919. Among the activities of Electra were musical and educational programs, dramatics, charity, and welfare work. Electra was active during both World Wars in Red Cross and other war relief work. The club also offered classes in swimming, cooking and dancing. A November 20, 1919, meeting was the scene of a debate on the subject: "Resolved, that the business woman makes a better wife than the girl who stays at home." Abbott, Doyle, and D. H. Miller acted as judges. The debate was decided, not surprisingly, in favor of the stay-at-homes. Of course, the point was moot as company policy required, with few exceptions, that a woman resign once she married. This policy was relaxed during World War II when women were needed to fill servicemen's positions, and eventually eliminated. Similar, subsequent restrictions regarding pregnancies were also loosened over time until they were eliminated in the 1960s.

97

The two clubs jointly held an annual dinner dance that provided the highlight of the company's social year, sometimes attracting more than 1,000 celebrants. Additionally, the Edison Club sponsored an annual Christmas party for employes and their children; golf tournaments; basketball and bowling leagues for both men and women; a men's softball league; chess and checker tourneys; and regular flower shows under the auspices of the Edison Club Horticultural League. There were card parties, a choral club, a drama club, a symphony orchestra, a tennis team. No hobby was too obscure, as the existence of a mandolin club will attest. News of the various recreational events filled several pages in each issue of the *Edison Round Table*, rating at

A 1920s cartoon by an unknown artist depicts employes enjoying themselves on Edison Club Night at Chicago's Medinah Temple.

least equal space with corporate news and reports of advances in electricity. The pages depict happy employes enjoying their lives, their work, and the entertainment the company provided for them.

From 1918 to the present, Edison has held recognition dinners or luncheons for long-time employes and service annuitants, though the gatherings now are not nearly as zany as they were in, say, 1933. That year the 57 employes who had reached 25 years of service came dressed as school children, replete with knickers, knee socks, middy blouses, and wigs. One man even wore a dunce cap. The *Edison Round Table* tells us they entered the annual party to the tune of "School Days," took their places in a mock classroom, "and presented nearly an hour of scintilating (sic) entertainment—including oral exams, recitations, songs, class yell, valedictory address, et al.—in return for which they were officially declared members of the Quarter-Century Club."

Insull believed in the importance of employes owning a share of their company. He not only encouraged employes to become stockholders themselves but urged them to enlist their families and friends as well. The employes, who could purchase Edison stock at an attractive discount, earned a commission on any stock they sold to non-employes. At the same time, new savings and loan and mutual benefit associations were formed.

In keeping with Insull's dictum to 'be a credit to your community,' top executives were expected to follow the boss's example and perform some sort of public service work on their own time. The executives, in turn, urged their subordinates to do likewise and so on down the line, to the extent that Edison employes became involved in practically every stratum of community life. "They were aggressively dedicated to public service," according to McDonald; "throughout the twenties Insull men were in the center or at the top of virtually every important community service activity in Chicago, and they continued to be so long after Insull was gone. Whenever volunteer workers were needed—as when Insull set out to democratize opera in Chicago—they would spread over the city like a cloud of benign locusts, and the job would be done."

The practice has changed little over the years. Today, one can find Edison executives serving on the boards of universities and colleges, participating in civic and charitable organizations, working for youth groups, promoting the fine arts, and contributing to a welter of associated projects. Other employes serve as scout leaders, Little League coaches, Big Brothers and Big Sisters, community development workers, and so on—all with the active encouragement of top management.

Altruism is the primary motive for these good works, although the company has always believed that it receives certain benefits, difficult to quantify, in return. The late Charles E. Wilson, chairman of General Motors and Eisenhower's first secretary of defense, made a memorable statement in the 1950s that caused no small amount of controversy. He said, "What's good for General Motors is good for the country." An arguable statement, certainly, but it works conversely for Commonwealth Edison and other utilities that operate as regulated monopolies. Beginning with the fact that everyone who uses electricity is a direct or indirect customer, Edison has long held that what is good for its service territory is good for the company. If the territory provides a good place in which to live, do business, and raise a family, business and industry will thrive, using kilowatthours and maintaining or creating jobs for workers, who use even more kilowatthours in their homes. If successful companies hire more people, new workers will flock to the territory and will become electricity customers. Healthy schools, municipal governments, and social amenities provide all the more reason for them to stay. Prosperity and pursuit of the good life translate into kilowatthour sales, so making communities within the service territory better places in which to live has added benefits for Edison and its employes. On the other hand, if business and living conditions are not favorable—if industry and workers pack up and leave the service territory—Edison cannot follow; for better or worse, regulated utilities are wedded to the territories they serve.

Today, there is no greater exponent of public service work than Edison Chairman James O'Connor, active in approximately two dozen civic, educational, and charitable organizations in Chicago and northern Illinois. The commencement speaker at Northwestern University's Kellogg Graduate School of Management in June 1984, O'Connor concluded his remarks by challenging the graduates to "involve yourselves in some activity which benefits the public good. Individually and collectively, this great class can do so much to make our world a better place in which to live. Long ago, Horace Mann said, 'Be ashamed to die until you have won some victory for humanity.' Don't deny your special talents to others when the need is so great—and don't deny yourself the tremendous satisfaction to be derived from making a contribution that will improve the lot of others. Help to stamp the culture of your company or your firm as an institution that cares...Get involved in the difficult, sometimes sticky, areas of race relations, health care, education and housing. Develop a sense of community—a sense of caring for others—do what you can to provide a sense of hope to those who despair."

The Chairman of Northwestern's Board of Trustees, Thomas Ayers, immediately preceded O'Connor as CEO of Commonwealth Edison and is one of the few Chicago corporate officers in recent times to be as active in community service as O'Connor himself. In addition to serving on the various boards and committees, Ayers vigorously promoted fair housing and equal opportunity employment in the mid-1960s, not the most popular of causes in Chicago at the time. Although he enjoys a game of golf, Ayers wouldn't retire to the links in 1980 when he reached the mandatory retirement age of 65 for Edison officers. He decided to cap his public service career by helping to bring a World's Fair to Chicago in 1992 to commemorate the 500th anniversary of Columbus' landing. Ayers realized that this would require every inch of his negotiating, diplomatic, and organizational skills. While other people his age warmed their hands by the fire, Tom Ayers led the private civic group that launched the Fair project—a job he tackled with the same energy and enthusiasm with which he ran Commonwealth Edison.

For all of their intense involvement in the business and public sectors, Ayers and O'Connor are both affable, no-frills individuals—liked and admired by their peers as well as their employes. O'Connor drives a medium-sized Chevrolet and often answers his own telephone. Both pride themselves on their concern for their people. In a farewell interview in *The Edison* magazine in 1979, Ayers spoke to the legacy he hoped to leave: "The most important ingredient any company can have is the selection, training and upgrading of people. . . . One thing I like to tell management is that to treat people fairly you have to treat them differently. No two people are alike." Then he recounted a story, actually a parable, that he had told many times before. "Back during the war years, one of our department heads wanted to fire two female employes because they were late half the time. I said he could fire them but first he should talk with

101

each of them about their tardiness for 20 minutes or so. Well, he came back and said that was the best advice he ever had. In his conversations with the girls, he learned that one was the oldest of seven children, whose mother had died recently, and she had to get her six brothers and sisters off to school every day before she came to work. The other kept late hours and couldn't answer the morning alarm. So we fired one and helped the other. Anyone who says he or she treats all people the same is in trouble."

Ayers' concern for people and their problems became finely honed over the years in industrial relations. Insull established the Industrial Relations Department in 1921 to handle the complaints and general welfare of the employes. Insull advertised an "open door" policy with regard to employes' problems, but in reality, he didn't have time to see everyone who had a grievance. He therefore established a hierarchy of personnel experts. Insull's biographer nonetheless maintains that "If an employe, no matter how lowly his station, complained that he was not getting adequate attention along the chain of command, Insull would see him, and the employee generally found Insull to be a soft touch."

In a later interview, Tom Ayers asserted that there exist any number of successful managerial styles and recalled "a fellow named Charlie Heller who ran the gas department in Western Division." According to Ayers, "Charlie was a rough, tough boss, and you would have thought that we would have all kinds of grievances because he didn't always operate by the book. Charlie Heller, in the years he was there, never had a grievance. He used to walk around with about $2,000 in his pocket, and if Angelo Labachi said his wife's mother was sick and could he get a $100 loan, Charlie would peel it off and give it to him. He never wrote it down, never asked a man to sign anything, and swears he never lost a nickel. If one of the members of his gang had a child in the hospital, you could be damn sure Charlie would be there, seeing what he could do. That was his style. I've known others who were tougher than hell as bosses and didn't have a dollar and a half in their pocket and were successful. By and large those that were successful were those who showed concern for the employe, helping the employe be what they would like to be."

102

Two groups of employes increased greatly in number during World War I—women and Blacks. Both groups replaced white male workers who had left for military duty. In 1918 more than one employe out of every four joined the service. When America entered the war in 1917, Edison employed about 375 women; a year and a half later, the number had nearly tripled. They filled positions of draftsmen, meter readers, meter repair technicians, and apprentice substation operators, in addition to the more traditional clerical jobs. Since the company had promised the workers who joined the military that they could have their jobs back when they returned, it temporarily found itself with more employes than it needed. However, Edison made room for everyone. Black workers who held the jobs of returning servicemen often received clerk positions in the company's appliance stores.

Electrical World magazine reported, in September of 1918, on the success of placing women as meter readers, despite the none too positive tone set by their instructors:

"During the selection of the applicants, every attempt was made to explain fully the arduous character of the work, even to the point of attempting to discourage (the women). Further elimination occurred during the three days of schooling, about 30 percent of the class being dropped during this period. It is notable, however, that of the applicants who have satisfactorily finished their schooling, only a small percentage have since found it necessary to drop out. This is in sharp contrast to the usual practice of the young men who were formerly used, as 40 percent of the male force was lost during August. While it is, of course, too early to as yet draw decisive conclusions, it appears that women will work out more satisfactorily than the class of male help available, being able to do as much work and being more accurate, principally on account of their greater sense of responsibility."

But the trial of women as substation operators drew criticism from the same source, in a January 1919 article:

"It may be remarked that substation operation is of such a nature that it is doubtful whether women are particularly adapted to it in ordinary times. This is especially true of a large city system like that of the Commonwealth Edison Company where the substations are often located in rather rough neighborhoods. In the case of a man operator, one person can be left alone in the substation if desired, and a man can go and com (sic) in any neighborhood at any hour of the day or night. This cannot be done so readily, of course, in the case of a woman."

Helen Norris, Dean of Women, on her 25th anniversary with the company in 1939.

But the influx of women workers had created a new set of circumstances. For one thing, there was only one women's restroom in the entire 20-floor Edison Building. The logic of the day deemed that a woman would best be able to handle the concerns of other women. In 1916 Insull chose Helen Norris, the daughter of a Board of Trade member, to interview and hire women applicants. Norris had been with the company since 1914, serving as the librarian. In 1921 Insull created the maternalistic-sounding post of Dean of Women and Norris stepped into it, adding to her existing duties the coordination of all women's activities within the company.

Many remember Norris as a strict, no-nonsense person. She was well-educated, having attended Lewis Institute and Vassar College, and held a Bachelor of Arts degree from the University of Chicago. Before joining Edison, she had helped her godfather compile a dictionary of the Aztec language which established a definite link between that language and the ancient

Sanskrit. Throughout her career, Norris attempted to instill her will to achieve in the women of Edison.

Because she reported to no one but Insull, she had great influence over the progress of women employes. In 1917 she caused the formation of the Women's Committee. With Norris as Chairman, this sub-group of the Advisory Committee increased the number of washroom and recreational facilities available, established a food service which set the precedent for the downtown employe cafeteria, and tackled the issues of proper dress and conduct.

Norris herself had a formidable demeanor. Her personal uniform consisted of a tailored, dark suit, a single strand of pearls, and, always, a hat and gloves. At one time, she recommended that the women in the company be required to adopt an official uniform, and representatives from Carson, Pirie, Scott & Co. and Marshall Field's were brought before the Woman's Committee to present options. The idea was debated at length, but eventually rejected because it took away individuality and added expense. Instead, the committee printed a card relating to business dress and thereafter, each woman employe received one.

That card read: "The Women's Committee suggests that all women employes avoid extremes of color and cut in dress for business and wear either one-piece dresses or waists of not too shear material, with moderate collars and skirts of medium length, and avoid extreme use of cosmetics during business hours. It is the business of the Chairman of the Women's Committee (Norris), to interview any employe who does not conform to the above suggestion."

Such a "suggestion" today would seem likely material for a lawsuit. But Norris believed her intentions were for the best for her "girls." Indeed, most of them were barely out of high school. The *Edison Round Table* invariably referred to female employes as "girls" regardless of their age, a practice considered inoffensive years ago but one that would draw a wince, or worse, from many of today's readers. For example, an early 1930s story about a First Aid class carried the subheading, "Diplomas Awarded to 401 Men, 21 Girls at Completion of Course." Or, from the same period, "Edison girl hikers enjoy outing."

Norris' purpose was to help female employes fit into a world that was, by and large, made for men. Remembers one annuitant: "Miss Norris was great on what she called deportment, the way we acted and the clothes we wore. We were not to be outstanding, we were really to fade into the background. Not because we were less than anyone else, but because we would then be accepted. I think that all along she was preparing you. Because if you were going into a business world, particularly one dominated by men, you absolutely had to blend in."

At the same time as she was working on outer appearances, Norris worked on opening up the women's minds. Given the nature of their jobs, most of the Edison women never ventured far from their desks and so had little opportunity to learn about the rest of the company. In 1921 Norris helped to bring the Women's Public Information Committee to Edison. WPIC was a national organization, a subsidiary of the public relations section of National Electric Light Association (NELA). At Edison, committee members invited company executives to speak to women employes on subjects pertaining to the industry.

In September 1924, the Women's Committee sponsored an essay contest among the women on "Women as Builders of Good Will." Seeing the excellent response, the committee decided to build a regular working committee around it, and so, on October 21, 1924, the Woman's Information Committee (WIC) was born. The purpose of the new organization was to educate the women to make them better employes and, in doing so, improve public relations through their contacts with customers. Through WIC, the women attended lectures by company executives, toured generating stations, and formed their own public speaking group. The work of the WIC was carried on into the 1970s. The public speaking group became known in later years as the Vocettes.

That women were a novelty in the utility business is further illustrated by Edison Historian Seymour, who devotes a half-page to a woman named Mattie L. Fish, a stenographer and one-time missionary in China who retired in 1935. Her 38 years of service were not unique among the total work force, but she was the first woman to achieve that longevity with the company and only the ninth female annuitant. The Silver Service Club, of which Mattie Fish was the first president, was organized in 1934 to honor women employes with 25 or more years of experience. The club still holds regular meetings today.

106

It took women somewhat longer to climb the ladder of success than it did men. Some of those who rose to prominence in their day and their service dates were Anne Bryce (1915–1951), who started with Edison as a junior clerk, became Supervisor of Stenography and Typing (1924), and rose to become an interviewer in the Industrial Relations department; Edith Mattson (1922–1953), who spent all but two years of her career as Edison's librarian; Mercedes Hurst (1929–1949), who joined Edison with a bachelor's degree in liberal arts from Indiana University and put her considerable public speaking skills to work in Public Relations and Home Service; and Lora Briggs (1929–1964), who served for 20 years as editor, first of the *Edison Round Table* and then of its successor, the *Edison Service News*.

In 1927 the *Edison Round Table* did a special "Women's Number." In it, Helen Norris wrote:

"A survey of the titles of positions held by 1,159 women employes shows an interesting development in the company, as compared with the positions occupied by the 176 women employed in March 1914. There are 34 titles in which we find women today which either did not exist in 1914 or for which women did not then seem fitted.

"Some of the classifications represent the normal growth of the company and consequent growth in or development of departments such as: Assistant Librarian, Assistant Teller, Bill Ledger Typist, Junior Lamp Renewal Clerk, Senior Lamp Renewal Clerk, Payroll Clerk, Stenographic Secretary, Supervisor, Telephone Services; Assistant Cook, Bus Girl, Counter Woman, Checker, Waitress, Head Waitress.

"Other positions now held by women represent growth in the scope of company activities, such as: Appliance Saleswoman, Head Demonstrator, Coupon Canvasser, Edison Studio Staff Artists.

"And still other jobs it would seem have developed from the reasons mentioned above and are filled by women—not so much because they are women's jobs or that women have served a long time—but because they have applied themselves to the tasks assigned, and have studied and trained so they were entirely capable of the responsibilities for direction and execution demanded in the following list:

"Supervisor of Stenography and Typing, Assistant Supervisor of Stenography and Typing, Bookkeeper, Chief Clerk, Head Bookkeeper, Head Budget Control Clerk, Head Clerk, Interviewer, Proof Reader, Senior Service Clerk, Statistics Clerk, Supervisor, Electric Shop; Supervisor, Lunchroom; Teller."

One unique area in the company had its day-to-day operations run solely by women—the Correspondence Department.

Legend has it that one Saturday Insull came to his office to finish some work and found no secretary available to assist him. The following Monday, Insull called in James Rice, who had been writing construction bulletins for meter readers, and told him to form a new department which would have secretaries available every day of the week except Sunday. No longer would any executive come to work and find no one there to do the clerical tasks.

At its inception in 1921 the department was staffed with 19 women. It had grown by 1927 to a staff of 82, including a supervisor and two assistants. Of all the women who held the supervisor's spot in the Correspondence Department, perhaps none is so well remembered as Genevive Dooner. Despite her father's misgivings about higher education for women, Dooner had studied science at Mundelein College and the University of Chicago, then embarked on a career at Edison. Her first position was junior grade typist in the Correspondence Department. She rose through the clerical ranks, moving into Plant Records in 1939 as a Grade B typist. An anecdote Miss Dooner tells of her first day in that spot foreshadows the indomitable character that was to mark her career:

"I arrived on the job and Vince Cole sat me down and said, 'Stay here. We need to get these things done and I don't want you to move. If you need anything, ask the office boy.' So, after a while, I saw this rosy-cheeked young fellow and I stopped him and explained that he was to get my supplies, and I gave him a list of what I needed. And he ran off and got everything. Well, I later learned that that 'office boy' was Leonard Spacek, the auditor in charge of the reorganization of the Auditing Department, and later managing partner of Arthur Andersen & Co."

Dooner's knack of getting people to do things her way would prove valuable in one of the many roles she performed over the years—coaching everyone from executive vice presidents to contractor representatives in the fine art of public speaking. Her task was to organize meetings of the Management Committee, a vehicle for Edison officers and managers to learn more about company-related activities outside their own. The programs were to last exactly one hour, which they did, because Dooner timed each speaker down to the minute at rehearsals held the week before the meeting. She also suggested improvements.

"Two years ago, I got a letter from a man I had coached at one of the Management Committee meetings," Dooner said in a 1986 interview. "In it he remembered going on and on with his talk until I asked him to please button his lip until his mind had made up what it wanted to say. After all this time, he said he still tries to put that advice to work."

Another time, a construction man was having a difficult time pronouncing some of the words in his speech.

"I sent him away with a few gentle suggestions to work on for the final rehearsal on Monday. When he came back, I knew things were not going to work as they were. I didn't want him to put up a bad appearance, so I said, 'Listen, is your Sunday suit and fancy tie all ready?' He said yes. I said, 'All right, I'm going to keep a copy of your speech and make a few changes.' I went back to the office and redirected the entire talk and had it typed triple space. Then I took my green pen and phoeneticized the troublesome words in the spaces. Then I made sure he got a copy of that at home. When I talked to him Tuesday night on the phone, I told him, 'As soon as you have supper, I want you to go into the basement and stand in front of the water heater and read this speech over a minimum of 40 times.' You see, I wanted to get him away from the family and I didn't want him standing in front of a mirror.

Well, I guess he took me seriously because the next day he was wonderful. You never would have known he didn't graduate from the University of Chicago school of speech. After it was all over, I was walking back through the office and my boss' secretary said, 'What on earth did you do today? The boss came by and said, I don't know how Dooner does it.'. . . You just had to work with people."

When World War II broke out, Dooner left her typewriter to serve her country in the newly organized Women's Marine Corps. When she was discharged, she carried the rank of first lieutenant, and upon retirement from the Marine Corps Reserve, she was one of four women in the country to carry the rank of lieutenant colonel.

Soon after returning to Edison, Dooner took over as the supervisor of Stenography and Typing, and many women at Edison today remember training at her hands. Her military background spilled over into her work life, for most remember her as strict and extremely disciplined. But there is also a great respect for her and pride at having been one of "Miss Dooner's girls."

One woman recalls an incident in which Dooner met an opponent she almost couldn't beat. The story goes that Dooner had the right of way in a downtown intersection when a turning car failed to yield, and bore down upon her. Dooner, feeling that right was might, refused to give way. Unfortunately, the driver was equally stubborn. Just before she was struck, she flung her heavy briefcase into the car's windshield. Though Dooner suffered no serious injury, the car's windshield was smashed.

It was this kind of tenacity by which Dooner lifted herself up to serve, for twenty years, as administrative assistant to the secretary, and finally, in 1973, to become assistant secretary until her retirement in 1977.

"I started at the bottom, but my education helped, and I wasn't afraid of anything," says Dooner. "And, despite the fact that I had red hair, many times if somebody created a problem for me I'd give them a smile and say 'Oh, my goodness.' That wasn't my nature, but I'd do it because it was part of the job."

Dooner is remembered more fondly than Norris. During World War II, Industrial Relations announced that due to anticipated shortages, women employes could wear sox instead of silk or nylon hose. One IR veteran recalled that Miss Norris "was madder than hell," claiming it was indecent for women not to wear stockings.

110

"Look, Miss Norris," the IR man said, "there's a war going on and it's going to be harder and harder to get stockings!"

"That isn't true," she said.

"Well, it's going to be true, the kind of stockings that you wear you aren't going to be able to get," the IR man asserted.

As anyone who remembers those days will recall, it turned out to be true. The dispensation stood.

After the war, in 1947, an historical milestone of sorts was achieved when the legendary Dean of Women retired after 33 years. Her job title, mercifully, did not survive, but her role was carried on, first by Anne Bryce, who served as chief women's employment interviewer, then, in 1954, by Hazel Stevenson as supervisor of women's activities. Stevenson was responsible for the coordination and guidance of women's activities, including personnel counseling. So the legacy of Helen Norris was carried on until 1972, when Stevenson's title and duties were changed to supervisor of employe activities.

Times had certainly changed during Norris' tenure. At an after-work service recognition dinner for veteran employes and annuitants, an outraged Norris, then in her 80s, confronted the speaker and complained that some of the men were "plying the girls with liquor."

"These 'girls' were at least 60," recalls the executive who was the recipient of Miss Norris' ire.

'If Mr. Insull knew this, he'd be spinning in his grave,' Norris said.

'Miss Norris, the world has changed,' the speaker replied.

"She was kind of a throwback to another age," the Edison man concluded. "She was just out of touch".

Stevenson, on the other hand, was a thoroughly modern woman, who enjoyed bowling and golf, and was an enthusiastic White Sox fan. Stevenson joined Edison in 1942 as a member of the steno pool in Correspondence. She worked there about a year before being assigned as a stenographer to Norris herself.

"In one of my first days on the job, Miss Norris gave me exactly six pieces of personal letterhead and six envelopes to match. The point was clear. . .there were to be no mistakes."

Apparently, Norris was satisfied, because Stevenson was recommended for a job with the manager of Industrial Relations, Roy A. Dingman. When he became vice president, Stevenson was promoted to be his secretary, a unique development because throughout most of Edison's history, very few women had been secretaries. These positions were usually held by rising male stars.

The lot of the clerical worker at Edison changed radically in the early 1970s, Stevenson recalled.

"It was an era of total change. The girls wore mini-skirts, they went from pantsuits to blue jeans. And it changed some men's attitudes. If they dressed that way, they were not just pretty little girls anymore. In a way, they were defiant, and they had to be reckoned with."

Helen Norris would be spinning in her grave.

Seven

Halcyon
Days

"By 1890 every urban political machine not operated by morons had in it, somewhere, a coal company."

That is the blunt conclusion of Forrest McDonald, Insull's biographer. The Chicago political apparatus, not operated by morons, had the Peabody Coal Company, run by Francis S. Peabody, "sometime ward heeler, sometime sheriff, usually Democratic national committeeman from Illinois," according to McDonald.

Insull, certainly no moron either, served as a big customer for Peabody Coal because smart politics demanded that he do business with a political heavyweight. But about the time Fisk Station came on line, in 1903, the Edison chief realized he might gain more from the relationship than political advantage. Fisk, with its unprecedented size, and the other large generating stations that would follow within a few years would require huge supplies of coal. Edison needed to guarantee a long-term supply.

Peabody had another agenda. He wanted to become a large-scale mine operator as well as a distributor of coal, but he lacked capital. His friend Sam Insull could get capital, so a deal evolved: Peabody would keep Edison supplied with all the coal it needed, well into the future, for cost plus a reasonable profit. With such a contract in his pocket, Peabody could then borrow the money to buy the mines that would enable him to keep his part of the bargain.

According to Seymour's history of Commonwealth Edison, the company itself purchased coal properties in 1903 and 1904 totalling some 40,000 acres in Christian and Sangamon Counties in Illinois and Vigo County in Indiana. Edison created a subsidiary called the Illinois Midland Coal Company in 1905 to own the properties, which included two mines that produced about 3,500 tons of coal a day and the four-mile-long Pawnee Railroad, constructed in 1881 to haul farm products. Insull and Peabody headed Illinois Midland jointly, with operation of the mines remaining the responsibility of the coal baron.

The contract called for Peabody to produce nearly 10 million tons of coal between 1905 and 1915, with the Edison Company to receive half. Due to Edison's insatiable appetite for coal, the result of the service territory's insatiable appetite for electricity, two more mines, with a daily output of 4,000 tons each, were opened later. In 1904, Edison consumed approximately 300,000 tons of coal; 10 years later the amount had passed the 1.25-million mark.

One of the first lessons Sam Insull learned about the coal business taught him that a large part of the price is for transporting the coal from the mine to the point of consumption, in this case the Edison generating stations. Accordingly, Insull and Peabody developed the little Pawnee Railroad into a connecting line to carry their coal from central Illinois to Edison's generating plants in Chicago. They named the newly acquired railroad the Chicago and Illinois Midland after its corporate parents, Chicago Edison and the Illinois Midland Coal Company. Originally, the C&IM connected Edison's coal properties with the trunk line railways running to Chicago.

In 1926 the C&IM purchased the right-of-way of the bankrupt Chicago, Peoria and St. Louis Railroad, extending from Springfield to Pekin, by way of Havana, to complete the railroad as it exists today. The C&IM operates on 121 miles of track between Pekin and Taylorville, presently employs 350 people, and owns five locomotives, 10 cabooses, and approximately 1,200 coal cars. As demands for power and coal grew, Edison built a rail-to-barge transfer facility at Havana on the Illinois River, 40 miles downstream from Peoria, enabling the company to supply its river stations by the less expensive water route.

In the mid-1960s Edison built Kincaid Station across the road from Peabody Mine No. 10, near Taylorville. Coal once hauled by the C&IM to the Havana dock now literally moved across the street by conveyor. Shortly after the startup of Kincaid, however, the federal Clean Air Act became law, effectively prohibiting the burning of high-sulfur Illinois coal in metropolitan areas. Kincaid, in a sparsely populated part of the state, was the only Edison coal-fired station not affected. As a result, the C&IM received a new lease on life and today serves as a terminal carrier for Edison's low-sulfur western coal, which the company began using to comply with the Clean Air Act.

Some of the coal destined for Edison's generating stations originates in the Black Butte mine in southwestern Wyoming, where the Union Pacific Railroad transports the train to Council Bluffs, Iowa, then turns the cars over to the Chicago & North Western Railway. The C&NW then moves the train from Council Bluffs to East Peoria, where the C&IM crews steer the train toward Havana or Powerton Station, near Pekin.

Edison constructed Powerton in the late 1920s along the C&IM right-of-way. Before the new environmental regulations, coal moved from an Edison mine in central Illinois, onto an Edison train, and into the Edison power plant a comparatively short distance away. As an Englishman, Insull in particular would have appreciated the "coals to Newcastle" analogy suggested by the change to western coal. As a businessman, he would have been less than appreciative of spending considerably more to bring coal to one of the world's richest coal deposit regions.

Today, coal also comes from the Decker and Big Horn mines in southern Montana and northern Wyoming. The Burlington Northern then carries the fuel to East Peoria, where the C&IM crews board the BN train and take it to Havana or Powerton. Upon delivery at Havana, the coal is dumped into 15-barge tows, the equivalent of two 110-car unit coal trains. The coal moves by barge up the Illinois River to Edison's generating stations in the Chicago area.

The relationship between Commonwealth Edison and the Chicago and Illinois Midland Railroad benefits both parties. Edison, on the one hand, provides the C&IM with an almost guaranteed source of business. Hauling coal for Edison accounts for approximately 97 percent of the C&IM's business; local freight runs make up the remainder. The C&IM, in turn, helps Edison keep fuel transportation costs down and pays the parent company a fair dividend.

Edison, in partnership with Peoples Gas, acquired a second railroad in 1924, the Chicago & Illinois Western. The C&IW, with only 11.5 miles of its own track, would provide connections between coal carriers and Edison's Crawford Station, on Chicago's Southwest Side, as well as an adjacent gas manufacturing plant. Edison sold its interest in the C&IW in the late 1940s.

Acquisition of the Chicago and Illinois Midland and the central Illinois coal mines required some structural changes at Edison. The company was not authorized by charter to operate coal mines or railroads, so it had to establish subsidiary corporations which it controlled through stock ownership. Other subsidiaries followed, and presently Edison has six in addition to the C&IM. Commonwealth Edison of Indiana owns State Line Generating Station in Hammond; Edison Development Company holds coal reserves. As the name suggests, Commonwealth Research Corporation researches important issues such as the chemical cleaning of nuclear power stations, with the help of funds from the U.S. Department of Energy (DOE) and the Electric Power Research Institute (EPRI). Cotter Corporation serves as Edison's uranium mining and milling operation in Colorado, while Edison Development of Canada holds uranium ore reserves. Finally, Concomber Ltd. is a nuclear and workmen's compensation insurance corporation.

Thanks to the Edison-Peabody decision to acquire a railroad and coal mines a dozen years earlier, Edison could get through World War I without the shortages or high prices that plagued nearly every other utility in the country. During the war years, the company's coal reserves averaged about 400,000 tons—a three-month supply. In fact, Edison's reserves were so healthy that during the winter of 1918–19, when shortages threatened a cold winter for millions of coal-burning households, Edison came to the rescue by selling coal at cost for home heating, considerably under the market price. The scene would repeat itself in the 1970s, when a coal miners' strike cut off fuel to generating stations in the eastern United States. Edison, primarily on the strength of its nuclear units, could move sufficient power to the East to avoid school closings, factory shutdowns, and other disruptions.

Edison also had its coal mining labor problems in the post-World War I era. In the summer of 1919 a series of wildcat miners' strikes hit the Illinois coal fields but left Edison-Peabody untouched, largely because of the companies' generous treatment of their miners and good rapport with union leaders. But all the goodwill in the world couldn't save Edison-Peabody that fall, when United Mine Workers president John L. Lewis called a nationwide strike, demanding a six-hour day, a five-day week and a 60 percent increase in wages. A lot of workers got a six-hour day, all right, but not miners—they were employes of Chicago business houses forced to scale back their hours because of the strike. Many Chicago factories closed altogether, throwing some 25,000 people out of work. Coal rationing was imposed throughout the area. The Illinois Public Utility Commission finally settled the local dispute at far less than the miners had sought.

Another wave of strikes followed in 1922, closing the Edison-Peabody mines from April until August. For the first time in years, Edison had to buy coal on the open market at much higher prices than the company had paid under the Peabody contracts. The extra cost amounted to more than $1.6 million. Ironically, Edison's long-term coal and oil contracts, designed to provide uninterrupted fuel supplies at reasonable prices, would come under fire from the Illinois Commerce Commission (ICC) and others in the early 1980s, when spot market prices unexpectedly dipped below the contract prices.

The Peabody Company settled the 1922 strike by cutting a private deal with Frank Farrington, boss of the Illinois mine workers and archenemy of John L. Lewis. Peabody offered something to both the miners and their leader. For the miners, the company agreed to boost the basic daily wage well above that of miners elsewhere in the country. At the same time, the coal company offered Farrington a $25,000 annual gratuity. Farrington happily accepted both. The men returned to work, and Commonwealth Edison never had to deal with a coal miners' strike again, even though infighting among union leaders would continue for years. In 1927, for example, Lewis found out about the annual gratuity to Farrington, obtained documentary proof, and had Farrington thrown out of the union. Farrington, in turn, staged a comeback later and led a group that toppled Lewis as the mine workers' leader.

Labor relations at Commonwealth Edison over the years have been far more placid. The only strike against the company occurred at the start of the 1956 Christmas season and involved only the employes at State Line Station, incidentally members of United Mine Workers Local 50. A "catchall" union, Local 50 had no connection with coal mining. The remainder of Edison's union employes were and are represented by the International Brotherhood of Electrical Workers (IBEW). Today, the United Steel Workers of America represent State Line.

The strike began when Local 50 demanded, and the company refused to grant, a contract that called for a higher wage scale than that of IBEW. Tom Ayers, commercial vice president at the time, recalled that "there were about 300 employes in that union (UMW), and the Edison system had 11 or 12 thousand union employes. We took the position that we wouldn't treat them any better or any worse, but there is no way 300 are going to swing 11 or 12 thousand. You get into a ratcheting process if you do that." UMW believed the company was trying to move the workers into IBEW, so Edison would have to bargain with only one union. If that happened, employes who liked working at State Line feared being transferred to another plant.

The State Line employes went out on a frigid Saturday morning, November 24. Jim Walsh, one of three union trustees who counted the ballots, couldn't believe the approximate eight-to-one margin in favor of the strike. All three trustees had voted "no." As he counted, Walsh told the other two, "You guys must have all the 'no' votes, because all I'm getting are 'yes' votes." The nearly empty treasury increased Walsh's disbelief. He theorized that many of the workers who voted "yes" did so to posture as hard-liners, but thought that the majority would vote against the strike.

"The first morning of the strike, there was a big Nash Ambassador blocking the road to the plant," Walsh recalled. "There was a 'State Line on Strike' sign in the window. I got into the car to warm up, and the driver, who was about 58 or 60 years old, gave me a pep talk about how this strike was going to separate the men from the boys."

Under police protection, the company moved in a skeleton crew of management personnel to keep the plant running. Once inside, they remained for the duration. On the second day of the walkout, 22 union members broke ranks and entered the plant by boat from Lake Michigan. "One of them was the guy in

118

the Nash," Walsh remembered wryly. The company trucked in large quantities of food, including a lot of steaks, to the men on the inside, who agreed that the provisions were better than they were used to eating at home. State Line had a good-sized coal pile at the start of the walkout, and an additional train shipment arrived after the picket line had gone up. Police arrested three strikers who tried to block the shipment, and successfully assured passage of the train to the plant. The company could get the coal inside the station because a couple of the managers knew how to operate a bulldozer.

Vern Stone, one of the managers on the inside, believed the strikers knew they had lost when they saw smoke coming from one of the stacks, indicating that he and the others had been able to start a unit, formerly out of service. Jim Walsh agreed with that observation, adding that two more indications arose—reports that another 35 strikers would enter the station the following week and that some of the older workers feared losing their pensions.

Walsh himself didn't cross the line, heeding the advice of his father, a streetcar man who had taken part in a bitter strike in 1919 and who warned his son that anyone who broke ranks would incur the longtime enmity of his fellows. According to Walsh, his father turned out to be right: members read the names of the linecrossers at union meetings for years afterward.

The agreement ending the strike called for no recriminations by the company. Walsh himself provided living proof of that. He eventually moved to management and retired in 1984 as manager of Industrial Relations at Edison's Chicago South Division. He also served as vice president of Commonwealth Edison of Indiana, the subsidiary that operates State Line.

"We settled (on November 30)," Tom Ayers remembered, "and offered every employe the chance to borrow up to the total amount of the wages he lost, interest-free. As I remember, we gave them 18 months to pay it back. We didn't negotiate the offer with the union; we simply said it was available. We weren't trying to embarrass the union, but fellows had kids who were looking forward to Christmas. It put us in great standing with the people at State Line Station.

"It was popular in the '30s, '40s and early '50s to say, 'Well, the union takes care of the employes, and that's not management's job.' In the Edison group of companies, we never took that position. "If they have problems or needs, we have to address that and not turn over the concern about the employes exclusively to the union.

"I can remember sitting next to the head of U.S. Steel at a dinner in the 1950s, and we got to talking about labor relations. I said that we had made what I thought was an absolutely great agreement with our union. If people were knocked out of a job because of technological changes, they would suffer no loss of pay, and we would find other work for them. In return, if we made a technological change, the union had the right to grieve about what pay rate was set, but not to grieve about whether or not we made the change. Now, the fellow from U.S. Steel thought this was the dumbest thing he ever heard of. I saw him 10 years later in a New York hotel. He said he remembered our conversation and had thought about it for years. He told me as things turned out, that would have been the smartest thing the steel corporation could have done."

In the 1920s Commonwealth Edison and Public Service of Northern Illinois acquired the land on which State Line Station was built after a study by the two companies indicated the wisdom of having generating stations outside the city of Chicago. For one thing, there was practically no place left to build in the city. For another, the availability of condensing water seemed doubtful in the city. A U.S. Supreme Court order in 1929 would, in fact, reduce the amount of water permitted for diversion in the Chicago River and the Sanitary and Ship Canal. That decision all but ruled out the expansion of Crawford Station or any other plant on the river or canal, and there were no available sites on Lake Michigan within the city limits. On the other hand, large sites with almost unlimited water supplies existed north and south of Chicago, respectively, at Waukegan and Hammond, Indiana, in addition to the Powerton site on the Illinois River, south of Pekin. Edison pushed ahead with plans to develop each of these sites to meet anticipated future demand.

Edison chose the State Line site for its rail facilities and its proximity to Chicago, as well as for its location on the lake, along the Indiana side of the state boundary. It offered the further advantage of lying in the growing industrial belt that extended from Chicago's Southeast Side to Gary's mighty steel

120

furnaces and coke ovens. The generating station's parent, the State Line Generating Company, became a part of Edison, Public Service of Northern Illinois, Northern Indiana Public Service, and Interstate Public Service in March 1928. The plant sat upon 75 acres of landfill and went into service in July 1929. With a rating of 208,000 kw, State Line Unit 1 was the largest operating unit in the world and for 25 years held the title of largest generating unit in the United States. The unit generated electricity for 22 years without interruption because of a unique design consisting of one high-pressure and two low-pressure steam turbines. This permitted one set of turbines to be taken out of service while the other two operated.

State Line Unit 2 went into service in 1937, following a delay of six-and-one-half years due to the depression. Rated at 150,000 kw, the new unit was the largest hydrogen-cooled generator in the world and the most efficient of its type ever built to that time. The company added a third unit in 1954 and a fourth in 1962. State Line became a wholly owned subsidiary of Commonwealth Edison in 1939. In 1957 its parent corporation became known as Commonwealth Edison Company of Indiana.

Historic Unit 1, retired in 1978, took its place alongside Fisk Unit 1 as a National Historic Mechanical Landmark designated by the American Society of Mechanical Engineers. Unit 2 was retired the following year.

Leaving Hammond and following the northwestern curve of Lake Michigan, some 40 miles north of the northern Chicago city limits, one will find Waukegan Station, built in 1923 when the press described it as "the last word in modern station construction." It moved Public Service Company Historian Whetstone to flowery prose. "Within, it is light, clean and spacious," she writes. "The white tile walls of the turbine room, the terra cotta parquetry, and the sheen of highly polished metal, compare with the elegance of an ocean liner. The walls, ceilings, pipes and even the huge machines have been toned in shades of buff, light green and grey, to make the whole exceedingly pleasing to the eye. And over all is the pulse and throb of the machines, as tirelessly as night and day, they carry on; translating coal into light and power.

"Today, enclosed, overhead mechanical conveyors, electrically operated, carry the coal from the crushers and deliver it to the automatic stokers, which in turn feed the coal to the furnaces in the exact proportions required to maintain combustion at white heat, and steam at 600 pounds pressure; a heat so intense that colored glasses must be used when looking into the combustion chamber."

Thirty-five years later, the addition of 305,000-kilowatt Unit 7, the largest generating unit in the country in 1958, would dwarf Waukegan Station's original unit, rated at 25,000 kw. A single boiler, 16 stories high and burning more than 3,000 tons of coal a day, produced steam to power the new turbine and generate enough electricity for 500,000 homes. Unit 8, at 300,000 kw, was added in 1962.

As with State Line, Powerton Station was built by Commonwealth Edison in shared ownership with three other companies, Edison's share being 30 percent. The partnership, formed in 1924, was known as the Super-Power Company of Illinois, later the Powerton Electric Generating Company. Edison acquired full ownership of the plant in 1942. The first of two 50,000-kilowatt units went into service in 1928, the second the following year. A 220,000-volt transmission line connected Powerton to the Chicago system.

The first of the great post-World War I generating stations, Calumet Station, went into service in December 1921, on the west bank of the Calumet River at 100th Street, on Chicago's Southeast Side. Calumet Unit 1 was rated at 30,000 kw. By 1933, six units, totalling 187,000 kw, functioned, but the company did not require all of the capacity.

Edison shut down Calumet altogether in the summer of 1932 because of a drop in demand caused by the depression. Though the plant provided for small loads the following winter, it ceased again in the summer of 1933. Fired up again the following winter, Calumet operated only a few units, exclusively on weekdays, until 1940, when wartime production caused a sharp increase in demand on the Edison system. Among its achievements Calumet can list the first pulverized fuel-fired boiler on the Edison system and the first cyclone-type coal burner. Calumet Station was retired in 1975.

Crawford Station, located on 72 acres at 35th Street and Pulaski Road, formerly Crawford Avenue, in Chicago, on the north bank of the Sanitary and Ship Canal, went into service in

November 1924. Previously a farm, the property retained much of its former character, for poultry and animals continued to roam the grounds during construction. They must not have raised too much protest, because workers completed the plant in 20 months—amazing by today's standards, but typical of the times. The first unit, rated at 60,000 kw, immediately preceded units of 50,000 kw and 40,000 kw. According to Edison historian Rice, the three units "were the greatest generators ever manufactured up to that time, and put Crawford Station in the limelight as the greatest in the world for a long period."

Formal opening ceremonies for the station did not occur until the following May, when all three units would be in operation. The company planned a big civic luncheon and invited a slew of state, county and city officials, including Mayor William E. Dever, as well as many prominent members of the financial and engineering communities—about 400 in all. Some 250 of the VIPs rode out from the Loop on a special Illinois Central train. Insull prepared to wax eloquent, as always. However, reminiscent of the shaky startup of Fisk Station more than two decades earlier, when Fred Sargent had feared that the plant might blow up and the dignitaries had to be ushered out, things did not proceed as smoothly as planned.

The day before the dedication ceremonies, the last of the three units to come on line went through a trial run. It lasted for 26 minutes. The unit began again and ran for several hours before, according to Rice, "The commutators, brushes and brush holders, and both exciters were badly burnt. It was necessary to remove the armature for rebanding and to replace some of the brush holders."

So, with fingers crossed, the Crawford station hands fired up the errant unit, praying that it would last through the ceremonies. Although they could not immediately replace the destroyed brushes, the unit started well. Everyone enjoyed lunch. Insull made his speech. The station hands looked at their watches. Dever made his speech. The station hands checked the time again. The mayor completed his remarks. The event was over. Once the last of the dignitaries went out the door, still marveling at the precision and efficiency of these new machines, the troubled unit was brought down and stayed down for repairs for two months.

Like the farm creatures before them, animals seemed to haunt the place, causing odd encounters. Three related anecdotes crop up in a carefully prepared history of Crawford covering the period 1922–1937 and written by its longtime chief electrician, Bill Moore.

In the spring of 1926, charged with the maintenance of several acres of lawn adjacent to the station, chief engineer W. J. Weyker began lobbying for a power mower, something of a novelty at the time. However, the board of construction engineers in charge of purchasing new equipment repeatedly turned him down. With grass growing taller by the day, Weyker had just about given up when he got an urgent call to come to the plant store room: the lawnmower had arrived, but there seemed to be some problems with it.

"On reaching the storeroom," Moore recounts, "his gaze fell upon a shipping crate, and within it, eyeing him belligerently, stood a seasoned and well-developed ram ... According to the shipping memoranda attached, this animal purported to come from the Rambler-Roaming Lawnmower Co., Munchenchewit, N.Y. Directions for its care and use together with a description of the mechanism were also attached."

At that moment, about two dozen of Weyker's co-workers stepped out of hiding to needle him. One of the men had bought the ram for his farm and figured to send it there after everyone had had a laugh. But Weyker elected to keep the ram as a station pet, naming him Oscar and feeding him hay along with his diet of grass.

"Oscar possessed certain qualities which in a lawnmower we considered to be faults," Moore continues. "First, he was imbued with the notion that the grass was greener beyond the length of his tether. He refused to stay put and was continually wandering off the job. One favorite hideout and feeding place was the 440-volt switchboard room where he would be found gnawing at the fuses and switch handles with the greatest of relish. He enjoyed his own crude jokes which through want of variation became monotonous and dull, his favorite being a flying tackle from the rear without warning of the play. Furthermore, being a sheep and not a dog, Oscar was not housebroken and made not the slightest attempt to learn the niceties of good behavior and deportment."

124

During the winter, the station hands kept Oscar in an old locomotive house. The following spring, according to Moore, the ram ended his hibernation by glutting himself with too much green grass and died "without ever viewing the promised land of Mr. Casey's farm."

Another unusual creature paid a visit to Crawford in July 1933. In the early evening of an otherwise routine day, a 12 kilovolt (kV) transformer in the outdoor switchyard failed, and the watch electrician set out to investigate. When he reached the transformer, he couldn't believe his eyes. "On the stone floor," Moore relates, "huddled in forlorn abjection, sat a slightly singed monkey, blinking its eyes and sadly shaking its head. It offered no resistance nor attempted to escape . . . The transformer was examined and several square inches of glazing found burned from a bus support insulator, along with burns on the nearby supporting steel; this at a height of about 20 feet. Two thousand amperes had flowed through the fault established."

The watch engineer reported his discovery to the load dispatcher who enjoyed a good laugh, then asked the real cause of the problem. The engineer repeated his story. The dispatcher said, in substance, "Look, pal, we're starting to get busy. That's a funny joke, but what's really going on?" The electrician assured him that he wasn't joking. The conversation began to get heated, and Moore says the men would have come to blows if they hadn't been separated by distance. Somebody finally verified the story, and the police were called. They removed the monkey to the dog pound. The animal was later returned to the University of Chicago, more than 10 miles away, from where it had wandered off, "whether to continue his studies in electrical engineering or to turn to some other line, we never learned," Moore reports.

The third of Moore's animal incidents occurred in May 1936, when a screen attendant at Crawford Station, probing the swirling water near the intake screens, came up with an unusual catch on his pike pole. According to a *Chicago Tribune* account of the incident, "Workmen for the Commonwealth Edison Company pulled the body of a 35-pound octopus from the Drainage Canal at 35th Street and California Avenue (sic) yesterday. The sea creature was blocking the water intake screen of the

Edison plant at 3501 South Crawford Avenue.* Walter H. Chute, director of the Shedd Aquarium, said the octopus probably is one preserved and displayed frequently by roving museums. They cannot live in fresh water and it would be impossible for one to reach Chicago through the lake or rivers."

With five of the most advanced generating stations in the world rising under its corporate domain, with booming sales and despite periodic aggravations such as coal miners' strikes, the 1920s were halcyon days for Commonwealth Edison. Many believed they were halcyon days for the country as well. The War to End All Wars had passed; the country was back to normalcy, according to Harding; legal booze had evaporated but illegal booze flowed; the business of America was business, according to Coolidge; prosperity reigned; people who had never owned stock jumped into the market with both feet; radio sales took off; automobiles buzzed across the land like so many four-wheeled insects; it was the Jazz Age, the Lost Generation, and the Golden Age of Sports rolled into one; it was an age of greats: Paul Whiteman, Bix Beiderbecke, and Louis Armstrong; Ernest Hemingway, F. Scott Fitzgerald, and John Dos Passos; Jack Dempsey, Red Grange, and Babe Ruth. And Sam Insull. He was to the business world, according to McDonald, what Dempsey, Grange and Ruth were to the sports world. In this era of hero worship, the biographer writes, "The people—butchers, bakers and candlestick makers who invested their all in his stocks—fairly idolized him, and even titans viewed him with awe. He measured up to America's image of itself: a rich, powerful, self-made giant, ruthless in smashing enemies, generous and soft-hearted in dealing with the weak. His doings, small and large, became a great spectator sport, and they were reported and followed accordingly. . . .

"When a generous act came to a reporter's attention— such as the time Insull sent a young Negro singer to Europe to study at his expense or sponsored a European trip for his favorite Pullman conductor—the event was treated with all the reverence due Babe Ruth for hitting a home run to save the life of a hospitalized child."

*The intake is near Pulaski Road, then known as Crawford Avenue, 1½ miles west of California Avenue.

126

Such were the times.

In the decade of 1919 to 1929, the number of Edison customers rose from 415,000 to 950,000; output rose from 1.60 billion kwh to 4.28 billion kwh; gross operating revenue from $30.36 million to $83.49 million; generating station capacity from 519,000 kw to 1,268,000 kw; and peak load from 433,000 kw to 1,000,000 kw.

In 1923 the company witnessed its largest net increase in the number of customers, nearly 78,000. The summer of that year saw Edison's version of that great American pastime "Keeping Up With The Joneses"—the opening of a model electric home at 97th Street and Hamilton Avenue in Chicago's fashionable Beverly Hills neighborhood. Tens of thousands of actual and would-be homeowners flocked to the display to see what modern living was all about and to learn how electricity could help them live more comfortably and economically. In addition to the latest type of radio, phonograph, electric range, electric dishwasher, the model home contained a couple of features particularly ahead of their time—an automatic garage door opener and a fire detection system. Later in the 1920s Edison unveiled the first electric apartment, at 2130 Lincoln Park West. Like the model home, it was enormously popular with the public, as were additional model electric homes that Edison and Public Service Company showcased in the '20s and '30s. The Public Service displays took place in River Forest, Joliet and Waukegan.

Another milestone, a long-term agreement in 1923 to furnish electricity to the Illinois Central Railroad's south suburban commuter line, marked the company's biggest sales coup since the agreement to supply electricity to the streetcar and elevated lines a decade earlier. The contract called for Edison to furnish 30,000 horsepower for the electrification of the IC, enough to power a typical city of 125,000. To help supply the electricity, Edison constructed seven substations along the IC right-of-way. Spurred upward by the addition of the IC as well as by the increasing popularity of modern home appliances, Edison's load underwent its largest annual increase, nearly 250,000 kw, in 1925. In 1929, Edison installed its one millionth meter in, of all places, the new *Chicago Daily News* Building at 400 W. Madison St. Coincidence? Or was the fine hand of public relations expert Bernard Mullaney showing?

Another major development in the 1920s was the interchange of power between Edison and other electric utilities in adjoining states. The interchange would maintain reliable service during emergencies—in case a storm or accident knocked out a transmission line, a generating unit had to shut down unexpectedly or, in later years, a prolonged hot spell built up the demand for air conditioning. Today, Edison belongs to the Mid-America Interpool Network (MAIN), a group of 16 interconnected utilities in Illinois, Wisconsin, Missouri, and Upper Michigan with a combined electric power capacity of more than 40 million kw.

Numerous other technological breakthroughs by Edison in the 1920s included: a system for the remote control of substations, invented by the company's Engineering Department; extensive use of underground cable; the first 60-cycle rotary converter to supply 230-volt direct current; establishment of a special Training Division in Industrial Relations; establishment of a high voltage AC testing laboratory.

Edison was a pioneer in a brand-new industry that would change the living habits of Americans almost as much as electricity itself had done a generation earlier. Edison teamed with Westinghouse to build and operate the first commercial radio station in Chicago, KYW, in 1921. KYW was only the second radio station in the United States, the first one another Westinghouse operation, KDKA in Pittsburgh. The original KYW studio was on the 18th floor of the Edison building with the transmitter on the roof. A one-hour concert by artists of the Chicago Civic Opera Company served as the first program, broadcast from the stage of the Auditorium Theatre. The announcer, Edison employe E. H. Gager, later became the station's chief engineer. The operatic recitals continued periodically, other programming consisting of records played in the studio. Additional early broadcasts included concerts by the Edison Symphony Orchestra under the baton of Morgan L. Eastman, who later became a station manager, and a children's program called The Air Juniors Radio Club featuring Irma Glen and Everett Mitchell. An annual Christmastime highlight of the Air Juniors show, a letter writing contest, encouraged children to address the topic "Why Electric Tree Lights Are Better than Old Fashioned Candles." Letters were read on the air, and prizes included electric trains, miniature electric ranges, and toy electric irons.

In 1925 KYW moved to the Fine Arts Building at 410 S. Michigan Ave. In 1930, the studios and offices of the station, now known as WENR, the "Voice of Service," moved to three floors of the new Chicago Civic Opera Building. Edison announced the sale of its interest in the station in 1936 as part of an overall plan to reduce investments in outside companies.

A particularly high point for Edison came in 1926, when the company received the Charles A. Coffin Award from the National Electric Light Association (NELA) for the "greatest progress in the use of electric light and power for the well being of the public and the benefit of industry." Edison thus ironically received an award named after a man who had helped squeeze Tom Edison and Sam Insull out of their electric manufacturing company in the early 1890s and whose early corporate policy, according to McDonald, "was scarcely distinguishable from theft." Interestingly, the company's application for the Coffin Award concentrated on achievements in marketing and advertising. "Popularizing the use of electricity in the home has been effected by advertising, education and intensive sales effort," the application declared, pointing out that the average annual residential use of electricity in 1925 was 494 kwh. Today, that figure represents slightly less than the average *monthly* residential use, a fact that would have made the Edison strategists and sales people of the '20s proud because they had just begun to redirect their efforts. By 1925, 94 percent of the homes in the city of Chicago had electric service. "This fact has caused the company to center its efforts on increasing the use of electricity among the 94 percent," Commonwealth Edison informed NELA. "Where this close approach to 100 percent is reached, it means that the remaining six percent would require a very disproportionate investment to serve them ... It is therefore to the greater advantage of the industry and of the community rather to have an increased use made of existing investment by present customers."

The Coffin Award application also focused attention on the industrial sector and the emergence of a new breed of sales experts—the marketing engineers. These people composed "a corps of specialists" who studied new applications for electric service to give the customer expert advice. "This includes men who specialize in electric furnaces, heat treating, commercial cooking, industrial oven applications, electric vehicles, electric ventilation, illumination, electric refrigeration, basic steel, industrial specialities and others. The development of this corps is largely responsible for the large increase in industrial load taken on in the last year."

A Christmas window display in the Edison Electric Shop at Jackson and Michigan (1930).

The lengthy NELA application touched all bases. A significant lighting contract concluded in 1925 would make downtown State Street the most brilliantly lighted thoroughfare in the world with the installation of special street lamps of 2,000 watts each. The application also touted the fact that the company sold $4 million worth of electrical appliances at its 13 electric sales shops and door-to-door. The merchandise included curling irons, grills, fans, toasters, washing machines, vacuum cleaners, and other conveniences. Finally, the Utilitarians, a newly formed group in which employes developed their public speaking abilities, received notice in the report to NELA. Even landscaping at generating stations and substations was mentioned, without reference to Crawford's pet ram.

130

One more 1925 development was the creation of a foreign language section in what would later be known as the Customer Service department. When a call came in from a person who spoke poor English or none at all, a battery of Edison linguists who could converse in most any tongue spoken in Chicago would take the calls. In later years, with the influx of a large Hispanic population, the company would establish a Spanish Hotline.

Enjoying music at the Electric Shop in the Edison Building. Phonographs were just one attraction for browsers.

To a company that, above all else, has prided itself on rendering reliable, courteous service and maintaining customer goodwill, it is especially noteworthy that in 1925 it pioneered the use of a tool that is widely utilized today—some would say excessively—the public opinion survey. Edison reasoned that improved relations with the public would require understanding of the present state of public attitudes in its service territory. To that end, the company retained an outside polling firm to conduct the first comprehensive measurement of public attitudes. More than 5,000 customers responded to a wide variety of carefully prepared questions. After the results were analyzed, one conclusion stood out: the public believed that employe performance is the most vital factor in good public relations and that employe training is the essential method of improving performance. The results reinforced what Commonwealth Edison had believed—and what Sam Insull had preached—for some time. The company stepped up the training of employes who had regular contact with the public. The large majority of these employes were and are customer service representatives (CSRs), who principally communicate with customers on the telephone. Through meetings, training sessions, contests, and other methods, Edison reminds CSRs of their critical role in forming customer attitudes toward the company. In the Spring 1984 issue of *The Edison* magazine, James O'Connor recalls the 1925 survey in support of his argument that public attitudes toward the importance of employe performance have remained virtually unchanged over the years. In his regular chairman's letter in this issue of the magazine, O'Connor hails the contemporary men and women of Customer Service by citing current surveys showing that 91 percent of the customers rated Customer Service employes excellent in courtesy; 81 percent rated them good to excellent in competency; while 80 percent regarded the company's performance good to excellent.

In the years immediately following World War I, death came for six of Sam Insull's archbishops. They included Fred Sargent, the brilliant engineer who, in addition to masterminding Fisk Station, helped to pioneer virtually every major advancement in central station development for 25 years; Frank Baker, the lawyer who convinced Insull to expand into the suburbs, then became vice president and general manager of Public Service Company of Northern Illinois; Roger Sullivan, the Chicago Democratic powerhouse who had first tried to scalp Insull, only to become his friend and one of his closest political advisers; William Beale, partner in the law firm of Isham, Lincoln and Beale, who was perhaps Insull's closest adviser of all; Francis S. Peabody, the coal magnate who entered the mining business with the Edison chief; and Arthur Young, Insull's British-born ace accountant. Insull himself suffered a nervous breakdown during this period but recovered by taking an extended vacation to Scotland.

McDonald maintains that the loss of these six lieutenants was mitigated by the continued presence of what he describes as Insull's "triumvirate of 'no' men"—top-drawer outside executives John J. Mitchell, James A. Patten, and John G. Shedd, for whom Chicago's renowned aquarium is named. According to McDonald, these three men appreciated Insull's brilliance as a businessman but acted as a check "when his daring threatened to be merely dangerous and his radicalism merely reckless."

Yet these men would die within a two-year period. Mitchell was killed in an auto crash in 1927—causing Insull to experience, in McDonald's words, "the panicky fear a seaman knows when he loses his rudder in a gale." He wept when told of Mitchell's death. Death weakened the Insull empire in still another way. Between 1924 and 1927, the older generation of Chicago's banking elite passed away, almost to a single man, leaving less experienced managers to face the unprecedented financial crisis that would explode within a few years. These newer banking leaders were not nearly as familiar with the Insull regime as were their predecessors. An Insull bookkeeper once remarked that the old-timers used to call up the way the grocer would, asking whether the company, "needed some nice fresh money today."

Insull had no one to fill the shoes of Mitchell, Shedd, or Patten, although he still had six or seven outsiders on whose advice he could rely. He couldn't do much about the changing of the guard at the big banks, but within his Big Three companies —Edison, Public Service, and People's Gas—he still had a well-stocked pool of talent with which to compensate for the loss of Baker, Sargent, and the others.

Two men who predated Insull at Chicago Edison headed this list—Louis A. Ferguson and John F. Gilchrist. Ferguson, inventor of the revolutionary fuse that bore his name, had slowed somewhat because of a serious illness in 1914 but remained a pioneer in urban distribution. Gilchrist, Insull's marketing genius, was one of the few high command members born in Chicago. Like Ferguson, he served as both a Commonwealth Edison vice president and a Public Service Company director.

Two other Public Service directors doubled as high-ranking Edison executives, Charles A. Munroe and John H. Gulick. Munroe claimed the distinction of being the only one of the entire lot fired by Sam Insull, and it came about in a curious way. While Insull was overseas in the mid-1920s, Munroe, ever the eagle eye, learned that he could save a foundering gas company in St. Louis for a mere $1.5 million. Munroe made some fast calculations and saw that he could rescue the firm in much the same way as People's Gas. Once the gas company turned around, Edison would reap gigantic profits. He didn't have to think twice. He borrowed the money on the old man's credit and bought the company in both Insull's and his own name. When the Edison chief returned, he hit the ceiling. Insull had always admired Munroe's panache, but this time he went too far. Even the prospect of huge profits didn't mollify him, so he fired Munroe. According to McDonald, the younger man left —and took the deal with him, clearing an incredible $26 million profit in three years. The incident stands as one of the few times that Insull let his emotions interfere with sound business judgment. He didn't speak to Munroe for nearly 10 years. A lesser man might have celebrated his good fortune by thumbing his nose at Insull. Munroe, on the contrary, would come to the chief's assistance years later, when Insull's world would begin to collapse and supposed friends would treat him like an invisible man.

Tall, courtly bachelor John Gulick, a particular favorite of Mrs. Insull, served as financial vice president for Public Service and vice president for accounting at Commonwealth Edison. Historian Whetstone credits Gulick's financial acumen with keeping Public Service alive and well during World War I, when many other utilities collapsed. "He would sharpen his own pencils," one veteran recalled. "He would come to a meeting with a bad cough, and someone would fix him up with cough drops, and he would later find out where he got them and come all the way down and return the little box."

Rounding out Insull's top command in the '20s were Ed Lloyd, the industrial sales expert; E. J. Fowler, ace statistician; Bernard Mullaney, public relations pioneer; Fred Scheel, who masterminded the program to sell Insull stock to customers; Edward J. Doyle, who started as Insull's office boy and rose to succeed him as president of Commonwealth Edison when Insull became chairman in 1929; George Mitchell, who followed a similar career path to become president of Peoples Gas in '29; Britton I. Budd, who ran the elevated and interurban railroads as well as Public Service Company and Middle West Utilities; and finally Samuel Insull Jr., who handled a variety of executive duties under the watchful eye of his father.

The outsider who acted as Insull's social conscience and political lawyer was Daniel J. Schuyler, law partner of Chicago corporation counsel Samuel Ettleson, who was, according to McDonald, the brains behind Mayor Thompson. The social conscience of Insull and Schuyler finds voice in their efforts on behalf of the city's Black population, swelled by a post-World War I migration from the South. With the aid of friends and associates, they founded a community center on the South Side and later on, the South Side Boys' Club. In those days, one did not often hear of efforts by the white business establishment on behalf of minorities.

"The obvious reason was human decency," McDonald explains, "but that was not the sole reason." The biographer goes on to state that both Insull and Schuyler anxiously wished to avoid a repetition of the race riots that plagued Chicago in the summer of 1919. Helping the newcomers adjust to urban life, they figured, would lessen the threat of violence. Another reason was good business: if the city's growing minority population could do well, so much the better for utility sales and transit ridership. Finally, Insull and his "political lawyer" foresaw as early as the '20s that the rapidly increasing Black population would become an influential voting bloc, and when it came to politics a public utility couldn't have too many friends. "All these considerations, and more, Insull instinctively grasped," McDonald concludes. "And in such matters, Schuyler's hyper-sensitive social antennae were perfectly attuned to Insull's own."

The social consciousness of Insull and Commonwealth Edison extended to a variety of other endeavors during the period. McDonald tells us that in the late '20s, when the chief earned almost half a million dollars a year, he gave away more than that to charities, some a bit unconventional, such as the Chinese YMCA and the education of African doctors.

In the cultural sphere, opera received the most from Insull's benevolence. His biography tells us that as a youth in London, he would skip meals in order to raise enough for a ticket in the upper gallery. In Chicago, he had been a longtime box holder and minor guarantor when the principal backers of Chicago's opera company, Harold and Edith Rockefeller McCormick, withdrew their support in 1922. Insull, with his friends Shedd and Mitchell, moved to fill the vacuum. In fact, Insull plunged in, the way he involved himself in almost everything. He sharply increased the number of guarantors, raised large sums of money, put the company on a more business-like footing and brought about various economies. He even fought with the director of the Chicago Civic Opera, the celebrated prima donna Mary Garden, causing her to leave Chicago in a huff. She preferred the French repertoire: he, the German and Italian. Always the politician, Insull's preference had more to do with demographics than taste. There were far more Germans and Italians than French in Chicago.

Just as the Pharaohs had their pyramids, so, too, would Sam Insull have a monument built in his lifetime. Instead of a tomb, it would be a magnificent structure to house grand opera in Chicago—a 42-story office building with the Chicago Civic Opera House on the ground floor. The opera building rose on a site bounded by Washington and Madison Streets, Wacker Drive and the Chicago River, which previously was occupied by the old Chicago Arc Light and Power Company plant and two auxiliary buildings acquired by Edison in the early 1890s. Insull would finance the building by selling $10 million in first mortgage bonds to the Metropolitan Life Insurance Company and $10 million in preferred stock to the public, both of which held in trust for a non-profit foundation. Rentals of office space would pay the interest and dividends, with enough left over to finance the opera.

Construction began in January 1928. As the building took shape, it began to resemble a giant throne, facing west, away from Wacker Drive and toward the river. The building quickly earned the nickname "Insull's throne," as if the person who would occupy the throne wanted to turn his back on something. The street below? Downtown Chicago? Numerous theories have risen up over the years. The most credible seems that Insull wanted to turn his back on the Eastern United States, more particularly New York, and most particularly the New York banks. Over his long tenure at the helm of Commonwealth Edison, he had shunned involvement with the New York banking community. If he could not finance a particular undertaking in Chicago, he would turn to London—never New York. No doubt the bitter memory of the House of Morgan's role in forcing Tom Edison out of the electrical business had burned into his soul like acid. According to McDonald, "not only did he refuse to look to New York for leadership and financial backing, he expressed contempt for New York bankers in both his words and deeds." But the cloth cut both ways. There were those in New York who had long waited eagerly to give Insull his comeuppance. Soon they would have their chance.

"Insull's throne," containing the new opera house, was completed in the fall of 1929. In keeping with Insull's program to "democratize" opera in Chicago, and to the surprise of many, the house had no side boxes. The first production, Verdi's *Aida*, opened on November 4. A photograph of Insull with philanthropist Stanley Field, Edison board member and nephew of Marshall Field, makes them look like a pair of stuffed penguins in their white ties and tails. Neither looks particularly happy. Nor, undoubtedly, did too many other first-nighters from the Chicago establishment. One week earlier, as the theatrical trade publication *Variety* so aptly put it, Wall Street had laid an egg. The Great Depression was underway.

Eight

The
Fall
Of
The
Empire

President Hoover assured the nation that prosperity was just around the corner. At a White House conference shortly after the crash, Sam Insull assured Hoover of the same thing. He promised the President and other business leaders that his companies, including Commonwealth Edison, would spend approximately $200 million in 1930 on plant construction and expansion, an increase of some $50 million over the previous year. Astounding as they may have seemed, these figures represented, according to the chief, "a reasonable indication of the faith we operating people have in the future of the country and the utility business. . .In looking ahead, we view the present business depression as only temporary. We feel that this depression will have relatively little effect upon the growth of our business over a period of years."

Over the short run, Insull was correct. The banks would still lend him all the money he wanted; the Insull companies experienced no difficulty selling stocks and bonds; and while total kwh sales, revenue, and the number of customers dipped from 1929 to 1930 for the first time in the company's history, residential sales continued to climb briskly. "Therefore," he concluded, "we feel that the public shares our faith in the future of our business." After the banks had refused to take a chance on the tax anticipation warrants of the City of Chicago, a public hearing illustrated that the financial community also shared the faith.

"Do you mean to tell me that the credit of the City of Chicago is not as good as that of Samuel Insull?" an alderman demanded of Silas Strawn, partner of the prestigious law firm, Winston and Strawn.

"Exactly that," Strawn replied from the witness stand.

139

And he was right. In January, with the city facing bankruptcy, Insull extended $50 to $100 million in credit so the government could pay the police, firefighters and schoolteachers. In April he undertook the mammoth task of bailing out, integrating, and modernizing the city's transportation system, a venture that would ultimately cost $500 million.

Insull periodically sought to reassure the Edison employes. On January 8, 1930, a record 1,200 members of the Edison Club and Electra filled every table in the Grand Ballroom of Chicago's Palmer House to witness Insull's first appearance before the clubs since 1922. Hardly a wake, the occasion included dining and dancing as the groups held their annual installation of officers. Insull's only reference to the crash, strangely enough, provided the only moment of levity in a talk so dry, so punctuated with statistics even by Insull standards, that even the most loyal employe must have wished for the music to begin.

"It is a pretty difficult thing to get up on one's feet and talk about our business, and especially to our own people, without having something to say about the unpleasant happenings in the stock market the latter end of the fall. (Laughter.) I am very glad you are able to smile at it. (Renewed laughter.) It was no smiling matter when it was going on—from the president down to the office boy." (Laughter.)

Insull's message: "Hold onto your Edison stock. If a business is worth devoting your lives to working for, its securities are worth holding." As it turns out he had given them good advice. Stockholders of Edison, Peoples Gas, and Public Service who held on for the entire course of the depression lost only a fraction of one percent of their investment. But hundreds of thousands of people who had money invested in Insull holding companies faced a far different fate. Looking back on that dinnerdance nearly six decades ago is a bit like looking back at the shipboard festivities on the *Titanic* after the first reports of icebergs in the area.

Insull, supremely confident that his companies could navigate through the icebergs, continued to take to the bully pulpit. In late 1930 he told the Chicago Jaycees, "In times of depression, men lack a proper sense of proportion in financial matters. They forget the experiences of the past and doubt the possibilities of the future. The psychological effect of bad business and unemployment is to deprive them of courage to deal with problems of today and is to throw doubts on their hopes of tomorrow."

He reminded the younger businessmen of Chicago's condition when he arrived in 1892 and how it had grown and prospered—always a favorite topic of his. "In 1893," Insull lectured, "some people were fearful that we would never get over the effects of the panic of that time. Yet, as I have just shown you, investors have put 48 times as much money into the electricity business as was invested in it in 1893, and we have 214 times as many customers. This absolute proof of growth and expansion that I have given you shows that business depressions, even panics, are passing things. The natural resources of America are too great for any business depression to hold back their development for any extended time."

Insull delivered that sermon throughout 1930 and well into 1931. He not only delivered it, but believed it, in spite of several business moves he made during this period that paved the way for disaster. On the surface, however, things progressed well enough at Edison for the company to establish a relief fund for the unemployed in Chicago. In November 1930 employes began contributing one day's pay a month for six months. The funds went to charitable organizations for distribution to the unemployed, with Edison bearing the total cost of overhead. The contributions, employes were informed, were tax-deductible. Within a few years, Edison employes would receive a 10 percent pay cut.

No one would have to hold any tag days for Insull. He sat on the boards of 85 companies, chaired 65 of them, served as the president of 11, and through his holding companies controlled 6,000 power units in 32 states. The empire also included textile mills, a paper mill, ice houses, and a hotel. At the time, Commonwealth Edison itself ranked as a $400 million company. Insull's two other operating utilities, Peoples Gas and Public Service of Northern Illinois, were valued at $175 million and $200 million, respectively. In addition, Insull controlled Middle West Utilities, with several hundred subsidiaries supplying electricity and gas in some 5,000 communities around the country, representing an investment of $1.2 billion; and Midland Utilities Company, a holding company whose subsidiaries represented an investment of $300 million and provided electricity and gas to about 700 Indiana communities. Then came the elevated railways in Chicago, three interurban rail lines that connected the city and suburbs, and the North American Light and Power Company, which linked Insull's properties with those in the St. Louis area controlled by other utility interests. Thus the Insull empire added up to nearly $3 billion worth of utility properties with about 600,000 stockholders and some 500,000 bondholders. The companies served more than four million customers and produced approximately one-eighth of all electricity and gas consumed in the United States. Insull's personal fortune rose from $5 million in 1926 to $150 million, on paper, in 1930. Two years later it would be zero.

Like the fall of the Roman Empire, the fall of the Insull empire was the culmination of many events, some caused by Insull himself, some outside of his control. Political missteps by Insull or brother Martin, rare but costly, contributed to the fall, as did financial miscues, committed with the best of intentions in the belief that the depression was, indeed, "a passing thing." Other factors resulted from Insull's family pride: he was intensely loyal, but Sam Jr. and particularly brother Martin didn't always measure up to the responsibilities the chief placed upon them.

According to McDonald, the longest-simmering cause of Insull's downfall was the mutual antipathy between the Edison chief and the New York banking establishment, at whose core stood his old nemesis, J. P. Morgan and Company. "No one has ever quite successfully described, or even identified, the inner circle of financial power in New York, 'the Club,'" writes Insull's biographer. "It could neither be seen nor touched, but its influence was everywhere; among its identifiable attributes were eastern seaboard aristocracy, the Ivy League (especially Harvard), Wall Street, Washington; the adhesives to its web were secret syndicate lists and blacklists, social connections, marriages. . .For outsiders, it had two simple rules, and it neither forgave nor forgot transgressors: (1) Do not upset the order of things, and (2) Look to New York for financial leadership. Insull violated both rules, and countless minor rules, regularly and on a huge scale."

For a long while, New York considered marketing utility bonds as small potatoes. Only one or two of the large banks bothered to do so with any regularity. The boom years of the 1920s, though, changed that as the nation's utilities borrowed large sums of money and expanded as never before to meet soaring demands. Suddenly, the utility bond business became extremely lucrative, and the New York bankers tripped over themselves to get in on the action. Into these turbulent waters, like a huge, silent shark, moved the House of Morgan, determined to impose order and have it all. This movement caused the creation of a single, Morgan-dominated super-holding company called The United Corporation, a sort of AT&T of the electric gas and utility business. Indeed, Morgan held exclusive control over AT&T's bond business as well. With a capitalization 20 times that of U.S. Steel, United was the biggest venture ever undertaken by Morgan. In short order and through a complex set of directorships, United either acquired or influenced most of the major utility holding company groups. The only major exception, none other than Sam Insull, represented an annual bond business of hundreds of millions of dollars.

As New York simultaneously coveted this prize and chafed at its inability to devour it, Insull gave the shark's tail a twist. Instead of being devoured, he did some devouring of his own, acquiring two holding company systems that operated in 14 Eastern states, in the very shadow of Wall Street itself. Although the systems fitted in nicely with Middle West Utilities' properties and with each other, they were "extremely and dangerously pyramided," according to McDonald, who likens Insull's move to Napolean's invasion of Russia.

Martin Insull had suggested the acquisition of these properties and Sam approved. The chief himself primarily dealt with operations in the Chicago area. He had a penchant for being at the center of things, loved the feeling of "hands-on" control, and disliked dealing with long-distance problems. To a large degree, he let Martin run Middle West Utilities and arrange the financings to acquire the additional properties in distant states. Martin, jealous of his brother and anxious to escape the giant shadow he cast across the Chicago scene, relished the responsibility. Sam, however, never knew about Martin's jealousy and would resent any criticism of his brother even more than an attack on himself. Consequently, no one within the Insull companies would dare criticize Martin Insull. That fact, coupled with Sam's intense fraternal loyalty, left Martin without any effective checks and balances and gave him a virtually free hand to get into trouble.

Emmett Dedmon, in *Fabulous Chicago*, tells us that Martin Insull was not popular with Chicagoans. "Most of them distrusted him because of his pronounced preference for the English way of doing things; it was frequently pointed out that Samuel Insull had become an American citizen in 1896 but Martin never took the step." Martin, who had a reputation as a ladies man, raised fine horses on his farm near Highland Park and was frequently photographed wearing English riding clothes. How Chicago's Irish must have loved him! Martin's British citizenship proved particularly ironic because in the late teens and early '20s Sam conducted campaigns to encourage all of his employes who were not U.S. citizens to become naturalized. By 1923 only 11 Edison employes were noncitizens, and nine of them were ineligible.

About the time Middle West was staging its Eastern invasion, the Insulls committed a political blunder. The historians disagree as to whether Sam or Martin made the greatest mistake. The setting was the 1926 Illinois political campaign. The Republican primary for United States Senator pitted Illinois Commerce Commission Chairman Frank L. Smith against Senator William McKinley, a downstate utility operator who had feuded with the Insulls for years. Dedmon maintains that Sam Insull was in Europe as the campaign warmed up, and that Martin and some subordinates cabled the chief for advice on how to help defeat McKinley. Dedmon says that Sam gave Martin and the others *carte blanche*. McDonald, on the other hand, mentions nothing of Sam's absence and indicates that the move came from him alone, based on his long-time hatred of McKinley.

Regardless, the Insulls contributed $125,000 to Smith's campaign, while McDonald says Sam kicked in another $33,735 for propaganda against the World Court, opposition to which provided Smith's principal campaign issue. These massive contributions might have gone unnoticed had not an uproar in Pennsylvania over even more lavish campaign funding occurred. In a bitter factional war between liberals and conservatives, the progressive Republican governor, Gifford Pinchot, lost a primary bid for the Senate, along with the man who had Pinchot's blessing to succeed him in the state house. No stranger to controversy or publicity, Pinchot cried foul and claimed that his rivals spent millions of dollars to defeat him and his running mate. Newspapers around the country reported the charges.

The accusations were good news for Pennyslvania Democrats but even better news for Democratic Senator James Reed of Missouri, a powerful, controversial national figure with his eye on the 1928 presidential nomination. With potential headlines aplenty to fuel his bid, Reed formed a special committee to investigate the charges of campaign funding abuse. Originally, he had planned to concentrate on Pennsylvania, but two developments caused him to widen his scope to Illinois. First, Pinchot had charged that his opponent's campaign fund had come from utilities, implying that utilities across the country had their hand in corrupting elections. Second, in a well-publicized speech, Senator Caraway of Arkansas, a close friend of McKinley's, claimed that Sam Insull had contributed $500,000 to Smith's campaign and hinted that a $20 million utility "deal" was involved.

Actually, Smith had never done any favors for Insull. In his five years as ICC chairman, he had allowed no rate increases to Insull companies and had either ordered or allowed five rate reductions totaling $42 million. Insull always maintained that his sole motivation in contributing a large amount to Smith was his hatred of McKinley.

In any event, Reed came galloping into Chicago on the proverbial white horse, determined to brand Insull as an outlaw. The Edison chief didn't disappoint him. According to McDonald, Insull so frankly admitted contributions to the Smith campaign "that newspapers all across the country clucked editorially that he was 'brazen,' 'insolent,' and 'arrogant.'" Insull did, however, decline to answer questions about his contributions to local political figures. With Chicago's municipal elections looming the following spring, Insull didn't want to do anything to harm the chances of his friends. He continued to dodge questions about local politics at subsequent sessions of the Reed Committee in Washington. Finally, Insull was cited for contempt of Congress, but he avoided prosecution by supplying the information in January 1928, with the local elections safely out of the way.

As for Smith, he went on to capture the election of November 1926, only to find the Senate doors barred, his victory nullified because of the excessive amount of money spent in his behalf. Ironically, McKinley himself spent more than half a million dollars in utility money in his battle to defeat Smith, while Sears, Roebuck chief Julius Rosenwald offered Smith $550,000 to get out of the race and support a third candidate. According to Dedmon, the nullification of Smith's victory "gave Illinois the besmirched distinction of having two senators turned down because their victories were bought; Senator William Lorimer had been expelled from the Senate on much the same grounds a little more than ten years earlier."

Reed's hearings notwithstanding, the 1928 Democratic presidential nomination went to Governor Alfred E. Smith of New York. However, the Reed committee hearings and subsequent report created tremors felt by the utility industry for years to come. When the full Senate received the report, Senator Norris of Nebraska thundered, "God only knows how many senatorial campaigns Mr. Insull has financed." Senator Walsh of Montana demanded a full-scale Senate investigation of the "power trust," a buzzword immediately seized upon by the press and other politicians. For example, an exchange of correspondence between Martin Insull and other utility executives, suggesting that Senator Glass of Virginia be given the industry's point of view on public power, became "Senator Glass Threatened by Power Trust" in the banner headline of the Hearst papers after the correspondence became public. The news story itself presented events much more accurately.

Sam Insull consistently ignored attacks by the press and particularly those of politicians. As a matter of fact, William Randolph Hearst was a personal friend, and while the Hearst papers railed against the "power trust," Hearst visited Insull to assure him that he meant nothing personal by the campaign. Insull understood. The situation recalls Mario Puzo's novel, *The Godfather*, in which the murder of errant mobsters was considered "business" and not "personal." With regard to politicians, Insull understood that posturing was just part of their trade, and the louder they barked, the less likely they were to bite.

Martin Insull had different ideas. He barked back, frequently with a vengeance. Occasionally, however, Martin

146

demonstrated perceptivity through wit. For instance, Senator Norris charged that electric utilities in the United States overcharged residential customers by some $750 million a year. Martin remarked that Norris must have thought that the utilities should pay their customers, because the *total* annual bill for residential electric service was $650 million. Usually, though, his attempts to parry the politicians' thrusts hit much more heavily. In February 1931, Martin went on nationwide radio in a broadcast sponsored by Halsey, Stuart & Co., the Insulls' principal bond house, to denounce attackers of the so-called power trust. He described the trust as a myth conjured up by politicians, including some governors, for their own purposes.

The one particular governor who made the most noise about the power trust, though, was not just any governor. He was the governor of the great state of New York, Franklin Delano Roosevelt: FDR himself. Roosevelt had made speeches against the utility holding companies and had even denounced a proposal by the utilities of his own state to cut rates in order to stimulate electricity use. Utility people, including the Insulls, could not determine Roosevelt's purposes. They ruled out pure politics because his attacks didn't follow the same line as those of the other politicians who milked the power trust issue. Roosevelt also leveled some of his attacks at companies outside New York, so they couldn't conclude that he only wished to curry favor with his constituents. Perhaps he wanted to improve his national image for his presidential run the following year. However, according to McDonald, utility men most often asserted that Roosevelt bore a grudge against holding companies, and indeed, no matter how the theme of his wrath varied, he invariably aimed at holding companies. His ire reportedly began in 1928, before he decided to run for governor. Roosevelt went to see Howard Hopson, leader of the multi-billion dollar Associated Gas and Electric Company, to ask for a top-level job. Hopson apparently laughed Roosevelt out of the room, and FDR became a man bent on revenge. Whatever the reason for FDR's attacks, Martin Insull rose to the industry's defense, repeatedly jabbing the governor in attacks that received wide coverage in the press, a circumstance Roosevelt would not forget two years later when he would be first a presidential candidate, then President-elect.

In his nationwide broadcast, there was no doubt that Martin Insull had FDR in mind when he lashed out at senators, governors and college professors who used "this sinister, threatening trinity of words—the power trust. I have never seen an attempt to describe a goblin, and. . .I don't believe that you can recall in any news dispatch, speech, or editorial, a real effort to explain what the power trust is. The power trust must therefore remain a myth until the politicians, professors, and editors who talk about it so glibly condescend to give more definite information about it."

Martin proceeded to lecture the 'professors and politicians' as to how half of the nation's 21 million residential electricity customers paid an average of five cents a day—the price of a package of chewing gum—for their service; the other half about 12 cents a day, the price of a pack of cigarettes. He also explained that electric utilities are regulated monopolies and, as such, cannot be a "trust."

"The success of the American plan of running the electric light and power industry is attested by the fact that the growth of the industry has been such that Americans, who number about one-seventeenth of the world's inhabitants, use about one-half of the world's output of electricity. Every foreign commission that has come here to find the reason for America's industrial supremacy has included in its report that an important explanation is 'cheap electric power, anywhere and everywhere,'" Martin concluded.

A hint, both to Sam Insull's long-range plans for his empire and to one of the major causes of its demise, came in 1929, at the start of one of his excursions to Europe. When his boat docked, a cable from his brother waited for him. Martin asked for approval to raise an additional $50 million for Middle West Utilities, repayable at a rate of $10 million a year for five years. Much of the proceeds would support, not utilities, but rather related business activities, such as the revival of the textile business in New England. Martin was "inebriated with the magic of paper and credit," according to McDonald, and Royal Munger, one of the savviest Chicago financial journalists of the era, blamed the eventual collapse of the Insulls on Martin "spending too much time on Pullman trains, expanding into all parts of the country, instead of studying the books." Be that as it may, Sam responded to his son, whom he had installed as vice chairman of Middle West. "If you and Uncle Martin want to fail, do what you want," he wrote. "I am only an old man." Martin and Sam Jr. ignored his advice and plunged ahead.

The old man had never spoken outright of a dream to turn over the empire to his only child, but the indications were there. McDonald maintains that Insull began dreaming of a dynasty as early as 1912, when Sam Jr. was 12. Insull Jr.'s decision to make a career of the utility business, without pressure from his father, and his subsequent capable performance undoubtedly crystalized the father's thinking, as did Junior's marriage in 1926 and the birth of a son. In fact, in late 1928, when the Insulls created a holding company called Insull Utility Investments (I.U.I.), their press release stated flatly that they had taken the move "to perpetuate the existing management of the Insull group of public utilities."

As the Opera House neared completion in 1929, Sam Insull approached his 70th birthday and his 50th anniversary in the electric business. What better occasion than opening night to cap his long, illustrious career, turn most of his operations over to his son, and play the part of elder statesman and patron of the arts? If at one time Insull had planned it, the crash changed it, so that the old man decided to stay on until conditions improved. They wouldn't, of course, in his lifetime, but how could he have known that as he settled back to listen to Rosa Raisa sing *Aida*?

The I.U.I. holding company, which the Insulls had established to perpetuate themselves, served to defend them as well. In the summer of 1928, Insull became increasingly concerned about the takeover of utility holding companies by the eastern banking establishment. Naturally, his concern centered on his old nemesis, the House of Morgan. Initially, Insull sat in the right church but the wrong pew. The forthcoming move came not from Morgan, but from Cleveland financier Cyrus Eaton, a smaller though no less dangerous predator. Eaton had built and managed small utilities for 20 years and by the mid-1920s had acquired two utility holding companies. Beginning in late 1927 and continuing into 1928, he quietly began to accumulate large blocs of stock in the Insull companies—Commonwealth Edison, Public Service, Peoples Gas, and Middle West. By mid-1928

Eaton's holdings grew to an amount several times larger than Insull's.

Gradually, Insull became aware of Eaton's huge holdings but puzzled over his motives. Although Eaton never did try to seize control of the Insull companies—he later testified under oath that he never had any intention of doing so—Insull came to believe that was his intention. In retrospect, the conventional wisdom stated that Eaton wasn't the type of person who wanted to run things; he just wanted the money. Insull, on the other hand, didn't care that much about money; he just wanted to run things. Eaton even testified that if he had sought control, he still would have wanted Insull to operate the companies, because he regarded him as the best utility operator in the world. The Edison chief, however, presumed that Eaton marched to the same drummer as he did and braced for a takeover attempt.

Thus, I.U.I. came to life as an investment trust, as the tip of a pyramid to box out interlopers. Insull had stepped into the dangerous and unfamiliar world of stock market operations. The Insulls exchanged all of their utility holdings for common and preferred stock of I.U.I. They also received an option to buy a large additional bloc of I.U.I. common. "It was good business to control the greatest possible assets with as little capital as possible. The best way to do so was to engage in pyramiding and to see to it that outside shareholders (like Eaton) had as few rights as possible," according to Leonard S. Hyman.

I.U.I. went on the market and began its dizzying ascent prior to the crash. On the first day of trading, January 17, 1929, I.U.I. common opened at $25 a share and closed at $30. By summer, it traded at $150 a share. Over the same period, Edison common stock rose from $202 to $450 and Middle West from $169 to $529. Unfortunately, the boom grossly inflated the prices I.U.I. had to pay for Insull stocks, making it increasingly difficult for the Insulls to maintain the upper hand. This led to creation of a second investment trust called Corporation Securities Company of Chicago (CORP), organized along the same lines as I.U.I. CORP and I.U.I. partially owned one another, and as additional insurance against Eaton or other would-be raiders, Insull control of CORP was assured through a voting trust. In the final months before the crash, I.U.I. and CORP sat atop the Insull pyramid.

"The Insull interests controlled 69% of the stock of Corporation Securities and 64% of the stock of Insull Utility Investments," Hyman explains. "Those two companies together owned 28% of the voting stock of Middle West Utilities. Middle West Utilities owned eight holding companies, five investment companies, two service companies, two securities companies, and 14 operating companies. It also owned 99% of the voting stock of National Electric Power. National, in turn, owned one holding company, one service company, one paper mill, and two operating companies. It also owned 93% of the voting stock of National Public Service. (The two Nationals were the holding company systems that operated in 14 Eastern states.) National Public Service owned three building companies, three miscellaneous firms, and four operating utilities. It also owned 100% of the voting stock of Seaboard Public Service. Seaboard Public Service owned the voting stock of five utility operating companies and one ice company. The utilities, in turn, owned 18 subsidiaries.

"With a capital investment of about $27 million, Insull controlled at least half a billion dollars of assets in 1930. What made that job so easy was that voting stock constituted a small portion of the capitalization of the constituent corporations within the empire. One could argue, in fact, that Insull controlled the lowest operating companies by means of an investment equivalent to less than 0.01% of the securities issued by those subsidiaries."

Demand for electricity continued to grow for more than a year and a half after the crash, particularly in rural areas, which didn't feel the industrial cutbacks as quickly as urban areas. Utilities, therefore, had to expand to keep up with the demand. In this context, the crash did have one apparent benefit: large quantities of money became available at low rates, and the Insull companies headed for the well, much to their later chagrin. Besides having to meet growing demand, Sam Insull seriously strove to meet his pledge to President Hoover that his companies would spend $200 million in capital investment in 1930. During that year, I.U.I. and CORP borrowed $60 million and $30 million, respectively, right on the heels of Martin Insull borrowing $50 million for Middle West Utilities.

Insull had such good credit that the financial community caught its breath in time to snap up virtually every issue. Halsey,

Stuart handled the sales at an estimated minimum profit to itself of $10 million. New York, as usual, was excluded from the action. Then, for good measure, Insull let loose with a blast against the concentration of financial power in New York when he spoke at the annual dinner of the Chicago Stock Exchange in May 1930. The newspapers gave the story widespread coverage, interpreting it as a call for the Midwest's financial liberation from Wall Street.

At this point Cyrus Eaton re-entered the poker game with plenty of chips—160,000 shares of stock in Edison, Peoples Gas and Public Service worth approximately $52 million. Eaton opened with an offer to consolidate all of his holdings with those of Insull. The Edison chief would remain the boss, no strings attached. Such a move would have greatly benefited both men, but Insull didn't believe in the Tooth Fairy, the Easter Bunny, or Santa Claus. What he did believe was Eaton's reputation as a corporate raider. So he turned down the offer without realizing what Eaton's real goals were—possibly the Clevelander wanted a chunk of Harold Stuart's bond business—because he saw himself as the target.

Eaton next offered to sell his holdings to Insull for $63 million, some $11 million above the market value. If Insull refused, Eaton hinted that he would sell the securities to a syndicate of New York bankers, a prospect that disturbed the Edison chief no end. Insull mulled conflicting advice from his inner circle on how to handle Eaton and agonized over a decision for a couple of months.

Enter Donald R. McLennan, a director of both Commonwealth Edison and Continental Illinois National Bank, which had become Insull's bank when it merged with Illinois Merchants Trust Company after the death of Insull's close friend and advisor, John Mitchell. McLennan held much of Insull's insurance business and now wanted Eaton's. It certainly wouldn't harm his sales efforts, he figured, if he did Eaton a favor—such as talk Insull into buying Eaton's holdings.

McLennan tried four times in mid-1930 to convince Insull to buy, assuring him that Continental, now the largest bank under one roof in the world, stood solidly behind him. Four times Insull said no. The fifth time Insull gave in, and in doing so, went back on a promise to consult with Stuart before making such a decision. Stuart, who had sailed for Europe, wanted to discuss the means of financing so large a purchase.

Both parties agreed on a price of $56 million, a compromise between Eaton's original asking price and the market value of the securities. McLennan, however, could not back up his word that Continental would finance the entire transaction. In fact, the deal could not come together within the Chicago banking community. With no time to go to London, they turned to New York, which loaned $20 million of a total debt of $48 million undertaken to help transfer Eaton's holdings to I.U.I. and CORP. The securities of the holding companies provided the collateral. Insull had disposed of Eaton, but at considerable cost. Worse, the hated New York bankers finally had a foot inside the door of the Insull empire. Yet $20 million comprised a mere fraction of the empire. If New York wanted to increase its influence, the price of the stocks of Insull companies would have to decrease. That would require the holding companies, I.U.I. and CORP, to put up more securities against their bank loans. The companies had a total combined portfolio of nearly $400 million. If the market fell far enough, the bankers would have as collateral all of the stock owned by I.U.I. and CORP, and that, in turn, would give them control of the Insull empire. At this time, the two companies together held only about 17 percent of Commonwealth Edison's stock. According to McDonald, the New York bankers began a ruthless, protracted campaign, marked by rumors and dirty tricks, to drive down the price of the Insull stocks.

Though formidable, the Wall Street crowd did not face an easy task. The Insull utilities not only survived the immediate aftermath of the stock market crash, they flourished. Their earnings for 1930 exceeded their record earnings of 1929 by 15 percent. Then, too, the New York crowd had to reckon with Fred Scheel, Insull's stock market expert. Scheel's job was to hold up the price of the Insull stocks at all costs. He would buy the stocks on the market, then sell them in small blocks to small investors, many of whom still believed Insull walked on water. Hardly a day passed when they didn't mail money directly to Insull, asking him to invest it for them. But Edison faced a losing battle. As Scheel himself admitted, "You can't go on buying your own stocks forever. Sooner or later you run out of money."

Nevertheless, he had one more ace up his sleeve—selling short. As McDonald explains, "If Peoples Gas was pegged at $300, Scheel could sell short 20,000 shares at $295, stop buying, let the stock slide to $270, and buy his 20,000 at that price to deliver at his short selling price, clearing $500,000. New York could drive the price of every Insull stock all the way to zero; en route, Scheel could make a billion dollars and break every bank in New York."

While Insull was away, Scheel got Insull Jr.'s permission to give the scheme a trial run. When the old man returned, he exploded. According to a Scheel-McDonald interview, Insull demanded to know what the devil was going on, and the stock market whiz laid it out in detail.

"And what will happen to the market in our securities?" Insull asked.

"Well," said Scheel, "if New York is crazy enough to keep on fighting, we'll end up with all the money and the market will slide to nothing."

"Scheel, we can't do that," said Insull. "That would be immoral. We've got a responsibility to our stockholders. We can't let them down."

"Mr. Insull," Scheel said, "they're going to be let down anyway. Unless we go short, we can't possibly win."

"Well," said Insull, "we've got to try."

Thus McDonald insists that Insull, in spite of allegations to the contrary, morally could not sacrifice his shareholders in order to save his own hide.

Like the boy with his finger in the dike, Insull and Scheel waited for relief. Only in this case, help never came to relieve the pressure on the dike. It finally burst in the summer of 1931, when England went off the gold standard. Insull happened to be in London at the time. The New York Stock Exchange panicked, the alarm fueled by rumors of Insull lying dead or dying in London. Stocks of the Insull companies embarked on a steep plunge, dropping by $150 million that first week alone. Julius Hecht, now vice president for operations of Public Service Company, reportedly lost $140,000 on the market in a single day. The stocks continued their descent until they passed the point where they would no longer cover the bank loans. Every last cent in the I.U.I. and CORP portfolios landed in the hands of the

New York bankers. Insull reacted frantically, borrowing to the hilt on his personal credit to shore up his companies, shifting money around from one company to another, reorganizing and slashing expenses wherever possible. But unlike the Peoples Gas rescue effort, these attempts proved feeble and finally impotent altogether when the Chicago banks, some deeply in hock to their New York colleagues, defaulted leadership to Wall Street.

Two quite different celebrations took place at Christmastime 1931. The New York bankers celebrated because, from now on, they completely controlled I.U.I. and CORP. In Chicago, perhaps oblivious to the intricate financial jockeying or perhaps just trying to forget for awhile, Commonwealth Edison employes took their families to the company's annual Christmas party. More than 10,000 parents and children filled Medinah Temple twice on December 19—afternoon and evening—for a two-hour performance by clowns, acrobats, jugglers as well as other circus acts and, of course, a visit from Santa Claus, played by William A. Durgin, newly named manager of Industrial Relations. Each youngster received candy and a toy from St. Nick.

The annual inaugural dinner for officers of the Edison Club and Electra, whose members had laughed at Insull's references to the stock market crash two years earlier, did not match the relatively joyous mood of the Christmas party. The gathering, about half as large as the one that had listened to Insull, learned from President Edward Doyle that their clubs were being 'temporarily inactivated' because of the depression. The Edison Club office closed, but several activities, including the horticultural club and bowling league, continued. Employes received notice that the full slate of activities would resume when "all the clouds that beset the industrial world will finally have passed away."

In what would be his final annual message in the *Edison Round Table*, Insull addressed himself to "Courage, Steadfastness and Advancement." "We look back over the happenings of the past year without bitterness," Insull wrote. "We go onward in our fulfillment of our obligations to the public, and to those whose trustees we are in the management of property committed to our care. We look to the future with abiding faith that our civilization is dedicated to progress...We have clung to our original determination to serve our public to its very best advantage in accommodation and cost; we have been earnest in our endeavor to give the men and women who own the company confidence in the soundness of their investment and to insure them a fair return thereon."

He concluded with a piece of advice "in the spirit of the season:" buy Edison stock. "The highest stimulant of hope is a stake in your company and your community, and those who reap the profits of good times are those who invest their goods, their faith and their efforts in the bargains of hard times."

Concurrently, Edison announced the sale of still more stock to additional customers under a customer ownership marketing plan devised by Fred Scheel. "Current stock market conditions have brought about bargain prices for even the highest grade investments," the *Edison Round Table* explained. "While these conditions have affected quotations, they have also demonstrated the soundness and stability of Edison Service as an industry, and Edison stock as an investment."

The New York bankers bided their time in the early months of 1932, in no hurry to deliver the death blow to Insull and his empire. They had no desire to seem like a monster crushing a corporate structure with half a million small shareholders. The American public was still looking for a scapegoat for the depression, and would have to wait until November to sweep Herbert Hoover out of office. New York certainly didn't want to take on that role, but it did find someone to cast as the villain before the election campaign revved up—Samuel L. Insull. It had to make Insull look like the pirate in the eyes of the public while casting itself in the part of the rescuer.

Such staging required more of an effort than New York had anticipated. Insull's personal popularity, both with his stockholders and the general public, still ran high. In February, faced with a large number of bitter and hostile shareholders, he turned the annual meetings of his companies from a potential disaster into a resounding victory, complete with enthusiastic applause and a vote of confidence. On the civic front, Insull Jr. headed up an emergency fund-raising drive that raised more than $10 million for Chicago's poor and unemployed. Insull Sr. capped this effort by peerlessly lobbying influential members of the General Assembly and obtaining passage of one of the country's first and best statewide welfare programs. Clearly, New York would have to root out some serious dirt to tarnish this man before the public.

In March, under the guise of attempting to rescue the Insull companies, the bankers installed a new auditor to supervise expenditures and maintain relations with creditors. The auditing firm primarily functioned, however, as watchdog, instructed to report any improper transactions it might discover. Discover it did—one "improper transaction" after another, usually in the form of loans between Insull companies in the frantic days immediately before the banks had gained control. Disclosures of these transactions found their way into the press, but they lacked appeal, and Insull's personal reputation for honesty remained intact. Then the auditor hit upon a much more damaging sequence of events.

Russell, Brewster and Company, the firm that handled much of Middle West Utilities' security operations and served as Martin Insull's personal broker, found itself in trouble with the New York Stock Exchange. Russell, Brewster had overextended themselves and faced possible suspension by the NYSE following an upcoming audit. The firm was so closely identified with the Insull empire that many thought it was an Insull company. According to McDonald, the Edison chief feared that suspension would set off a final wave of panic selling that would wipe out all Insull stockholders. In a futile effort to stave off such a calamity, Sam Insull signed a check for more than half a million dollars on a subsidiary of Commonwealth Edison as an unsecured loan to Russell, Brewster. In the meantime, Martin's account went under, creating the impression that Sam had tapped company funds to cover the margin of his brother's personal brokerage account. The loan eventually proved to be worthless anyway. Now the bankers had found their scandal: the Insulls' embezzlement. The revelations in the newspapers became more frequent and more spectacular.

Insull realized that I.U.I. and CORP would have to go into receivership to satisfy in part the bank creditors and holders of I.U.I. debentures. In April, he and Harold Stuart travelled to New York for a series of meetings to arrange the financing of a $10 million Middle West Utilities note coming due on June 1. (The note was an installment on Martin's controversial textile venture.) Unlike the other two companies, Middle West had remained in reasonably good shape, and Insull figured he would have no trouble lining up the financing. He figured wrong.

On April 8, a meeting took place in the office of Owen D. Young, chairman of both General Electric and the New York Federal Reserve Bank. Young served as mediator of a gathering that, in addition to Insull and Stuart, included Chicago and New York bankers and representatives of creditors. After the meeting had started, Morgan's people began to arrive, singly and in small groups. Surprised to see them because they presumably had nothing to do with the $10 million note, Insull was even more surprised when he and Stuart were asked to step outside and wait in an adjoining room. In a few moments, the Chicago bankers were asked to do likewise. An hour later, Young emerged from the meeting to tell Insull that no one would put up any money. The Edison chief couldn't believe his ears. He asked Young whether that meant a receivership for Middle West. Young replied that it did and expressed his regrets. Insull and Stuart silently shuffled out. Neither man uttered a word until they were aboard a train, halfway back to Chicago. Stuart, in an interview with Insull's biographer, said that he finally broke the silence by suggesting a bold counterattack:

"The first thing I'd do," he told the old man, "is hire the Chicago Stadium. And then I'd get Mullaney and all his publicity people together, and I'd announce in every newspaper and on every radio station around Chicago, I'd announce that I was holding a mass meeting of everybody who owns any kind of Insull securities. It would draw 50,000 people, at least. And I'd go before them and tell them exactly what these bankers are doing to you, and to them."

"What good would that do?" Insull asked.

"It might not work at all. But even if it didn't, you'd at least have your side of the story before the public, and it would stick, no matter how the bankers lied about it. But I think it would work, and if it did, one of two things would happen. What I believe is, they'd get the money for you, and we could save Middle West. And if they couldn't, the next morning they'd pull such a run on the Chicago banks that they'd break every God damned bank in Chicago, and maybe in New York, too." Stuart confided that for a moment Insull's eyes lit up, as if the old fire horse were going to answer the alarm one more time.

But then he slumped back in his seat and said, "Aw, hell. Somebody would just shoot me."

Insull's state of depression continued after he returned. Gordon Corey, relating a scene conveyed to him by his one-time boss, George R. Jones, head of Western United Gas & Electric, describes how Jones, Insull, Louis Ferguson, and other officials sat at a table in Insull's office mulling the effects of the bankers' action:

"Ferguson kept asking Mr. Insull for more information on the finances of the company. The old man finally yelled, 'Stop browbeating me!' Insull put his face in his hands, broke down and sobbed, then put his face on the table. We all sat there for a little while and we finally got up and left."

Now I.U.I., CORP and Middle West had vanished, and National Electric Power, Insull's eastern operation, would soon follow. More than 300,000 shareholders lost most or all of their savings. Insull remained in solid control of the three operating companies, Commonwealth Edison, Public Service and Peoples Gas. Although each stood in hardy financial shape, in spite of the depression, a new attack on Insull waited to descend. As with previous challenges, Insull did not perceive its nature or direction. This, the final thrust, would come from within. Martin wouldn't be around to help. His resignation as an Edison director, dated April 27, was accepted by the board on May 17.

The outside directors of the three companies had plotted a palace coup with bankers from Chicago and New York, ostensibly because the credit of the companies would vanish if Insull remained in charge after the receiverships and scandal. Four of the directors also served on the boards of Chicago banks. They decided to make their move during the first week of June, when virtually all of the electric utility executives would be attending a NELA convention in New Jersey. Harold Stuart would be on vacation. Except for Insull himself, Britton Budd would be the only important person left in Chicago. The bankers and outside directors elected Insull's old friend and fellow opera buff, Stanley Field, to deliver this message. On Saturday afternoon, June 4, 1932, Field visited Insull in his office and, speaking on behalf of the others, demanded his resignation. Insull balked at first, but Field insisted. Finally, the old man relented but informed Field that he "wouldn't do it through the back door on a Saturday afternoon," and signed a one-sentence letter of resignation from the Edison chairmanship, "to be accepted at the pleasure of the Board." He then instructed Field to call special meetings of all Insull boards the following Monday.

Just as a woman had urged him 40 years earlier to apply for the job, now another woman urged him to fight to keep it. Sam and Gladys sat up until six o'clock Sunday morning. Sam got her to sleep only by promising that he would try. But what would his strategy be? True, the outside directors were a minority at all three companies. Of the insiders, Sam Jr., of course, and Stuart would back him to the end. On the middle ground stood Gilchrist, Ferguson, Doyle and Budd, loyal employes all, but could he count on them? Would he be asking too much of them to make such a decision? He decided to take a straw vote of one. Remembering that Budd had remained and lived only a few blocks away from the Insull's Gold Coast apartment, the chief telephoned him at 6:15 a.m. and asked him to come over. Insull formed a simple plan. He would tell Budd what had happened and watch for his immediate reaction. If Budd showed signs of fighting, Insull would fight. If Budd reacted otherwise, well, that would decide it.

Roused from his sleep, Budd reached Insull's door 15 minutes later. Insull led him into his living room overlooking Lake Michigan and explained the situation. As Budd remembered it later, he listened carefully, then replied, "Well, Mr. Insull, I'm sorry. But you've built a monument they can't tear down."

That was all Insull needed to hear.

"Thank you, Budd," the chief replied. "I'm counting on you fellows to keep my memory green."

On Monday, June 6, Insull sat at the head of the long directors' table in his 17th floor office at the Edison Building. Sam Jr. sat at his side, trying to control his emotions. Throughout the day, various groups of directors assembled around the table as secretaries, carrying bulky minute books, hurried in and out of the room. From morning until late afternoon, Insull dictated and signed resignations from some 60 corporations, and each time the directors framed a suitable resolution, thanking him for his long years of meritorious service. At noon he presided over the regular meeting of the Edison Board's Executive Committee at which routine business was transacted. Not till 4 p.m. did a special meeting of the board convene to accept his resignation. The directors, with Insull still in the chair, first ratified the recommendations made by the executive committee. Then, in his last official act, he called on Field to act as temporary chairman while he placed his resignation on the table. It was adopted unanimously, with Sam Jr. abstaining.

Samuel Insull's formal letter of resignation.

Field called for nominations for a successor. Insull himself offered the name of the director already chosen by the insurgents, expressing his "great pleasure in nominating. . .a citizen of high repute." The new chairman, in turn, praised Insull for his 40 years of service, recognizing "the tragedy of this moment." The other outside directors present—Field, McLennan, John Mitchell Jr. and Sewell Avery—joined in the eulogy. Only faithful old Louis Ferguson, stating he had known nothing of the coup until "an hour or so ago," spoke for the insiders: "(W)e hope that this relief from your burdens may restore you to the same old strength and vigor you used to have. Mr. Insull, we

161

shall miss you." Insull urged the directors to close ranks behind the new chairman, predicted better times for the company, and bid them all goodby. Outside the door, swarms of newspapermen kept a death watch, noting that some of the directors had tears in their eyes as they left the room.

When Insull had signed the last of the resignations, an office boy blurted, "You will be back in six months, Mr. Insull. Your stockholders will demand it."

"No," Insull replied. "I will not come back. I am through."

Then he got up and left the room to face the newspapermen waiting outside. A hush came over them when Insull appeared in the doorway. His parting statement was one sentence:

"Well, gentlemen, here I am, after forty years a man without a job."

He started down the hall, then turned to an aide and said, "I guess you'd better call Mrs. Insull and tell her." He started off again, then said, "But she may be asleep. Never mind. I'll tell her myself." Then he left the Commonwealth Edison building for the last time.

Eight days later, accompanied by personal secretary and confidant Philip McEnroe, he took a train to Montreal. Corey quotes McEnroe as saying Insull had $25,000 cash in his pocket —everything he had left after signing away all of his other possessions, including his city house, Libertyville farm, and several Steinway concert grand pianos belonging to his wife.

"No other place but America could this happen to someone who started out from scratch," Insull told McEnroe.

From Montreal Insull traveled to Paris, where Gladys later joined him. The two settled into an apartment hotel, worked out arrangements to live on his modest pension from the operating companies, and passed a quiet summer. The quiet ceased with the end of summer as the 1932 election races heated up. Insull provided an easy target for campaigning politicians, particularly incumbent Republicans who feared getting swept out of office in a voter backlash against the depression and Herbert Hoover. One such Republican was John Swanson, the state's attorney of Cook County, a friend and admirer of Insull's. All summer his advisors had urged him to launch an investigation of Insull's collapse and all summer he had resisted. Finally, facing almost certain defeat in November, Swanson relented and consoled himself with a now familiar rationale: Sam would understand that it was politics and not personal.

On September 15, Swanson opened his investigation and dominated the front pages of the Chicago dailies for the next several weeks. Not to be outmaneuvered, the Democrats took up the crusade against Insull. Less than a week later, Franklin D. Roosevelt delivered a scathing attack on the deposed Edison chief, and Democratic candidates all the way down the ballot took up the chorus.

Roosevelt hammered away at Insull for a week as his campaign moved from the West Coast toward Chicago and an important meeting with Mayor Anton Cermak. The Democratic presidential contender apparently had planned to deliver a major blast at Insull in the latter's hometown. But on the eve of Roosevelt's arrival, wily John Swanson released a list of local VIPs whom Insull had permitted to buy I.U.I. stock for half price in 1929. The name of Mayor Cermak headed the list, so that Roosevelt quickly deleted any mention of Insull from his planned remarks.

Insull, in the meantime, closely followed these events from Paris. He perceived that he was being lynched *in absentia* and decided not to return to Chicago. In early October, while Sam Jr. joined his father in Paris, urging him to take a cut in his pensions at the request of the new management of the operating companies, the Cook County Grand Jury indicted Sam and Martin Insull on charges of embezzlement and larceny. Encouraged by his son to leave Paris, Sam set his sight on Greece because that country did not have an extradition treaty with the United States. Sam Jr. accompanied his father as far as Milan, then put him on a plane to Greece, where the elder Insull remained for the next year and a half. Determined to keep his father abroad until the political uproar had subsided, Sam Jr. returned home to fight the extradition proceedings. Gladys, meanwhile, rejoined her husband in Athens. Presently, the directors of the Chicago operating companies, fearing political retribution, cut off Insull's pensions altogether. Sam and Gladys subsisted mainly on support from Sam Jr. as well as gifts and loans from friends. Charles Munroe, who had become alienated from Insull 10 years earlier, cabled $5,000.

The federal government indicted Insull three times in 1933. Martin, who had fled to Canada, Sam Jr., and Harold Stuart were co-defendants on some of the charges. Martin, as a British citizen, could be expelled from Canada only after a long, technical proceeding. The only family member left in the country, Sam Jr. alone had to face the quiz of a hostile Congressional committee, undergo the systematic harassment of Internal Revenue Service agents, and worry about the threat of the President-elect to "get" the Insulls. In the midst of these travails, Sam Jr.'s wife died at age 36 after a brief illness, leaving him with a two-year-old son.

The battle to avoid extradition involved many complexities. Throughout, Insull insisted that he would voluntarily return once convinced he would receive a fair trial, not a political trial. Following many legal maneuvers and intense pressure by the Roosevelt Administration, the Greek government finally agreed to expel, but not extradite, Insull, who chartered a Greek vessel with money borrowed from friends. For a week he sailed the Mediterranean, contemplating his future. He had received an offer to become the minister of electricity in Romania. He could also seek asylum in the Middle East. Any decision soon became moot, however. When the ship put into Istanbul for provisions, Turkish authorities seized Insull at the request of the U.S. State Department, which had put out an all-points bulletin for the deposed utility chief. That Turkey, like Greece, had no extradition treaty with the United States didn't seem to matter. The authorities turned Insull over to the U.S. embassy and put him aboard a ship to the states.

As soon as he arrived in Chicago, Insull was booked at Cook County Jail. With bond set at $100,000, according to his lawyers, Sam Jr. had already arranged to have the money on hand. However, bond was set at $200,000 instead. In lieu of that amount, Insull ended up in a cell with a variety of criminals, including a murderer. When his lawyer came to visit and offer his apologies, he assured Insull that he would come up with the additional money, posthaste. Insull told the incredulous attorney, no—he planned to spend the night in jail. Since public opinion as much as juries would determine the outcome of the case, the spectacle of an ailing 74-year-old man being thrown into the slammer with common criminals would do much to soften the public's impression of him as a callous embezzler. His sense of public relations had remained as keen as ever. Insull was later transferred to the jail's hospital ward, and released on bond soon afterward.

The first federal trial began on Oct. 2, 1934, and ended on Nov. 24 of that year, not long after Insull's 75th birthday. It took the jury all of five minutes to find the defendants not guilty of all charges. The jurors thought better of returning so quickly, for someone might think they had been bribed, so they held a little coffee-and-cake party for one of their panel who was marking a birthday and rendered their verdict two hours later.

The *Chicago Times*, a staunch supporter of President Roosevelt's New Deal, summed up the verdict by proclaiming: "Insull and his fellow defendants—not guilty; the old order— guilty. That was the Insull defense, and the jury agreed with it." Gladys Insull offered her own postscript: "He has been a great sport through it all. It is character that counts and not money."

Two more trials remained. In March 1935, Sam and Martin were acquitted of the first state embezzlement charge. The state's attorney threw out the remaining counts. Three months later, Sam, his son, and Stuart faced trial on the remaining federal charges. The case ended in a directed verdict of acquittal. At last, Sam Insull was a free man. Legally free, yes, but not free of the past, of the controversy attached to his memory to this day.

After the trials, Gladys refused to live in Chicago or London, so the couple settled in Paris, returning to Chicago periodically to visit their son. Money was no problem, because the boards of the operating companies had Insull's pensions restored once the verdicts were rendered. Boredom was the problem. He followed American business and politics with sharp interest, but after decades at the top, could only watch and wonder, from a long distance at that. In 1936 he tried a come-back with a plan to form a radio network in the Midwest, but the venture fell through.

On the morning of July 16, 1938, Insull entered a Paris subway station and while waiting for a train suffered a fatal heart attack. His body remained unidentified for several hours.

His pockets contained neither a wallet nor identification, unusual for a man who habitually carried large amounts of cash. This circumstance led to speculation that he had been robbed after being stricken, but the Paris police report mentioned nothing of robbery:

> "An unidentified man was found in a state of collapse on the platform of the Tuileries subway station near the Place de la Concorde. He was neatly dressed in a gray suit with red stripes, wore a brown felt hat and had (about 85 cents) in his pocket. He was of medium size with white hair. He had no identification papers but the initials 'S.I.' were on his handkerchiefs and underclothing."

An unceremonious end indeed for a man whom the fates plucked from a London subway, afforded unequaled power in the American Midwest, and dropped back in a Paris subway nearly 60 years later. In the end, a man like all men. Ashes to ashes, dust to dust.

II

Nine

Picking
Up
The
Pieces

L ike any other place, Chicago has claimed its special breed of patriarch—Richard Daley and George Halas come readily to mind along with Sam Insull—men who dominate an office or an organization for so long and become so synonymous with it that some people subconsciously think the individual will never die or leave or, approaching the incredible, get fired. In Mayor Daley's final years, it was difficult, if not impossible, to visualize Chicago or the local Democratic Party without him. Shortly after Daley died in 1976 and Michael Bilandic became mayor, a reporter in Ireland reportedly called City Hall to arrange an interview with the Mayor. Hearing of the request, an old-time payroller was said to have remarked, "What's the matter with those people over there? Don't they know the Mayor is dead?"

Insull departed Commonwealth Edison and the other companies in 1932 as suddenly as if he had died but with infinitely less ceremony. If he had gone out feet first, an elaborate civic funeral would no doubt have graced his exit, and accolades would have poured in from around the planet. As it was, Insull immediately became a non-person to "official" Edison. Except for occasional discussions about his pension, Insull's name never reappeared on the record nor came up in *The Edison Round Table* between his "retirement" in 1932 and his death in 1938. This was the immediate legacy of a man who had been chief executive officer of 77 different companies, involved practically to the point of deciding how many paper clips each of them used.

The rank and file, however, present a different story. Long after the shock of Insull's sudden departure had worn off, countless employes remembered him fondly, particularly because of the innovative pension plan he had engineered. The day

Insull died, Thomas G. Ayers, future Edison chairman, was working on a farm line construction crew as part of a field training program for new college graduate employes. "At lunchtime," Ayers recalled, "a farmer came along and said to us, 'I see where that old bandit, Sam Insull, died.' Well, the men in the gang really took after him and said what a wonderful man Mr. Insull was. The farmer said he was a crook, but the men said no, it was the bankers who did him in. The crew really stood up for Insull, which was quite surprising to me."

When Stanley Field and the outside directors decided to dislodge Insull, they faced the obvious problem of finding a replacement. How do you replace an institution, even a tarnished one? They decided to turn to a community pillar, a good, gray individual known and respected by the business world and the public.

James Simpson, the merchant prince, succeeded Insull as chairman in 1932.

The man who would be king had not attended an Edison board or executive committee meeting since the Feb. 29 annual stockholders' meeting. Handsome, square-jawed James Simpson, who had never worked a day as a utility employe, was tiger hunting in India when the other outside directors notified him by telegram of his annointing as their standard-bearer. According

170

to a conversation between Corey and Budd, Simpson, upon his return, met with the others at his Winnetka home. Simpson told them that at 58 he had thought he would taper off from his work load—now he was being asked to tackle two jobs, the Edison chairmanship and his present position, chairman of the board of Marshall Field & Company. He further asserted that he would not chair an organization headed for bankruptcy, but finally agreed to assume the Edison post when the bankers on the board agreed to refinance an Edison loan that was coming due. If he had foreseen the final suspense connected with the transaction two months later, he might have had second thoughts.

Simpson relinquished the Field's chairmanship when he assumed the Edison gavel from Insull. He had served as an Edison director since 1927, succeeding John J. Mitchell, the Insull confidant who had died in an auto accident. Simpson had started as a teen-aged clerk at Field's and rose through the ranks, succeeding Insull's good friend, John G. Shedd, as president when Shedd retired in 1923. Simpson had become chairman in 1930. He expanded Field's sales and oversaw construction of the Marshall Field Annex building and the mammoth Merchandise Mart, completed in 1929 as the world's largest private office building. He also served on the Chicago Plan Commission and the Federal Reserve Bank of Chicago board, in addition to the usual blue-ribbon list of civic and charitable organizations.

Simpson's new position seemed ironic in at least two ways. First was the fact that Insull had harbored a longstanding distrust of Scots. Born in Glasgow in 1874, Simpson came to Chicago with his family in 1880. Second, the original Marshall Field, who had bankrolled young Sam Insull when he arrived in Chicago, had also marked Simpson for great things, selecting him for his personal staff less than a year after Simpson had joined the company and about the same time Field was loaning Insull a quarter of a million dollars.

Simpson tabbed fellow Marshall Field director Charles Y. Freeman, member of a prestigious Chicago law firm, as architect of the legal and financial reform of the Insull companies that would survive. But recovery would take time. For awhile, Edison and the other companies moved by inertia.

"It was just a shambles," according to George A. Travers, an Edison employe for nearly 50 years, who spent his early days

171

working for another architect of the recovery, Edison Secretary John W. Evers. "I remember Mr. Evers saying that you could have no idea of the state of disrepair these other companies had fallen into. If it weren't for the fact that we had this tremendously successful company (Edison) underneath us—almost without executive direction itself, but getting the power back on in case there was a failure, getting the wires back on in case of a storm, buying the coal, doing all the things they had to do—there would have been virtually no executive direction whatever. A lot of these things were happening in a leadership vacuum at the top. Mr. Insull had said that a lot of people had no idea how complicated the structure was because nobody told them how complicated it was. It wasn't until the lawyers and auditors and the federal people got into it that they realized how criss-crossed these interlocking directorates were and who had money in what." Under seven years of the Simpson administration, the number of Edison companies would drop from 77 to 12.

In early 1933 the Edison Board enlisted another outside business leader to help pick up the pieces. George A. Ranney, vice president of International Harvester Company since 1922, resigned that position to become vice chairman of Edison. Recognized as a financial expert, Ranney also became vice chairman of Peoples Gas and Public Service. At Edison he replaced Sam Insull Jr. who, in turn, became assistant to the chairman. Stanley Field and President Edward Doyle submitted their resignations as directors. In the continuing reorganization, the size of the Edison board fell from 14 to nine members.

The Simpson regime got off to a good start in at least one regard. As the bankers had promised Simpson, Edison was able to sell $18 million of 5.5 percent first mortgage bonds in quick order. The Chicago *Evening Post* commented: "Although it was generally conceded that the company's strength was not impaired by the personal troubles of the Insull family, yet it might have been possible that there may have been a question in the minds of some people. Several developments, however, served to dispel some of the doubts. The election of James Simpson as chairman to succeed Samuel Insull placed the management in the hands of a man whose business life has been one of continued success, and brought returned confidence. The willingness of bankers to advance the necessary funds to meet bond maturities, although there was doubt whether new bonds could be sold for some time, was another helpful factor. But what was probably the greatest influence was complete frankness in presenting all facts." Not reported by the newspaper, however, was Jones' recollection that the bankers balked at the last minute. Edison officers had to wait at Continental Bank until four o'clock in the morning, increasingly fearful that the financial people were reneging, before the bank officials finally agreed to refinance the loan.

At his first annual meeting of stockholders, Simpson had the unpleasant task of explaining that earnings per share had undergone their sharpest drop since the outset of the depression, from $10.57 in 1931 to $6.24 per share in 1932. The figure had stood at $12.99 in 1929. Simpson quite logically blamed the sharp decline on the depression and on the decrease in electricity use caused by a reduction in the number of residential customers and collapses of industrial and manufacturing plants. He vowed to turn the earnings trend around by instituting economies including pay cuts for officers and employes. Operating costs decreased in 1932 and held steady in '33 and '34. Maintenance charges in '32 were more than 40 percent lower than in '29.

At the same time, the new chairman aired his concern over two irritants that would nag Edison for several years—the comparatively high amount of taxes paid by the company and efforts to extract a further rate reduction. Simpson blamed much of Edison's financial woes on a 36.9 percent increase in state and local taxes from 1931 to 1932. In answer to Illinois Commerce Commission calls for a rate reduction to ease the effects of the depression, he pointed out that the cost of living in 1932 was 38 percent higher than in 1913, but the kilowatthour rate was 43 percent lower. Of course, monthly residential bills had risen, Simpson admitted; residential consumption had increased by 134 percent over the same period. Annual electricity use averaged 740 kwh, with an average cost per kwh of 4.43 cents and a total annual bill of $32.78. The company had 15,000 bondholders, 8,000 employes, and 888,000 customers of all classes, in addition to more than 63,000 stockholders, the majority of them customers.

The company presented these and other facts to the ICC in April of 1933 when Edison and 16 other utilities had to show why rates should not decrease. The company explained that it had reduced wages and dividends and effected "the most drastic operating economies," but these measures had not offset falling revenues. Edison followed up with additional testimony showing that its workforce had shrunk by 3,800 employes since 1929 and that quarterly stock dividends had dropped by nearly 40 percent. The company slashed the dividend still further—to one dollar a share payable Aug. 1, 1933—down 25 cents from the dividend in effect for the previous year and half of its amount before the depression. At this time, the ICC accepted Edison's compromise offer to reduce large commercial and industrial customers' rates, to assume a three percent federal tax on electricity sold to residential and small commercial and industrial customers, and to make additional voluntary reductions in those last two rates when increased revenues permitted. The initial moves reduced annual revenues by about $2 million of a total $70 million.

The ICC, however, was only temporarily satisfied. In October 1934 Edison again found itself in a rate justification proceeding. The first evidence introduced included a 50,000-word history of the company tracing its growth from a three-story brick building on Adams Street, "Old 139," to a giant metropolitan utility serving 750,000 residential customers as well as thousands of businesses and factories. The history also strongly emphasized the numerous rate reductions over the years, stressing that between 1908 and 1933, the average residential customer increased his or her use of electricity by more than 300 percent while the average kilowatthour cost fell by 55 percent. Of 37 cities in the United States with a population of more than 250,000, Chicago ranked eighth lowest in the typical monthly electricity charge for a four-room dwelling. The history cited lower taxes, the availability of hydropower, and close proximity to coal fields as reasons why other, smaller cities had lower rates.

After more than 200 hearings, covering over 20,000 pages of testimony, the ICC ordered a rate reduction in October 1936 totaling $3 million for the coming year—$2.5 million for residential customers and $500,000 for commercial and industrial users. The Commission also directed the company to pay the three percent Illinois utility tax, amounting to another $1.5 million a year, thus reducing Edison's revenues by a total of $4.5 million. The monthly bill for a typical four-room dwelling using 100 kwh a month would now be $3.65 instead of $3.72 and for a six-room dwelling using 200 kwh per month, $5.90 rather than $7.08. However, the ICC handed the company a tool with which to not only make up the shortfall but possibly increase revenues. The tool formed the third step of a declining block residential rate pegged at only two cents per kwh, rather than three cents, for all electricity over 100 kwh a month.

A model lighting display in the Adams Street Electric Shop window (1933).

The company didn't require an economics professor to explain what it needed to do—SELL. Sell toasters, dryers, and electric fryers. Sell refrigeration. Sell better lighting. Sell all manner of electrical household conveniences that would increase living comfort while saving time and money. After a fashion, the ICC enabled Edison to recreate the early days of Sam Insull, when he set rates so low that people couldn't afford **not** to use Edison service. And in addition to the more common household appliances, entirely new markets opened up.

In 1933 Edison conducted a thorough study of how residential customers utilized electricity. The results showed that

51 percent of the electricity used in Chicago homes operated appliances, while 49 percent provided lighting. Electric flatirons proved to be the most popular appliance, with fully 97 percent of the homes owning one. The next most prevalent item, the electric vacuum cleaner, ran in 88 percent of the residences.

With a foot in each camp—lighting and appliance—Edison in the 1930s advanced the sale of improved illumination and electric ranges. In the fall of 1933 the company, in cooperation with the Edison Electric Institute, launched the "Better Light—Better Sight" campaign, the outgrowth of an earlier suggestion by Edison President Edward Doyle. A stepped-up advertising campaign wielding newspapers, billboards, and direct mail proclaimed the importance and economy of proper lighting. Additionally, the company began a program to furnish residen-

An Edison appliance store in 1940. Floor lamps sold for $12.95, with 50¢ down.

tial customers—later, commercial and industrial customers as well—with up-to-date information on the proper methods of lighting in the home and workplace. As part of this campaign, engineers from the company's Lighting Sales Department con-

176

ducted an experiment at the Meissner Manufacturing Company, 2815 W. 19th St. They installed improved modern lighting in one section of the plant and compared production results with the other areas. A 16 percent increase in the production of radio coils and a reduction in the number of improperly wound coils in the test area resulted. The Meissner Company promptly installed the new lighting throughout the plant, while Edison offered the same demonstration to other commercial and industrial customers. Although the "Better Light—Better Sight" campaign didn't start until the final quarter of the year, Edison felt that the program had a lot to do with the Lighting Sales Department obtaining some 6,000 kw of load more than it did the previous year. The "Better Light—Better Sight" campaign continued for several years and expanded to the other Edison group companies: Public Service, Western United, and Illinois Northern Utilities.

Later in the '30s, capitalizing on the third step of the residential rate structure, two-cents-a-kilowatthour, Edison began a big push to sell electric ranges. Full-page newspaper ads, billboards, transit car displays, and company publications emphasized the advantages of electric cooking—cool, clean, fast and economical. Capacity crowds jammed the range display sections of the Edison Electric Shops. For the first time, the company had cooperated with appliance dealers to sell electric ranges, virtually unknown to Chicago homes at that time. Edison provided numerous sales promotion aids and displayed Hotpoint and Westinghouse ranges in the company's sales shops. Toward the end of 1937, 221 stores throughout Chicago sold electric ranges. Edison marketers made it clear that a customer who used more than 100 kwh a month and who used at least another 100 kwh for cooking would only have to pay two dollars a month for all electricity over the first 100 kwh. "Cooking Advisors" from Edison's Home Service Division offered to demonstrate the ranges immediately after installation. The advisors also conducted periodic cooking schools well attended by homemakers. *The Edison Round Table* ran a regular feature titled "Why I Like My Electric Range..." showing the photo of an Edison employe's wife alongside her range, explaining the benefits of electric cooking. "I used to think I could bake good cakes," said Mrs. H. H. Jesperson, whose husband worked in Lighting Sales, "but my results are considerably better now, and I never have to peek in the oven to be sure everything is all right."

The attractive two-story brick home at 6809 S. Euclid Ave. did not look markedly different from others in Chicago's then-affluent South Shore neighborhood. Beneath its tiled roof lay seven rooms, a finished attic and a basement recreation room. This, the home of the Roland G. Schmitt family, would never find a place alongside the John Doane home in Chicago history, but it was a pioneer just the same. Earlier in 1936, it became the first completely air conditioned home in Chicago.

Actually, "artificial weather," a name given to air conditioning in its early days, had taken its time in penetrating the home market. While some theatres, restaurants, and other establishments had already had air conditioning, 1932 marked the beginning of more widespread use. The first four floors and basement of the recently completed Field Building at 135 S. LaSalle St. included air conditioning. A pilot system cooled the office of Edison executive Edward W. Lloyd, vice president for Electric Light and Power Sales, to facilitate customer demonstrations and to provide cost and operating data. In July, some 40,000 persons attended a two-week air conditioning exposition at Edison's main Electric Shop. Twenty-six manufacturers exhibited their equipment, most of it for home use.

The Edison Service logo used in the early 1930s.

In 1933, the Woolworth store became the first State Street merchant to add air conditioning. During the first seven months of the year, 26 large air conditioning installations went into use, representing a total load of more than 1,100 kw. Then, in July alone, 36 more installations started up. The boom was on. Another 158 units came on during the first half of 1934, including a system at the big Sears, Roebuck store at 63rd and Halsted streets, the first local department store completely air conditioned. By the spring of 1936, installations passed the 1,000 mark, representing a load of some 40,000 kw. Four Edison employes— F. F. Sharp, Treasury-Collection; O. D. Westerberg, Architects Service Bureau; William J. Niemann, Engineering; and Edward A. Eul, Customers Accounts—followed the lead of the Schmitt family and built completely air conditioned homes, all on the Northwest Side of Chicago. Still, decades remained before home air conditioning would prevail.

The long decline in electricity sales bottomed out in 1933. The following year, overall sales increased 7.3 percent. Revenue climbed $3.3 million over '33, but net income went up only $113,000. The smaller decrease resulted mainly from increased taxes which claimed 15 cents of every revenue dollar. The same pattern held in 1935: sales continued to climb, revenues rose another $3 million, but net income increased only $3,000. In 1936, peak load hit a new record for the first time since 1929, up 4.4 percent over the year of the market crash. Sales mounted another 8.5 percent. By 1937, taxes ran $100,000 per business day. The annual tab for the year amounted to $24 million, more than twice as much as in 1933. As in other recent years, the growing tax burden highlighted Chairman Simpson's annual address to shareholders. "You, as stockholders," he declared, "can observe that your contribution to the cost of government and toward decreasing the cost of living was $20 million greater in 1937 than in 1933—$13 million of which was represented by tax increases and $7 million by rate reductions."

For all of Edison's complaints, preaching to the choir had about as much effect on taxes as talk on weather. On the bright side, revenues rose another $9 million, but dipped slightly the following year because of a recession. Nonetheless, Edison's good health allowed it to increase the annual common stock dividend from $1.25 to $1.60 per share in November 1938. Simpson further noted that the wages of Edison employes receiving $300 a month or less had increased by some 20 percent over 1932, while millions of other Americans were unemployed. "Thus, all parties in interest have participated in the improved conditions of the (Edison group of) companies: customers by reduced rates; general public by the increased taxes paid; stockholders by increased dividends and employes by increased wages," Simpson informed the annual meeting of April 1939.

Edison employes had received some good news in August 1933, thanks to a provision of the New Deal called the President's Re-Employment Agreement. To comply with the edict, the company put most employes on a five-day, 40-hour work week with no reduction in wages. The new arrangement meant Saturdays off for many employes who had previously worked a 48-hour week. A year later, the company restored one-third of the pay cut imposed in 1932. Vice Chairman Ranney tactfully reminded the employes that the reductions had amounted to much less than those imposed on workers in most other industries.

What would an Edison employe do with an extra day off? Why, go to the World's Fair, of course!

After five years of preparation, Chicago opened the doors to its second World's Fair on May 27, 1933. While the 1893 Fair had commemorated the 400th anniversary of Columbus' landing, albeit one year late, the 1933 Century of Progress marked the centennial of Chicago's incorporation as a town. And while the Columbian Exposition had occurred in Jackson Park, on the mid-South Side, the 1933 Fair took place closer to the central city, on the lakefront from 12th to 37th Streets.

"The three-mile by 600 foot strip on which the Exposition was to be built was an area of waste land, relieved only by clumps of weeds and an occasional straggly poplar, with a narrow strip of planting along Leif Eriksen Drive," writes Lenox R. Lohr, the Fair's general manager. "It was entirely man-made. The fill above the lake bottom averaged from 20 to 30 feet in depth and varied from a miscellaneous assortment of junk and rubbish to good sand. Part of the site had been filled in by dumping refuse, and under the surface were found rusty bed springs, tin cans, radiators of old automobiles, discarded phonographs, coffee pots, odds and ends of every description; even a submerged scow was encountered while piles were being driven for the Foods and Agricultural Building."

The other principal component of the fairgrounds, artificially made Northerly Island, became the site of the present Meigs Airport. Lack of funds ruined plans for the construction of additional islands.

From Day One, Edison participated in the planning, construction, financing and operation of A Century of Progress. Sam Insull was a charter member of the blue-ribbon Organization Committee formed in late 1927, for what blue-ribbon civic

The Electrical Building at the Century of Progress exposition (1933, 1934) shines as a beacon of hope amid the gloomy fog of the Great Depression.

committee at that time would have excluded him? Insull also became chairman of the General Finance Committee. Private funds entirely financed the Fair; from the outset, taxing bodies neither sought nor received a single nickel. Early in 1928, to test public opinion as well as get the project rolling, the Fair board started a five-dollar membership drive headed by Jack Peabody, the coal magnate. By the end of the year, according to Lohr, "118,773 citizens paid in five dollars each for a fair that was still several years distant. The funds received from this source were not used for financing any of the Exposition's operations, but were held intact until the opening of the fair was assured." By opening day, Insull had to follow the developments from the newspapers in his Greek exile.

181

Although Doyle modestly described Edison's relationship to the Fair as "nothing more than the addition of another large customer," the extra load of 18,000 kw represented the equivalent demand of a city the size of Evanston, Chicago's largest suburb at the time, and required construction of a special substation. By contrast, the limitations of the company's direct current system and the use of on-site power plants by exhibitors had made Edison a virtual bystander to the 1893 World's Fair.

Electric lighting stole the show at the Columbian Exposition and stimulated an unprecedented period of progress in the field of illumination. Nevertheless, the 1893 Fair had excelled most in architecture. At the city's second Fair, though, architecture played a minor role, with lighting outshining everything else. A Century of Progress literally became a Festival of Light. More than 3,000 kw of lighting equipment—incandescent lamps, searchlights, neon and mercury vapor tubes—illuminated the grounds. Their function, according to Lohr, was "to vitalize buildings and landscaping and blend the whole into a gorgeous color symphony, to present to awestruck and footsore crowds a satisfying glory of joyous light."

The man whom Fair management tapped to oversee the planning of the Exposition's electrical features, Edison Vice President Lloyd, assembled a first-rate team of Edison lighting engineers headed by Edwin D. Tillson. The company also offered the use of its laboratory for testing and demonstration of various lighting suggestions.

A ray from the star Arcturus, whose light had started toward earth 40 years earlier at the time of the Columbian Exposition, set A Century of Progress ablaze on opening night. Powerful telescopes in four observatories around the country captured the ray of this star 225 trillion miles distant, converted it into electrical energy by photo-electric cells, and amplified it to operate the switch that transformed the Exposition grounds into a wonderland of light. Fireworks augmented the display. One Edison supervisor remarked, "Now they can start another generator at Fisk Station."

One of the most popular attractions at the Fair was the Electrical Building on Northerly Island. Sponsored by the electric light and power industry, the Electrical Building housed an "Electricity at Work" exhibit covering some 8,000 square feet.

182

The exhibit included a model electric kitchen containing 15 electric appliances; a model home's laundry, basement, and living room; half a dozen model stores; a model beauty shop and even a model hospital operating room. Another feature at the Electrical Building, a 90-foot diorama, depicted the production, transmission, distribution, and use of electricity in towns, cities and farms. A miniature electric generating station anchored the extensive interconnected electrical system. Edison contributed a huge map showing the electrical system of Chicago and northern Illinois on an illuminated, translucent canvas dotted with cartoon figures of city buildings, generating stations, farms, farm animals, and other illustrations. A combination of searchlights, an electric fountain, and mercury vapor tubes that created the appearance of a waterfall adorned and illuminated the exterior of the Electrical Building. Above the artificial waterfall, 17 giant searchlights formed an aurora borealis, their rays intersecting above the fountain in a brilliant silver fan. The fountain itself was a tower of water and light, surmounted by a cone of polished metal 50 feet high that reflected the sparkling colors of the water.

Edison employes, able to purchase discount ticket books years in advance, enjoyed their own special memories of the Fair. The employe publication *Watt's Happening* marked the 50th anniversary of A Century of Progress by asking annuitants and employes to share their recollections.

James Williams, retired from Chicago Central Division, had no problem remembering opening day: it was his own wedding day.

"At about noon when we returned from church, the wedding party sat down to a breakfast at my sister's home and enjoyed seeing all the airplanes that flew over the Michigan Avenue parade fly over our party. We jokingly said they knew we were just married."

Guy Trulock, retired General Office executive, recalled that Oakley V. Morgan, longtime head of the Edison employes' Horticultural Club, "was loaned to the Fair on a full-time basis to help lay out their prize-winning gardens and was responsible for their design and development."

Others remembered the Sky Ride from the mainland to Northerly Island, the Avenue of Flags, the Hall of Science, the

Fort Dearborn replica, the arrival of Marshall Italo Balbo and his squadron of seaplanes from Rome, and, of course, Sally Rand and her fans. "(She) was friendly and gracious when I met her between acts backstage at 'The Streets of Paris,'" said retired General Office engineering employe Merle Goedjen, who worked as a guide at the Fair. "It never occurred to us that the handsome young man who pulled a rickshaw and knew many guides would someday become movie star Tyrone Power."

The 1933 Fair was such a fabulous success—higher attendance than any previous exposition, millions of dollars pumped into depression-rocked Chicago, satisfied exhibitors, enriched concessionaires—that officials decided in mid-October, with only about a month to run, to continue the celebration for another year. All previous American fairs had operated for only one year and had lost large amounts of money. But this was Chicago—Sandburg's "City of the Big Shoulders," which Burnham had urged to "make no little plans." So the following spring the Exposition offered a new look that would lure back old visitors as well as attract new ones, particularly from other parts of the country.

The lighting engineers in 1934 responded to the challenge with, "You ain't seen nothin' yet." They increased electric illumination by more than 50 percent over 1933. When asked what they considered the greatest improvement of the '34 edition over the previous year, many visitors mentioned the lighting effects first. On a sweltering day in July, electric industry employes enjoyed special guest privileges at the Fair—reduced ticket rates and half a day off in order to attend "Electric Day." There were bands, fireworks, ceremonies, and welcoming speeches by Mayor Kelly and Edison President Doyle.

When A Century of Progress closed for good on Halloween night, more than 39 million visitors had passed through the turnstiles, making it the largest American fair to date. The 1893 Columbian Exposition had drawn 21 million. The '33 Fair also wound up with a $170,000 surplus, subsequently distributed to various scientific institutions.

Lenox Lohr maintains that, "The Fair was a bright spot in a world of gloom. It did much to redeem the reputation of Chicago from its stigma of the prohibition era. Two hundred million dollars of fresh capital poured into Chicago, rescuing many of its institutions from bankruptcy. It showed the millions of visitors that Chicago is a grand city to bring their business to and settle down in with their families."

On closing night, Chicago showed quite a different face to the world. An odd thing occurred—Lohr calls it "a remarkable phenomenon in mass psychology"—something repeated across America in more contemporary times after championship sporting events. But in 1934, no one had heard of such a phenomenon. The huge crowd decided to cap the '33–34 Fair with a full-scale riot.

"Until 11:30 at night," Lohr remembers, "the enormous crowds packing the grounds behaved just as they had on all the days preceding. Then as if by magic, over three-and-one-half miles of Fair front, pandemonium broke loose. Everything that could be moved was taken; signs, some with letters six feet tall, light fixtures, benches, chairs, ornamental facades, curtains, anything which they could pick up, reach, or climb to. Of the 65 huge pennants along the Avenue of Flags, not a shred remained. Guards at the gates made those leaving deposit all bulky objects on the ground, and nearly an acre was covered." Everyone wanted a souvenir, it seemed. The private security force fought a valiant but losing battle, so that by dawn, nearly every one of them required hospital treatment.

"The most interesting part of the whole proceeding," Lohr continues, "was the fact that the destruction was done by well-meaning peaceful citizens who were simply caught in a mass hysteria and gave vent to a hitherto submerged destructive instinct." Happy Halloween!

Thus, with a bang instead of a whimper, did the two-year party end. All the while Edison put considerable manpower and material into the Fair, realizing added revenues. While employes enjoyed a pleasant diversion from duty and the depression, work continued on the primary corporate goal—moving Commonwealth Edison out of the Insull Era.

In January 1934, financial Vice President John H. Gulick, 66 and chronically ill, retired. One of the earliest of the top Insull men still around, he had started as a bookkeeper with a predecessor company in 1898. Having been with Insull so long, and in the financial limelight at that, Gulick was not the most popular man in Chicago after the fall of the empire. Less than two months later, he was dead.

Purcell L. Smith, who came to Edison from the City Company of New York, Inc. replaced Gulick. Smith had spent much of his early business life with Insull's North American Light and Power Company, which bound the old man's properties to utilities in the St. Louis area. North American would also produce Smith's successor in 1937—the brilliant, explosive Willis D. Gale, who would finally lead Edison out of the post-Insull shambles into the dawn of the nuclear age.

In the interim, other key changes took place. In November 1935, Simpson stepped aside as chairman of Peoples Gas, a post he had assumed the same day he took over the Edison reins. He explained that, in his judgment, more efficient management of the city's gas and electric utilities dictated they should be separate. And so they split. George Ranney took over the gas company leadership after resigning as Edison vice chairman, a position immediately abolished. Simpson resigned as a gas company director and Ranney as an Edison director. Lingering like a youthful ghost of the earlier era, Sam Insull Jr. was relieved of his gas company duties and assigned to Edison and Public Service responsibilities exclusively.

On New Year's Eve, 1935, two of Sam Insull's technical giants, the formidable Louis A. Ferguson and William L. Abbott, called it a career. Abbott, chief operating engineer since 1899, stepped down two months after becoming the first employe to mark 50 years with Edison and its predecessors. He had been the chief engineer of the old Harrison Street Station who 'was kept broke' buying cigars for his men each time the plant reached a new record load. He also became the only Edison employe ever to have a generating station named for him. The University of Illinois at Champaign-Urbana dedicated a campus power plant, located west of Memorial Stadium, to Abbott in recognition of his 18 years of service on its board of trustees and 14 years as president. Vice President Ferguson, who had worked under Fred Sargent on the construction of Harrison Street, had more than 47 years of service that included landmark achievements such as the refinement of the demand meter, invention of the Ferguson fuse, and the technology of stepping up and stepping down electrical current.

186

Alex D. Bailey, patron saint of the famed Chicago Edison clock, replaced Abbott, while Ferguson's duties fell to both Harry B. Gear and Augustus G. deClercq.

At the 1936 annual meeting, the ubiquitous Stanley Field began a second tour of duty as an Edison director. At the same forum, Simpson announced major strides in paring down the corporate structure:

- When he took command, Edison had holdings in 44 nonutility related companies; now it had 17;
- Edison had disposed of its interest in suburban real estate projects and scuttled plans to build a block-square office building in the Loop;
- The company had sold radio station WENR, as well as a truck manufacturing company;
- Edison had liquidated the apparatus for selling stock to customers and employes;
- Executives had dissolved two intermediate holding companies and placed controlling interest of Western United Gas and Electric and Illinois Northern Utilities directly under Commonwealth Subsidiary Corporation;
- The company had sold large blocks of stock in Peabody Coal Company and had become primarily a purchaser with a long-term contract.

"It is our present intention," Simpson declared, "to carry on with such (a streamlining) policy, to the end that the portfolio will be confined to investments properly related to a public utility, thus enabling the management to center its full attention upon the company's fundamental business of supplying electricity."

These moves preceded yet bigger things that year. In December the chairman announced the first step toward the merger of Public Service, Western United, and Illinois Northern under the leadership of Commonwealth Edison, although he denied any eventual merger. The complex plan called for Edison to acquire ownership of all of the securities of Western United and Northern Illinois, both stocks and bonds, and all of the stock of Public Service as well as a substantial portion of its funded debt. In other words Edison would own it all—except for an insubstantial amount of Public Service bonds. Commonwealth Subsidiary Corporation, a wholly-owned subsidiary of Edison, already owned approximately one-third of the common and preferred shares of Public Service and Illinois Northern and all of the common of both Western United and Northern Illinois.

In phase one of the new plan, Edison would acquire complete ownership of Public Service's voting block. The directors of both companies believed that since the operating relationship between city and suburbs had drawn so close, tighter corporate ties would, in Simpson's words, "insure the continuance of the benefits arising from the many operating arrangements. A more closely knitted utility operation in the great metropolitan district served would also be possible."

Edison directors recommended a four-for-one stock split and offered three shares of the new stock for each share of Public Service. Edison stockholders who voted at a special meeting in January 1937 gave near-unanimous approval to the bold plan. The number of Edison stockholders grew from about 57,000 at the end of 1936 to more than 100,000 only four years later. Substantial decreases in interest charges resulted, as did an increase to nearly 50 percent in the total consolidated capitalization represented by Edison stock, compared to only 26 percent at the announcement of the financial consolidation plans.

More upbeat signals marked the times. In late 1936, employes received a 2.5 percent pay increase plus a 2.5 percent bonus. Then the company kicked off the new year by announcing it would spend $20 million for construction over the next 12 months. The big ticket items included $4 million for enlargement of State Line Station, $2.6 million for expansion and modernization of Fisk Station, $2 million for completion of the Humboldt Park distribution station, and $1.1 million for underground transmission cables linking State Line and Calumet Stations. Separately, a new 66,000-volt transmission line—stretching for 15 miles and probably then the longest high-voltage underground line in the world—began transmitting between State Line and Fisk.

The company rode the crest of reasonably good times once again as it celebrated its 50th anniversary on April 29, 1937. Unlike the Silver Anniversary, when Sam Insull held court at Orchestra Hall, the half-century event appeared low-key. The headline story in *The Edison Round Table* notes that the birth of Chicago Edison had rated only a three-line item in a newspaper listing of new corporations. The papers of 1887 gave more coverage to a windstorm that had killed three persons and injured many more and to Sarah Bernhardt's opening in "Camille." So it was and so it is when the Mississippi stays within its banks and utilities quietly go about their business.

Edison did stage at least two events, both sales-related, to mark its first 50 years. A Golden Anniversary exposition, which included electric cooking schools, an exhibit of antique electric appliances, and a blind home economist who cooked a complete meal on an electric range, took place at the downtown Electric Shops. The exposition drew the largest crowds in the history of Edison's electric shows. The company also built and displayed a Golden Anniversary Electric Home, complete with white picket fence, that could have passed for the set of "Ozzie and Harriet" or "Leave It To Beaver" some years later. Located at 63rd and Sangamon Streets in Englewood, the home featured all the modern electric conveniences, including electric range and air conditioning. It drew more than 100,000 visitors during the first three months it was open. The home also featured an attic ventilation fan for summer cooling. Edison would again promote attic cooling fans in the mid-1970s as a way of limiting air conditioning demand and reducing peak load.

With questionable timing, The Edison Symphony—at age 15 the oldest radio program on the air—ceased broadcasting. Two "lower-brow" offerings, "Charlie on the Spot" and "Everywoman," replaced the symphony. "Charlie," a.k.a. WMAQ announcer Charles Lyon, did a 15-minute live broadcast three times a week from the Electric Shops. He invited questions on any subject from the audience and when he didn't know the answer, quite frequently so, he would pay the questioner a crisp dollar bill. "Everywoman," which aired three times a week on WBBM, featured Kay Brinker as Mrs. Julia Brown, who dished up "a day-to-day diary of the amusing events, trials and tribulations in the life of an average suburban family," according to the Round Table.

Only seven months into the company's second 50 years, the man who would do the most to set the agenda for the second half-century joined the company. Thirty-eight-year-old Willis Gale, lawyer, certified public accountant and one-time college economics instructor, came to Edison from North American

Light and Power, where he had served as financial vice president since 1932. He succeeded Purcell Smith as Edison's financial vice president. Smith resigned to become chairman of Middle West Corporation.

Colleagues at Edison and Public Service Company, where Gale also worked as financial vice president, soon found that behind the wire-rimmed glasses and the austere, business-like manner stood two Willis Gales. One was the brilliant intellect, the razor wit, the probing mind, the wordsmith. "A genius," recalled George Travers, veteran aide to several of Edison's top executives. "Absolutely beyond confusing. He could separate the wheat from the chaff very quickly. You could never snow the man, confuse him with a lot of gibberish or garbage. He could see through it. He was the best words craftsman I ever worked with. Everything was so tightly written, no errors, not a lot of art, but a great deal of facts packed into every paragraph." Travers is himself a writer who has drafted material for Edison executives from Gale himself to Jim O'Connor.

The other Willis Gale did not suffer fools gladly. He soon came to abhor the regular gatherings of the Quarter Century Club with their costumes and horseplay, deeming them a terrible waste of time, effort, and money. However, the extravaganzas continued for some time after Gale joined the company but were eventually discontinued, not because of his displeasure, but simply because they became too large and cumbersome, requiring division between noon hour and supper hour.

When Willis Gale's finely tuned sense of order and precision was upset—when anyone rubbed him the wrong way —his other side quickly became apparent. "It was a strange thing," Travers mused. "You would not think that a guy—a lawyer, an economist, a college teacher—would have that kind of a personality. But get on the wrong side of him and he became an absolute maelstrom of cursing and anger. He just had a very, very low boiling point, a short fuse, and he was extremely articulate in his vituperativeness. He was the world's champion swearer. His language sounded like the Nixon tapes without the 18 minutes deleted."

Gale practiced winning through intimidation long before that style became the subject of a popular book by that name.

"His wife, Gertrude, was probably the only person who was not intimidated," according to Travers, "and she was a delightful and charming person—very easy to be with."

High on the list of people who *were* intimidated sat an Edison Treasury executive who had done something particularly offensive to Gale; Travers never learned what it was but assumed it had to do with money. "They met in the hallway while I was nearby, and Gale called him every name in the book—in front of me, and I'm just an office boy. It was totally unacceptable behavior. Gale called him four-letter expletives from here to breakfast. The poor guy on the receiving end was very mild-mannered, a sweet sort of man, who was just like a lily in a windstorm. He just collapsed."

Travers recalled another incident in which an aide explained to Gale that he had been on vacation when some adverse event occurred. "Why don't you take two (expletive) vacations?" Gale raged. "Six months—back to back!"

Even female employes could not escape his wrath. According to Travers, he would swear in front of his secretary, Kathleen Keating, by no means a soft woman. "She managed to survive this guy," Travers added, "but he would curse her up one side and down the other for some minor infraction or other."

Gale would wait many years before advancing beyond vice president for finance, and longer still before getting a shot at the top. Even then he had to force his way up in what Travers described as the only management power play in the history of Commonwealth Edison, a classic between Young Turks and the Old Guard. While Gale was still settling into his new company as the 1930s ended, neither he nor anyone else knew that Edison would not make a change at the very top for a decade. Although no Sam Insulls reigned this time, a lot of people, Gale included, must have again felt that certain individuals would never retire, die, or get fired.

One month after Gale signed on, Charles Y. Freeman, already the top lawyer for the company in private practice, took on the newly created position of general counsel while retaining his association with his firm, Wilson & McIlvaine. Freeman, who had received his undergraduate degree from Princeton the year of Gale's birth, would also perform the duties of the Edison chairman in Simpson's absence or disability. The new general counsel's grandfather had been one of the original 39 Edison stock subscribers.

The dissimilarities between Gale and Freeman merit comparison. Gale was just under 40, 6'1", athletically built, a good golfer, and a fine table tennis player. Freeman was 60, looked it, stood even taller at 6'5"—and was thin almost to emaciation. Gale hailed from Wisconsin, Freeman from New York. Gale demonstrated little emotion other than anger and was limited to comments like, "That's a nice game." Travers tells of having written a major speech for Freeman toward the end of the older man's career. When finished delivering the address, Freeman received a standing ovation, then walked over to young Travers. "This big, tall, lanky elderly man actually put his arm around me and gave me a big hug and thanked me for all the work I had done on that speech. I tell you, I was about nine feet tall, getting that kind of accolade from a man who was not used to doing that sort of thing. Gale would never do anything like that."

According to Travers, the incident revealed C. Y. Freeman's real nature: his austere, humorless exterior was not the true measure of the man. "It wasn't until you got to know him that you realized he was quite a warm, genuinely friendly soul, but he was afraid of people in a way. He wasn't a social person; he was a very private person. He kept meticulous records of everything he did. Every letter he ever wrote was kept in book form—acknowledgements of gifts, a transmittal letter of a check. Nobody else I ever knew around the company did that sort of thing."

Three days before Christmas 1938, Chairman Simpson had occasion to issue a statement on the "resignation" of Sam Insull Jr. as assistant to the chairman to take a job with a LaSalle Street insurance broker. Simpson expressed his regrets, wished Insull success and hailed his service as "most satisfactory." The company then abolished the position of assistant to the chairman. Actually, Simpson had fired Insull but did it "so subtly that for years I thought I had quit," Insull remembered. According to Corey, Simpson's reason for sacking Insull was somewhat frivolous. "Insull Junior—everyone called him Junior—would always come up with the answers," Corey related. "Simpson finally called Gale aside and said, 'Look, no guy can always have the answer to everything,' and he fired him," four months after the death of Insull Senior. After 46 years, the personal association of the Insull family with Commonwealth Edison ended.

In Europe, another era also came to a close—the brief period of peace between the two World Wars. Nazi Germany had annexed Austria and part of Czechoslovakia without firing a shot, but the clouds of war continued to gather and would burst on Sept. 1, 1939, when Hitler would invade Poland. Late in 1938, representatives of the National Defense Power Committee in Washington met with Edison officials to urge the installation of additional capacity. The company agreed to the request and held a special shareholders meeting to discuss the plans. Simpson explained that Edison had a 30 percent reserve margin—more than enough to meet present demands—but warned that rapid load increases could wipe out that cushion in short order. He spoke of "a continuation of the recent upturn in business" but only hinted at the possibility of war. The chairman proposed to spend $25 million on construction over the next two years in addition to the $50 million the company had expected to spend. The biggest items planned included the addition of a fourth unit, rated at 105,000 kw, at Powerton Station, as well as the addition of 90,000 kw and the modernization of another 55,000 kw at Northwest Station. A month after the outbreak of war in Europe, the company published a newspaper ad assuring the public of an adequate supply of electricity. The addition of the new capacity, the ad made clear, would bring the reserve margin to 46 percent, adequate for "the demands of almost any tomorrow." The statement thus only hinted at the possibility of America's involvement in the war.

The specter of war notwithstanding, peaceful uses of electric service continued to develop. In late December 1938, work began on Chicago's subway system—a job that would last some five years. Edison service supplied electricity used to operate drills and hoists, to charge locomotive batteries, to light work sites, and to charge the compressors that maintained safe air pressure in the tunnels.

In the spring of 1939, Chicago got its first look at a gadget that would eventually revolutionize the nation's living habits—television. Edison played host to a traveling demonstration by the Philco Corporation. Company officials and members of the press could see "this new electrical marvel" in Edison's assembly hall. On three following days, members of the public could also view the demonstration, which featured singer Virginia Gibson performing on stage before the camera while also monitored for viewing by the "studio audience."

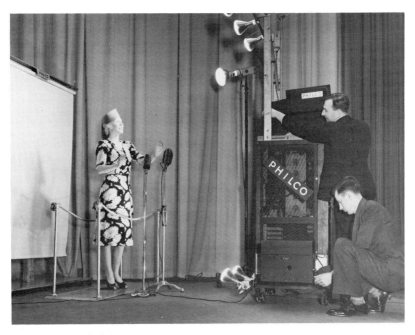

Singer Virginia Gibson and Philco Corp. technicians demonstrate television at the Edison Building in 1939.

A Chicago sports trivia question that would undoubtedly stump most fans is, "What famous event took place on Aug. 14, 1939?" Clue: It happened at Comiskey Park, home of the White Sox. Answer: The first major league, regular season, night baseball game played in Chicago. Under 768 floodlights, mounted atop eight steel towers, the Sox knocked off the St. Louis Browns, 5 to 2, and according to the Chicago newspapers, the fans enjoyed the lights as much as the outcome of the game. "Night baseball made a spectacular debut at Comiskey Park on August 14, and 30,000 fans, most of whom were previously unable to attend weekday games, voiced their approval," the *Chicago American* reported. "The big crowd was an enthusiastic one which seemed to endorse night baseball in a hearty way."—*Chicago Tribune.*

194

"There are more than 30,000 eyewitnesses scattered around today who will testify that major league night baseball is a fixture in Chicago."—*Chicago Herald and Examiner*. Well, a fixture on the city's South Side, at least. The North Side Cubs, under the ownership of the Wrigley family, remained the only major league team to play day-only ball because, the Wrigleys believed, *that* was the way Abner Doubleday had intended it to be played. After the Tribune Company bought the team in the 1980s, the Cubs made an about-face and sought to install lights in Wrigley Field, only to have to fight with tenacious neighbors and local politicians, who caused the passage of a state law prohibiting night baseball there.

At his first annual meeting as chairman in 1933, James Simpson had to break bad financial news to the shareholders. At his final annual meeting in 1939, he could reflect upon the improved condition of the Edison companies. A hallmark improvement, the program of financial consolidation and simplification had netted a substantial reduction in interest and preferred dividend requirements, an enhanced credit standing, and a simplification of capitalization by substitution of four new bond issues for 25 bond and preferred stock issues retired. The program involved the sale of more than $420 million in mortgage bonds and debentures, chiefly for the refunding or retirement of securities in Public Service Company, Western United, and Illinois Northern.

The corporate streamlining would remain Simpson's legacy; on Nov. 25, 1939, he died of a bronchial ailment at the age of 65, following an illness of several months. Charles Freeman, who had run the companies during Simpson's illness succeeded the former chairman at Edison. Freeman's position of general counsel was discontinued. Freeman was formally elected to the Board of Directors at the annual meeting in April, as was President Edward Doyle, following a hiatus.

The new chairman told the annual meeting that the company would add 147,000 kw of capacity at Fisk Station for operation in 1942, bringing to 360,000 the amount of kw in the company's three-year construction program. The increase at Fisk would come about by the replacement of four vertical turbo-generators, which had revolutionized the young electric power industry in 1903, with a single new unit supplied with steam from two pulverized coal-burning boilers, the largest on the Edison system at that time. When the job was finished, Fisk added to its rich history by simultaneously housing the four principal types of turbo-generators that had evolved over nearly 40 years: the vertical turbine, the horizontal turbine, the topping unit, and the high-pressure, high-temperature condensing unit.

Separately, a new 220,000-volt, 147-mile transmission line, linking Powerton and Crawford Stations, began service in September 1940. The longest and largest transmission line on the system, it represented an increase of more than 65 percent in voltage and approximately 50 percent in capacity, compared to the largest existing lines.

During the year preceding Pearl Harbor, talk of war and the company's ability to meet wartime demands began to displace the sale of appliances as a corporate focal point. More and more pictures of men and women in uniform appeared in *The Edison Round Table*. In November 1940 Vice President Harry Gear told a meeting of the Illinois Public Utilities Association that the state's electric utilities were "fully alive" to provide power for national defense, citing a projected 22 percent increase in statewide capacity over the next three years. "Of the (estimated) 1,111,000 kw of capacity which is coming into service in the United States this year, about 750,000 kw is in the war material areas," Gear reported.

When Freeman addressed the service annuitants at their luncheon in January 1941, he also spoke of Edison's role in national defense, one of many pep talks on the subject by Edison officers over the next several years. "The country is in the process of being turned into a huge arsenal," he noted. "Chicago-land with its great steel mills and workshops is an important unit in the country-wide plan for the production of equipment for defense."

In April, Freeman told the annual meeting that demand from defense contractors had gone from about zero the year before to 58,000 kw and counting at present. He announced a three-year construction program totalling $120 million, approximately one-third towards additional capacity. The chairman said Edison expected to add the additional facilities without further outside financing.

To Ralph E. Weaver, Merchandise Sales, went the distinction of being the first Edison employe drafted under the Selective Service Act of 1940. Weaver and four others were inducted in January 1941, among 3,670 Edison employes who had registered for the draft to that time. Another 63 company employes, members of the National Guard, Army Reserve, or Navy Reserve, were also called up. In March a delegation of Edison executives, headed by Vice President deClercq, joined a throng of friends and relatives at the Illinois Central Station to bid farewell to Company B, 108th Engineers, many of them Edison employes, as they left for training at Camp Forrest, Tennessee.

A welcoming ceremony took place in September—for the drum and bugle corps of Edison's American Legion post, which had won its third national Legion championship in competition in Milwaukee. The corps, in their white cavalry uniforms with wide-brimmed campaign hats, paraded through the Loop to the Edison Building, where they presented a musical salute to employes, passersby, and Edison officers and directors atop a second floor reviewing stand. A giant 75-pound victory cake, prepared by Edison lunchroom baker Joseph Sigmund, and other refreshments were served at an informal reception.

Even with all the emphasis on the military, Edison did not forget the consumer. Robert Plowe, manager of publicity and advertising, reminded everyone that during 1940, Edison's promotional advertising suggested one billion times that a greater use of kwh would make living easier in the home, contribute to the comfort of workers in stores and offices, add to business profits, or increase industrial efficiency. After stating unabashedly that Edison's advertising department existed to sell more kwh, Plowe proceeded to describe the difference between appliance and promotional advertising. "Our appliance advertising specifically calls attention to products which are for sale in our retail stores at definitely stated prices, and already have public acceptance, such as toasters, washers, vacuum cleaners, lamps. The purpose of our promotional advertising is to bring to the attention of users and prospective users new and improved ways for employing electric service in their homes, in business, and in industry." Plowe could have added one more product to his list: in late 1940 and early 1941, manufacturers began turning out large numbers of FM radios. Some 30 FM stations around the country, including several in Chicago, had received licenses, with 50 more awaiting approval.

About this time, Edison unveiled still another way of telling the story of electricity and its uses to the public. The company signed a contract with the Museum of Science and Industry to provide an electrical exhibit covering more than 5,300 feet of space, making it one of the largest displays in the museum. According to Freeman, the main theme of the Edison display would be the tremendous increases in the use of electricity during the previous 50 years, its contributions to progress in business, industry, and agriculture, its milestones, and its important role in everyday life. The Edison exhibit has remained a popular fixture at the museum over the years, with periodical updating, most recently in 1985.

After drawing a record attendance averaging some 1,000 visitors a day, Edison closed its model electric home at 3305 N. Marshfield following a two-year run. The home attracted more than 700,000 persons from all of the states as well as 15 foreign countries. Number 700,000, Gertrude Engel of Oakdale Avenue, received an electric range from Edison.

If there were ever any competition between guns and butter (or electric appliances), it ended when the bombs fell on Pearl Harbor. "(W)ith the country geared to the gigantic job of war armament, our obligation to serve has been greatly magnified," Freeman declared. The company turned up the power for national defense, pushed its construction program and sent its men and women off to the armed services. Photos and news items of employes in uniform displaced many of the traditional features about sports participants, vacationers, and the like on the pages of *The Round Table*. The publication began to look like *Stars and Stripes*. Employes who remained at home undertook a variety of war-related activities. They bought savings bonds under a new payroll deduction plan implemented by the company one week after the U.S. declared war. The Edison American Legion Post organized a civilian defense corps to assist in fire fighting, first aid and police patrol duty. A *Round Table* cover photo showed a platoon of the volunteers, dressed in civilian clothes and standing in ranks, looking deadly serious but a bit over the hill, their hands touching the brims of their fedoras in salute. Shortly afterward, the magazine cover went to the opposite extreme and featured a shot of General MacArthur. The company briefed executives on civilian defense in chemical warfare, conducting training sessions in the generating stations. The safety division ran an article on how to put out fires caused by incendiary bombs. Employes participated in scrap collection campaigns. Edison women sewed bandages and knitted sweaters for the Red Cross, sold "victory corsages," and mailed cartons of cigarettes to employes in the service.

World War II Red Cross volunteers.

"During the past year, the employe body has displayed a devotion to duty of which it can well be proud," declared Chairman Freeman in his 1941 year-end message. "The company's strong financial condition has been maintained and its plant and equipment have been expanded and strengthened to meet the emergency.

"In 1942, we face still harder work and greater sacrifice to do a good job even better . . . With an ever-deepening sense of responsibility let us renew our pledge to do our part for our country, our community, and our company."

Ten

Mr. And Ms.
Edison
Go To
War

In the February 1942 *Edison Round Table*, on the same page but in different stories, lie photos of a smiling, dark-haired man in early middle age, dressed in evening wear, and a smiling, gray-haired, older man, a kindly-looking, grandfatherly sort, dressed in a business suit. Nothing explains why the younger man is dressed in formal wear. Was he photographed at a wedding? An anniversary? A banquet? His attire has nothing to do with the story. He was a soldier, but so were hundreds of other Edison men and women whose pictures appeared in the company magazine during the war. They appeared in uniform. So it seems particularly odd that the obituary of Army Captain Alvin Hamilton, the first Edison employe killed in action during World War II, shows a man in a tuxedo. Undoubtedly, no other photo was available. Hamilton, a line installation engineer for the company, died at Corregidor on the second day of the new year. A 14-year Edison veteran, he had served as a reserve officer since graduation from Kansas State in 1927. Hamilton left a wife and daughter. He was 39.

The older man is Charles Freeman, shown making the first application for the purchase of a Defense Bond from a cashier in Customers Hall. The photos of Hamilton and Freeman symbolize Edison's double-edged devotion to the war effort—many of its people going off to fight, still more participating in an intensive support campaign on the homefront. One can understand their intensity. In the bleak, early days after Pearl Harbor, the possibility of the United States losing the war did not seem remote.

In March the company unveiled an Honor Roll in Customers Hall that already listed the names of more than 500 employes in the service. Along with the name of Alvin Hamilton, those of Donald Cooper, George Fairley, Daniel O'Malley,

Customers Hall in 1941. Note the
Edison clock on the third level.

and Raymond Stults had stars in front of them. All together, 98
Edison group employes would lose their lives. Not included in
this count, but mourned by general office employes just the
same, was the newsboy who had sold papers outside the Edison
Building. Freeman himself would lose a son, Lieutenant Donald
Freeman, killed in action in Germany.

In November Marie Weismantel, Merchandise Sales, and
Hester Henry, Treasury, joined the WAVES. Myrtle Ryker,
Industrial Relations, joined the WACS. They became the first
Edison women to enlist.

By the end of the conflict, a total of 4,266 men and
women of the Edison group of companies would serve in the
armed forces—a microcosm of the nation's total fighting machine. Each month, the pictures of some of these distant "Edison
boys and girls" would appear in the magazine, showing them in
jeeps, alongside aircraft, holding rifles, standing outside barracks,
even astride camels, and usually smiling. Their photos reminded
one of a line from a Lyndon Johnson speech about another war, a

202

later generation of young people, in which he said that he had seen their faces on a thousand streets in a hundred towns.

In the early days of the war, everyone considered an enemy air attack on the Chicago area a distinct possibility. Chicago conducted its first general blackout in August 1942, causing a brief drop in Edison's electrical output of more than 50 percent below normal. Although the blackout took place from only 10 to 10:30 p.m., many residents heeded the request of civil defense officials not to turn off all their lights abruptly at 10 or turn all of them back on when the all-clear was sounded. Edison and the civil defense people anxiously wished to avoid any damage to company equipment or service interruptions caused by too sudden a plunge in load. No serious trouble occurred as the load began to drop sharply at 9:00, about half an hour earlier than usual. By 9:54, when the warning sirens ceased, the load had receded to one million kw, about 300,000 lower than normal. At 10:05, just before the defense plants turned their lights back on after a token five-minute blackout, the load bottomed out at 590,000 kw, approximately 700,000 kw below normal. By 11:00 conditions had returned to normal.

Edison's civil defense expert, engineer H. E. Wulfing, witnessed the blackout from a plane flying 4,000 feet above the city. From there, Wulfing recorded, "Chicago just before the blackout presented a beautiful sight, aglow with light, the colored signs standing out like precious jewels in the city's lighting pattern. It was somewhat startling to see the signs begin to disappear, then the street lighting, until, as residences and industrial plants extinguished their illumination, darkness gradually settled over all. The darkness was not complete immediately because in residential areas occasional householders had forgotten to turn off porch or garage lights and these left pinholes of light in the blanket of darkness."

Chairman Freeman informed the annual meeting that there might be power curtailments having nothing to do with air raid drills. Without going into specifics, he cautioned that the company might require some restrictions during certain hours of the day by the following winter. Freeman raised the possibility of curtailments because of steadily increasing war production demands coupled with the company's inability to obtain new generating equipment, because the production facilities of the manufacturers served defense interests. He estimated the demand on Edison for war production as 300,000 kw and predicted that the figure would grow to more than 500,000 kw by the winter of 1943–44, or approximately 45 percent of Edison's total output. Less than four months earlier, war work had accounted for only about 15 percent of the output.

Freeman also mentioned that an average of 30 employes a week left for the military. As in the First World War, Edison hired large numbers of women to fill the vacancies, "releasing men to stand behind America's guns." Women took over as truck drivers, meter testers, storeroom keepers, and postage meter machine operators, to mention just a few changes. The company instituted a special training program to acquaint the newcomers with operations and corporate organization. Tom Ayers, at Public Service, visited suburban high schools in an effort to hire more female employes, telling the school administrators "what kinds of things we did at Public Service and how we would be positioned to look at their graduates. We were one of the first companies to do that in high schools." Ayers recalled that Public Service ran a bus for women employes between Evanston and the company's Northbrook headquarters.

The USO almost caused some minor difficulty for the Edison companies. "They were always looking for hostesses," Ayers remembered. "We had women working here who were working at the USO at night. Sometimes the supervisors thought they looked pretty sleepy in the morning, but everything worked out all right."

Public Service conducted a placement service of sorts for military-bound employes, according to Ayers. "We pretty well populated the CB (the Navy's Construction Battalion) with our linemen and cable splicers," he said. "They were looking for certain kinds of people, particularly craftsmen and engineers. We were able to send a lot of these employes to the commander who headed up CB recruitment here."

By the spring of 1942, 97 percent of Edison's employes had purchased war bonds. In fact, the company relentlessly urged employes to buy bonds or war stamps. In "An Open Letter to Johnny. . .who doesn't work here any more," a war bonds poster assured the fighting man that his job would still be there when he returned and that, "there's not one of us who doesn't think of you when payday comes and we save part of our pay in U.S. Stamps and Bonds. . .it helps you get the fighting equipment you need. (Signed) The Folks at Home."

The Folks at Home continued to respond enthusiastically throughout the war. During 1942 alone, employes who had subscribed through the payroll deduction plan received nearly 45,000 bonds. Edison launched an all-out campaign to encourage employes to commit at least 10 percent of their salaries to bonds. More than 38 percent subscribed for that figure or more, representing seven percent of the company's total payroll. In one bond drive alone, the seventh, employes rolled up a total of $1.14 million in bonds at issue price. The investment would provide the men "over there" with a B-29 bomber, six pursuit planes,

Shirley Benson of Statistical Research prepares to christen the "Chicago Edisonnaire" B-29 with a 1,000-watt light bulb. Looking on (from far right) are President Edward Doyle and Chairman Charles Freeman.

and nearly 300 blockbuster bombs. In an airport ceremony, the B-29 was christened the Chicago Edisonnaire by Shirley Benson of Statistical Research, who smashed a 1,000-watt bulb across its nose as Freeman, Doyle, and other dignitaries looked on. Employes had provided the name in a contest.

To hype the sale of bonds, the company held a series of patriotic rallies, or war shows, for employes and their guests in the Assembly Hall, featuring movies, talks, and appearances by war heroes as well as radio and movie stars. The nine shows attracted a total of 5,000 people. The stars also came out at Treasury Center, 9,000 square feet of space in Edison's downtown appliance store which the company had donated to the U.S. Treasury Department to promote the sale of bonds. The Center gave Chicagoans an opportunity to see the type of war materials their bonds bought. Instead of the electric ranges or washing machines of pre-war days, visitors could inspect an Army jeep, a torpedo, a 500-pound bomb, and a model of a tank. Mr. Yankee Doodle Dandy himself, James Cagney, helped open the Center, which would become a sort of mini-Hollywood Canteen. Jack Benny, Fred Astaire, Chico Marx, Lawrence Welk, Constance Bennett, and Hildegarde entertained along with other celebrities at Treasury Center during the course of the war. WGN Radio broadcast the programs, which drew thousands of spectators.

In addition to buying war bonds, Edison employes dug deep into their pockets for the Red Cross war fund. In 1942, Edison donated more than $100,000 to the cause—over $40,000 coming from individual employe donations and $60,000 from the company itself. Edison also maintained its own Red Cross unit.

Then there were the scrap drives—for rubber and metal, even keys and hosiery. In mid-1942 the company amassed more than 123,000 pounds of rubber, over 78,000 pounds turned in by company departments and the remainder brought from home by employes. The total amount, combined with the required addition of new crude rubber, could have equipped 267 flying fortresses. Later in the year, employes relinquished some two million pounds of metal. This time, the amount represented an average of 192 pounds per employe, enough total scrap metal for 38,000 machine guns. R. L. Staggs of the Construction Department was pictured brandishing a two-handed Samurai sword, promising to "send it back to Japan" where he had obtained it 37 years earlier. By the end of the year employes had turned in more than four-and-a-half million pounds of scrap metal. Nicholas Werer of Construction led them all with 211,000 pounds to his credit. By mid-1943 the total soared to 12 million pounds and Fred Blum, Lighting Sales, grabbed the individual lead with 750,000 pounds. The Edison Jaycees conducted a knife-collecting drive, and Edison women turned in their used hosiery. The women learned that silk hose could be used for the manufacture of gunpowder bags, nylons for parachutes, and glider tow ropes.

During the war Edison continued to provide the service of maintaining customers' appliances, a task increasingly complicated by the fact that Americans had grown accustomed to many conveniences now either difficult or impossible to obtain. War production consumed practically all materials used in the manufacture of appliances. That meant that the Joneses' electric iron or vacuum cleaner or radio would have to last for the duration. If it broke down, Edison had a team of service repairmen go to the home to fix it. Appliances not repairable in the field went to the company's repair shop, which also received appliances that customers turned in at local Edison branch stores. During a one-year span, the Service and Repair Department handled 162,000 calls, fixing nearly 70,000 appliances at the shop. Given the scarcity of replacement parts, the ingenuity of Edison's Mr. Fix-Its continually faced new challenges.

Toward the end of 1943, the company hit on another way to ease the shortage of appliances—a swap campaign in which Edison urged people to comb their attics or basements for broken or forgotten electrical appliances. Those who turned in old appliances at the stores of participating dealers received war stamps as compensation. The appliances were then repaired, if necessary, and resold to people unable to buy the necessary item elsewhere.

By the time Christmas 1942 rolled around, the possibility of power curtailments in the Chicago area had eased considerably. Freeman attributed the improved outlook to five factors: a slower than anticipated pace of war-related construction, less than expected power demands by war industries, a slowdown in non-war manufacturing due to a civilian manpower and materials shortage, the introduction of daylight saving time in winter, which reduced the evening peak load, and the requested curtailment of outdoor Christmas lighting.

Edison headed into 1943 with a 20 percent reserve capacity after two downward revisions of the estimated winter peak. Nevertheless, the company held to its estimate that war production would account for about 45 percent of the demand on the system. Four defense plants under construction—one with the equivalent demand of a city of 375,000—would soon increase load. Helping to meet the load would be the new 145,000-kilowatt unit at Fisk Station, announced at the 1940 annual meeting. Known as Unit 17, the new machine went into service in December 1943, more than a year behind schedule because of the war. Operating at a speed of 1,800 rpm and at a steam pressure of 1,300 pounds per square inch, the Fisk unit was strictly state-of-the-art. Two pulverized coal-fired boilers with a combined capacity of 100 tons of coal an hour drove it, giving it the capability of delivering 1.5 million pounds of steam in the same period. At the dedication ceremony, Freeman said, "We know the kilowatthours it generates will help hasten victory."

Edison had already begun to think ahead to that day, realizing that the end of the war would mean thousands of employes returning from the service, a renewed demand by consumers for appliances that had been unavailable, and the need to upgrade the company's production facilities with equipment and services diverted to the war effort. But final victory lay more than a year-and-a-half away from the day Fisk 17 began turning out power.

In the meantime, the company's civil defense activities continued as if an enemy invasion were likely. The Edison Rifle and Revolver Club held instruction classes at its range on the near South Side for any employe who wanted to learn the basics of shooting. Hundreds of generating station hands underwent training for defense against chemical warfare "in the event that military gases are released in the Chicago area." The company issued a safety message instructing employes on how to fight a fire in the home caused by an incendiary bomb. The Civil Air Patrol dropped 216 paper "bombs" on four generating stations, signaling the start of a mock air raid that brought nearly 700 members of the company's defense corps into action. Fire trucks extinguished the imaginary blazes, the "victims" received first aid, ambulances rushed them to emergency field hospitals, and crews wearing gas masks and protective clothing neutralized "gases" released from the "bombs."

Historians have cited a number of critical turning points in World War II—victory in North Africa, the Battle of Stalingrad, the Normandy invasion, and, in the Pacific, the Battle of Leyte Gulf. All severely undermined the Axis and hastened the end of the conflict. However, the true turning point, when everyone at Commonwealth Edison could taste victory, occurred on July 11, 1944. On that day the Edison defense corps was disbanded following two-and-a-half years of volunteer service, its members never having been called upon to deal with a real incident. At a testimonial dinner, Freeman attributed that good fortune to "our magnificent Army and Navy and those of our Allies (who) have been able to turn back our foes." Freeman and other company executives, along with representatives of the Army and Chicago Police and Fire Departments, nonetheless lavishly praised the corps members for their patriotism and continued readiness. Each man received an award certificate.

At the other forums, Freeman and Assistant Vice President Alex Bailey promised an aggressive load-building campaign among residential, commercial and rural customers to take up the expected slack in industrial demand when war production declined and ultimately ended. Bailey predicted that the relatively new uses for electricity would become available on the job, citing an anticipated post-war marketing blitz by the makers of freezers, electric ranges, water heaters, and air conditioning units. Still, because of an industrial downturn, he foresaw a dip in total system load for the Edison group, with the companies not returning to their record levels of 1943–44 until approximately three years after the shooting had stopped.

Total kwh sales for 1943 increased 12.8 percent over 1942, and sales to large industrial customers led the way with a 22.1 percent jump. The following year broke another record, showing a climb of 5.7 percent in overall sales and 9.8 percent in sales to the big customers. War production demand peaked at 40 percent of the total.

Bailey reported in April 1944 that more than 20 percent of Edison's work force served in the military, a considerably higher average than that of the electric utility industry as a whole. If World War I were an accurate barometer, he observed, about two-thirds of the employes would return to their former jobs. The actual return rate settled at more than 90 percent. What about the women who had filled many of those spots? A lot of them had married servicemen, according to Bailey, and would "be anxious to resume their housekeeping activities when the war is over. As in the case of World War I, the returning soldier and sailor will find a job waiting for him with his old gang ready and happy to welcome him back." The company placed returning veterans on the payroll at the rate of pay, plus increases, that they would have received if they had stayed. Edison also gave them credit for their military time toward their pensions.

II

While Chicago and the rest of the country celebrated V-J Day, Edison had already begun to gear up for the post-war consumer boom. Cardboard replicas of electrical merchandise had replaced all wartime displays in the windows of the downtown appliance store 10 days earlier. Soon afterward, customers took advantage of their first opportunity since the war to inspect new electrical products. An estimated 20,000 spectators a day streamed into the downtown store for the Postwar Electric Appliance and Radio Show, which displayed the products of some 100 electrical manufacturers. Television attracted quite a bit of attention, as it had in its debut six years previously.

The company also set its sights on the national market by creating the Territorial Information Department to attract new business to the service territory. "In order to do this," Freeman explained, "we must keep informing the country of what a really great community we have and what an opportunity it offers for expansion." Edison stressed many themes in newspaper ads in major cities throughout the country, especially Chicago's position as the railroad center of the nation, as a great central market with $8 billion in annual trade, as an outstanding financial center with an adequate labor pool, and, naturally, plenty of electric energy, totalling 2.5 million kw. And more kilowatts were on the way. As the war ended, construction approached full speed on the new, 107,000-kilowatt Unit 7 at Calumet Station which would go into service in 1947 at a cost of some $13 million.

Edison thought small as well as big. With the removal of wartime restrictions on gasoline, the company resumed the delivery of light bulbs to customers. The company had discontinued the service in early 1942 to save on tires as well as gas.

The "Jane Foster" service, begun in early 1945 to help housewives save money and rationing stamps and cope with various wartime problems, continued after the conflict. In real life, Jane was Madeline Mehlig, Edison's Director of Home Economics, "mother and homemaker (who) knows and understands housewives' problems." The company's newspaper ads carried Jane's recipes as a regular feature and invited the public to consult her about any homemaking tasks. Toward the end of the war, Edison also sponsored a cooking show on television starring members of the Advertising and Home Services departments. Jane Foster got her own TV cooking show in 1947.

Since its creation in 1930, the Home Service department had expanded its public relations role. Starting with a staff of 16 women, the department was actually a consolidation of existing activities, such as home demonstration of major appliances, home lighting service and appliance surveys, exhibits at fairs and expositions, operation of model homes, and demonstrations in Electric Shops. The women traveled throughout the service territory, calling on appliance dealers, demonstrating new appliances to social and civic groups, offering cooking classes. Their activities created a lot of goodwill for the company and helped move many a new appliance from the dealer's floor. When Home Service was phased out in the late 1950s, some of the women representatives went to Marketing school and entered management ranks through the Marketing areas.

One of the most popular exhibits, right to the present day, at Chicago's Museum of Science and Industry has been Yesterday's Main Street, opened to the public during the war with an assist from Commonwealth Edison. The company provided for the installation of a small power plant, an early 1900s model used in small towns. Electricity for the entire exhibit came from a 17.5-kilowatt generator directly connected to a steam power unit. Five other longtime companies joined with Edison and the museum to create the atmosphere of 1910. In addition to the vintage power plant, the exhibit included storefronts of the period, old-time cars parked in the street and illumination produced by carbon filament lamps.

211

A man whose tenure with the company extended for nearly a quarter of a century before the time re-created by Yesterday's Main Street, John F. Gilchrist, retired at the close of 1942 after 55 years of service. He joined Chicago Edison only a few months after it was organized in 1887 and went on to write the script for the commercial advancement of electric power. A vice president since 1914, Gilchrist became chairman of the Chicago and Illinois Midland Railway upon his retirement. He died in August 1945 at the age of 77.

Gilchrist was succeeded as vice president by one of those solid, hard-working types who seem to be able to do anything, without fanfare, and who would play a major part in reorganizing Commonwealth Edison for the second half of the twentieth century. John W. Evers Jr. had already been with the company for 29 years, the last 18 of them as secretary, deftly performing mundane but critical tasks away from the limelight. He rewrote the Edison pension plan from scratch in the late 1930s; when the Social Security System appeared, he handled Edison's participation. He also helped administer the Mutual Benefit Association and the Savings and Loan Association, and served on the boards of several subsidiary companies.

Six years after he joined the company in 1913, Evers became Sam Insull's secretary. Better stepping stones might have existed in those days, but none come readily to mind. Five more years and he would have the same title with a capital "S." Perhaps the fact that Insull had started life as a secretary— first at the London newspaper and later to Thomas Edison— made him further the advancement of his own secretaries. A previous Insull secretary, Edward J. Doyle, had become company secretary and treasurer and ultimately president. To carry the relationship a step further, Evers once served as Doyle's secretary.

Like any good secretary, Evers excelled at detail and would perform an infinite variety of tasks, even after he became vice president. He wrote speeches for Freeman, and served as a sort of super-PR man and ambassador-at-large.

"Evers always ran the interviews and discussions with the New York press," according to Travers, who once worked as his secretary, too. "That really wasn't the function of a corporate secretary, but he would always go to New York as the advance

212

man and set things up. Then he would brief Freeman on all the questions that would be asked and suggest the answers."

John Evers had still another feature in his favor—a close personal friendship with Freeman, Doyle, and Gale. In a sense, Evers was to the scholarly Freeman what Insull had been to Tom Edison—the man who made the organization work.

"Freeman did not have a super executive secretary, he had a lady named May Boyle," Travers continued. "She didn't come up through the company; she didn't understand the company; and she didn't care about the company. All she cared about was Mr. Freeman. Anything that had to do with the running of the company, she couldn't care less about. So John Evers stepped in to fill the gap, since Mr. Freeman didn't have any staff assistant, as such."

When Evers moved up to vice president, he received the responsibility for Purchasing and Stores, Transportation, Fuel, Revenue Protection, and the Central and Northern Service buildings. He continued as secretary but resigned as assistant treasurer.

Much closer in age to Gale than to Freeman or Doyle, Evers enjoyed a particularly close relationship with his fiery contemporary. Evers and Gale belonged to a small circle of friends in the Highland Park area which included Edison Comptroller Otto Gressens. They met every Saturday to play golf in the morning and table tennis in the afternoon, capping off the day by going out with their wives for cocktails and dinner. Travers, invited to play table tennis at Gale's home on several occasions in spite of his youth, saw Gale as a totally different person in that setting and figured that intimidation might be simply his leadership style.

Curiously, though Evers had never completed high school, he had befriended a man who held a Ph.D. and an L.L.B. Beyond golfing and table tennis, Travers believed that Evers and Gale got on so well because they were "intuitively street-smart fellas. They were absolute peers." And together they would move even higher in the company, Evers at the expense of Gressens, with whom he and Gale would have a falling out of the first magnitude in the early 1950s.

Wearing his secretarial hat, Evers signed the first collective bargaining agreements between Edison and a national labor union, the International Brotherhood of Electrical Workers. The first contract, signed in April 1944, covered only employes at Powerton Station. Powerton's clerical workers, not included in the first agreement, joined a union later. In November, Edison concluded a contract covering the remainder of Edison's production and maintenance employes.

The pacts with IBEW replaced the company's Employe Representation Plan, a system established in the early Insull days under which co-workers elected employes in various departments to serve on a kind of cooperative council that met regularly and conveyed its ideas and concerns to management. In 1943, an employe in Edison's substation department filed an unfair labor practice charge with the National Labor Relations Board (NLRB), attacking the company's use of the Employe Representation Plan. The NLRB responded by ordering the discontinuance of the Plan. The move opened the way for an organizational drive by IBEW, affiliated with the American Federation of Labor (AFL), and the independent Utility Workers Union (UWU). Following hearings, the NLRB set up two collective bargaining units within Edison: the "inside plant" which included employes of the Generating and Substation departments and the "outside plant" which covered the Construction, Service and Repair, Meter, Transportation, Purchasing and Stores, Stone Conduit, Revenue Protection, Testing, Merchandise Sales, Electricity Sales, Service Buildings, and Revenue Accounts departments. The NLRB ordered an election held under its jurisdiction in each of the two units. Employes had to choose between IBEW or UWU—or no union at all.

IBEW triumphed among the inside employes by a margin of almost two-to-one. UWU won narrowly among the outside group, but the NLRB threw out the results after a challenge by IBEW. The NLRB then certified IBEW as the collective bargaining agent for both groups. Later, IBEW organized Public Service, Illinois Northern, and Western United. No other union competed with IBEW; employes only voted yes or no on the electrical workers union. Meanwhile, United Mine Workers Local 50 organized State Line Station.

Negotiation of the Edison contract lasted from July through November 1944. The pact provided wage increases, time-and-a-half for overtime, double-time for extra time on a holiday, premium pay for early morning or late night work,

214

overtime for returning to work on short notice, and other wage benefits. Ayers, who worked hard on the contract, recalled that though the negotiations were "not bloody," things got stickier soon after the handshakes.

Thomas G. Ayers attends his last annual meeting as Chairman in 1979.

"In the early days, there were lots of grievances which caused a lot of difficulty," Ayers noted. "Edison had a job evaluation plan which I later succeeded in getting rid of when I came over to Edison (from Public Service, after the two merged). This plan gave points to people for various jobs. Once the union got in, they questioned all the points that were low, and we had a real donnybrook on wages that took several years to calm down. One of the ways we got it calmed down was to follow a practice throughout the system that had been inaugurated by Public Service—create a first class job in the various trades, like the first class turbine operator, first class boiler operator, first class machinist, . . . and so on, all at the same rate. This got us away from the argument that this job or that job should pay 10 cents more. We were just arguing all the time on that kind of thing.

"I think unions are a very useful way of being able to deal with employes as a group. It isn't what you pay a bricklayer; it's how many bricks he lays an hour that counts, and I think that we get good production out of our people. You occasionally have someone who doesn't do well and you can't understand how he ever got into the business. But I once told Mr. Gale, 'Don't be so tough on me about the people we hire. Even the Good Lord couldn't choose 12 good ones.'"

215

An employment interviewer and manager of industrial relations for Public Service, active in labor-management relations most of his career, future board chairman Ayers formed some strong, perhaps unorthodox opinions on issues debated within and outside the company over the years:

On a frequent claim that unions exercise too much authority over corporate managers: "It probably has some validity, but I think mostly it speaks of a weak supervisor who is hiding behind that excuse rather than doing his job and getting people to follow him. I think that the boss would just like to say, 'This is the way we are going to do it,' and get no back talk. But in today's world you get lots of back talk, whether you are talking about the kids or anyone else. I think it takes unusual ability as a supervisor to not have that happen."

On the decline of unions: "I think there are several things that are causing that. Of course, there is a general decline in manufacturing activity in this country, some of which is probably permanent. But then you have situations like on the airlines and railroads where they arbitrarily established how many miles constituted a day's or week's work. Maybe there ought to be some restriction of how much a pilot flies, but I'll be damned if I think that ought to apply to the person who is serving in the cabin."

On women in Commonwealth Edison management: "I think we are going to have a time not too far off when we are going to have women in leadership positions. I fully expect that we will see a woman officer before too long. The difficulty we find is that a number of very good young women we have hired have left for any number of reasons, and therefore the training you give them is kind of wasted. I remember one young woman who I thought was just absolutely a sure winner to be a division vice president in a short time. But her husband was transferred out-of-state, and she went with him. I still get Christmas cards from her, and my wife is suspicious. Now she has three or four kids, and she isn't working. Overall, our experience has been that women are very good supervisors, and men do not object to working for them. That was one of the things we used to worry about in the early days."

In 1946, Edison had to contend with a labor problem far beyond its own control, a problem that nearly brought the entire

216

country to its knees. With the nation no longer at war, United Mine Workers boss John L. Lewis, craggy-browed nemesis of Sam Insull and countless other captains of industry, began flexing his muscles once again. Lewis took the miners out on a nationwide strike beginning April 1.

The walkout caught Edison in a precarious position. Early in the war, the company's coal supply stood at more than 120 days. However, wartime allotments imposed by the government had pared the supply to approximately 50 days, or about one million tons, by the time the strike began.

After the mines and their employes had remained deadlocked throughout the month of April, the Illinois Commerce Commission ordered immediate restrictions on the use of electricity to help assure that power would be available to protect public health, safety and property. The ICC decree curtailed the use of electricity for purposes such as decorative and flood lighting, showcase illumination, air conditioning, and interior lighting above minimum requirements. The commission confined the commercial use of electricity to 2 until 6 p.m., Monday through Saturday, industrial use to 24 hours a week. Edison workplaces conformed along with the rest, as employes spent part of their time working by candlelight or kerosene lantern.

Calls from customers seeking interpretations of the dimout restrictions bombarded Edison's switchboards. Nearly every member of the sales departments had to assist commercial and industrial customers. The company also ran a series of full-page newspaper ads to keep the public informed about the fuel situation. Ever so slowly, demand decreased until a reduction of 45 percent below normal output was reached on May 9.

But it wasn't enough. Edison realized that unless the strike ended shortly, the unthinkable—the total cutoff of electric service—would occur on or about May 21. The company did everything possible to stave off such a calamity. It purchased coal from every available source. On two days in early May, more than 700 truckloads arrived at the Loomis Street yard alone. Natural gas, purchased from Peoples Gas, helped keep some of the turbines running at Calumet and State Line Stations. At Fisk and Northwest, the company scrambled to install oil-burning equipment. Retired Vice President John Eilering, who had worked on both jobs, remembered that the company's construction and engineering forces teamed up with Sargent & Lundy, the architect/engineer, "designing in the field, buying equipment and converting what we had in warehouses. We had equipment coming in from everywhere." The crews worked double shifts and got the job done in seven days. "Quite a dramatic story," according to Eilering. Then Edison rushed in fuel oil by rail and tank truck. The combined emergency measures enabled the company to save more than 86,000 tons of coal by May 10, when the coal operators and the miners reached a truce. The first coal delivered to Edison after the truce arrived at Crawford Station on May 15.

Oil burning accounted for 225,000 out of the 323,000 kw of former coal-burning boiler capacity at Fisk, 135,000 of 215,000 kw at Northwest. Not till May 28, long after the strike ended, did the company convert both stations completely back to coal. "We had a lot of (oil) pipes there for a long, long time," Eilering recalled. All restrictions of electricity use were lifted by the ICC following the walkout, and Edison ran a final newspaper ad thanking customers for their understanding and cooperation during the Great Coal Emergency of 1946.

During the summer of 1948 the specter of electricity shortages loomed again, but for a different reason. Company planners began to see trouble brewing as early as the final quarter of 1946. A funny thing happened to those predictions that a plunge in sales to heavy industry would drop Edison's total load below 1943–44 levels for some three years after the war. Surprisingly, industrial sales began to rebound briskly toward the end of 1946, much sooner than anyone had estimated. A decline during the first three quarters more than offset the upturn, and sales to the big customers fell 12 percent over the year. But booming residential sales, a phenomenon that the company had foreseen, held the overall decrease in sales to only 1.2 percent for the year. By the spring of 1947 Edison sales to the large commercials and industrials hit an all-time high. "It was generally believed . . . that the postwar requirements of industrial customers would ease off enough to provide some capacity for the anticipated sharp increase in the residential and small commercial fields," Freeman explained to shareholders at the annual meeting, adding that the exact opposite was occurring. The answer to the unexpected turnabout was clear: build more capacity.

Freeman announced plans to build a 107,000-kilowatt unit for the Joliet Station of Public Service Company. Studies for an additional 150,000-kilowatt unit (ultimately Ridgeland Station) had already begun. In addition, Edison would continue the construction of the 150,000-kilowatt Fisk Unit 18 and the 107,000-kilowatt unit nearing completion at Calumet. But could Edison complete them in time to keep up with mounting loads? Total sales for 1947 increased 11.5 percent, powered by an 18.6 percent rise in the small commercial and industrial category and a 13.7 jump among the large commercial and industrials. Edison had to purchase power from neighboring utilities to meet the peak load that December.

Freeman told the 1948 annual meeting that the construction program had progressed as rapidly as possible, but obtaining the necessary equipment from manufacturers who also experienced overloads in their production facilities remained a problem. Building the new plants also cost a lot. The chairman informed the stockholders that the construction budget for the years 1948 through 1951 would substantially exceed the $300 million reported earlier in the year, and that the company might have to raise as much as $175 million in outside capital. The budget soon soared to $400 million. The company now planned to add a second 150,000-kilowatt unit at Ridgeland, bringing to 557,000 kw the amount of capacity expected in service by 1951. Of that total, 407,000 kw remained locked in various stages of construction.

Since the mammoth building program came at a time of record prices, Freeman emphasized that the company had no alternative. "Had we any choice," he declared, "our entire construction program would be postponed until shortages became less acute and the purchasing power of the dollar becomes greater. But because of the nature of our responsibility, we must stand ready to supply the present demands of the territory we serve and to build for its foreseeable requirements."

With the new Calumet unit in service since September 1947, the next unit scheduled for completion, Fisk 18, would not join the system until the spring of 1949.

"This means that any increase in peak load demands next winter will have to be carried by our present system without the benefit of additional capacity," Freeman warned. "This is not a comfortable thought to harbor...."

The peak load did increase—by 45,000 kw over 1947. As a matter of fact, the annual peak, in December 1948, rose to about 28,000 kw above the total net system generating capacity, a wider negative reserve than that of the previous annual peak. The company could only carry the load by reducing voltage, practically unnoticeable by customers when done in small increments, and by tapping into the "overload capacity" of certain units. Earlier in the year, on a dark, hot day in September, Edison actually had come up short.

An unseasonably heavy load at that time coincided with a substantial decrease in capacity due to plants placed out of service for scheduled overhauling. For about four hours, customer demand outstripped available capacity. Neighboring utilities could offer no help this time because they, too, fell short of capacity due to the heat wave. Edison compensated for the shortage by implementing a plan worked out earlier in the summer under which large commercial and industrial customers would curtail their use of electricity when conditions got especially tight, so that there would be enough power for essential community services and for the general public. Edison had contacted some 7,000 big customers to seek their cooperation and to determine their minimum requirements. The company asked only 43 of that number to cut back in September. In later years, the company would offer a formal tradeoff to large industrial users—a reduced rate in return for allowing the company to cut their load on short notice, for no more than a given number of times and hours each year. This load management tool would normally be used routinely a few times each summer, when the reserve margin would grow particularly thin.

A month after the September 1948 experience, the Edison group of companies announced plans for a program to deal with possible future shortages. The companies bought radio time in advance so, if necessary, they could issue an emergency plea to their 1.5 million customers, urging them to cut back on their use of electricity. If no emergency arose, the companies would use the time to air general public service announcements.

220

One company message stated, "With full cooperation by all customers, it is expected that any shortage can be met without serious inconvenience to any customer. Shortages, if they occur, are likely to be of short duration, prevailing only during the hours of heaviest use of electricity. At night and on Saturdays and Sundays the load normally drops to such an extent that capacity is far in excess of demand. This program has been developed so that customers will be asked to curtail only when and if it becomes necessary for them do so, and for no longer periods than is absolutely essential."

In the 1980s Edison reinstituted this program under the title "Peak Alert." Conservation appeals would reach listeners when the company expected a particularly heavy demand on the system, when it would have to use older generating equipment and more costly fuels to meet the load. By then, however, actual shortages were less likely because of healthier reserve margins and stronger interconnections with other utilities provided by the MAIN network. So Peak Alert reminded customers that they could save money by using less electricity on a hot summer day, rather than warning them of the consequences if they did not cooperate.

Total kwh sales for 1948 rose 6.8 percent over the previous year. The increase in customer demand had now grown 48 percent since 1940, while the Edison system had increased its capacity by only 22 percent over the same period. Thus the game of catch-up continued. The company would fulfill its new construction budget of 667,000 kw of capacity with the addition of a 110,000-kilowatt unit at Waukegan Station in 1952. The capacity crunch let up somewhat in July 1949 when Fisk 18 went into service. Addition of the 150,000-kilowatt unit made Fisk, at 473,000 kw, the largest of the Edison group's 10 generating stations. About the same time, Fisk obtained a new conveyor system which linked the plant directly to the Loomis Coal Handling Plant. The conveyor could carry up to 800 tons of coal an hour at speeds of 500 feet a minute.

Between 1946 and 1951 electricity consumed by residential and rural customers increased by 54 percent, primarily due to the influx of more than 100,000 residential customers, a corresponding building boom to house the newcomers, and the growing use of labor-saving devices on the farm and conveniences in the home. The commercial field showed similar increases, as places of business made their locations more attractive and comfortable to customers. The postwar industrial boom continued through 1949, dipped, then came back strongly in 1950 and 1951 as the Korean War brought about a sharp upturn in defense manufacturing.

Two major factors triggered the postwar stampede in residential sales: a rate reduction and the enormous popularity of television. In March 1946 the ICC ordered a rate reduction for the Edison group that averaged approximately seven percent for residential users and four percent for commercial customers. The commission also imposed a uniform declining block rate system that replaced a method in which kwh charges for residential customers were based on the number of rooms in the home. The new rates were five cents per kwh for the first 25 kwh, three cents for each of the next 75 kwh, and two cents apiece for all kwh over 100. To a war-weary public already yearning for consumer goods, a rate reduction and continuation of a dirt-cheap third block in the rate structure not only placed the proverbial feast before the starving, but gave them a tip for eating it.

With these incentives, television sets in the Chicago area multiplied like dandelions in spring. Edison realized the potential of this new medium early on. The Merchandise Sales department conducted a survey in the summer of 1946 that indicated an immediate market among Edison customers for a quarter of a million TV sets. The Edison survey jibed with a national tally by the Federal Communications Commission (FCC) which predicted that more than four million sets would come on the market within the next 18 months with 10 to 15 percent of them purchased in Edison's service territory. The Edison study further showed that the typical TV set would use an average of 280 watts an hour, compared with a radio's average of 65 watts an hour. Following through with the projection, Edison estimated that by Jan. 1, 1948, annual usage by TV sets would surpass 23 million kwh, far exceeding any other appliances connected to the system by the same date. By mid-1946 an amazing total of 20 television manufacturers had set up shop in the company's service territory alone.

Chicago's first TV station to go on the air, WBKB, climbed to 35 hours of broadcast time a week that year, a record for the country. Not long afterward, the city had four stations. The number of TV sets in the Chicago area reached the 1,000 mark in February 1947; by November they had increased eight-fold; during 1948, the number grew to 89,000; and by the end of April 1949, more than 142,000 TVs in the region beamed the Milton Berle show, Howdy Doody, the Friday night fights and—how could anyone forget?—Edison's Telequizicalls and Jane Foster to a fascinated audience.

III

The Television Age was not the only epoch that began in the mid-40s. While not underestimating the profound and subtle changes television would work on generations to come, the flight of the Enola Gay over Hiroshima would alter the course of history far more than the glowing box in the living room and present humanity with the awesome option of destroying itself or harnessing this genie for untold human benefits. The first formal public mention of the peaceful use of the atom in Edison circles apparently came from a military man, Major General William E. Keppner, deputy commander for Army and Navy aviation. "Atomic energy is at present at about the same stage of usefulness to civilization as was electricity when Benjamin Franklin slid his key down the kite string," General Keppner told a meeting of the Edison American Legion Post early in 1947. "We must approach the problem of atomic energy intelligently as we did with electricity." On the negative side of the equation, he said that science stood at the mere threshold of creating atomic weapons far more destructive than the ones whose tests he had commanded at Bikini Atoll the previous summer.

Even this early in the Atomic Age, Edison had begun to investigate the potential for generating electricity with atomic power. Beginning in June 1948, the Edison group of companies invested $100,000 over a five-year period in the University of Chicago's Institute for Nuclear Studies where, under the west stands of Stagg Field in 1942, scientists had first succeeded in splitting the atom. Edison became a member of the Institute through the Utilities Research Commission (URC), the research arm of Commonwealth Edison, Public Service, Western United, and Illinois Northern. URC became the 12th largest organization to join the group, entering the ranks of Westinghouse Electric, U.S. Steel, Standard Oil of Indiana, and others. Scientists at the U. of C., in turn, kept the companies informed of their most recent research.

Vice President Alex Bailey, URC Chairman, said that it was high time utilities got on board. "Companies producing or transmitting power should, in the public interest, participate in this research work," he stated. "Any substantial progress in the harnessing of atomic energy for power production, even though it may be 25 to 50 years ahead, will be of great importance to the industry." Neither Bailey nor anyone else at that time had any inkling of just how quickly events would unfold. Within less than 10 years, Edison would begin to build the world's first privately-financed commercial nuclear power station, and actually generate electricity from the plant in a little more than a dozen years.

Even one year later Chairman Freeman still spoke as if nuclear energy would not come about for quite some time. In answer to a shareholder's question at the 1949 annual meeting, Freeman replied: "Atomic power is still a 'top secret,' and even those in the electric utility business do not know about it. We do know, however, that what they are working on now—which I think Chairman Lilienthal of the Atomic Energy Commission said publicly not too long ago would not be available for four or five years—is simply a pilot plant, as they call it. At this moment, so far as we know, they do not have any definite plan for developing a generating unit of any such size as we require; one, that is, with a capacity of 150,000 kw. From the public statements that have been made, I think that it is a long way off, although just how far off, I do not know and I doubt if anyone else does."

With the next generation of power production coming of age faster than Freeman and most everyone else could recognize, Edison and the rest of the industry and country paused in 1947 to glance backward and honor, on the 100th anniversary of his birth, the remarkable man who had started the whole electric scene. The company built a Thomas Edison centennial exhibit, at the downtown store, which included a model of the 1882 Pearl Street Station, an early phonograph that played cylindrical records, a bipolar motor, a nickel-iron alkaline battery, and an

224

early light bulb. More than 700 representatives of business and industries which sprang from Edison's inventions paid homage to the Great Man's memory at a dinner at which Freeman and Illinois Governor Dwight Green spoke.

Looking again to the future, Edison began a modernization of the Edison and Marquette Buildings. Work included the installation of new elevators and air conditioning and a reconfiguration of Customers Hall that added 20,000 square feet of floor space. With the Edison Post drum and bugle corps playing and company officials waxing patriotic, an honor roll of employes who had served in both World Wars found a temporary home in the Customer Room on the first floor of the Edison Building. The plaque settled permanently in a lobby after the installation of new elevators.

Edison's franchise to supply electric light and power in the city of Chicago, the 50-year plum that Sam Insull landed when he outmaneuvered the Gray Wolves and bought up their Commonwealth Electric Company for a song, expired in 1947. The City Council granted a temporary extension, and public hearings began the following month. By all accounts, some hard bargaining took place, but there were none of the ham-handed tactics by aldermen that had strained Insull a half century earlier. For one thing, the alternative to a new franchise, which had posed a serious threat to infant utilities, municipal acquisition and operation of power facilities, was no longer considered practical: Edison had approximately 1.5 million customers and a net income for 1947 of more than $27 million. The city, nevertheless, held some trump cards.

To continue providing electrical service, the utility needs the ongoing cooperation of municipal authorities who regulate street openings, construction, and many other day-to-day utility operations. The franchise serves as a contract between a municipality and a utility. Without a franchise, a municipality with a penchant for mischief could threaten or actually hamstring a utility in any number of ways. For many years, Edison has provided service to city buildings in its territory outside Chicago in return for a municipal franchise. Chicago remains the only place where the company pays a franchise fee.

During the 1947 renewal hearings, Gale, Evers, Bailey, and other Edison executives made eloquent statements about the quality and dependability of electric service, about the $28 million in local, state, and federal taxes Edison paid in 1946, about the estimated $186 million plant expansion and improvement program. All well and good, but when the ink on the new franchise had dried, in June 1948, it showed an increase in the annual compensation paid to the city by Edison from three to four percent of revenues. In the year that followed, the city realized about $1.2 million more than it would have under the old agreement. The new franchise would run through Dec. 31, 1990.

J. Harris Ward succeeded John Evers as secretary in the late 1940s and later became chairman of the board.

While the franchise negotiations continued, John Evers gave up one of his hats to a fellow negotiator, someone whose star at the moment was rising even faster than his own. The board of directors elected J. Harris Ward, assistant to Vice President Gale, to succeed Evers as secretary. Evers would devote full time to his vice presidential duties. Holder of an MBA from Harvard's Business School, Ward marked 10 years with the company, all of it as a member of Gale's staff except for time spent with the War Production Board and as an Army major in the European theater.

226

"He was much less aloof than Gale and more of a good fellow," George Travers remembered. "But he was a modest sort; he had difficulty meeting people. Harris Ward was witty to the point of being almost incomprehensible. He would give you only as much as he wanted you to know, and liked to play puzzles or little games with you. He would give you some clues as to what he was thinking about, but if you didn't read him it would be very difficult to know what he wanted you to do. He was so quick and cryptic; he would not repeat himself. He would give you the two or three things he wanted you do do, and you were dismissed; somebody else was sitting in (his office)."

In September 1949, the board elected Gale, long chafing under the septuagenarian leadership of Freeman-Doyle-Budd, to the newly-created position of chairman of the finance committee. He received a similar post at Public Service, with his former position, financial vice president, abolished. Other committee members included Freeman, Doyle, and Budd, as well as outside directors Walter Cummings and Solomon Smith.

A new 132,000-volt line from Edison's Kewanee substation to Illinois Northern's new Rock Falls substation symbolized the ever-closer ties between the companies in the Edison group. The new line would reinforce the power supply to Illinois Northern's system. Illinois Northern's Dixon Generating Station and energy from Edison's Powerton Station, delivered from Kewanee over an existing 132,000-volt line from Public Service Company's Waukegan Station to Belvidere, supplied the system's load.

In November 1950, Freeman announced plans for the merger of Western United Gas and Electric Company and Illinois Northern into Public Service Company. "This integration will provide an organization better able to meet the continuing increased demands for electricity and natural gas in this growing territory of northern Illinois," a company statement maintained. Britton Budd, president of Public Service, would head the enlarged organization, though he had opposed any merger with Commonwealth Edison, putting him at loggerheads with Gale. The other two companies became operating divisions of Public Service. Murray Smith and George Fluehr, respective leaders of Western United and Illinois Northern, stayed on to direct the divisions from their headquarters in Aurora and Dixon.

227

The 77 companies that Sam Insull ran at the time of his departure had now dwindled to four major concerns: Commonwealth Edison, supplying electricity to 1,032,000 customers in Chicago; Public Service, providing electricity to 612,000 customers and gas to 387,000 customers across a wide area of northern Illinois outside the city; the Chicago & Illinois Midland Railway; and the Chicago District Electric Generating Corporation, later Commonwealth Edison of Indiana, owner and operator of State Line Station.

The 11,000-square-mile territory served by Edison and Public Service enjoyed rapid and continuing growth. During the six-year period ending Dec. 31, 1950, 684 new industries had arranged to locate their plants in this territory. Edison estimated that the new industries alone provided employment for more than 100,000 workers and contributed approximately $9 million a year in electric and gas revenue. More than 140 newcomers arrived in 1951.

The Industrial Development department carried out the selling of Chicago as a desirable location for commerce and industry. Now known as Marketing Services, this arm of the company continues to maintain voluminous files and data on available sites in the area to assist companies expanding their operations or considering a move to northern Illinois. From these sources the department can supply up-to-the-minute information about locations, transportation facilities, the available workforce, public utilities, demographic figures, and other items. Edison has regularly run advertisements in national publications urging prospective customers to contact the department for assistance.

The Chicago Fair of 1950 provided Edison with a unique opportunity to use a lakefront setting visited by thousands of people to showcase the service territory as a good place to do business. Although by no means as world-class as the 1933–34 extravaganza, the fair opened on June 24 to enthusiastic crowds who would break the attendance mark set the previous year by a Railroad Fair held on the same grounds. The Edison companies sponsored one of the principal displays at the fair, demonstrating the advantages of doing business in Chicago and northern Illinois, and featuring a stage show. "Electricity—the Wonder Worker" had company employes demonstrating the "magic" of electricity in an air-conditioned Electric Theatre. In an adjacent

228

theatre a movie dramatized the industrial, commercial, agricultural, and residential advantages of the service territory, while in still another area a model milk house and a small scale model of an all-electric barn illustrated how modern farmers were putting electricity to work.

Edison introduced a new twist, in February 1950, not highlighted at the fair but which affected all Commonwealth Edison customers—postcard billing. By switching from envelopes to postcards, the company reduced billing costs and still provided the customer with the necessary information, including the present and previous meter reading, period covered by the bill, amount of electricity used, past due date, and, of course, the "bottom line."

A movie and stage show was among the attractions at the new electricity exhibit which Edison and Public Service presented to the Museum of Science and Industry in late 1951. Similar in approach to the companies' presentation at the Chicago Fair, the new exhibit told the story of electricity in modern life in an Electric Theatre, which took more than a year to construct and covered 6,800 square feet of floor space. A brief motion picture depicting electricity generation in a modern coal-fired generating station preceded a 40-minute stage show demonstrating how electricity can produce different types of wave energy—electric, radio, infrared, visible light, ultraviolet, gamma, cosmic, and x-ray. Outside the theatre, in a foyer and exhibition hall, visitors could test their knowledge of electricity on quiz boards. A bicycle-driven electric generator, pedaled by the visitor while a meter registered the amount of electricity produced, put stamina to the test as well. Visitors who pumped fast enough to produce electricity at the rate of .5 kw for a few seconds received a coin stating that if they had continued the exertion for one hour, they would have produced only one cent's worth of electricity. In 1985 Edison introduced a completely redesigned exhibit featuring a film about the basics of a nuclear generating station.

Six months after the opening of Edison's Electric Theatre, the Museum officially entered the Atomic Age. A Centennial of Engineering pageant titled "From Adam to Atom," celebrating the founding of the first civilian engineering society, began a five-year run. It told the story of humanity's scientific advance-

229

ment—"from the cave dweller who snatched fire from a light-
ning-blasted tree to the nuclear scientists who split the atom."

IV

For all practical purposes, the second half of the 20th
century for Commonwealth Edison began on Dec. 7, 1950, on a
96-acre tract along the Sanitary and Ship Canal, at 4300 S.
Ridgeland Ave. There, on that date, Ridgeland Station, the most
advanced generating plant in the country at the time, was
officially opened as the company's first completely new generating station since 1929. Ridgeland began operation with one
150,000-kilowatt unit. Edison added a second unit of equal size in
June 1951. Two additional 150,000-kw units came on line in
1953 and 1955, making the 600,000-kw plant the largest on the
Edison system.

Some 2,300 members of the Edison organization and their
families attended two open houses to obtain a first-hand look at
this state-of-the-art facility. A separate inspection tour for VIPs
included Freeman, Doyle, outside company directors, and officials of Westinghouse, Sargent & Lundy, and the Illinois Commerce Commission. In one photo, the dignitaries stand gathered
around a panel in the first centralized control room on the
system. Located between the boiler and turbine rooms, the single
nerve center controlled the boilers, turbine-generators, and high-
voltage transmission terminal. From the moment coal reached
the furnaces until power flowed through the transmission lines,
central operators recorded and guided every step. For the first
time, operators used television to give them a continuous view of
water gauges atop the boilers. Each of the two boilers, 13 stories
tall, was fired by four cyclone furnaces which Edison pioneered
in developing. The four consumed approximately 750 tons of
coal a day, in pea-sized pieces blown into the furnaces by blasts
of pre-heated air, creating a swirling or cyclone motion as it
burned. The flames roared out of the furnaces into the boilers
"like a giant blowtorch," according to early accounts.

To handle a substantial part of Ridgeland's output, Edison
built the Jefferson Substation, one of the largest installations of
its kind in the country. The new facility, located on the near
Southwest Side and bounded by Cabrini, Arthington, Desplaines,

and Clinton Streets, displaced 20 substandard buildings and now occupies most of two blocks bisected by Jefferson Street. Because high voltage transmits electricity most efficiently and economically, current was stepped up at Ridgeland from 14,400 to 138,000 volts and transmitted to the substation, which reduced it to 69,000 volts for redistribution. Intermediate substations stepped down voltage for use by homes (120 volts) or industries (the largest at 4,000 volts). The company built two new underground transmission lines, one from Ridgeland to Jefferson, the other from Crawford Station to Jefferson.

Big things also brewed at the northern and southern ends of Public Service's territory. The company began the year 1952 by adding a new 110,000-kw unit at Waukegan Station, bringing the plant's total net capacity to 388,000 kw. It also announced plans to build Will County Station on a 216-acre tract along the west side of the Sanitary and Ship Canal, between Lockport and Lemont. Initial plans called for the installation of two 150,000-kw units. They went into service in 1955, joined by a 250,000-kw unit in 1957 and a 500,000-kw unit in 1963.

A global development that would alter the lives of many employes and profoundly affect the way the company did business overshadowed the many important company advancements at mid-century. In June 1950 the United States once again found itself at war, or as official Washington described it, involved in a "police action." Waves of North Korean troops stormed across the 38th parallel into South Korea. The United States, under the umbrella of a United Nations peacekeeping force, quickly came to the aid of the Seoul government.

Less than a month after the fighting started, three Edison members of the Naval Reserve Squadron at Glenview were called to active duty. Raymond Beck of the Materials Accounting division, Edward Neteland of Mail and Information, and Harold Wodak of Revenue Accounts sat down side by side and smiled for the *Round Table* photographer. They survived the war, but five other Edison employes did not.

The first casualty occurred in a training accident at Camp Breckinridge, Kentucky. Army Private John Granahan, 25, an Edison Building elevator operator, died in an explosion. A native of County Mayo, Ireland, Granahan had lived in the United States and worked for Edison only two years when drafted.

Another Army private who had worked as a groundman in Construction-Overhead, Frank Marassa, was the first Edison employe killed in action. He was 23. Marine PFC Joseph Ballard of Correspondence, Seaman Richard Dollen of Mail, and Airman Joseph Seger of Revenue Accounts also lost their lives.

When the Korean War began, Edison still struggled to adjust to the post-World War II sales boom. Nineteen forty-eight, a turning point for the national economy, had seen supplies of consumer goods finally catching up with demands and prices beginning to level off. In Edison's service territory, this had led to a moderate decline in business activity, which had continued through the first half of 1949. But when prices began showing signs of stabilizing, an impressive rebound occurred, and the outbreak of fighting found the company at its peacetime busiest.

"With the passing of months," Freeman told the annual meeting of 1951, "it became evident that we were faced not only with the immediate military action in Asia but also with the establishment of a mobilization economy to enable us to resist further aggression there or in other parts of the world." The latter focus of resistance apparently referred to Europe, where the Soviets had already imposed the unsuccessful Berlin blockade and where the Cold War had taken off. By this time the Soviets had already startled the world by testing an atomic bomb, years before anyone in the west thought they would have the capability to do so. Ever ready, Chicago's civil defense organization reacted to the perceived Soviet threat by responding to a mock attack to test its efficiency. Three hypothetical "atom bombs" fell on the city during a 13-hour period. According to the *Round Table*, the explosions had remained "on paper," unlike the paper bombs dropped during the World War II mock air raid. The lead in the *Round Table* story nevertheless chilled its readers all the same: "Chicago will stand its ground to fight the effects of the atom bomb. There will be no wholesale evacuation, no plan to make a ghost town of the nation's second largest city." A diagram showed that the atom bombs—firecrackers by contemporary military standards—dropped on the Southwest, Near West, and Mid-North sides of the city would leave the majority of Chicago's landscape undamaged.

In its primary role in the civil defense apparatus, Edison would work with other utilities, police, fire and medical authorities to restore electric service as quickly as possible to hospitals, pumping stations, and sewage disposal systems. Under the conditions in the test case posed by federal authorities, Edison estimated that it could supply emergency service to undamaged hospitals within 24 hours. The company figured it would take from seven to 14 days to restore electric service to all except severely damaged sections of the city.

In late 1951, Edison appointed key people in every department to serve as air raid wardens, firefighters, and first aid administrators. All received instructions in how to protect co-workers and company property in the event of an attack. "No one knows whether an enemy attack will occur in the next few months or be ten years away or will never occur, but we want to be ready now—not the day after such an attack," a company statement declared.

As in earlier wars, Edison servicemen got a lot of support from the home front. The company encouraged employes to "bake Jane Foster's cookies to send to your favorite serviceman." Jane recommended cookies that would not break easily and explained the best way to package them. (She suggested tins or sturdy cardboard boxes lined with wax paper.) A group of women from the Correspondence department got together regularly in the evening to prepare packages of food, magazines, and gifts for Edison's fighting men. Again, employes bought savings bonds and donated blood to the Red Cross, but the Korean conflict did not bring the all-out scrap drives of World War II. As always, page after page of photos in the *Round Table* depicted smiling Edison men and women in uniform.

The production facilities of the service territory and the nation operated at full capacity to meet the effects of stockpiling, defense orders, and plant expansion. Company operations reached record levels during 1950. All categories of sales rose well above those of 1949, with industrials leading the way. Total kwh sales went up 8.2 percent, sales to large commercial and industrial customers, 11.3 percent. Edison led all electric utilities in the country in kwh sales and peak load.

Nationwide, the electric utility industry's generation in 1950 doubled that of 1941. Moreover, an expansion program unequalled by any other industry in history would add more than 31 million kw of capacity over the next few years. A survey showed that by mid-century, post-World War II expansion of the electric and gas industries far exceeded that of 16 other industries, nearly triple the growth in petroleum, the closest competitor.

Edison made 1950 a signal year in spite of another coal strike. The company's coal reserves began to dwindle in July 1949, when John L. Lewis decreed that working time at nearly all mines in the country be reduced to three days a week. A complete suspension of production from mid-September until early November followed this action. Edison began buying coal from new sources as far away as Ohio, Pennsylvania and West Virginia. When it became apparent that these supplements wouldn't suffice, the company again turned to oil, with shipments coming from as far west as Oklahoma and Wyoming. Fisk, Northwest, and Powerton Stations could still burn oil, and now Calumet could as well, making it the one station on the system equipped to use all three boiler fuels—coal, oil, and natural gas. By the time the miners went on strike in February, Edison had slashed its normal supply of 1.5 million tons to less than 500,000 tons. Before conditions could become as grim as they did in 1946, the walkout ended, just one month later. Edison had approximately 167,000 tons of coal in storage, or enough for about 20 days.

After a long period of relative inertia, changes in the high command came all at once. In June 1951, J. Harris Ward came to bat again, elected vice president while continuing as secretary. One month later, bigger moves came about.

Gale had lobbied Freeman for several years to let him replace either Doyle as president of Commonwealth Edison or Budd as president of Public Service Company. Now he had finally run out of patience. According to Travers, Gale gave Freeman an ultimatum: unless he were named to either of the two positions, he would quit. Neither man spoke publicly about what had transpired, but Freeman had to realize that he, Doyle, and Budd, all in their 70s, wouldn't last forever and that Willis Gale stood as an increasingly powerful figure in a company which could ill-afford to lose what Travers called "his unbelievably powerful mentality and gifts of leadership, which he alone possessed in the top cadre of officers." In any case, Freeman agreed. At a Board of Directors meeting on July 6, Gale became president of *both* companies. Doyle and Budd moved upstairs to the newly-created positions of vice chairmen at their respective companies, with a private understanding that this arrangement would only last a year.

In the same power shift, Evers was elected to the new post of executive vice president. Edison employes received only the basic information about the changes, but the rather terse announcement did spell out what had occurred if one disregarded the euphemistic statement about the "promotion" of Doyle and Budd. Gale, the announcement read halfway down, "will be in direct charge of the affairs of the company," Evers "will act as Mr. Gale's principal assistant," and Doyle "will assist Chairman Charles Y. Freeman in the performance of his duties." Where that left Freeman remained unclear, except that for all appearances Gale now had everything but the chairman's title, and that would not elude him for long.

"There had been no talk whatever about a changing of the guard," Travers said. "There was no talk at all from Evers, in particular, and he confided in me a great deal about those things."

Evers' promotion spelled the end of the Highland Park Table Tennis and Chowder Society. Vice President and Comptroller Otto Gressens became enraged because Gale had selected Evers over himself as executive vice president. Gressens thought he understood his friend Willis Gale and had figured that he would obtain the next promotion. But, according to Travers, very few people at Edison really knew Gale.

"Otto quit that very afternoon," Travers recalled. "He wrote out his resignation in longhand. His secretary typed it up, and it was handed to Willis Gale that afternoon. It was handed to a lawyer in the Board meeting, and by three o'clock Gressens was cleaning out his desk."

Gressens quickly signed on as financial vice president of Peabody Coal Company, which not only was still supplying Edison with a substantial amount of its needs, but had recently seen its contract with the company extended to 1981. Into Gressens' comptroller shoes stepped Gordon Corey, a University of Wisconsin business administration graduate with a master's degree from Northwestern. Corey, assistant comptroller since January 1950, would become a major power in the company later on.

"In Mr. Gressens the Peabody Coal Company gains an experienced accounting and financial officer," *The Edison Round Table* graciously explained.

"This power play, this interplay of personalities, took place within a matter of seven or eight days," Travers noted. "It was a very crucial time for the company."

The Freeman-Doyle-Budd triumvirate had reigned for 13 years. Doyle and Budd, of course, went back a lot farther than that. Doyle had served as president since 1930, two years before Insull left. He had started with the company in 1896, four years after Insull had come to Chicago, two years before the Spanish-American War, and seven years before Fisk Station had gone into service. Budd had been around, in Travers' words, "since the beginning of time," but actually since pre-World War I, when Insull chose him to run his newly acquired elevated railroads.

"Having such a long history, they were reluctant to step down" (or up, to be euphemistic again), according to Travers. "It was up to Gale to force their hand. It was a coup, the only time in the years I have been in this company where I have seen something happen that had the distinct aroma of a power play. I am sure Gale threatening to leave and possibly take people with him is what forced the issue."

Doyle and Budd held on for another year. Their retirements were announced jointly after a board of directors meeting of both Edison and Public Service in June 1952. Doyle continued as an Edison director, Budd as a director of both companies.

A week earlier, at the annual meeting, stockholders approved an increase in the number of company directors, from nine to 12. The new slots were filled, not surprisingly, by Gale, Evers, and Herbert Sedwick, executive vice president of Public Service.

The directors' meeting that sent Doyle and Budd into retirement also elevated a man who would redefine utility public relations for the first time since Sam Insull had laid down the gospel a generation earlier. Morgan F. Murphy, Public Service vice president, became a vice president of Edison with responsibility for the company's contacts with the news media and publication of the *Round Table*. Travers became his staff assistant. Murphy, whose son, Morgan Jr., would become a United States congressman representing a district on Chicago's Southwest Side, came to the company at the time the career of a good friend and fellow alumnus of De La Salle Institute, Richard J. Daley, was also on the ascent. Daley would become chairman of the Cook County Democratic organization the following year and mayor of Chicago two years after that.

At the 1952 Edison Management Conference, Murphy delivered a talk that has set the theme for the company's community relations program to this date. Taking a page from Insull, he emphasized that maintaining good relations with the public is the responsibility of everyone in the Edison system. He elaborated, explaining that the company actually deals with five "publics"—customers, the press, community organizations, public officials, and stockholders. To the corporation, he added, employes form another of its publics, but to the public, these employes *are* the company.

"We are different from most industries," Murphy maintained, "in that our customers are confined to a definite area, and practically everyone in the area is our customer. We serve them day and night, and each of them forms a daily impression— consciously or unconsciously—of the company."

Citing "Mrs. Brown" as a typical customer, Murphy pointed out that Edison keeps her good will by supplying her with continuous electric service. Only when something goes wrong and her service is interrupted do the company's relations with Mrs. Brown become tense. When she calls to complain that her lights are out, a customer service representative has the option of retaining or losing Mrs. Brown's friendship. If he or she does the job right, Mrs. Brown realizes that this big electric company actually cares about her problems. A half hour later, when Edison crews have corrected the fault, Mrs. Brown is again a completely satisfied customer. Murphy stressed that each employe is "Mr. Edison" or "Miss Edison" to the customer.

Murphy stated that developing the best possible relationship with all members of the news media lies in Edison's best interest because of their influence on the thinking of the general public. Notice he spoke of "members of the media," or individuals. For all his innovative PR concepts, Sam Insull had had little

Three top company executives of the 1940s and '50s—(from left) John Evers, Willis Gale, and Herbert Sedwick—discuss nighttime load patterns in the Power Supply Office on the sixth floor of the Edison Building (circa 1953-54).

use for newspeople as human beings. Murphy also remarked that Edison's participation in civic activities promotes the company's image as a good corporate citizen. He cited the participation of employes in chambers of commerce, business associations, service clubs, and the like.

Turning to public officials, he pointed out that because of the nature of the utility business, Edison must constantly remain in contact with them. He mentioned an example of Edison crews having to "rip up and repave streets and alleys where our distribution facilities are being installed or repaired." The company needs franchises from municipalities to perform such work.

Finally, Murphy turned to Edison's 126,000 shareholders. He suggested a program that keeps them informed of company activities so that they, too, can be PR representatives of Commonwealth Edison. "We are doing our level best to cultivate friends who take our daily presence in their lives for granted," he concluded. "We want them to know that all their electric utility needs are being met by us. We want them to have confidence in our ability to continue, and if necessary, improve our high standards of service, come what may."

In January 1953, Gale completed his rise to the top, as the board elected him chairman and chief executive officer of Commonwealth Edison and Public Service. Freeman became chairman of the executive committee of the companies and would, according to the announcement, "continue to take an active part in the management of the companies and in the formulation of their policies." Evers became president of Edison and executive vice president of Public Service. Sedwick, in turn, would serve as executive vice president of Edison and president of Public Service. The latter title, however, would change to president of the Public Service Division, once the merger of the two companies became complete. At the same meeting, the directors elected Gordon Corey as vice president, though he would keep the post of comptroller. Public Service Vice President E. E. Lungren received the additional position of Edison vice president. Two months earlier, Ward had been named treasurer, succeeding George Williamson, who retired. Fred Baxter became secretary, replacing Ward, who kept his vice presidency.

The proposal to merge the two companies went public in November 1952. The change that had evolved for 15 years would be largely a formality, since Edison owned nearly 99 percent of the stock of Public Service. Stockholders would have to approve. Gale explained that the merger would produce advantages in administration, efficiency, and economy, but he stressed that "Commonwealth Edison must continue to be identified as one of the important business assets of the city of Chicago. Likewise, Public Service must continue to be recognized in each city, town, and village as a local enterprise."

Gale assured the annual Management Conference that the merger would only simplify corporate matters, leaving personnel and operations unaffected. How many in the audience accepted that rather bland judgment at face value remains unknown. In fairness to Gale, he did hasten to add that organizational changes would occur from time to time, as always, "but while we are going to do everything we can to get the best possible efficiency, we are not going to do it at the expense of those who have spent a substantial part of their lives in our organization."

Travers remembered that the actual merger of the two organizations didn't "leave any blood on the doorstep," but there was resentment on the part of Edison people who tended to be older than their opposite numbers in Public Service. "People came over from Public Service to take jobs on a parallel basis with fellows who were older and much more experienced. Many Edison people felt they were being pre-empted by Public Service people. I suppose if you talked to people who had a Public Service background, they would feel as though they were pre-empted by Edison, the big company from Chicago taking over. I'm sure both of those feelings were there, depending on an individual's personal history or how he moved or didn't move at that particular moment."

In a foregone conclusion, stockholders of both companies overwhelmingly approved the merger at special meetings on March 17, 1953. Commonwealth Edison, which began by serving a small area of downtown Chicago, presently extended across some 11,000 square miles of northern Illinois. Now Gale and his new management team would have to integrate the organizations, overcome the personal resentments, and make good on the promise of a streamlined, more efficient utility.

Two other items loomed large on the new chairman's agenda. Soon, the company would have to go before the Illinois Commerce Commission and seek the first rate increase in its history following years of decreases. And he would have to decide on the future of a small team of Edison employes who had worked on a project since May 1951 with no publicity whatever, and whose very existence the company did not even acknowledge until late 1952. They called themselves the Nuclear Study Group.

Eleven

Atoms
For
Peace

I

One day in the spring of 1951 Bill Kiefer, a 35-year-old electrical engineer with the company for 12 years, was working at Ridgeland Station when he got a call from his supervisor. Kiefer had spent many of his years with Edison specializing in instrumentation and control. He went from station to station, maintaining the electronic telemetry equipment that fed power readings from each unit to the central load dispatcher's office, which would use the information to determine regulation of the entire system load. Kiefer and the people under him also participated in the research and development of new applications of electronics, particularly in electrical transmission.

Kiefer's supervisor told him, without elaboration, that he was to report the following morning to the corporate office of Murray Joslin, assistant to the president. Kiefer was puzzled. Someone in his position normally wouldn't be invited to the office of a corporate executive for any reason. At first, he didn't connect the invitation with a task he had been performing since the waning days of World War II. Since the first stories had appeared in the newspapers about the bombing of Hiroshima, Kiefer had kept a clipping file on atomic power. Someone in the corporate office—he didn't know who—had decided such a file might come in handy and had further decided that the assignment belonged with the Testing department. The department head, Charlie Hejda, had given the task to Kiefer, who dutifully clipped and filed everything he could find in the papers and technical journals about atomic energy, including early references to the possibility of building nuclear generating stations.

Bill Kiefer's scrapbook had grown at least three inches thick when, six years after he had started it, Murray Joslin called him downtown. By then, he figured that he had read as much as anyone in the company on the subject of atomic energy.

Kiefer's apprehension about sitting down with someone of Joslin's standing in the company quickly disappeared. He found the 49-year-old Iowa native friendly and approachable, and soon relaxed in the presence of a fellow electrical engineer.

Joslin explained that Edison and Public Service were forming a small, elite group to explore the possibilities of producing electric power from atomic reactors and to report its findings to the Atomic Energy Commission (AEC). He added that the companies would select employes with various backgrounds, including engineering, finance, and management, who could evaluate any portion of the classified material the government would reveal to them. Joslin, who would serve as project manager, told Kiefer the names of the others he had invited on board: Bob Gear, who would act as technical director, and Les Evers, who would be secretary, together with Gene Bailey, George Redman, and Edson Jones from Power Production; D. Robert Bower from Finance; Marion Oldacre and E. L. Tournquist from Research; and Fred McCloska from Sargent & Lundy—the 11 men making up Edison's atomic football team.

The project leader went on to explain that the group would work in a special office whose location for the time being would remain unidentified. Team members were not to discuss their assignment with anyone, including their families, nor were they to disclose the location of the office. Since the group would work with large quantities of classified documents, Joslin explained, they would need a thorough security clearance from the AEC. Then Joslin added an additional note of caution: in spite of the sacrifices and the unconventional nature of the project, which would require the full-time efforts of the group, the ultimate future of their work would remain, at best, uncertain. Kiefer, however, was already hooked; he accepted on the spot.

Nuclear power, at this stage, had at least one significant handicap: the 1946 Atomic Energy Act prohibited private ownership of facilities for production of fissionable material. The act created a five-member civilian board—the AEC—to watch over the government's atomic monopoly, which had been totally military in nature. But now that the war had ended, the civilian commission took charge of the country's atomic program. The AEC, in turn, reported to a panel of senators and congressmen—the Joint Committee on Atomic Energy—which served as a public watchdog over the nuclear program.

The ban on commercial nuclear development nothwithstanding, private companies anxiously wished to explore its possibilities. Westinghouse and General Electric had already received hefty military contracts for nuclear work and saw the prospect of additional money in the civilian sector. However, the government wanted to maintain its world monopoly on the secrets of atomic fission. Washington believed that monopoly would vanish if it shared those secrets with private industry at large, outside the comparatively narrow scope of the GE and Westinghouse defense work. Nonetheless, the two companies continued to research commercial nuclear power, looking forward to the day when the government would lift the ban. In October 1947, AEC Chairman David Lilienthal created the Industrial Advisory Panel to oversee the agency's own research into civilian nuclear reactors.

The Soviet Union's atomic detonation in 1949 initially hampered, but then spurred participation by private companies in commercial nuclear research. In response to the Soviets' literal and figurative bombshell, President Truman issued a directive in 1950 ordering a dramatic increase in the production of atomic bombs as well as the development of the next generation of nuclear weapons—hydrogen bombs. The beginning of the Great Arms Race shoved the government's commercial nuclear research into the background for the time being. On the other hand, it also led to a solidification of this country's military alliances. In 1949, the North Atlantic Treaty Organization (NATO) was established to counter the Soviet threat, and Washington started to share more of its atomic information with its European allies. Some American manufacturing companies began to wonder out loud how their government could give foreigners information that it withheld from them. What would prevent these other countries from using the data to develop their own commercial nuclear power programs and leave the United States behind?

The AEC responded to this rhetorical question and to continued political lobbying by forming its Industrial Participation Program. Companies could peek under the tent for the first time, but they would have to judge for themselves what, if anything, to do with what they saw.

Edison's first personal contact with members of the AEC staff was through Alex Bailey, chief of power production and patron saint of the historic clock. His interest began to grow, along with that of Gale and Sedwick, who received his reports. Gale undertook a personal study of nuclear power and became well informed about the technology. Once the company had decided to form the study group, Sedwick boosted Joslin, a rising young star in Public Service but virtually unknown at Edison, to the job of project leader. He was an experienced engineer, a quick study, an effective speaker, a pleasant person, and a good manager. Gale and Bailey agreed with Sedwick's choice of a proper man for the task.

Edison and Public Service comprised one of four separate corporate groups that the AEC invited to investigate the possibilities of using atomic power for peaceful commercial purposes. The others were Detroit Edison and Dow Chemical, Union Electric (St. Louis) and Monsanto Chemical, and Pacific Gas and Electric and Bechtel Corporation. Edison's early interest stemmed from a concern over possible future problems with the transportation and ash disposal of coal, not to mention a defect of coal burning that would become even more vexing—air pollution.

The Edison group began meeting on the sixth floor of the Marquette Building, under strict security and in the austerest of surroundings. The office had an outer room where the secretarial group worked, a meeting room for classes and discussions, and a large area with desks, files, and safes with locks impenetrable by ordinary drills. Two team members were assigned to each desk under the erroneous assumption that one of the two would always be in the field. A gate with an electronically controlled lock operated by the secretaries in the outer office protected the work. Like the study group members, the secretaries needed security clearances because they also handled the classified documents. Before the establishment of a permanent secretarial staff, any classified material that needed to be typed went to the Correspondence department, where the supervisor would assign each page to a different typist, seated at least two desks apart. The permanent secretaries also served as de facto security officers, recognizing everyone who had a clearance. If any visitors arrived while the group members had classified material on their desks, the secretaries would stop them in the outer office. However, few visitors bothered them in the first year or so because nobody outside the group itself or top management knew the location or the activities.

"We were allowed to give our co-workers a phone number so they could get in touch with us if they needed help with a problem on our regular jobs," Kiefer remembered. Was anyone curious about where he was spending so much time? "I just told them that I was on special assignment for the company," he related. "They never pressed me to reveal anything further. I guess they just respected that."

The AEC conducted surprise audits to make certain all of the classified documents on loan to the group had not crept off somewhere. Each night, a member of the team checked everyone's desk to make sure all of the documents were locked up. If a document was found on anyone's desk, that person drew the next inspection duty. Even the engineers' notebooks had confidential status. Les Evers carried them in a briefcase chained to his wrist. The Edison people prided themselves in never losing a classified document.

The government severity about security seemed apparent from the problem Kiefer had getting a security clearance. At first he didn't think anything was wrong, but he began to wonder when one colleague after another got permanently assigned to the sixth floor office while he remained on the outside, except for some orientation sessions. Following inquiries that lasted several months, the government had cleared all the others. Finally, Joslin contacted the AEC to ask what the devil was going on with the FBI's investigation of Kiefer. As a result of Joslin's urging, Kiefer was asked to appear at a special hearing at the security office of Argonne National Laboratory, southwest of Chicago, to get to the bottom of the matter.

"It was formal, almost like a court in some senses," according to Kiefer. "They had several security people there, as well as the FBI's investigation material. They also had a court reporter, and everything I said was recorded. I was quizzed for a full afternoon. They kept asking me certain types of questions, and when I responded in a way that they obviously didn't think attested to my loyalty, I really thought I ought to hire a lawyer. I couldn't convince them that I was who I was. I could sense that in the emotion of their faces."

In what could have passed for the plot of an Alfred Hitchcock movie, the FBI had mistaken Bill Kiefer—softspoken, bespectacled electrical engineer—for a man with the same name, right down to the same middle initial, suspected of being a member of a German spy and sabotage ring during World War II.

"I learned more about this later, when I inquired around and talked to the people with whom the FBI had spoken," Kiefer said. "This man was a member of an organization whose associates were persons whose relatives had managed to get to Germany during the war, and were going to spy school there. I think this man was one of them—I'm not positive—but there were others in that group that did that. As you may remember, some graduates of a German spy school were actually placed in a rubber boat from a German submarine off Long Island. Two days later, a couple of them showed up in Chicago, but the government found them. One of these men had some drawings and information on public utilities—telephone, gas, and electric facilities—in the Chicago area. He might have planned to sabotage them, so I can see how the FBI was concerned about these people and this man with the same name.

"They worked on my security clearance all summer. I kept hearing from friends and relatives about visits by these people."

The FBI submitted the results of its investigation to the AEC which would ultimately decide whether or not to give Kiefer a clearance. That preceded his taking the witness stand.

"Later on, I got to know the hearing officer, who was the chief of security for the AEC in the Midwest. He told me the reason the proceeding took all afternoon was because they kept asking me whether I knew a man named Sam Burke. They would always come back to Sam Burke, and I always denied that I knew Sam Burke. So I said, 'Who *is* Sam Burke?' 'Oh,' he said, 'Sam Burke was the man you bought gas from when you were in college. He had a gas station three blocks from your home. He knows you well.' When Sam said he knew me—and I said I never knew him—they obviously thought that I was the wrong man; you know, the man they didn't want to give the security clearance to. Well, I bought gas from that man for three years and never knew his last name. He was just Sam. It was kind of amusing, but it also shows how you can have your reputation destroyed by some quirk of fate."

While Kiefer waited for the AEC to unravel Edison's version of "The Wrong Man," the company hired Dr. Lyle Borst, formerly in charge of the government's experimental reactor at Brookhaven National Laboratory in New York, to help train the study group in the basics of nuclear technology. Borst was one of the scientists who had worked on the original atomic research project at the University of Chicago that led to the splitting of the atom. He had to prepare the group for visits to several government laboratories around the country to see reactor experiments. Following the inspection trips, the group would make a recommendation to the AEC on the feasibility of constructing an atomic generating station with the dual purpose of producing power for electricity and plutonium for weapons.

George Redman, who became part of a closely-knit threesome that included Kiefer and Evers, was a 24-year-old engineer at Waukegan Station in 1949 when he was invited to attend a series of eight lectures by experts in the nuclear field. About 40 Edison and Public Service employes attended the talks in Chicago, presented by Enrico Fermi and scientists from Argonne. Redman had to juggle shifts to attend. The speakers couldn't go into detail because of security regulations, but what they did say whetted Redman's curiosity. When the series ended, Marion Oldacre, director of research, asked for a critique. Redman expressed his interest in anything that might develop and went back to work on the technical staff at Waukegan where, among the duties, he tested the efficiency of the boilers. "I thought I'd never see the end of boiler gas samplings," he admitted.

He did—in the spring of 1951—when he joined Kiefer and Evers, already setting up shop on the sixth floor of the Marquette Building. Before Redman joined the group full-time, Evers had continually sent him reading material on nuclear energy and reactors. Redman recalled a division among higher management over the makeup of the group.

"Some of our people thought there should be a group of very knowledgeable, experienced, old-time engineers. But I think Murray Joslin himself had the idea that there should be some younger blood in there. I was certainly proof of that. So we wound up with some other younger fellows and some older fellows, too.

"I don't think we would have gotten into nuclear power if it wasn't for Joslin," Redman continued. "He was whatever we needed. He opened up the doors for us, particularly with the Atomic Energy Commission. When we needed to go someplace, he was with us. Gave us anything we wanted, anything appropriate to nuclear power."

Kiefer remembered his favorable impression of the group when all of them came together for the first time. One of the older members, he had worked with several and knew nearly all of them. "A great team. . .I was happy to be with them." At that first meeting, Roy Hegnen of the AEC explained what they would see at the government's Hanford, Washington, facility, the first stop on their itinerary.

They would see the original reactors built to produce Uranium-235 for making atomic bombs. Kiefer and the others felt privileged. They realized that they witnessed things that had made history just a short while before. They had seen simple conceptual drawings of the bomb-making process in newspapers and technical journals, but, according to Kiefer, seeing the operation first-hand proved to be quite an emotional experience.

"We had access not only to the reactors and how they were designed, but we were also shown in great detail how they were operated. Nothing was held back. We also visited the process plant where they made the fuel pellets to put into the reactors. The technology was good, but there wasn't much automation in the manufacture. It was more like a massive human effort instead of conveyors or anything like that. It was almost like a few steps above a blacksmith's shop, but it worked perfectly in the movement of the materials in the different processes, coating this, chemically treating this, heat treating that. It was like a ballet, all these men and women in masks and white protective suits. They had big clocks with hands that moved between different sectors, and during certain periods the pellets would have to move from one process to another. The

250

workers had tongs to pass the pellets from one to another as they watched the clock. It was just fascinating.

"The pellets had uranium inside and were covered with aluminum. At one end of the process, they were shoved into the reactors and went through a nuclear chain reaction inside. The pellets were gradually pushed through to the other end, where they would drop out. Then they had enough Uranium-235 to make (atomic bombs) and to make it worthwhile to chemically reprocess the pellets (to obtain plutonium for more bombs)."

The group's travels also took them to a government reservation near Idaho Falls, Idaho, called the National Reactor Testing Station. Before it became a nuclear experimentation site, the Navy had used the desert reservation to test 16-inch guns, which provides some clue as to its expanse and barrenness. Redman came there in March 1952, as the group's one-year study assignment drew to a close, to participate in the startup of a materials testing reactor (MTR). He spent three months working with the staff on experiments that tested the effects of radiation on a wide range of materials. An experimental breeder reactor, which produces more fuel than it consumes, and an experimental ship reactor were also being tested, but Redman did not participate in those experiments. He found the MTR a "pretty simple plant" compared to a power reactor, but nevertheless obtained a lot of background. "I had a rather free hand," he disclosed, echoing Kiefer's observation of the visit to Hanford. Two years later, Cliff Zitek would travel to the Idaho site for the all-important reactor safety experiments that would lead to commercial development of the boiling water reactor, the type of power unit that Dresden I would utilize as the world's first privately-financed commercial nuclear generating station.

While in Idaho Redman first became acquainted with nuclear contamination, something he did not regard as any great consequence. The military had conducted an atomic test in the Nevada desert, and some of the fallout drifted over the Idaho site, causing radiation detectors to sound. "We went around in little booties and had to take off our shoes when we went into the cafeteria," he recalled. "I wasn't concerned, but I could see that the health physicist was excited about it. For awhile they didn't know how long of a problem it would be. It certainly exceeded the limits they had for contamination levels, but it died off rather rapidly."

Logically, the study group made a number of visits to Argonne, in Chicago's southwest suburbs, where primarily design and analysis took place. Some of the fundamentals studied by the Edison team included conceptual designs for improving the control of reactors. But according to Kiefer, the most valuable resources at Argonne were human, not mechanical or scientific. The group became closely acquainted with Dr. Walter Zinn, the prestigious director of the laboratory, and Dr. Samuel Untermeyer, the colorful father of the boiling water reactor (BWR) who was working with reactor controls at the time. Both Zinn and Untermeyer took a keen interest in the work of the Edison team and frequently visited the Marquette Building office. Edison eventually hired Untermeyer as a consultant. "Very fertile mind, and a bit of a character, too," said Kiefer.

Following the preliminary visits to all of the government labs, seeing all of the work in progress—some of it in the embryonic stage—the study group visualized several types of reactors.

"The one we thought about first was a helium-filled reactor," Kiefer recounted. "We made the first design for that and convinced ourselves it would work. We really had just a conceptual design. We thought we could work out the major technical problems later on."

The study team issued a formal report on its first year of activities on May 1, 1952, while Redman was still in Idaho. The group did not endorse the helium-filled reactor or any other type, but urged generally that the atomic research be continued. The company used the report as the basis for a plan to move ahead with the design, construction, and operation of a nuclear reactor that would produce both power and plutonium. Edison envisioned an atomic generating station with a reactor paid for and owned by the AEC, which would also furnish the uranium fuel, extract the plutonium, and dispose of the waste. Edison would select the site and own the conventional power facilities, such as the turbine-generators and the transmission lines, and the plant would be connected to the Edison generating system. The company would pay the AEC for the uranium fuel used to generate kwh. Edison made it clear to the AEC that the company was not making a formal proposal, since it considered commercial atomic power to still be in the discussion stage. Consequently, Edison made no recommendation as to cost, capacity, location, or design.

Details of Edison's tentative plan and the work of the study group finally became public through a major address Joslin delivered to the National Industrial Conference Board in New York. After that, according to Kiefer, he no longer had to tell his wife he had to "go out to Hanford or someplace else." Of course, he never told his wife what Hanford was, other than to caution her that it involved a project that the company wanted to keep quiet for a while. The scene undoubtedly occurred in the other households as well.

"There was a longtime Edison employe who lived two doors from me," Kiefer related. "When this (account of Joslin's speech) came out, I came home from work that evening, and he rushes over and says, 'I wondered about you. I never knew what you were doing!'"

Upon submission of the first year report, Edison and the AEC immediately extended their agreement for another year. Bob Gear became project manager, replacing Joslin; Evers moved up to Gear's old slot as technical director; and Kiefer took over from Evers as secretary. New members added to the group for the second year's study included Sinesio Zagnoli from the Gas department, Cliff Zitek and Roger Dreffin from Testing, Ed Koncel and Al Veras from Engineering, and Norm Wandke from Power Production.

It now became the job of Kiefer, Redman, and Evers to train the newcomers in what they themselves had learned over the past year. Consultants taught classes once a week. Ed Koncel remembered that the three "old-timers" led the group well and "kept things moving." However, he had a difficult time at first because his electrical engineering background didn't help him understand the early discussion, much of which centered on mechanical and chemical principles. Koncel joined the group about the time his wife gave birth to their first child, and remembered holding his daughter and feeding her the bottle while reading his textbook. He and the others went through the same exhaustive background investigation as their predecessors, then traveled the national lab circuit.

With the first year progress reports from Edison and the other companies in hand, the AEC's interest in nuclear generation began to grow. International events also exerted an influence. Britain had joined the Soviet Union and the United States as members of the nuclear club. Now more than just the big corporations such as General Electric and Westinghouse found themselves concerned that other countries, particularly the Soviet Union, would dominate the future nuclear power industry; AEC and national security officials publicly and privately warned that unless the United States got moving, power-starved nations of the third world would turn to the Soviets for nuclear technology. Furthermore, Dr. Alvin Weinberg, director of the Oak Ridge National Laboratory, argued that the development of a commercial nuclear power industry would greatly increase the overall economic strength of the country. His declaration came to the attention of the Joint Committee on Atomic Energy, which began extensive hearings on commercial nuclear power in late 1952. In early 1953, shortly after President Eisenhower took office, the National Security Council concurred with these arguments. A secret memo called for the quick development of nuclear energy as a means of maintaining American superiority in the total atomic field.

On July 1, 1953, Edison's Willis Gale added his voice to the chorus. Appearing before the Joint Committee, he declared that the country's leadership in nuclear power called for construction of a full-sized atomic power plant in the near future. Gale told the committee that after two years of research, Edison's study group had come up with three preliminary reactor designs, two of which appeared to have the best economic promise—one that would use natural uranium fuel with a heavy water coolant and another that would use slightly enriched uranium fuel with an ordinary water coolant. The first would have a net capacity of 211,500 kw, the second, 246,000 kw. He recommended the pursuit of more than one design.

Gale recommended that the first atomic plant or plants be full-sized power producers, not pilot versions, and should be built under a partnership between the government and private industry. He said industry could not afford to spend up to $100 million on a plant without any real knowledge of fuel costs. The Edison chairman listed several advantages to an early start of

254

construction. It would (1) help establish America's leadership in the nuclear power field to complement the nation's leadership in atomic weapons, (2) hasten the day when nuclear power would become competitive, (3) help the nation gain knowledge from the actual experience of operating a full-scale plant, (4) provide a standby facility for producing weapons-grade plutonium in the event of a national emergency, (5) provide a facility to produce fuel-grade plutonium for other reactors, and (6) contribute to the advancement of reactor technology in general, and in particular the use of atomic power to propel ships.

Atomic-powered ships already had a formidable advocate in Captain (later Admiral) Hyman Rickover, father of the nuclear Navy. In the late 1940s, Rickover spearheaded development of the atomic submarine. He enlisted Westinghouse to perform the bulk of the work, beginning with Navy contracts for reactor coolant systems and eventually an AEC contract to develop the reactor of the *Nautilus*, the world's first atomic-powered submarine, launched in 1953. Its skipper, Captain (later Admiral) Eugene Wilkinson, would become a member of Commonwealth Edison's Board of Directors in 1984. While work progressed on the *Nautilus*, Rickover had another brainstorm: development of nuclear-powered aircraft carriers. He sold the idea to the Joint Chiefs of Staff, who made the program a military requirement. Rickover proposed to use the light water reactor and Westinghouse, as he had in the submarine program.

After AEC Chairman Lewis Strauss, whom Eisenhower had selected early in his administration to succeed Lilienthal, became acquainted with Rickover's aircraft carrier proposal, he had a brainstorm of his own. With the decision of the President's National Security Council to push nuclear power uppermost in his mind, Strauss, and the AEC, decided to utilize Rickover's carrier reactor design for a commercial generating station. The same concept had already succeeded on a smaller scale in the submarine program, so the reliability of such a plant seemed certain. It was high time the United States showed its superiority in commercial nuclear energy to the rest of the world, Strauss and the AEC determined. The Joint Committee agreed. Strauss, himself a retired admiral and Wall Street financier, provided the memorable quote that nuclear power would be "too cheap to meter." Though the public has forgotten Strauss, the quote has lived on, used by latter-day critics of the nuclear industry in an effort to show that the advantages of nuclear energy had been oversold in the early days. They never identify Strauss as the source, for they wish to imply, erroneously, the private utility industry's responsibility for the statement.

At Strauss' behest, the AEC chose Westinghouse as the prime contractor and Rickover as government manager of this country's first civilian nuclear reactor. Shortly afterward, the AEC designated the Duquesne Light Company of Pittsburgh as the plant's operators and Shippingport, Pennsylvania, as the construction site. In September 1954, President Eisenhower himself signaled from a televised ceremony at the White House for construction to begin.

The 72,000-kilowatt Shippingport plant was basically a landlocked version of Rickover's aircraft carrier, minus the ship and the planes. The core of the reactor and its other features mirrored the essential nuclear submarine propulsion system on a larger scale. But if anyone thought of Shippingport as a potential learning experience or building block for the rest of the commercial nuclear industry, reality proved him wrong.

"Shippingport was built by Navy people under Navy rules," explained Dr. A. David Rossin, Edison's Director of Research in the late 1970s. "The steam that came out of the pipe was sold to the utility to generate power. Duquesne Light had no real role in the plant; they were just a purchaser of steam. I think the Navy was really interested in showing that this technology in which they had taken the lead had real applications for the future. That was Rickover's dream, but they had no intention of letting anybody else get involved with that project. With the exception of Westinghouse, the rest of the nuclear industry had no access to the design features.

"Westinghouse used its Navy experience to design a pressurized water reactor nuclear plant, but they wanted to do some things differently. First of all, they didn't want to use the highly enriched uranium that the Navy reactors used because that was classified material, the type of stuff that would never be free from government control because it was in the weapons range. They knew that on a ship you had to minimize weight. Commercial plant weight was unimportant, so you could do things more efficiently by allowing more size—bigger buildings, bigger pieces of equipment. That made it possible to use very low enriched uranium, something more economical. So they tried for the lowest cost fuel cycle. They also recognized that big plants would have to have a containment building around them. A submarine, of course, was a different story. So that was the kind of design Westinghouse went to work on.

"There was a lot of information in the Navy program that probably would have been very valuable commercially that the industry had to reinvent. The Navy always felt that if you released enough information about technology, inevitably some of the critical design features would get out, and they felt they couldn't afford that. The Navy was successful because it kept out of the public debate. They didn't want any part of it. Otherwise, they feared they would have people questioning whether we needed submarines or not."

On the same day in July 1953 that Willis Gale testified before the Joint Committee on Atomic Energy, an even more important milestone in Edison's progression toward nuclear-generated electricity took place. Edison and four other companies formed a Nuclear Power Group (NPG) to study the AEC's power reactor program and report back to the member companies with recommendations for private participation. The informal group merged before any of the companies had any clue about what was the best type of reactor and before any of them had any immediate plans of building a nuclear power plant of their own. Sixty employes of the companies, including 22 from Commonwealth Edison, undertook five major design studies on a full-time basis. On Oct. 27, 1953, NPG signed a formal contract with the AEC under The Five Company Agreement. The other four companies were American Electric Power, Bechtel, Pacific Gas and Electric, and Union Electric. Illinois Power, Central Illinois Light, and Kansas City Power and Light joined the group in June 1955. Gale sat on the original executive committee; Edison's Titus LeClair served as secretary.

A number of people assigned to the group took graduate level courses in nuclear engineering. The first Edison employe to attend the government's Oak Ridge reactor technology program, Norm Wandke, spent a year at the Tennessee installation in 1954–55. "It was a nine-month, graduate level, academic program, followed by a three-month project," Wandke recalled. "It was just like going to college." However, he was excused from the project because he had already been working on nuclear conceptual designs for several years, and assigned instead to the operations department of Oak Ridge National Laboratory, which at the time had the highest density of reactors in the world. Wandke most vividly recalls a tour of what the government called its Y-12 project, of World War II vintage.

"They separated the Uranium-235 isotope using electromagnetic separation, somewhat like a beaver sticking his tail in one pond and wringing it out in another. They used these magnets with dozens of vacuum chambers that could be rolled in place. The chambers were small, maybe half the size of a telephone booth. A tiny speck of uranium was placed on a little carbon block, placed in the chamber which was hooked up to the vacuum line, put into the magnetic field, and controlled for a number of hours by an operator who was in a control room the size of a phone booth. He didn't necessarily know what he was doing; he just kept some gauges within limits. After the hours had gone by, this tiny fraction of a gram of uranium had been split spectroscopically into U-235 and U-238, placed on another carbon block, then that was subsequently processed to reclaim Uranium-235. It was a fantastic effort. That was one of the ways they prepared the fissionable material for the weapons program."

Just as Murray Joslin had admonished Bill Kiefer three years earlier, Wandke and his classmates went through their training at Oak Ridge with no assurance that Edison or any other company would build a nuclear generating station. Wandke and the others viewed nuclear power as an exciting new technology growing in national importance, but on the other hand shared the fear of the private sector that the government itself would build and operate the plants. Private industry feared that the AEC would use nuclear technology as a lever to spread government-owned power at the expense of investor-owned utilities. Industry wanted some assurance that the government would allow a private nuclear power industry to develop, but certain companies remained skeptical.

"Some companies participated in some of the projects kind of tongue-in-cheek," according to Wandke. "They didn't really think it would develop into anything. I saw that our company had a sincere interest in nuclear and sought its potential, but I know that at least one of our Nuclear Power Group partners had the view that it was transient. They wouldn't even commit one of their own people to work with us. They hired an engineer off the street and assigned him to a project. When the project ended, they dismissed him. Many years later that company did build its own nuclear plant."

While Wandke pursued his nuclear education at Oak Ridge, Cliff Zitek, a chemist and metallurgist, spent a year at the government's Idaho reservation, the site of an experimental boiling water reactor called BORAX I, under construction for the benefit of Dr. Zinn and his Argonne scientists, who needed a remote site. The experiments with BORAX I in the summer of 1954 particularly contributed to the development of nuclear energy because they dealt with safety. Argonne tried to learn all it could about controlling a boiling water reactor under emergency conditions. As a public relations aside, the scientists used power from the reactor to light the small town of Arco in southern Idaho for about an hour. It was the first use of nuclear-generated electricity in the private sector, predating Shippingport. The power line that fed the town lost so much voltage, however, that the illumination remained dim, and the scientists quickly terminated the experiment.

BORAX consisted of an open tank with a reactor core and control rods inside—"a boiling pot". In a nuclear reactor, the rods control the chain reaction by absorbing the neutrons which bombard and split the uranium atoms. Under normal circumstances, control rods are withdrawn slowly to initiate the reaction but can be inserted quickly, in case the reactor has to be shut down in an emergency. Engineers designed the control rods on BORAX, though, for fast *removal*—to deliberately cause fast surges of power. When that happened, the reactor shut itself down anyway, because the water would flash to steam—and neutrons require water to travel. Proof of that safety principle went a long way toward demonstrating the boiling water reactor as a viable power source and, in the jargon of the nuclear engineer, wouldn't "go super-critical" or "run away."

By the fall of 1954, the BORAX I team decided that they had obtained all possible experimental data. So as a grand finale, they decided to blow up the reactor. They wanted to see just how bad an accident they could create and check whether the results jibed with the expectations of the scientists. If they didn't, serious questions would arise concerning the safety of such a reactor.

Causing the accident was no easy matter. The control room sat in a trailer about a half mile from the one-megawatt reactor, with nothing but desert and tumbleweed in between. Monitors, placed in the surrounding area, could check the levels of radioactivity. The last person at the reactor before the experiment began, Zitek, placed foils between the fuel assemblies to determine the energy level produced. Since the reactor sat in an open vessel, the force of the blast would have a clear upward route and therefore would not produce any shrapnel.

"To blow it up, we had to eject one of the five control rods from the center of the core," Zitek described. "We found that we could force the center control rod out fast enough to give us the effect that we needed."

It took five tries before the experiment finally succeeded. The core melted, and extremely radioactive fuel blew high into the desert air. "All we could see was a big spout of water, like Old Faithful, and a couple of control rods which were blown out."

After the initial radioactivity subsided, Zitek and several of the others went into the reactor vessel to pick up the pieces. Most of the fragments had fallen to earth within a radius of just 200 feet. "The radioactivity level was not great enough to prevent us from looking for the damaged fuel assemblies and picking up the pieces," Zitek continued. Radiation monitors downwind showed negligible amounts of activity. They measured no meaningful fallout more than 500 feet away. Zitek was also able to retrieve the foils he had placed in the reactor. "I don't remember the energy output we measured, but it was a sizeable amount."

The results of the final BORAX I experiment were exactly as the scientists had predicted. Among other things, it proved that the fallout would not have escaped from a containment building with its steel-reinforced concrete walls. BORAX II, built on the same site, went into operation in the spring of 1955. This experimental reactor allowed the team to collect and analyze generated steam. Zitek performed a number of experiments. All of the data he obtained went, with the government's permission, to General Electric chemists in San Jose, California. BORAX II, their only source of information, vitally contributed to the development of what would become Edison's Dresden Unit I.

Zitek returned to the Chicago area in the summer of 1955 to work on the experimental boiling water reactor being built at Argonne under the direction of Doctors Zinn and Untermeyer, who had masterminded the BORAX units and the safety experiments in the desert. The success of these experiments made Edison decide to abandon consideration of the other designs and pursue the boiling water reactor (BWR) as the most promising model for a commercial nuclear generating station. The BWR also proved to be the most economical. The NPG members at regular weekly meetings in Chicago discussed each of the reactor designs. The final decision came down to the BWR and the pressurized water reactor (PWR) developed by Westinghouse and used by the Navy. In addition to the perceived safety and economic advantages, the BWR made the final cut because of its simple design. At this point, Westinghouse, primarily on the strength of its work for the Navy, recognizably outdistanced all other nuclear manufacturers. To say that General Electric greeted the NPG with open arms when the group proposed a joint study of a commercial nuclear generating station would be an understatement.

II

The technical breakthroughs at Argonne and in Idaho occurred against a backdrop of political breakthroughs. On Dec. 8, 1953 President Eisenhower delivered his historic Atoms for Peace address to the United Nations General Assembly. On that occasion, Eisenhower said: "I would be prepared to submit to the Congress of the United States, and with every expectation of approval, (a plan for international cooperation) that would:

"First, encourage worldwide investigation into the most efficient peacetime uses of fissionable material, and with the certainty that they (all nations) had all the material needed for the conduct of all experiments that were appropriate;

"Second, begin to diminish the potential destructive power of the world's atomic stockpiles;

"Third, allow all peoples of all nations to see that, in this enlightened age, the great powers of the earth, both of the East and of the West, are interested in human aspirations first, rather than in building the armaments of war;

"Fourth, open up a new channel for peaceful discussions, and initiate at least a new approach to the many difficult problems that must be solved in both private and public conversations, if the world is to shake off the inertia imposed by fear, and is to make positive progress toward peace.

"Against the dark background of the atomic bomb, the United States does not wish merely to present strength, but also the desire and the hope for peace."

International response to the President's proposals was overwhelmingly favorable, spawning discussions that led to the formation of the International Atomic Energy Agency (IAEA) in 1957. At home, the Atoms for Peace address brought about an even quicker result. In February 1954 Mr. Eisenhower submitted recommendations to Congress that would finally lift the restrictions imposed by the Atomic Energy Act of 1946 on the peaceful development of the atom. The President said his recommendations would enable "American atomic energy development, public and private, to play a full and effective part in leading mankind into a new era of progress and peace."

Congress agreed. It approved the Atomic Energy Act of 1954, and the President signed it into law on August 30 of that year. Among other things, the new law allowed corporations to build and own nuclear plants and equipment, conduct nuclear research, and use nuclear fuel. The government, however, retained control over the latter. The act also prohibited the government from building its own nuclear plants to generate electricity, allaying the fears of the investor-owned utilities.

To get the commercial power ball rolling, the AEC announced a Power Development Reactor Program in January 1955. The government offered to cooperate with private industry towards the development of prototype nuclear generating stations which would answer many of the questions that needed resolution before commercial nuclear power could move full speed ahead. The AEC would provide much of the money, receiving as a return continued American superiority in the development of commercial nuclear power, consistent with the objective set forth by the National Security Council two years earlier.

In this favorable climate, Edison submitted a proposal to the AEC on behalf of the Nuclear Power Group for the construction of a full-scale BWR nuclear power plant. The proposal, submitted on March 31, 1955, called for General Electric to build a 180,000-kilowatt plant owned by Commonwealth Edison. Bechtel would act as engineer/constructor for GE.

George Travers remembered the meeting in the Board Room on the 18th floor of the Edison Building* at which Edison's nuclear pioneers urged the company to move ahead.

"Murray Joslin and others made a pitch to Gale, Ward, Evers, Sedwick, and a number of vice presidents who were not involved in nuclear," Travers stated. "After an all-day presentation, Mr. Gale decided that he would then come to a decision. About a week or two later, the board met, and Gale made the presentation with help from Joslin. The board decided to support Mr. Gale's recommendation."

Gale required conditions that private funds entirely finance the plant. He also stipulated its economic parity with the latest coal-fired plant on the Edison system—at least within a few years. Ed Koncel, who had drafted the proposal the company made to the AEC, made an economic study based on Gale's dictate of competitiveness. He received help from a number of quarters, including other team members, Bechtel, Sargent & Lundy—and GE. According to Bill Kiefer, all of these companies worked together on detailed designs which paved the way for the best possible estimates at the time. Eventually, the GE people returned to their headquarters in Schenectady, New York. Koncel estimated that Edison could invest a maximum of $30 million in the plant.

"The group of companies (NPG) contacted General Electric again, although they had been working with (us on) these estimates all along," Kiefer noted. "We told them what we wanted to do, and that we wanted an estimate they would be willing to stand by if we gave them an order. A whole team of estimators from Schenectady showed up in our office late one

*Edison Building floors were renumbered during remodeling in the early 1950s, the 17th becoming the 18th floor. The Board Room did not change location.

263

afternoon and wanted to borrow one of our calculators to take over to the Palmer House and use it all night 'long to fine-tune their estimate. Their company wanted them to come back in the morning to make a solid deal. So we loaned them the machine, and—mysteriously—their detailed estimate was exactly the same as the one we had made!

"They were very anxious to get started with somebody and show that this sort of (BWR) technology was possible," Koncel added.

Formal contract negotiations with General Electric followed, some of the sessions lasting far into the night. The negotiators made it a practice to postpone dinner until they had cleared up all points under discussion. The Edison team joked that they won the negotiations because they were in better shape than their counterparts.

One of the final sticking points was who would pay for the electricity used at the construction site—Edison or GE. Edison resorted to a bit of a bluff to settle the dispute, according to Kiefer. One of Edison's negotiators made a seemingly innocuous telephone call from the meeting room as a signal to Gale. After an appropriate interval, Gale "just happened to drop in to see how the discussions were going." Ever so casually, he mentioned the construction site power issue. "Ralph Cordiner (GE president) and I settled that chickenshit in Texas last week!" Gale barked convincingly. GE paid for the electricity.

GE contracted to build the plant for $45 million on a fixed-price or "turnkey" basis. Edison would pay $30 million, members of the Nuclear Power Group $15 million. Cost of the land and other charges, however, brought the company's actual total to $36 million. In return for their investment, the other companies would gain technical information, experience, and training obtainable only from day-to-day participation in designing, building, and operating a full-scale power plant.

"We had cost figures that showed the plant would be slightly more expensive than a coal-fired plant, and we didn't like that," Ayers recalled. "General Electric took the position that we didn't know how to figure construction costs, and they would be willing to build the plant on a turnkey basis. So we said, 'Be our guests.' They took a pretty bad bath on that."

Edison Treasurer D. Robert Bower, who drew up the contracts, possessed such skill that insiders called the fine-tuning of a pact "Bowering." Nevertheless, as soon as Gale and Cordiner shook hands on the deal, each man instructed his people to find loopholes in the contract—GE to open them, Edison to close them. They found few, if any, and Edison President John Evers and Francis McCune, vice president and general manager of GE's Atomic Products division, signed the agreement on July 22, 1955. The AEC approved the pact two-and-one-half weeks later.

"Our philosophy was to build a plant that did not push the technology but one we could use to learn how such a plant would operate and one that would be extremely reliable," Ayers maintained. "We said we would build a Model-T."

The plant would stand on a 950-acre site near the confluence of the Kankakee and Des Plaines Rivers in Grundy County. It would take its name from the nearby Dresden locks on the historic Illinois and Michigan Canal. Senior Vice President Ray Maxson, who would head up the construction project, was primarily responsible for choosing the location. The Nuclear Power Group analyzed the site, checking population, water sources, wind conditions, seismic characteristics, and other criteria. The plain title of the group's report—NPG-126—belied its historical significance. The Dresden document was completed some 13 years before the government would require such environmental impact statements for nuclear power plants.

"There were never any concerns on the part of the residents near the site," according to Ed Koncel. "Our people were very aware of radiation and were desirous of being good neighbors."

The AEC issued a construction permit for Dresden on May 4, 1956—the same day it issued a similar permit to New York's Consolidated Edison for construction of its Indian Point PWR plant. By then, Commonwealth Edison had acquired the full 950 acres for Dresden and had made some test borings. Construction work would begin late the following spring.

Only one roadblock remained—insurance liability in the event of a major nuclear catastrophe. Appearing before the Joint Committee on Atomic Energy, Gale stated that the likelihood of such an incident was extremely remote, but should it occur, the potential damage might be extreme. For that reason, Gale said,

Congress had to solve the problem, not just for the sake of the electric utility industry, but for the country as a whole.

"Some of our leaders tell us that there is grave danger that other countries may forge ahead of us in the development of nuclear power," he testified. "We believe that private industry can help keep America in the forefront of this development. We are anxious and willing to do our part." And that meant passage of legislation to provide reactor operators with insurance against the possibility of atomic catastrophe. Such legislation failed to pass Congress in 1956, but Gale pledged that Edison would go ahead with Dresden without a single day's delay, confident that Congress would solve the problem in 1957. The lawmakers didn't disappoint him. Faced with the prospect of seeing commercial nuclear energy—and America's leadership in the field—die in birth, Congress passed the Price-Anderson Act of 1957 as an amendment to the Atomic Energy Act. The act limited corporate liability in case of a reactor accident to $60 million and total liability to $560 million. At the same time, the Act provided a guarantee that the federal government would review the need for compensation beyond that amount. The Price-Anderson Act balanced the benefits of public protection against a predictable level of financial exposure for the industry. Over the years nuclear utilities have opted to buy the maximum amount of liability insurance available. If damages from an accident exceeded that total, each licensed nuclear plant would be assessed up to a maximum amount, bringing the total coverage to the ceiling provided by Price-Anderson. Since the inception of the act, the public has received more than $30 million in claims from industry insurance pools, most of the payments stemming from the accident at Three Mile Island. The federal government has never paid out a penny in claims to the public.

With Price-Anderson on the books, Dresden steamed ahead at full speed. Major construction proceeded in early June 1957, following several months of ground clearance and excavation work. Ceremonies on June 12 marked the start of construction. About 400 dignitaries, some arriving by helicopter, others aboard a train from Chicago dubbed the "Dresden Special," gathered at the site to watch workers erect the first of 21 steel columns. The columns, 55 feet high and two feet in

266

diameter, would support the 190-foot steel sphere which would house the Dresden reactor and which would become famous in its own right as a symbol of Edison's pioneering efforts in nuclear energy. Chairman Gale, GE Vice President McCune, and Illinois Governor William Stratton jointly swung a huge wrench to fasten the base of the first column. Other VIPs included Congressman Carl Durham of North Carolina, chairman of the Joint Committee on Atomic Energy; Congressman Melvin Price of Illinois, committee member and co-author of the Price-Anderson Act; and the Most Reverend Martin McNamara, bishop of the Catholic Diocese of Joliet, whose invocation asked the Almighty to "help us realize that the knowledge of atomic energy is one more gift from Thy Fatherly love...Help us to more fully appreciate Thy wisdom which designed the atomic structure of the universe." Edison President John Evers served as master of ceremonies.

It was a festive day, with flags flying and the Edison Post drill unit performing. Large tents containing refreshment stands, luncheon facilities, and a model of the Dresden reactor surrounded the seating area on three sides. Wearing hard hats and relaxing on bulldozers and other equipment, some of the project's 600 construction workers watched the ceremonies from the sidelines. Many of them had also worked on the experimental boiling water reactor at Argonne, a condition not particularly unusual in an industry becoming more and more cross-pollinated.

As the Dresden construction work progressed, Edison's people maintained close liaison with the scientists working with the Argonne experimental reactor. Edison also obtained data from reactor research at GE's Vallecitos Atomic Laboratory near San Jose, as GE had once benefited from knowledge Zitek and company had gained from the BORAX experiments.

Norm Wandke, one of Edison's engineers who monitored the GE research efforts in California, explained Dr. Sam Untermeyer. "It was by virtue of Sam Untermeyer's influence that GE got involved in the boiling water reactor. They wanted a reactor concept different from Westinghouse. They didn't want to play follow the leader, so they picked the boiling water reactor. They used the technology Argonne was developing because of the important work Argonne had done with the (BORAX) test reactors in Idaho. GE wanted to have as much of this technology as possible in a proprietary fashion, so that's why they built the Vallecitos reactor."

The Vallecitos unit, only one-fortieth the size of Dresden, furnished steam for generating electricity to customers of Pacific Gas and Electric. PG&E installed the turbine-generator.

One week after the ceremonies that marked the start of major construction at Dresden, Edison sponsored a luncheon in Chicago attended by 1,200 persons to further commemorate the occasion. Vice President Morgan Murphy, who had made the construction of Dresden Station a political and public relations undertaking of the highest order, obtained all the mileage he could. AEC Chairman Lewis Strauss told the gathering that Chicago had good claim to the title of atomic capital of the world, commending the "bold vision and enterprise of Commonwealth Edison and its associated companies and their confidence in our atomic future." Chicago Mayor Richard Daley additionally declared that "it is fitting and proper that Chicago, where this great power was born, should continue to lead in development of nuclear energy." Later, Murphy would conduct an inspection tour of Dresden for a large delegation of Chicago aldermen.

By fall, the plant took shape. The turbine-generator building rose, and plates for the famed sphere—already the focal point of the site—were hoisted into place. The plates were welded in units of three on the ground, forming components that measured 30 by 30 feet and weighed 23 tons. The 3,500-ton sphere would be a "skin" for the reactor. Within the skin, an eight-foot concrete enclosure would shield the reactor.

The following spring Senior Vice President Maxson, who had run the Dresden project all along, became a senior consulting engineer for both Sargent & Lundy and Edison, heading up Sargent & Lundy's nuclear power section in a move that brought the two companies closer together.

As 1959 began the vanguard of engineers who would operate Dresden started arriving for permanent duty—16 members of an operating force that would total 95. Prior to this time, Edison's only direct involvement with the GE project had consisted of a four-man team consisting of Wandke, John Eilering,

Al Veras, and Joe Poer as leader. Eilering oversaw construction, Wandke and Veras nuclear details. Harlan Hoyt, a veteran of 22 years with the company, all of them in generating station work, became superintendent. Zitek, the only person in the company with reactor operating experience, became assistant superintendent.

"Harlan told me to just take care of the reactor and he would take care of running the station," Zitek related. "I was concerned that I didn't know much about electrical distribution, but Harlan said, 'We have an electrical operating engineer to worry about that.'"

George Redman would head the technical staff. Ben Stephenson was instrument engineer; John Hughes, radiation protection engineer; Warren Kiedaisch, chemical engineer; Frank Palmer, thermal engineer; and Jack Bitel, Al Veras, and Norm Wandke, nuclear engineers. The shift engineers were Charlie Mago, Joe DeLeo, Howard Gann, Bill Barthelmes, and Nick Kershaw.

"It was a learning process for everyone involved," Kershaw remembered. The training for actual plant operations took place at Argonne, Vallecitos, and Hanford, according to Kershaw, with the first reactor operator licenses issued at Vallecitos. GE conducted additional training programs, as did Edison. Training continued at the plant as the staff familiarized themselves with the various systems and participated in preoperational equipment testing.

"There were courses in health physics for people who were going into that," Kershaw stated. "The people who were in chemistry had chemistry training, operators had operator training, so that they were all very well trained."

Well enough?

"You look back upon all the people who were involved, whether they were bargaining group or management people, and you see that they have progressed very well within the Edison Company, not only in the nuclear field, but in other areas as well."

When Kershaw, Zitek, and the others came aboard in January 1959, they found a plant about 70 percent complete. About one-third of the 488 nuclear fuel assemblies sat on-site, awaiting initial reactor loading. The reactor itself arrived on

March 11, after completing a 3,600-mile trip by water that took 24 days. Built by New York Shipbuilding Corporation at Camden, New Jersey, for GE, the reactor rested on a barge for its long journey down the Atlantic coast, through the Gulf of Mexico, and up the Mississippi and Illinois Rivers to the site. After it reached the plant's loading dock on the Illinois, workers rolled it one-third of a mile along a roadway to the sphere.

Dresden achieved its first nuclear chain reaction on October 15, a milestone followed by several months of further reactor testing. Electricity first flowed into the Edison system on April 15, 1960. Although Edison did not ballyhoo this achievement, saving the fireworks for the official dedication ceremonies, the announcement of the first nuclear-generated electricity received heavy media coverage around the country. "History Is Made In Chicago," proclaimed the banner headline in the Chicago *Daily News*. A subhead stated, "First Power from Atom Lights Homes." It ran above large photos of the plant exterior and the turbine-generator. The main Dresden story in the *News* carried the lead, "Atomic power may be lighting your home or office today," and further down, readers found reassurance, "The electricity is the same kind as usual, despite its source." The paper even ran a sidebar, by its science editor, to further calm any unwarranted jitters. "Nuclear Electricity Won't 'Atomize' You," the headline declared, with a subhead adding, "It's the Same Old Stuff Produced in a New Way." The story began by recounting a call to the paper by a "nervous mother," asking whether nuclear-generated electricity would atomize her house. "You won't know atomic energized electricity from any other kind," the science writer asserted. "It won't change the color of your lights or make the television set work any differently." The concern by some members of the public recalls the early days of electricity itself, with those who feared that electricity "leaking" from the sockets could cause harm.

Four days later, Dresden reached half power, but not without some bugs along the way, according to Wandke.

"The thing that really impressed me were the tremendous resources that GE brought to bear on any problem. I remember we had a vibration problem with the downcomers to the steam drum (long, slender tubes that recirculate a combination of steam and water). These large pipes were tending to

270

swing. Once we knew we had the problem, it was just a matter of a day or two when large shipping boxes with test equipment began to arrive from all over the world. Specialists came to the site, worked on it for awhile, and had the problem solved. GE spared no resources in getting that plant up and operating properly. I believe the first load of fuel had to be sent back to San Jose twice to be reworked for some deficiencies, but the problems were overcome."

Dresden Unit 1, the world's first privately financed commercial nuclear reactor, was dedicated on October 12, 1960.

The station reached full power, 180,000 kw, on June 29. The following day, Gale received a congratulatory telegram from AEC Chairman John McCone, stating, "We believe the technical contribution of this plant, the largest of all nuclear power plants in the United States, will be of great importance to the achievement of economic and dependable nuclear power." The company placed Dresden in commercial service on August 1, four months ahead of schedule.

The company's pioneering efforts in nuclear power production, as well as its promotion of electric heating, brought

271

about additional recognition—the annual Edison Award, the electrical industry's highest honor, presented by the Edison Electric Institute. The citation hailed Dresden as "the country's first large reactor generating plant paid for by private enterprise—so soundly financed as to burden neither the customers nor the stockholders of the company, and for accomplishing the objective within the time and cost estimates. . ." A color cartoon of the period, on the front page of the *Chicago Tribune*, depicted a taxpayer surveying the new plant and asking a tradesman, "What did it cost me?" "Not a cent," was the reply.

Now came the biggest party of all—the dedication ceremonies—held, appropriately, on Columbus Day 1960. The mutual themes of Discovery or a New Age or New World were apparent, but none of the speakers belabored the point. In fact, the principal speaker, AEC Chairman McCone, spoke of military preparedness in the face of a fresh verbal threat by the Soviet Union. The day before, Soviet Premier Nikita Khrushchev had delivered an angry speech to the United Nations in which he boasted that his country was turning out missiles "like sausages." If the Soviets were actually doing that, McCone responded from the Dresden speakers platform, they must be violating a ban on nuclear weapons testing by conducting the tests underground. The AEC chief called Khrushchev's statement "a threat to all nations" and urged Americans to take up a renewed interest in their country's preparedness. Ability of the United States "to strike with devastating fury" had held the Soviets back in the past, McCone declared, but now this country needed to resume underground testing of the latest nuclear weapons. McCone's response came the same day that Khrushchev gained a footnote in history. In an encore to his speech the day before, he removed one of his shoes at the UN and angrily banged it on a table.

One cannot find what Gale, Ward or other electric utility executives on the platform thought about McCone's sabre rattling on this most illustrious day in the short history of peaceful nuclear energy. Although McCone apologized for using this "peaceful occasion" for his statements, his reply to Khrushchev upstaged or received at least equal billing with the dedication in news accounts that appeared around the world. He did, however, take time to convey President Eisenhower's personal congratulations and to praise Dresden as a tribute to the "boldness, courage, and foresight of American enterprise...a blueprint of the future." McCone also related that his Soviet counterpart, following a tour of the United States, had remarked that he wished he could take Dresden back with him.

Approximately 2,500 guests attended the ceremonies, including business, labor, and government leaders, as well as dignitaries from 14 foreign countries. A special 18-car train which carried many of the visitors from Chicago arrived nearly an hour late and delayed the start of the proceedings. Governor Stratton, in the final push of his campaign for a third term, arrived by helicopter. The copter also enabled Stratton to join Mayor Daley and other officials that day in dedicating the final leg of the oft-delayed east-west Congress Expressway (later the Eisenhower Expressway). The *Chicago Daily News* referred to the double dedication as "two spectacular feats of engineering." Helicopter or not, Stratton would lose to Daley's candidate for governor, Otto Kerner, by a half-million votes just three weeks later.

Highlighting the Dresden program, GE Chairman Cordiner presented to Willis Gale the original switch that had started Dresden's first chain reaction a year earlier. The switch had also started the first production of electricity and the first increase to full power. For his part, Gale praised GE, declaring that "if the Dresden project took courage on the part of Edison and its associates in the Nuclear Power Group, it took even more on the part of General Electric." J. Harris Ward also had kind words for GE: "Edison, which installed the first large steam turbine, has now, 57 years later, completed the nation's first full-scale, privately financed atomic power plant—and both were built by General Electric." Ward drew laughter from the assembly when he joked that it had been 56 years since the start of work on the Congress Expressway.

News accounts mentioned that a carnival atmosphere prevailed at the ceremonies. The tents, flags, and American Legion unit in evidence at the start of major construction work had reappeared. The seating area faced toward the sphere. "A bright sun shone over the aluminum colored dome and the red and white 300 foot chimney," the *Chicago American* reported. The sun also shone on the speakers platform, where Congressman Price held up a paper to shield his balding head. The reactor, which had already generated 180 million kwh of electricity, was shut during the dedication. Visitors could tour the plant and venture inside the sphere, but obviously not beyond the eight-foot thick concrete containment.

As the day wore on, the guests began to depart—McCone and congressional leaders to Washington, foreign dignitaries to their homelands, Governor Stratton off in his helicopter to the expressway dedication, various VIPs back to Chicago aboard the train (only 45 minutes late this time). Soon the plant had fallen back into the hands of the elite cadre chosen to operate it. How did they feel about all of the pomp and circumstance?

"We were there to do a job, and I don't think any of us were thinking of the glory of being the first ones," Assistant Superintendent Zitek mused. "We were all dedicated employes, and that was our job to operate the plant. I decided when I was on loan to the BORAX experiment that operating a nuclear power plant would be easier or as easy as operating a coal-fired plant. We certainly had a lot of distinguished visitors, but we just took it as a matter of course. After the visitors went home, it was just another job."

Twelve

Rearranging
The
Pieces

I

While the world watched with a mixture of curiosity and awe as Edison's nuclear program revolutionized power production, a simultaneous revolution—little noticed by outsiders but equally important to the company's future—radically transformed the way it did business. The St. Patrick's Day merger of 1953 marked the beginning of this second revolution whose objective was to unite two factions which often seem as mutually antagonistic as Cubs fans and Sox fans, smokers and non-smokers, motorists and pedestrians— namely, city dwellers and suburbanites. Needless to say, implementing the merger posed a major challenge, even for someone of Willis Gale's precise mind and organizational abilities. When one considers that Gale and his lieutenants rearranged the pieces against a backdrop that included the company's worst generating station accident, its first rate increase case, and a seemingly unquenchable demand for electric power, their accomplishment stands as one of the signal achievements of Commonwealth Edison Company.

The Chicago metropolitan area was not nearly as cohesive in 1953 as in 1986; the miles between city and suburbs were figuratively longer before the expressway system became everyman's main street, binding the two together and making an auto trip to The Loop, the museums, the ballparks, the zoos, and countless other places a matter of routine ease, traffic snarls notwithstanding. Before the expressways, getting into the city from the suburbs meant a ride on a commuter train or a stop-and-go car trip along arterial streets and, if the travelers lived farther out, on a state or county road as well. At the time of the merger, some people still referred to suburbs as country towns, and correctly so.

The 1950s saw massive population growth in the suburbs. Communities that numbered only a few thousand would balloon by five, ten, or more times over the succeeding decades. Some communities that would grow large didn't even exist in the early '50s. Acres upon acres of cornfields became subdivisions almost overnight. Shopping centers sprang up to serve their needs —and lure city shoppers who could get there easily on the expressways. Medium-sized industry began locating in the suburbs, often near the expressways, which now would carry reverse rush hour traffic, as city dwellers commuted by auto to their suburban jobs. The vicinity around O'Hare International Airport became a magnet for light manufacturing firms, in addition to modern office complexes and the inevitable hotels, motels, and restaurants. Though technically a part of the City of Chicago, O'Hare is an island, about one-quarter of which lies in DuPage County, surrounded by the northwest suburbs, linked to the city only by the Kennedy Expressway. At the time of the merger, Midway Airport, located in a residential neighborhood of the city's southwest side, was billed as the "World's Busiest." Chicagoans, if familiar with O'Hare, thought of it as a pasture. The advent of the commercial jetliner and its need for longer runways than Midway could provide changed the situation. Within less than a decade, O'Hare became the "World's Busiest Airport," and Midway a virtual ghost town, until its mini-revival years later.

In the 1950s the 41-story Prudential Building stood as Chicago's tallest, but the coming in 1962 of Marina City, the largest all-electric residential and commercial development to that time, followed by the John Hancock and Standard Oil Buildings, not to mention Sears Tower, not only dwarfed the older giant but stood as the most spectacular examples of a central district building boom that would radically change the Chicago skyline, with all but one or two of the dozens of structures all-electric. But while the skyscrapers rose and the suburban subdivisions multiplied, Chicago began to run out of space in which to build single family homes or small apartment buildings. Large, blighted areas, particularly on the South and West Sides, made way, with the help of the urban renewal wrecking ball, for block upon block of huge, squalid public housing projects. They provided homes for tens of thousands of members of Chicago's burgeoning Black population, its numbers growing during this period with the arrival of migrants from the South. The city's Hispanic population also began to increase substantially, while the number of white residents declined, many of them showing up in the suburban population explosion.

These, in brief, represent the trends at work in metropolitan Chicago as Edison began the task of integrating the two companies. Edison and Public Service each ran its own generating stations, as well as engineering, construction and customer service departments. Simply figuring out the right leadership positions presented a knotty problem. Strategists had to predict the individual animosities, the ruffled feathers, of people who felt that they deserved better treatment. Gale strove to minimize those feelings and accomplish the merger with peace and goodwill.

Gale and his architects admired the Public Service concept of divisionalization and decided to implement it throughout the newly merged organization. They also decided to drop Public Service Company's gas operation because it produced too little revenue in return for the manpower it required. But before the completion of these changes, a more pressing piece of business arose—the need to raise general rates for the first time in history.

On the surface, the financial picture looked all right. Sales of electricity and gas by the Edison system in 1952 had again reached new heights. Common share earnings had increased 32 cents a share from the 1951 figure of $1.93. Several factors had contributed to the increase: the introduction of bimonthly billing in August 1951, which saved an estimated $1.1 million in operating expenses in 1952; the wider availability of less costly boiler gas fuel; and the elimination of the federal tax on electricity. An increase in federal income taxes, though, offset some of the gains.

But these economies paled alongside the need to raise approximately $280 million through the sale of securities to help finance $500 million in construction over the next four years. Along with five generating units in various stages of construction, the company now planned to build a 191,000-kilowatt unit at State Line Station. The new unit, set for completion in 1955, would be the largest high pressure-type unit on the system and second in size only to a 208,000-kw unit at State Line. To carry out the construction program, Edison needed to improve the level of earnings in order to attract the required capital on favorable terms. That goal, the high command concluded, meant filing for the first general rate increase in the company's 66 years, following 26 electric rate reductions, the most recent in 1946.

The company filed with the Illinois Commerce Commission on June 25, 1953, for an annual increase of $16.4 million from electricity customers and $2.9 million for Public Service gas customers outside Chicago. Each increase would average about 6.5 percent. The typical residential customer, who used about 160 kwh a month, would see an increase in his or her bill of less than 50 cents a month.

"(W)e can no longer cope with prewar rates and postwar costs," Gale maintained. "Since 1940 our average pay per employe has more than doubled and so has the cost of coal, our principal fuel. In 1952 our tax bill totaled more than $66 million. (W)e earned but 4.82 percent on the money invested in our business by our bondholders and our stockholders."

To help put the case together, Edison retained a New York financial consultant named Marvin Chandler, a partner in the Wall Street firm of Reese and Chandler and widely experienced in utility ratemaking. Edison and Chandler couldn't have done much better. On Jan. 16, 1954, the ICC granted the total amount the company had requested, starting with meter readings on and after Feb. 1. The commission explained that public hearings, held over a four-month period, had conclusively proven the modesty of Edison's request in view of the continuous postwar rise in the cost of doing business. The ICC agreed that a 4.8 percent return would not attract enough new capital to complete a $1.1-billion postwar construction program. Furthermore, over half of the anticipated new revenue would go for taxes. The ICC also authorized Edison to include a fuel adjustment clause in electricity rates which would permit the company to raise or lower that component of a customer's bill as the cost of fuel fluctuated.

Gordon Corey gave J. Harris Ward much of the credit for carrying out the divisionalization of Commonwealth Edison.

According to Corey, Ward admired the General Motors and General Electric systems which had implemented autonomous divisions. He wanted Edison to follow the same procedure on a geographical basis and assigned an employe named Phillips Goodell to perform a year-long study to determine which components of the company should be decentralized and which should not. Tongue in cheek, Corey said, "Harris accused me of solving the matter by telling him the thing to do is centralize the stuff that should be centralized and decentralize the stuff that should be decentralized."

The company decided, for example, that financing, ratemaking, purchasing, and system planning run more efficiently on a central basis. In some cases, though, the company divided functions between the central office and the divisions. For instance, industrial relations remained a general office department while individual IR departments served each of the divisions. The division IR departments received the added responsibility of administering to the generating stations in their territory. In other regards the generating stations would operate independently of the divisions in which they were located. The divisions also retained local public relations responsibilities while corporate PR remained a general office function.

Public Service had already divided its territory into four operating divisions, with headquarters in Northbrook, Maywood, Joliet, and Dixon. Thirty-two districts, making up the divisions, contained 63 stores and 35 service offices. Now Edison created three new divisions within the city of Chicago. Each division would have its own vice president as well as a commercial, industrial relations, and operating manager. Because of their relatively small size, the city divisions did not have any districts. The project, according to Ayers, resulted in an operation that required fewer people, ran more efficiently, and provided means for monitoring work more closely.

"We began a system, in the divisions, of keeping score," Ayers recalled. "Each division had, in effect, a profit and loss statement. We introduced the idea of management by objective and having goals in every department, not only in the divisions, but in the general office departments as well.

"This whole shift in the corporate structure was carried out with a minimum of disruption. In a very short time, I think the managers and employes of the divisions felt that this was a better way to do business. We struggled over who ought to be in these various (new division) jobs, but by and large I think we chose well, because the divisions have functioned well."

John Eilering, former vice president of Chicago Central division, agreed up to a point. He found it personally rewarding to run one-seventh of a business as large as Commonwealth Edison, a section larger than many total corporations. On the other hand, Eilering stated, "you had a lot of traditionalists who couldn't grab the management by objective program because they had operated differently before. They just took the money and spent. Now, you had to set your goals and your budget, and if you didn't make it, you got called on the carpet to find out why."

Divisionalizing the city would also place the Edison employes who had contact with the public closer to the customers they served; in other words, it placed the company at the grass roots level instead of running it entirely from a downtown office.

"It seemed to us," Ayers explained, "that we were in a service business, and whether we are talking about a new arrival from the rural south or someone living on the Gold Coast, we ought to be an organization sensitive to their needs and desires."

Ward took charge of all commercial and sales activities of the Edison system, turning over his treasurer's hat to D. Robert Bower, the contract wizard, and all of his other previous responsibilities to nuclear dean Murray Joslin, who became a vice president. Shortly afterward, Ayers also became a vice president.

Chicago North, the first city division to centralize its operations, served all of the city north of North Avenue. Chicago South covered all of the city area south of 39th Street, with Chicago Central handling the territory between.

Chicago North established its headquarters in the Northern Service Building, an impressive red brick structure built in 1931 on the southwest corner of Addison Street and California Avenue. The building, constructed chiefly as a warehouse and garage, occupied the same tract of land as Northwest Station. Before Chicago North moved in, the first and second floors underwent extensive renovation to make space suitable for offices. The personnel, under the leadership of Guy Trulock, came from two other North Side offices as well as downtown. In addition to commercial offices, Chicago North headquarters, like the others, housed the Service and Meter, Transportation, Overhead, Meter Reading, and Stores departments. By the time everyone had gathered under one roof, the division had approximately 1,000 employes serving 400,000 customers.

Chicago North landmarks include Wrigley Field, home of the Cubs, Lincoln Park, and the Chicago Historical Society. Two others thrived then but have passed into history—the Riverview amusement park and the Edgewater Beach Hotel. The division boasts fashionable high-rise apartment buildings along Lake Shore Drive, single-family dwellings and small apartment buildings, small and medium industry, and the most diverse ethnic mix, not only in Edison's service territory, but possibly in the entire country. Primarily an Irish-German-Jewish-Scandinavian district in the 1950s, the area almost literally has become a United Nations, populated by almost every race and nationality.

Chicago Central and Chicago South headquarters found homes in identically designed new buildings on Polk Street, near Laramie Avenue, and at 76th Street and Lawndale Avenue, respectively. The buildings were constructed of brick and aluminum, and had large window areas. The main section of each headquarters offered 45,000 square feet of office space. A first-floor wing with additional offices added 30,000 square feet to each of the two-story structures.

The Chicago Central building became the reporting center for 750 employes under the leadership of Division Vice President Ralph Peterson. The smallest of Edison's seven divisions geographically, covering less than one-half of one percent of the company's total service territory, Chicago Central at its inception represented 21 percent of Edison's kwh sales. The Chicago Loop —world-class financial and shopping center, the home of city, county, state, and federal administrative offices, and the site of many of the major hotels that help make the city a major international convention capital—anchors the division on the east. Just outside the Loop stand the Art Institute of Chicago, Field Museum, Adler Planetarium, the Shedd Aquarium, Meigs Field, and the McCormick Place exposition center. To the north is the famed Magnificent Mile, the Michigan Avenue shopping promenade. To the west, one sees the University of Illinois-

Chicago Circle campus and the U. of I.-Cook County Hospital medical complex. Continuing west, public housing projects, single-family homes and small apartment buildings, and industrial plants. Many of these factories, including the mammoth International Harvester works at 26th Street and Western Avenue, have closed since the dawn of divisionalization.

In addition to a twin headquarters building, Chicago South had at least one other feature in common with Chicago Central: a small geographical area that returned big sales to the company. Covering only one percent of Edison's total service territory, Chicago South represented 22 percent of all kwh sales when it opened for business. Chicago South boasted the highest number of customers of any of the divisions. Its population of 1.5 million, living in 103 square miles, received service from an Edison work force of 903.

Fertile economic conditions greeted Division Vice President E. R. Lewis' new command. The shopping area around 63rd Street and Halsted Avenue ranked only behind State Street as Chicago's busiest. The Hyde Park redevelopment program had brought new housing, new streets, and other public improvements to the University of Chicago neighborhood, one of the few racially-integrated areas of the city. The old Stagg Field stands, where Enrico Fermi and his team of scientists first split the atom, made way for new developments at the University. The Lake Calumet area on the far South Side would become a world port with the completion of the St. Lawrence Seaway. Construction had begun on the Calumet Skyway and Dan Ryan Expressway. At the same time, Sandburg's "hog butcher to the world," the Union Stockyards, headed for the last roundup, later replaced by a modern industrial park. Another Chicago South landmark, the Museum of Science and Industry, reigned as the city's most popular tourist attraction until the Sears Tower Observation Deck deposed it.

Edison's Northern Division, stretching from the Chicago city limits to the Wisconsin state line, from Lake Michigan to beyond Crystal Lake, includes the affluent North Shore suburbs, other more modest subdivisions, the Waukegan-North Chicago industrial complex, and other large factories and farms, including the area where Sam Insull lived and conducted his historic Lake County Experiment. With headquarters in Northbrook, Northern Division had five districts—Crystal Lake, Evanston, Highland Park, Waukegan-Lake Villa, and Park Ridge-Barrington. Harold Otto served as the first division vice president.

Since 1945 the number of residential customers in Northern had increased by 109 percent, boosting division revenues by more than 274 percent. In the three years prior to the formation of Northern Division, an average of 15,000 new residential customers joined the Edison system annually, placing a strain on the engineering, construction, and customer service operations.

Elk Grove Village, just west of O'Hare Field, provided the most spectacular development of the period. Soon after its incorporation in the mid-1950s, 6,000 new homes began to rise. Northern Division worked with the village to install all of the electric distribution facilities underground. Not even a television antenna showed on the skyline, as each home had a built-in antenna in the attic.

"Formerly a relatively stable, even sedate area of better than average residential communities, Northern Division has been transformed in a few years to a bustling, booming expanse of development and change," the *Edison Service News* observed.

Western Division grew almost as rapidly as Northern, connecting an average of 13,700 new customers a year in the three years prior to divisionalization. In 1956, Western sold 185 million more kwh than Kansas City Power and Light. Stretching from the city limits to the far western suburbs and collar counties, the division covered 932 square miles and employed 1,150 people under the direction of Division Vice President Larry Pierron. Other Edison employes who worked within Western's boundaries, including Technical Center and substation personnel, brought the total to 2,200. The division originally had nine districts—Aurora, Cicero, Elgin, Elmhurst, LaGrange, Maywood, Oak Park, Summit, and Wheaton-Downers Grove. A new Glenbard district, later an Area, began in 1956 to meet the expanding needs of Glen Ellyn, Lombard, and surrounding communities, one of the fastest growing sections of the state. Comfortable suburbs, heavy industry at its eastern end and in the Fox River Valley, and the world-famous attractions of Brookfield Zoo and the Morton Arboretum all characterize the division.

Occupying an area about the size of Connecticut, or 35 percent of Edison's service territory, Southern Division plays host to large oil refineries, pipeline pumping facilities, steel fabricating companies, and glass container manufacturers, as well as some of the territory's richest farmland. The Sanitary and Ship Canal, a vital inland waterway running through the center of the division, helped bring in a profusion of new small industries at the time the new division became operational. Southern Division extends from the Chicago city limits through the Joliet-Lockport industrial corridor, to south of Pontiac and west of Streator. Covering an area of 3,750 square miles, Southern initially had six districts—Blue Island, Chicago Heights, Harvey, Joliet, Kankakee, and Streator-Pontiac. G. K. Hardacre served as the first Division Vice President. Southern can boast both Dresden Station and another "first" a quarter-century later—Illinois' first national park, the Illinois & Michigan Canal National Heritage Corridor. The Corridor now winds like a green ribbon through the most heavily industrialized sections of Southern Division, following the narrow man-made waterway the towboats traveled in the 1830s.

Illinois Northern Division, now known as Rock River Division, completed the new divisional arrangement as the largest in the territory, nearly 5,000 square miles or 45 percent of Edison's total area, and smallest in customer population, accounting for less than five percent of the company total. The *Service News* described Illinois Northern as "an area of rolling country, prosperous farms, scattered towns and thriving industry. The Rock River Valley and its Blackhawk Trail are abundant in Indian lore and historic landmarks." The division includes more than 1,200 acres of state parks.

Though small in number, the division's customers used a lot of electricity. The average use per residential and rural customer totaled more than 4,500 kwh a year, compared to the system average of 2,700 kwh a year. Illinois Northern supported a growing roster of industries which numbered more than 600 at the time of divisionalization, and included Northwestern Steel and Wire Company of Sterling, which would become Edison's largest customer.

In those days, Illinois Northern Division headquarters, commanded by Division Vice President L. B. Cappa, stood in Dixon with district outposts at Belvidere, Freeport, Sterling, and DeKalb. With a customer density of only 18 per square mile, the division's wide-open spaces posed operating and service problems. For example, customers contacted Edison through no fewer than 23 separate commercial telephone companies. Edison paid all charges for customer calls from outside the district headquarters town. To help cover an area more than 23 times larger than the three Chicago divisions combined, local representatives worked from 30 small towns. The service reps, at times the only company representatives in a 100 to 150 square mile area, performed many functions such as meter reading, bill collecting, switching, and line repairing.

Gale's decision to relinquish the gas business stemmed not just from the realization that gas revenues represented only 14 percent of Edison's revenues while taking up a far greater percentage of management's time. The move stemmed from the belief that the electric and gas business naturally competed and would do better if they operated as competitors. Some Edison employes, including those in advertising, public relations, and marketing, worked for both the gas and electric operations. According to George Travers, "They were involved in activities that were probably counter-productive to each other. It was like changing sides at halftime and rooting for the other side."

Gale considered yet another issue—long-term gas supplies. "Mr. Gale felt that down the line somewhere gas would become in short supply and very expensive, and like transit, put ink all over the face of a lot of utilities," Ayers observed. "He felt we ought to separate them, but we ought to do so by making the gas company a good, strong company financially."

Employes received a memo on Oct. 19, 1953, informing them of Edison's proposal to create a new corporation known as the Northern Illinois Gas Company, to own and operate the gas properties of Public Service. The memo reminded employes that Public Service's gas and electric businesses had operated separately, to as great an extent as possible, since the late 1930s. The new company would be the second largest gas utility in Illinois, after Peoples Gas. Commonwealth Edison would own all of its stock. Edison planned to separate the stock ownership of the new gas company, though, distributing the shares to Edison's common holders.

The ICC approved the spinoff on Jan. 19, 1954, and NIGCO (presently NI-Gas) officially began operating as an Edison subsidiary on Feb. 9. Corporate headquarters stood at 50 Fox St., Aurora, formerly the offices of Western United Gas and Electric. Initial capitalization consisted of $60 million in first mortgage bonds, $10 million of five percent convertible preferred stock, and $60 million of common stock. The 12 members of the NIGCO board of directors were all Edison directors with one exception—Executive Vice President E. E. Lundgren, who had directed gas operations for Public Service all along. Gale became chairman; Sedwick, president; and Freeman, chairman of the executive committee. Corey was elected vice president and comptroller; Ward and Ayers, vice presidents.

Eventually, the Edison people bowed out as NIGCO directors. Gale and Ward felt that someone with a strong financial background, but not necessarily someone with gas company experience, should head the new company. With the successful rate decision fresh in their minds, the Edison leaders turned to the star performer of the proceedings, Marvin Chandler. Ward and Corey traveled to New York to make the offer, and Chandler promptly accepted.

The final move separating the electric and gas businesses occurred in January 1955, when Edison's directors voted to distribute the company's five million shares of common stock in Northern Illinois Gas to Edison stockholders at a rate of three shares of NIGCO common stock for each ten shares of Edison. Directors also approved the private sale of the company's entire holdings of 100,000 shares of five percent convertible preferred stock of NIGCO to a limited number of institutional investors for $165 a share.

In the checkerboard manner in which some electric utility service territories evolved over the years, Central Illinois Light Company served the DeKalb-Sycamore area, an island located virtually in the center of Edison's service territory, while Edison provided service to the separate areas of Aledo and Lacon, at the extreme southwestern end of its territory, not far from CIL (later CILCO) headquarters in Peoria. Following the spinoff of the gas company, Gale next wanted to swap Aledo and Lacon for DeKalb-Sycamore. Both Edison and CIL agreed the swap would bring the respective territories closer to the power supply of each company and would result in shorter transmission feeds and better, more economical service. They made an even trade of properties with almost identical annual revenues of about $2.1 million. The Edison areas going to CIL comprised more than 1,200 square miles, 44,000 residents, 16,000 electricity customers, and 21 incorporated communities. In return, Edison obtained an area of about 400 square miles, 29,000 residents, 10,000 electricity users, and six communities. Employes working in each of the areas could either stay with their present utility or work for the acquiring company.

According to Corey, one of Edison's principal negotiators, "The beautiful thing about the trade was that our rates surrounding DeKalb and Sycamore were lower than Central Illinois Light's rates, and the Peoria area adjoining (our properties) was lower than ours. So the customers benefited in both instances. What we did was carve out enough territory from our Southern Division so that the revenues were approximately equal." The trade became effective on Jan. 1, 1956, following approval by the Illinois Commerce Commission.

II

Maintaining the proper amount of reserve generating capacity presents an ongoing challenge to any electric utility. A sudden surge in customer demand, the breakdown of a major unit, or both can quickly erase a comfortable cushion, as Edison has painfully learned over the years. Each of these factors created some close calls in the mid-1950s.

In late summer 1953 the company for the first time felt the impact of the gradually increasing air conditioning load. A long siege of hot, humid weather, resulting in heavy air conditioning use, produced unprecedented loads for that time of year. In fact, the summer peak of 2,903,000 megawatts (mw) on September 1 nearly equaled the peak load of the previous winter, 3,012,000 mw—a remarkable circumstance at that point in Edison's history. By that late in the summer, the company had taken a large amount of generating equipment out of service for scheduled overhaul, and the system could barely carry the load on several days. Kilowatthour sales for 1953 increased a healthy 9.1 percent over the previous year.

As usual, new capacity was about to come on line, but always, it seemed, one lap behind the latest close call in meeting demand. Only days after the unusual late summer heat wave, a new 60,000-kilowatt unit went into service at Dixon Station. The unit, which took about three years to engineer and construct, increased capacity of the coal-fired station from 65,500 to 125,500 kw.

Fisk Station, meanwhile, didn't add any new capacity but marked its 50th anniversary on the Edison system. The company gave a luncheon for 1,200 business and civic leaders at a down-town hotel and the following day held an open house at the station for employes and annuitants. Retired Vice President Alex Bailey, assisted by Vern Stone and Ray Maxson, unveiled a bronze tablet commemorating the "courage and vision which revolutionized the production of electric power."

A little more than a year after the late summer heat blast pushed Edison to the wall, another vagary of the weather created far greater havoc. Historically, flooding usually has not aggra-vated the Chicago area much. What's more, about the least likely time for a flood is October, one of the driest months. The Great Fire itself occurred in October, during a prolonged drought. All the more ironic, then, that throughout the night of Oct. 9, 1954, during the 83rd anniversary of the three-day inferno, one of the heaviest downpours in local history drenched the city. By Sun-day the 10th more than six inches of rain had fallen. The Chicago River overflowed its banks, and water poured into Fisk and Crawford Stations, not to mention thousands of homes. Edison crews piled sandbags at strategic spots, but to little avail. Water engulfed about 300 motors which operated auxiliary equipment such as boiler feed pumps, circulating water pumps, and fans, along with auxiliary switchboards, control circuits, and a variety of electrical devices. Fish swam in the turbine building at Crawford. The turbines themselves, together with generators and boilers at the two stations, escaped damage because they sat on the upper levels.

By late Sunday evening both stations stopped operating, reducing the system's capacity by about 25 percent, or 800,000 kw. Another 200,000 kw of capacity was out of service for routine overhaul and maintenance, typically performed in the fall because of lower demand associated with moderate temperatures. Edison issued a call for help. The company purchased power from five neighboring utilities and asked its large industrial customers to reduce their use of electricity by 50 percent. More than 100 employes in all divisions telephoned the customers, who graciously complied. At the same time, station workers, with help from the Chicago Fire Department, began to pump out the plants. Floodwaters in the basement of Fisk had risen to 30 feet. By Tuesday morning, workers had removed all water—hundreds of millions of gallons—from the two plants. The company then had to haul 250,000 gallons of uncontaminated water to Fisk from Ridgeland by tank truck for use as boiler feedwater, the efficiency of which depends on its purity. Meanwhile, hip-booted workmen began removing the recently-submerged motors, first cleaning them, then loading them onto trucks that would haul them to ovens for drying. Crews worked around the clock. The Central Service Building restaurant shipped 2,000 sandwiches, 4,000 cups of coffee, and 250 dozen rolls daily to the station hands.

The first two units came back Monday night. As others began to run again, the industrial customers could increase their use to 75 percent. Edison lifted all restrictions by 6 p.m. Thursday; by Saturday morning, all units were back in service.

"Anyone who saw the vast amount of equipment underwater still wonders how it was possible to get it cleaned up and back in operation in so short a time," Gale said in a written statement to employes. "The emergency is over, but the memory of an amazing accomplishment will linger."

Fortunately, only minor casualties occurred at Fisk and Crawford. However, an emergency at Ridgeland two months later caused far greater destruction. People present the night of Dec. 19, 1954, and early the following morning remember minute details, the way people remember exactly what they were doing the day of President Kennedy's assassination.

Vern Stone, in charge of all of Edison's generating stations, remembered that it was Sunday. He had gone downtown to the office to do some paperwork and planned to stop at Ridgeland on the way back home to watch the crew bring Unit 4 back on line after weekend maintenance work on its boiler. His wife had offered to pack a lunch, but he wasn't hungry. However, after working at his desk for awhile, Stone did get hungry.

"I went out to a little greasy spoon on Van Buren Street and had a tuna fish salad sandwich, a piece of cherry pie, and a cup of coffee. I went back to the office, and as the afternoon wore on, I felt worse by the hour. When I left the office, it was with the intent of going to Ridgeland. I drove out Ogden Avenue, but when I got to Ridgeland Avenue to go over to the plant, I felt so sick that I went home. I decided that the fellas didn't need me, and all I was going to be was a bystander. I was in the bathroom, getting rid of the sandwich and the rest, when the call came through about the Ridgeland disaster."

"It wasn't pandemonium, but there was confusion because nobody knew what had occurred," according to Nick Kershaw, who worked as an assistant shift engineer that night. "There was a loud noise, a lot of black and gray smoke, and two people were dead."

On December 19, 1954, the company suffered a major disaster: An explosion shattered Ridgeland Station Unit 4, killing two Edison employes and injuring six others.

The worst generating station accident in Edison history had occurred. At 11:19 p.m. the newest of the four 160,000-kilowatt turbogenerators at Ridgeland, the largest power plant in the Midwest, was ripped apart by an explosion that sent chunks of metal flying about the turbine room and through the roof. Flying debris killed two employes instantly. The victims, 34-year-old George Thorsen and 36-year-old Clarence Jorgensen, like Kershaw, were assistant shift engineers. Six other workers suffered injuries or shock. Workers had to shut down the other three units, damaged by the explosion, leaving Edison without its

290

largest single source of power for Christmas week, then the traditional period of annual peak demand.

The projectiles that caused much of the damage came from the 40-ton turbine spindle. One piece tore through one part of the turbine room roof and returned through another, shearing a large pipe off the condenser on Unit 1. Another chunk flew through the roof and buried itself in the coal pile outside the plant. Still another fragment that weighed some 200 pounds pierced the roof and sailed an estimated three-quarters of a mile into the air, imbedding itself in a residential street a half-mile from the station and barely missing the houses.

"The roof was kind of messy," Kershaw remembers. "You could see the great outdoors through it."

"That was a gruesome sight when I went in there that night," Stone recalled. "I knew the fathers of both of the men who were killed. I had encouraged them to go to school, and they did. They both graduated. Good students. Fine boys. It was just sickening."

Normally, Thorsen's and Jorgensen's shift would have gone off duty at 11. It was standard procedure for a shift synchronizing a unit to the system to turn it over to the shift coming on duty if they hadn't completed the job. However, the 3-to-11 shift boss, Bill Nicholl, had decided to keep his management team on the job past quitting time to clear up a problem with a mechanical vacuum trip, an automatic emergency shutoff device. In addition, since Jorgensen was performing the startup tests for the first time, Nicholl wanted to make certain he understood the process.

The unit had a low pressure and high pressure turbine. Bill Griesshammer, positioned at the throttle and stop valves at the head of the machine, controlled the unit. Nicholl stood between Griesshammer and Jorgensen, shoulder-to-shoulder, while Thorsen leaned on the low pressure turbine casing, reading instruments and relaying signals to verify the test results. Another station hand, Carl Stone, and a representative of Allis-Chalmers, manufacturer of the unit, also stood in the vicinity. Edison's non-management people who were working the job had knocked off at 11, adjourning to a nearby restaurant to celebrate Joe DeLeo's promotion from senior control operator to assistant shift engineer. So fortunately, they could return quickly to the plant to help restore order.

Griesshammer was to roll the turbines, synchronize the speed, then turn the unit over to the control room. He had finished testing the high pressure turbine and was bringing the low up to the appointed speed when "the low pressure turbine shell just plain exploded," according to Nicholl. "The whole thing went up through the ceiling," leaving a glowing blue-green hydrogen trail rising from the unit in the wake of the projectiles. The main force of the blast tore through the sides of the machine, taking out Thorsen and Jorgensen. Nicholl suffered a broken foot and little pieces of shrapnel embedded in his stomach and both legs.

"I was down at the vacuum trip, on top of the oil tank, with Barney Duggan, one of the other units' shift engineers, trying to figure out what the problem was," Kershaw recalled. "We were about 50 to 75 feet from where the rotor came apart, so the noise was quite heavy down there. We were shielded by the concrete foundation which was between us and the rupturing cylinder."

Before long, Kershaw was joined by Griesshammer, who had broken his leg.

"I wouldn't believe a man could walk down stairs with a broken leg, but he did," Kershaw stated. "He must have come down five or six stories to the basement, all the way from the operating floor, which was quite a way. It was unbelievable. I don't remember him ever saying anything to me except that his leg bothered him. There were two of us—I don't remember who the other fellow was—who took him into a room in the basement and laid him on the floor until we got somebody to take care of him and take him to the hospital. He really got racked up, but he lived through the whole thing."

Kershaw then joined Nicholl and others in making sure that all of the hydrogen was out of the generators. Nicholl found that he could hobble about if he kept his weight on the heel of his broken foot. The projectiles going through the roof provided both a boon and a potential bane; the holes constituted additional vents for the highly flammable hydrogen, but they also weakened the roof to the point of collapse, endangering those who remained behind to shut down the plant.

"The people in the control room did a very good job of shutting down the remainder of the equipment and putting it in safe condition so no more people got injured," Kershaw added.

According to Nicholl, the first report of the tragedy to the police came from an off-duty officer who was in the same restaurant as Joe DeLeo and the others. Nicholl believed the policeman overstated the seriousness because officers "from about 20 suburbs showed up," and some 30 ambulances lined Ridgeland's driveway, from the security gate to the plant entrance. The hospital was more than prepared, too, he remembered. About 10 or 12 doctors stood ready to treat two injury victims— Nicholl and Griesshammer.

Toward the end of a five-day hospital stay, Nicholl "was just beginning to realize the accident wasn't my fault. I must have reviewed everything we did that night 100 times. I was having my doubts until then. A nurse used to bring me coffee and rolls at two o'clock in the morning, when she and the others took a break, because she knew I would be awake."

Nicholl had another visitor as he neared the end of his confinement. "He looked kind of familiar, but I couldn't place him," he remembered. When the man appeared at the door of the hospital room, Nicholl was on the telephone with Cy Gorder, assistant chief engineer at Ridgeland, who warned that some type of investigator was on the way to interview him. Nicholl told Gorder someone was at his door already.

"Who is it, friend or jerk?" Gorder asked.

"The latter," Nicholl replied.

Gorder hung up. The man entered and said, "Mr. Nicholl, I'm awfully sorry to hear about your injury and for the loss of life at Ridgeland."

"Who are you?" Nicholl asked.

"I'm Gale."

"You work for the company?"

"Yes, I do.

"Where?"

"Well, I'm the chairman."

Nicholl started to laugh, and Gale asked why.

"I just called you a jerk."

"Maybe you have something," Gale replied.

The morning after the explosion—Monday—Edison again had to ask its large industrial users to reduce their power and consumption—this time by 25 percent. By noon, the company appealed to residential and commercial customers to voluntarily curtail their use of Christmas and store lighting. Edison met Monday's load, according to one news report, "by the skin of (its) teeth." By the time another 24 hours had passed, the all-out effort of repair crews, working around the clock, had resolved the crisis. Thursday evening, Edison lifted all restrictions on use, following restoration of two of the Ridgeland units. A third came back the following morning, about the time Nicholl got out of the hospital. A new Unit 4, paid for by Allis-Chalmers, did not function until November 1955, nearly one year after the accident. The investigation dislcosed that the 83-inch long rotor had a flaw in the forging which caused it to fly apart at high speed. Why were there no personal injury suits?

"The atmosphere was different then," Nicholl explained. "This was another world. We were company men; the loyalty was just unbelievable. We just accepted it."

Edison provided financial assistance to the Thorsen and Jorgensen families, and Mrs. Jorgensen obtained a job with the company.

As soon as he got out of the hospital, Nicholl, on crutches, went to visit Thorsen's widow and parents. He was shocked at what he encountered.

"They put me through a grilling, through the wringer, especially the parents," Nicholl recalled. Thorsen's father, Sam, was a retired Edison employe. "They weren't hostile; they were just groping for an answer. They thought sabotage might have been involved, that some sinister force had sabotaged the unit. They didn't single out anyone or anything.

"After I left, I was shaking so badly that I had to park the car for half an hour. I had planned to visit Mrs. Jorgensen afterwards, but I had to cancel because I was shaking so much. She wasn't happy that I broke the appointment. Eventually, I did visit, and there was no animosity."

A blue ribbon coroner's jury, convened shortly after Nicholl was released from the hospital, explored the possibility of sabotage but found that the tragedy had indeed been an accident. Nicholl felt that the explanation of the thorough testing procedures which he and the others followed as a matter of routine greatly impressed the jury.

Months later, under a bright blue October sky, some two dozen Ridgeland employes, with brushes, buckets and ladders in hand, visited the home of Mrs. Thorsen in Evergreen Park during their off-duty hours and gave it and the garage a fresh coat of paint. Along with Mrs. Thorsen, supervisors included her young son, Georgie, and his grandfather, Sam. One of the painters was Bill Nicholl. The following spring, the group built a garage at Mrs. Jorgensen's Northwest Side home, painted it, and put in a concrete driveway.

"I never met a group of guys like the Ridgeland startup group," Nicholl declared. "They were the cream of the crop on the Edison system."

Edison could have used every kilowatt of Ridgeland Unit 4 during the sweltering August of 1955. For the first time ever, the summer peak load exceeded that of the previous winter —not once but on three sultry days. Again the growing use of air conditioning, combined with healthy business and industrial performance, contributed greatly. The purchase of power from other utilities alone eased the capacity squeeze.

The record summer loads caused Edison to re-examine plans for future capacity additions and take a look at how heat-related loads affected the operation and maintenance of existing equipment. The company's operating people found that as heat waves created a rise in demand, they also reduced the ability to meet it. For example, warmer condensing water reduced the load-carrying ability of turbine-generators by as much as five percent. On the transmission and distribution side, the load-carrying performance of transformers, switches, cables, and other conductors is determined by maximum temperatures at which they can be operated safely. To prepare for future summers, Edison scheduled the overhaul of generating equipment throughout the year, with the bulk of work done in the spring and fall. The company also speeded up construction of transmission and distribution facilities, and looked ahead to the addition of a new 207,000-kilowatt unit at State Line which would go into service that November. A pair of 160,000-kilowatt units at Will County had gone on line in March and July, just in time for the late summer crunch. The soaring demand of August '55 caught Edison by surprise, as illustrated by a comment from John Evers, who wrote at midsummer that the new State Line and Will County additions, plus the return of Ridgeland Unit 4, "should give the Commonwealth Edison ... system a comfortable reserve for next winter." Even though his vision would soon be diverted to more immediate demands, Evers made another absolutely correct observation: "(T)he demand for electricity continues to grow seemingly without limit." After years of peak fluctuating between winter and summer, Edison had to adapt to summer peak loads, the norm from 1964 onward, to keep pace with change.

III

The summer of '55 also witnessed the arrival of the Computer Age. An IBM computer system, nicknamed an "electronic brain," found a home on the fourth floor of the Edison Building. The first of its kind in Chicago, the computer was also the first put into service by a public utility anywhere in the country. The *Edison Service News*, successor to *The Edison Round Table* following the merger, noted that, "The brain can read at the rate of a full-length novel in six seconds—and not miss a single letter in any word. It can multiply faster than a person could write down the figures involved." Initially, the 20-ton, 35-unit system served by computing and printing electricity bills at a rate of 40,000 each working day, enabling bills to be mailed two days after meter readings instead of the five days previously required. Later, the company obtained the 305 *RAMAC* (Random Access Method of Accounting and Control), which speeded billing for commercial and industrial accounts.

Edison also changed its marketing approach as a different type of "bill" debuted in 1955—Little Bill, the cartoon bird who would be Edison's spokesman for the next 15 years. Bill became a familiar figure on television, billboards and car cards, as well as in print ads: "a likable little fellow who is built like a light bulb and talks like a parakeet with a college education," according to the *Service News*. He proclaimed that electricity cost a lot less than it did 25 years past, delivering high value benefits, while the cost of just about everything else had risen. "I'm Little Bill. I work for pennies a day the electric way," one

296

billboard message proclaimed. Bill, whose call was, "cheap, cheap," came out of the newly retained Leo Burnett advertising agency working with Edison's Advertising department. After Little Bill had worked for less than a year, the Advertising department conducted a survey to see how the public accepted him. A total of 78 percent leaned favorably toward Bill, with only seven percent unfavorable and the rest having no opinion. A typical quote from the survey said, "His name, Little Bill, means that he keeps your electric bills little. It doesn't cost much to use lots of electricity."

"Cheap, cheap, Little Bill," Commonwealth Edison's symbol from 1955-1970.

In another campaign—not promoted by Little Bill— Edison made a million-dollar effort to encourage the use of modern 240-volt service in older homes. The program offered a three-wire, 240-volt wiring installation at a reduced price to customers who agreed to install a 240-volt appliance and a 100-ampere main switch. In most instances, customers realized savings of $35 or more as a result of the company sharing the wiring installation costs. The program succeeded through cooperation with electrical contractors and appliance dealers.

All things considered 1955 was a superb year for Commonwealth Edison. The largest addition of capacity in company history occurred with the first two Will County units and the new State Line unit placed into service; the contract for construction of Dresden 1 was signed; Ridgeland 4 returned; Little Bill made a successful debut; the computer arrived; the promotion of modern wiring progressed significantly; Edison obtained 50,000

297

new customers; peak load and kwh sales to all three major classes of customers increased; and Edison took the final step of the gas company spinoff.

The year also proved very good for Ward, who took over executive vice presidential duties and turned commercial matters over to Ayers. Edison President Evers and Public Service President Sedwick had been splitting the chores that Ward assumed. Gordon Corey became financial vice president, Murray Joslin engineering vice president. The following May, Charles Freeman retired as the chairman of the executive committee, the post he had held since he had turned over the corporate chairmanship to Gale in 1953. He continued as a director for one more year, stepping down at the 1957 annual meeting in favor of Ward.

Buoyed by the success of Little Bill, Edison continued to emphasize marketing. A luncheon sponsored by the company in early 1956 marked the Chicago area kickoff of the nationwide "Live Better. . .Electrically" advertising and promotion campaign. The program aimed at selling modern electrical products to consumers to enable them to "live better." Ayers presided over the local meeting, attended by some 700 business leaders, including builders, contractors, architects, realtors, and electrical equipment manufacturers and distributors. The Edison luncheon and others around the country appeared on a closed circuit telecast in New York, where "What's My Line" moderator John Daly and "Your Hit Parade" star Gisele MacKenzie emceed a program that dramatized how those present at the meetings could help the consumer live better electrically. The year-long advertising campaign received much publicity on TV and in print.

A remnant of the campaign, a "Live Better. . .Electrically" medallion, reappeared in an unusual context years later. Edison Chairman Jim O'Connor and his wife, Ellen, had received an invitation to a formal dinner in New York which called for "white tie with decorations." O'Connor understood how seriously the guests would regard decorations at this event, but he unfortunately had none. Ellen O'Connor came to the rescue. She dug out the old "Live Better. . .Electrically" medallion, fashioned it onto a sash, and pinned it onto her husband's coat. He said he held a drink or cigarette in front of it whenever anyone came near. As far as he knew, no one was ever the wiser.

298

In the seemingly endless challenge to keep capacity ahead of demand, Edison struggled like a man trying to outrun his shadow. As the company ordered and built larger, more efficient generating units, the public's appetite for electricity devoured the kilowatthours as quickly as they increased. Between 1950 and 1955, the air conditioning load on the Edison system had doubled from 255,000 kw to 584,000 kw. The number of window air conditioning units had grown during the same period from 30,000 to 165,000. Edison offered window units at sharply reduced prices to employes at the start of the cooling season. Employes could buy a one-half ton unit for $169.95, a three-quarter ton model for $199.95. Central air conditioning systems also became popular, with more than 1,000 of them added in 1955. In '56, air conditioning load jumped 30 percent, the most in a single year since 1945. By year's end, the size of the a.c. load had surpassed 750,000 kw. Room units numbered 222,000, central installations 4,500. For the first time in any calendar year, the system peak load in 1957 occurred in summer instead of winter. (The 1955 summer peak had exceeded the 1954 winter peak, but not the 1955 winter peak.) Unusually mild weather the last two weeks of 1957 also affected the peak load pattern.

That autumn also marked the start of a campaign to promote electric space heating, a campaign that has continued in one form or another to the present. Edison began the drive with a symposium attended by some 200 architects and engineers. In his opening remarks, Harris Ward said that the time had come to discard old-fashioned heating methods, just as modern society had discarded the gas mantle and the icebox. "Just as the electric light provided better seeing," Ward stated, "electric space heating will provide more comfortable living." One of the more popular displays at the gathering was an electric heat pump, the year-round comfort conditioning device whose promotion in later years would become a prime objective of the Edison marketer in the residential field.

The electric heating campaign received a boost when the Illinois Commerce Commission authorized a special electric space heating rate. The rate established a charge of 1.75 cents per kwh for all electricity used over 500 kwh a month, approximately 30 percent lower than the minimum average residential rate of 2.5 cents. Like charity, promotion should begin at home, Edison concluded, so the company offered an installation allowance of $25 per kw to the first 100 employes who installed complete electric heating systems in their homes. Under the offer, an employe could receive up to $500 toward the cost of the installation. Edison offered a special electric space heating course in which Chicago area electrical contractors learned the fundamentals of electric heating, insulation requirements, heat loss calculations, operating costs, and promotion ideas.

Edison's construction budget for 1957–60 reached $650 million, the largest in the company's history to that date. The plan called for outlays of $190 million in 1957 alone. The total program included Dresden Station and a 345,000-volt interconnection with the American Electric Power system. The 90-mile line between New Carlisle, Indiana, and Goodings Grove, Illinois, near Orland Park, would have the highest transmission voltage in the United States. The remainder of the budget concerned coal-fired generating stations and other transmission and distribution facilities. Fisk, Crawford, Will County, Northwest, Joliet, and Waukegan Stations all would undergo improvements that would bring Edison's net generating capability to more than 5.3 million kw by the end of 1960. Additionally, State Line planned to fill in 79 acres of Lake Michigan adjoining the plant to provide for additional coal storage space and for dock facilities to handle coal brought up the Illinois waterway by barge. And far to the north, the company purchased 300 acres of land in a little town on Lake Michigan near the Wisconsin state line which still reflects the influence of the religious fundamentalists who first settled there, with its ban on the sale of alcoholic beverages and its streets with biblical names. In announcing the acquisition in Zion, Illinois, District Superintendent Ted Kleisner said, "The system has no immediate plans for using the land. Because of the rapid expansion in our industry, the company frequently purchases property well in advance of the time it may be utilized."

Two communities to the south, Waukegan Station awaited the delivery of the largest turbine-generator ever ordered by the company, a 305,000-kilowatt machine built by General Electric at its Schenectady plant. Fisk, too, would add a 305,000-kw unit, almost on the same spot where the original 5,000-kw machine had stood. The construction budget rose to $700 million for the 1960–63 period.

Other company work locations also underwent changes. Edison moved out of the nine-story Central Service Building at 2233 S. Throop St., which it had used since 1927. The company leased the premises and moved the service and operating activities which had resided there to the new Chicago South headquarters. Shops and testing facilities found their home in the new Technical Center in Maywood. Before remodeling, Tech Center, the new home base for 900 employes, had been the General Shops building. The company built a new warehouse building, the General Warehouse, at the north end of the Ridgeland Station site. Finally, the company sold the Marquette Building, on the northwest corner of Adams and Dearborn Streets, which it had acquired in 1928. A number of Edison departments found themselves moved to the new division headquarters.

The burden of the huge construction program pushed Edison back before the Illinois Commerce Commission to seek another rate hike. In July 1957, the company filed for an increase in revenues of $26.4 million, or 7.3 percent. The ICC took the full 11 months it has under law to render a decision, then granted Edison the full amount. The increase came to less than 50 cents a month for the typical residential customer. The ICC found that a continuation of the company's actual rate of return for the previous two years would have made it difficult to raise the capital needed to finance the construction program. Federal income taxes and other taxes reduced the net gain to the company to about $11.9 million annually.

"Why make the customers pay $26.4 million more when the company only needs $11.9 million?" the *Chicago Tribune* asked in an editorial. "Because the tax collector, who had no part in asking for the increase, must nevertheless tap the wires for the lion's share, amounting to $14.5 million. . .

"When we see a company forced to make its customers pay more than double what it needs, the eternal price spiral which has been plaguing us seems a good deal simpler to understand," the newspaper concluded.

The increase had no visible effect on the consumption of electricity. Quite the contrary, for 1959, the first full year after

301

the boost, residential kwh sales climbed 11 percent and total sales by 10 percent. The company encouraged further sales by starting a program called IARAK—Increased Annual Residential Average Kilowatthours. The divisions set up sales clubs and committees which competed with one another for company honors. The IARAK program promoted the sale of 240-volt appliances such as electric ranges, water heaters, dryers, air conditioners, and heating installations.

In March 1958, 5,000 teenagers flocked to Chicago's historic International Amphitheatre, next door to the stockyards. They had not come to see Elvis Presley or some other star of rock 'n roll, but rather to help open a week-long Atom Fair and Nuclear Congress sponsored by 30 engineering societies. More than 100 nuclear energy exhibits filled the place, and inspection trips to Dresden and Argonne satisfied much curiosity. Many gave speeches, including Edison's Murray Joslin and Titus LeClair. Vice President Richard Nixon gave the principal speech at the banquet.

Later that year, on November 13, President Eisenhower himself, though not even in Chicago, helped draw a quarter of a million persons into State Street. The nighttime scene resembled New Year's Eve, as people stood elbow-to-elbow for blocks. Sitting in the White House, Eisenhower pressed a golden telegraph key, sending a signal from the Vanguard satellite to turn on the street's new $500,000 lighting system.

The following April, Edison added its two millionth customer. Unlike the one millionth, a newspaper, number two million had a young, smiling, human face. It belonged to Frank Flynn, a 23-year-old insurance salesman. Flynn, his 22-year-old wife, Marjorie, and one-year-old daughter, Catherine, went into the Edison record book when they moved into their new home at 10341 S. Sawyer Ave. in Chicago's West Beverly area. Evers played host at a special housewarming party. The Flynns received electrical gifts from Edison that included an air conditioner, an automatic washer/dryer, a refrigerator/freezer, a hi-fi set, and more. Ward used the occasion to remind employes that electricity did, indeed, cost less today, as Little Bill proclaimed. Ward pointed out that the average Chicago resident paid only $7.21 a month, compared to $11.10 in 1925, when customer one million came aboard.

The retirement in 1958 of Herbert Sedwick as Public Service president, following a 44-year career, marked the beginning of a series of executive changes that would give Edison new leadership at the top for the 1960s. Evers bowed out as Edison president the following year, after 46 years, and Ward succeeded him. At age 51, Ward had already served as financial vice president, commercial vice president, and had overseen operating, engineering, and construction activities. He had handled these varying responsibilities under Edison's executive rotation policy, i.e. that people go flat if they remain slotted, but grow in managerial ability with each new challenge. This policy came into play again in early 1960 when Vice President Tom Ayers and Murray Joslin traded jobs. Ayers assumed charge of production, construction, and engineering, experience that would prove invaluable later on as he presided over Edison's massive expansion in nuclear plant construction. For now, though, with Dresden about to come on line, Joslin retained his nuclear responsibilities while adding division operations and commercial activities to his duties. Ayers also retained responsibility for industrial relations. In the same shuffle, Hubert Nexon, the company's Boston-born lawyer who had joined Edison in mid-career, became assistant vice president, reporting to Gordon Corey. Wallace Behnke, another man on the move, was named manager of the newly-created Northwest Area with headquarters in Mt. Prospect. And Joe Poer assumed nuclear engineering duties previously assigned to Titus LeClair, who resigned to take a nuclear management post with General Dynamics. At the 1960 annual meeting, one more vestige of the Insull era faded as Stanley Field and Solomon Smith retired from the board of directors. One of their longtime colleagues, retired President Edward Doyle, died in July 1961 at age 81.

With the exception of LeClair's resignation, these changes stayed within the general scheme of things. However, a change that occurred later in 1961 definitely did not. After waiting so long to become the top man, Willis Gale voluntarily stepped down on November 2, turning over the title of chairman and chief executive officer to Harris Ward. Only 62 years old, Gale stayed on as chairman of the executive committee. In a written statement to employes, Gale characterized the change as keeping with the company's management development philosophy. He did not, however, tell the employes about his recent cancer operation.

"None of us knew if it was serious," Corey remembered. "As a matter of fact, I didn't know it was serious until a week before he died (in 1966)."

"With my retirement less than three years away," Gale told the troops, "the transition in responsibility for administering the affairs of the company should be effected well in advance of the completion of my active service." Gale had announced long before that he would leave the company at age 65. In fact, right when he became chairman, he made 65 the mandatory retirement age for officers. No longer would people hang on, well into their 70s, forcing the company to drag them away to make room for younger leadership.

According to Corey, Gale called him into his office and gave him the word of the change before revealing it to the rest of the company. Corey said Gale put the announcement in a "good news, bad news" context: the good news was that Corey would become executive vice president in 1962; the bad news that Ward would become chief executive officer.

"That doesn't sound like bad news to me," said Corey.

"Well, obviously you figured you might have it," said Gale.

Corey later recounted, "I was sufficiently younger than Harris, so it came as a surprise that he (Gale) would feel that way."

At the start of the new decade, Ward had speculated that Edison and the United States would enter the period of their greatest growth. In large measure he based his observation on the company's spectacular performance in 1959, which resulted in record kwh sales and revenues. There was no reason to doubt his view of the country's future. The nation had just completed eight years of "peace and prosperity," to use the Eisenhower Administration's phrase. They were, by and large, gentle times across the land, remembered nostalgically for hula hoops, cars with huge tail fins, the beginnings of rock 'n roll, cheap gasoline, crew cuts, pony tails, and the spectacular growth of television. Periodically, events jolted the country from its diversions—the Supreme Court's landmark school desegregation decision, the first warnings that cigarette smoking causes cancer, the Soviet

304

Union's launching of Sputnik, the Suez Crisis. But mostly, the country saw a time to forget World War II and the Korean conflict; a time to unwind, relax, and enjoy the growing benefits of a consumer-oriented society, many of them electrically-powered. Like the post-World War I era, Americans strove to return to "normalcy". The earlier period had brought bootleg liquor, the Charleston, the growth of spectator sports, roadsters, zany fads, and stockmarket speculation. Then came the 1929 crash, like a cold shower at six the morning after. Nothing akin to a stockmarket crash stamped the ending of the 1950s Eisenhower era and the beginning of the next.

However, despite the seemingly uneventful nature of the 1950s, the United States of January 1961, when John F. Kennedy took office, differed greatly from the United States of 1953 when Dwight D. Eisenhower took the presidential oath.

At home, while record numbers of Americans headed for the suburbs and enjoyed newfound prosperity, millions more remained stranded in the inner cities, feeling trapped in a cycle of poverty. Now television explicitly showed the poor what they lacked. Abroad, political conditions in a Southeast Asian country many Americans had never heard of and couldn't have cared less about deteriorated badly in the second half of the '50s. Had Americans only a clue to the price they would pay in a futile attempt to untangle the mess, they might have paid more attention.

Even Kennedy himself represented subtle change, the ill-defined coming of a new generation. The youngest president in history, he was also the first born in the 20th century. He brought to Washington the promise of vigor and the vision of Camelot. He meant to get America moving again, as he had said so often in the presidential campaign. Yet neither Kennedy nor anyone else foresaw the nation's most cataclysmic decade since the Civil War, a decade of unparalleled violence that brought rioting in the cities and on the campuses; the assassination of the President himself, his brother, and Dr. Martin Luther King Jr.; bitter racial confrontation; and a pervasion of the total fabric of American life to a greater extent than any of these other events, by the war in Viet Nam. More than anything else, the war turned many people against the "establishment." Yet countless other reasons existed for what the noted economist John Kenneth

Galbraith in *The New Industrial State* called "an interesting and widely remarked phenomenon of recent years. . .an ill-defined discontent, especially among students and intellectuals, with the accepted and approved modalities of social thought."

Elaborating on Galbraith's theme, historian William Manchester, in *The Glory and the Dream*, wrote, "Actually, by then (1967), blacks, radicals, feminists, and just about everybody else who felt systematically cheated by organized society had taken to calling it and all its works the 'establishment.' Often the word was used so loosely as to render it meaningless—shoplifting was called a blow to the establishment; the establishment was blamed for poor television programming. . ." And, Manchester might have added, for electricity bills that customers considered too high, for disconnections when the bills went unpaid, for power that occasionally failed when the bills were paid, for smoke from the stacks of the plants that produced the power. There was no way around it: electric utilities stood as prominent, highly visible, Class A members of the "establishment." When some people turned against the "establishment," utilities could hardly escape.

Thirteen

Days
Of
Wine
And
Roses

One after another, international and national events shattered America's sense of complacency in the early 1960s. The Soviets placed a man in orbit around the earth; President Kennedy vowed that the United States would land a man on the moon by the end of the decade. The Soviets erected the Berlin Wall; Kennedy traveled to West Berlin and told its citizens he was one of them. The Soviets installed offensive missiles in Cuba; risking World War III, the President forced Moscow to remove the weapons. Rioting greeted the enrollment of a Black student at the University of Mississippi; the President directed federal troops to quell the disturbances. Finally came the ultimate shock —the slaying of the President himself.

Despite these momentous events, Edison and the rest of the electric utility industry continued to do business in an atmosphere of tranquility reminiscent of the Eisenhower years. The company masterfully marketed its product; sales continued to boom; newer, larger, more efficient generating units began service to meet the rising demand; the cost of electricity declined and customers remained content. A turning point would come, but not yet; the times would remain uncomplicated yet for a little while, a second lingering of halcyon days like those savored by Edison in the 1920s.

"In 1945–65, America's energy consumption moved in line with its economic activity, and demand for electricity grew at roughly twice the rate of the economy," writes Hyman in *America's Electric Utilities—Past, Present and Future*. "Some might attribute the fast pace to the development of electrical appliances, to the discovery of the convenience and cleanliness of electricity, and to smart marketing by electric utilities. The above elements helped to create demand, which in turn allowed utilities to reach for greater economies of scale and operation, which in turn sufficiently lowered the price of power to encourage the development and marketing of new electrical devices. Whether the development of new markets occurred because of the drop in the price of electricity or vice versa is a chicken or egg debate. The reality is that the price for electricity declined not only on an absolute basis but also in relation to prices as a whole and to the price for competing fuels. And electricity usage grew far faster than energy usage as a whole."

In the early '60s the sharpest minds in the energy business foresaw no bending of the economic line that continued to move toward the upper right hand corner of the page. Speaking before an industry group in Chicago in the spring of 1963, Chairman Joseph C. Swidler of the Federal Power Commission declared: "The 80-year history of the industry has been one of constant growth, and in the last four decades the growth has averaged 7.5 percent per year. This phenomenal rate of growth seems likely to continue without substantial slowdown *at least to 1980 and perhaps beyond."* (Emphasis mine.)

Not quite that bullish, Ward pegged Edison's annual growth rate at six percent, following increases in kwh sales of 5.3 percent in 1961 and 8.7 percent in 1962. During the latter year, kwh sales cracked the 25 billion mark for the first time. Even at a six percent annual growth rate, Ward calculated, the six million kw of capacity that Edison had at the end of 1962 would have to become 17 million by 1980. He estimated that such expansion would cost $3 billion.

"We think that to prosper we must go on growing," Ward told the 1963 annual meeting. "We will continue our intensive efforts to reduce costs, lower prices, and expand sales. As long as we earn a fair return, lower prices are in the best interest of our stockholders as well as our customers. They enable us to expand volume and improve earnings."

Two-and-a-half months earlier, the company had reduced electricity charges to customers by approximately $2.7 million a year, bringing to $7 million the amount of reductions in the preceding year. The savings came through the fuel adjustment clause, which automatically passes on to customers the effect of changes in the cost of fuel for generating electricity. Also in 1963

Edison cut the electric heating rate for the third time in three years. The 16 percent cut saved the typical residential electric heat customer about $30 a year.

In his remarks to the shareholders, Ward also referred to the so-called "economies of scale," or the reduction of costs per kw as generating units increased in size. "A dozen years ago," he observed, "the cost of building a generating unit on our system was more than $200 per kw. In 1958, the cost was something more than $150 per kw. Our most recent addition at Will County cost about $130 and our two new Joliet units we hope will be under $115." He credited the progress to research and development by the manufacturers, as well as innovations by Edison's design engineers and good bargaining by the Purchasing Department.

The six million kw to which Ward referred represented three times the amount of capacity the company had at the end of World War II. Actually, the addition of two new 340,000-kilowatt units at State Line and Waukegan in mid-1962 pushed the total capability to 6,187,000. Waukegan, with 1,063,000 kw, became the first Edison station to top the one million mark. As even larger units neared completion, Edison discontinued power production at Aurora Station, which had begun operation in 1904, one year after Fisk went into service. The company took the step because of high production costs for the five small, obsolete units.

Waukegan didn't stay in first place for long. In May 1963 Edison added its largest unit ever, Will County 4. The unit's 510,000 kw boosted the station's capacity to 1,095,000 kw and placed it among the top units of all electric utilities in the United States. In the meantime construction continued on a massive project that would make Joliet Station the system's largest by 1966. Two 560,000-kilowatt units rose on the north bank of the Des Plaines River, across from the existing station. At the same time, on paper, studies explored the feasibility of building a mine-mouth generating station in the central Illinois coal fields, 200 miles south of Chicago. Those studies would come to fruition with the construction of Kincaid Station, which began operating in 1967. The two 560,000-kilowatt units, built at a cost of $100 million, received their coal by conveyor from Peabody Mine No. 10, located less than a mile away. By damming a local creek, Edison created a 2,700-acre, three-fingered lake to provide cooling water.

With the addition of more coal-fired capacity came a fleet of new rail cars to carry the coal and new transmission lines to carry the power. Two 345,000-volt lines tied Kincaid to Edison's service territory. The underground transmission system in Chicago grew with the addition of a 138,000-volt line that extended for 18 miles under the city's streets, from State Line Station on the Illinois-Indiana border at Lake Michigan to the Jefferson Substation, immediately southwest of the Loop. It extended farther than any other underground line on the Edison system and any other of its type in the country.

The purchase of 378 coal cars for use in integral train service to Joliet and State Line resulted in a saving of approximately $6 million passed on to customers through the fuel adjustment clause. Two 100-car-plus trains hauled about four million tons of coal annually from southern Illinois to Joliet. A third train delivered more than 1.5 million tons a year from the Indiana coal fields to State Line. Edison owned the $5-million fleet, but two rail carriers operated them under an arrangement that cut the company's coal carrying charges in half. The three trains made round trips of roughly 300 miles in each direction every 48 hours. Special unloading facilities and the installation of swivel couplings allowed workers to dump the cars without separating them.

"The company has long been active in the reduction of air pollution, conducting research in this area as early as 1927," the *Edison Service News* proclaimed in April 1962. Who could have foreseen how much more active it would become in a few more years, when the term "air pollution" would appear daily in headlines and newscasts? For the present the company proudly planned to spend $7 to $8 million on air pollution control equipment between 1962 and 1966, bringing the total expenditure for air cleaning to $30 million. The bulk of the total went for the purchase of electrostatic precipitators, huge electrical devices used to separate fly ash from boiler exhaust before it leaves the stacks. Forty-two precipitators operated or waited for complete installation as of early 1962.

At the General Office, the next generation of computer made its debut. The IBM 7080 had twice the memory capacity and four to six times the speed of the 705 computer it replaced.

As Commonwealth Edison completed 75 years of service, it added a new chunk of territory. Woodstock, the county seat of McHenry County northwest of Chicago, joined the system when the company purchased the municipal power plant which had operated since 1897. Ayers handled Edison's purchase of the $2.1-million plant. The company continued to operate the old plant until it connected the community to the Edison system the following summer with the completion of a new 40,000-kilowatt substation.

The company quietly observed its Diamond Anniversary in 1962 with a cover story in the *Service News* which included a spread of historical photographs and some written remarks by Ward, observing, among other things, that the average cost of residential electricity had dropped from 19.5 cents per kwh in the company's early days to less than three cents at the time.

Later that year Ayers became part of a troika with Gordon Corey and Morgan Murphy, when all three rose to the position of executive vice president. Ayers handled commercial and operating activities including overall management of the seven divisions. Corey took care of financial affairs, purchasing, fuel, and real estate, and Murphy headed up advertising, public information, and community relations. Interestingly, all three had begun their careers with Public Service Company, rather than with Edison. The next year, Nexon became a vice president, while John Eilering took over as manager of division operations under Murray Joslin and Ayers.

The promotions fueled speculation that would continue for a decade as to whether Ayers or Corey would succeed Ward as chairman. Murphy, who had already been with Edison and Public Service for nearly 40 years, was not viewed as a realistic contender because of his approaching retirement.

Many observers of the electric utility industry in the United States, including Hyman, point to 1965 as the year in which the industry began a long decline. Certainly the infamous Northeast Blackout in November of that year shook the industry to its foundations. However, Corey believes the downward trend began two Novembers previously, with the assassination of President Kennedy. In an address to the American Power Conference in Chicago in April 1985, after he had retired from Common-wealth Edison, Corey noted the "dismay and loss of confidence" that afflicted the country in the aftermath of the murder.

The dismay and loss of confidence over the assassination, Corey said, was "accelerated by the controversy over the Viet-nam War, (and) affected nearly all of our institutions and national goals. We began to question longstanding social objectives, in particular, the heretofore accepted goals of efficiency, productivity, and economic growth. The apostles of "small is beautiful" appealed to many who were disturbed by the explosive growth and urbanization of our society."

If Edison experienced any loss of confidence in the future, it did not appear in the records of the annual Management Conference, attended by some 1,200 employes, including Corey, less than three weeks after the tragedy in Dallas. "A stimulating, fast-moving program on selling and marketing our product," the *Service News* described the conference. Once again, the byword was growth, and the formula hadn't changed since uttered by Sam Insull.

"The more electricity we sell, the less it costs to supply," said Nexon. "The lower our costs, the lower the price at which we can sell at a profit. The lower the price tag on electricity, the greater our sales will be."

Vice President Larry Pierron stressed the same theme: "Growth in sales will bring growth in revenue and earnings. This will be good for everyone—customers, employes and stock-holders alike."

Pierron and other speakers also acknowledged increas-ingly fierce competition from the gas companies, particularly in the industrial and comfort conditioning sectors. Some accused the gas companies of resorting to false advertising in an effort to blunt Edison's sales advances and promised appropriate steps to make sure customers were not misled.

Nearly a year later the Federal Power Commission still adhered to the views set forth by Chairman Swidler. The FPC's National Power Survey envisaged "increased dependence on electricity as a source of energy in the daily life of every American...The electric utility industry...stands at the thresh-hold of a new era of low-cost power for all sections of our country...Larger and larger machines are being built...Extra high voltage. . .transmission lines can now move power economically for many hundreds of miles. . .(Thus, the) nation's rapidly expanding use of electricity is expected to more than double and perhaps triple by 1980. . ." And, for good measure, the FPC study endorsed the electric power industry's commitment "to a farsighted philosophy of maximum growth encouraged by reductions in rates and steady improvement in service. . ."

Edison gave its customers all of the above. The company reduced rates on an annual basis by a total of more than $36 million between 1962 and 1968, as kwh sales climbed an average of 7.6 percent each year. With regard to service improvement, Edison and other electric utilities formed MAIN, the Mid-America Interpool Network, in November 1964, pooling a total generating capacity of 31 million kw. The power-sharing network involved operations in 17 states, extending from Minnesota to Virginia. Ayers became chairman of MAIN. The organization had already operated informally when day after day of 90-degree weather in the summer of 1964 produced a succession of peak loads at Edison, culminating in a maximum demand of 6.1 million kw on August 3, a more than 13 percent increase over the previous summer's peak.

The Industrial Development Department, meanwhile, continued its work to attract new industry to the service territory. In 1963 the department helped 152 firms build new plants or expand existing ones. The biggest catch of that period, the $50-million Chrysler assembly plant near Belvidere, created 5,000 new jobs and set off a chain reaction of new payrolls, new homes, and new purchases that generated additional jobs. Edison's yearly revenue from the Chrysler plant totaled approximately $700,000.

Midway between Belvidere and Chicago, Edison opened a new district headquarters building in Crystal Lake to serve a growing area that covered 500 square miles and included about 40,000 customers and 28 municipalities. The building stood as the first in the service territory to feature "heat by light" space conditioning, a feature that downtown Chicago building managements soon found particularly attractive as one after another became electric heat customers. About 150 recessed ceiling fixtures provided high-intensity lighting while providing enough warmth to meet the Crystal Lake office area's needs when the outdoor temperature dipped as low as 10 degrees below zero.

These were "the days of wine and roses," Corey told the 1964 Engineering Conference. During the decade since division-alization and the gas company spinoff, generating station con-struction costs had reduced by half, sales had doubled, thanks to aggressive, innovative marketing by a team led by Paul Fenoglio; earnings had risen two-and-a-half times and the price of Edison stock had tripled. Corey, a thoughtful, perceptive man, neverthe-less began to realize that the good times couldn't last forever. "During the years ahead we face a more difficult job," he warned, "because we may be approaching a ceiling on our rate of return." He had spoken the closest thing to gloom spread by any company leader in those golden days.

Days of wine and roses lay immediately ahead for Corey himself, as well as the other members of the troika. All three rose to new positions at a Board of Directors meeting in Septem-ber 1964. Ayers became president, as Ward relinquished that title but kept the chairmanship. Corey became chairman of the finance committee and Murphy chairman of the executive com-mittee. The responsibilities of the three remained the same. Murphy moved into the slot vacated by Willis Gale, who had reached the compulsory retirement age of 65 which he himself had instituted.

Gale's predecessor, gentle, reclusive Charles Freeman, died earlier that year in Tucson, Arizona, at age 87. In the following year, 1965, death would claim two more retired of-ficers. Britton Budd, former president and vice chairman of Public Service Company died in Chicago at 93, and retired Vice President for Operations and Engineering Alex Bailey succumbed in Hinsdale at 83.

Freezing rains and sleet rolled through northern Illinois in late January 1965, leaving behind a coat of ice the like of which Edison had never seen. It clung like paint to streets, trees, utility poles, power lines—anything it could grip. Embrittled lines snapped like pretzels. Others able to withstand the winds fell under falling tree limbs. Throughout the storm and its aftermath, some 200 communities went without power, as did more than 250,000 residential and commercial customers, pri-marily in Chicago's northern and western suburbs. Downed lines, broken poles, and damaged transformers numbered more than 6,000. Edison switchboards handled nearly 100,000 calls reporting power outages.

After Edison had made good progress for the first 48 hours, the weather turned nasty again. For every broken line repaired, two other lines broke under the strain of ice and tree limbs.

Linemen restore service after a devastating ice storm in January, 1965.

The company put its Emergency Restoration of Power, or ERP, plan into effect for the first time on such a large scale. The program coordinates several departments and the seven divisions into one unified group—in this situation, more than 4,000 people and hundreds of vehicles. Edison kept 500 to 800 crews on the streets day and night, repairing the damage caused by ice and wind. Some 450 Edison crews received help from nearly 700 workers from other electric utilities and another 1,000 from private electrical and tree-trimming contractors. Linemen came in by truck and plane from other parts of Illinois, as well as Indiana, Wisconsin, Michigan, Minnesota, Missouri, Iowa, Colorado, and Pennsylvania.

The Transmission and Distribution Construction office at Tech Center in Maywood provided the nerve center of the recovery operation. Staffers analyzed damage in all areas, while dispatchers used the appraisals to concentrate crews where they were needed most. Other employes searched for downed power lines and performed additional support duties. Three helicopter crews looked for breaks in the distribution system and pin-pointed areas of heavy damage. The cost of the massive restoration effort came to more than $2 million.

The destruction and subsequent cleanup, however massive, only attracted local and regional interest, unlike the events in the Northeast a little less than a year later, Nov. 9, 1965. In a modern variation of Ben Franklin's advice, "for want of a nail...the kingdom was lost," the failure of a backup relay in a little box at a Canadian hydroelectric plant, four miles west of Niagara Falls, triggered a chain reaction that left 30 million people across an area of 80,000 square miles without electricity. That little box caused the worst power failure in the age of electricity, the utility industry's equivalent of the sinking of the unsinkable *Titanic*, at least in terms of public incredulity. Fortunately the blackout caused few deaths. Nonetheless, more than 800,000 evening rush hour commuters were stranded underground in the New York City subways; doctors operated by candlelight until emergency generators at hospitals kicked in. Some disturbances and looting upset the area. People varied widely in their initial reactions, including fear of an enemy attack, sabotage by anti-Vietnam War activists, and even an invasion from outer space! According to popular rumor, the birth rate surged dramatically upwards nine months after the blackout, but subsequent studies have, perhaps unfortunately, disproven this romantic story.

How did it happen? The failure at the Ontario hydro plant caused a mini-chain reaction that knocked out the lines running out of the station. Massive amounts of electricity, destined for Toronto, sought the path of least resistance and headed south, through the transmission lines of the Ontario, New York, and New England power grid, knocking out generating stations along the way. Those power-deprived areas, in turn, automatically demanded electricity from elsewhere on the grid, specifically Manhattan. The borough didn't have it to give.

Every calamity seems to have at least one irony. The man in charge of Consolidated Edison's power dispatching office at that hour realized what was happening and decided to push the eight buttons that would disconnect New York City from the grid and stop the "domino effect." As he reached for the buttons, the metropolis went dark.

William Manchester, in *The Glory and the Dream*, writes, "Except for Staten Island and one small Brooklyn neighborhood, the power was gone—all of it: illumination, appliances, subways; the works. In unaffected Montclair, New Jersey, a woman looking out her picture window had been admiring the fairy-like spectacle of Manhattan alight. She called her teen-age son to share it with him, and when she turned back to the window the city had disappeared. Above Kennedy International Airport, Captain Ron George of Air Canada was entering his glide pattern. He looked down at the runway, glanced at his instruments, glanced back—and saw only Stygian blackness. The airport, too, had vanished.

"In the early hours of that evening, virtually the only light in the grid was provided by candles, flashlights, automobile lights, and a full moon. Then the lights began returning, one area at a time."

Vermont and New Hampshire came back on first, after outages as short as half an hour. Other sections of New England followed. New York remained dark much longer; the various boroughs came back on throughout the early morning hours. Some of the New York suburbs went without power for over 30 hours.

The Federal Power Commission launched an investigation and concluded that the initial reaction to the blackout was general disbelief that it could have happened at all. Delving deeper, the FPC learned that the blackout had, in fact, been waiting to happen for several years. For one thing, the errant relay device at the Canadian hydro plant had remained set for power requirements of two years earlier, never readjusted as demand increased. The FPC found a great need for new power-pooling procedures, more generating stations, and more transmission lines. It also instituted new reporting procedures to track outages.

In Edison territory, the logical question of press and public was, "Can it happen here?" The company answered, "Extremely unlikely, but not impossible." Edison engineers explained that they could shed up to 700,000 kw of load automatically if the system frequency dropped. Load dispatchers stood ready to take the necessary action to prevent system frequency from dropping below 59 cycles (60 being normal).

The blackout gave Edison a chance to crow about the formation of MAIN only one year earlier, but company officials restrained themselves from making too many comparisons between the two parts of the country. Ward did remind employes that strong interconnections had saved the Midwest from serious trouble a number of times in recent years. He pointed out that in the spring of 1965, Edison used its 345,000-volt tie to the Indiana & Michigan Electric Company to supply power to tornado-stricken areas of Indiana. Without interconnections, he noted, Indiana customers would have had to endure longer, more serious outages. The situation reversed soon after the Northeast Blackout, when Edison instantaneously lost its largest and newest unit, 560,000-kilowatt Joliet 7. Interconnections with neighboring utilities helped Edison surmount the large capacity deficit within minutes, with no inconvenience to customers, who remained oblivious to the incident. "Our experience with blackouts has been confined to reading about their occurrence in other parts of the country," O'Connor once stated.

Joliet 7, centerpiece of a $700-million construction program, came on line in May 1965 as the largest ever installed on the Edison system. Joliet now joined Waukegan and Will County as stations with net generating capabilities of more than one million kw. When Unit 8 was added a year later, Joliet became the system's largest generating station.

The way Edison added capacity, superlatives such as "newest" and "largest" moved from unit to unit, station to station, the way the Indianapolis 500 crowns faster and faster champions. The Kincaid units would soon eclipse their counterparts at Joliet, but after Kincaid, Ward and Corey had a surprise up their sleeves.

At the beginning of 1965 Ward had hinted that the next unit following the two at Kincaid might be nuclear, but he didn't say much more, except that it possibly might rate in the 600,000-kilowatt range. In February the company announced plans to build a second Dresden unit. If Dresden 1 was a Model T, Dresden 2 would be a contemporary four-door sedan. The company said that it would ask the Atomic Energy Commission for a permit to construct a 714,000-kilowatt unit, but that the rating might eventually approach 800,000 kw, four times the size of the first unit. Again General Electric would build the plant, supplying the reactor, turbine-generator, and other major components, including the first two fuel cores. The new boiling water reactor unit would come on line in 1969 and would incorporate a number of technological advancements gained from Dresden 1 and other BWRs, including an improved, simplified reactor system and an advanced instrumentation system to monitor operating conditions. In his announcement, Ward predicted that Dresden 2 would generate electricity at a cost slightly lower than that of the company's newest coal-fired plants.

The decision to proceed with a second nuclear unit, four times larger than the first, was major news by itself. Edison, though, had contracted with GE to build not one, but *four* identical nuclear units—two at Dresden and two on the Mississippi River near Cordova, Illinois—each of which would be the largest in the world.

"It was a bold step for us to write a contract for four bigger reactors all of the same kind," nuclear pioneer Kiefer recalled. "That was just about the time the FAA was grounding all planes when they had a problem with the prototype."

Corey served as Edison's chief negotiator with GE. He remembered that the bargaining took place in his office on the 18th floor of the Edison Building over a five-day period, ending on a Saturday.

"It was three o'clock in the morning when Jim Young (GE vice president) phoned me and said, 'I've arrived in California and signed the contract.' He wanted the contract signed in California to avoid the service tax here."

The turnkey contract cost a remarkably low $100 per kw for each of the four units. Various additions, including company overheads and environmental backfittings, eventually raised the tab to about $160 per kw, a bargain all the same. GE still played catchup with Westinghouse in the commercial nuclear field and agreed to rock-bottom prices just to obtain business. Since GE had signed a turnkey contract with Jersey Central Power & Light in December 1963 to build the Oyster Creek plant, the competitive price surprised Edison people. Corey believed that deal helped pave the way for the favorable terms he obtained for Edison's four units.

"General Electric was very anxious to get into the business," he remembered.

One incident in the negotiations stands out in Corey's memory. In the talks, one of the GE negotiators would periodically say to his colleagues, "Give them (Edison) an evasive answer," and all of the GE people would burst out laughing. Corey finally became curious about the inside joke. The man who used the phrase explained, "It's a story about W. C. Fields. He had just finished a movie and was dead tired. He went up to his hotel room, ordered up a case of gin, and told the hotel manager not to disturb him under any circumstances. He pulled down the shade, climbed into bed, and there was a knock on the door. It's the manager of the hotel. Fields asks him what he wants, and the manager tells him it's Mr. Goldwyn on the phone, and he insists on talking to you. 'Look,' says Fields, 'give him an evasive answer!' The manager says, 'What should I tell him, Mr. Fields?' and Fields roars, 'Tell him to go to hell!' An evasive answer."

After the announcement of Dresden 2, Edison officials emphasized that the company would not switch to nuclear power exclusively, even though it soon would appear that way, and that Edison would consider all methods of power production as the need for more capacity arose. In announcing plans to build Dresden 3 a year later, Ward repeated that "our choice is likely to vary from unit to unit throughout the 1970s." He cited studies which showed that a companion nuclear unit to the one under construction would provide the lowest delivered cost of power— about five to ten percent below that of the newest coal-fired units —because of the economies gained from building identical units simultaneously. He announced that Unit 3, slated for service in 1970, would cost $79 million, $3 million more than its sister plant.

Dresden's honeymoon with the press, which began during the construction of Unit 1, continued after the announcement of plans to build Unit 3. In an editorial, *Chicago's American* proclaimed, "The success of the Dresden plant holds future promise of immense importance to the world—that of cheap and plentiful power no longer limited by supplies of fuel. The announcement of plans for Dresden 3 shows how speedily that future is approaching. . ." An editorial in the Joliet *Herald-News*

320

asserted, "We are especially happy that these power-producing plants are being built with private capital, the only concession from the federal government being a sort of insurance guarantee against possible large loss, due to a major catastrophe. The efficient functioning of Dresden Unit 1 has made it apparent that this guarantee will probably never be needed. . ."

With an annual growth rate of 7.5 percent (FPC Chairman Swidler was still closer to the mark than Ward), announcement of the remaining two nuclear units would soon follow, Edison divulged plans for Unit 1 of the present Quad-Cities Station only a few months after the announcement of Dresden 3, with Quad-Cities 2 coming to light only a couple of months after its sister unit. The units, owned jointly by Edison and Iowa-Illinois Gas and Electric, would come on line in 1970 and 1971, respectively. Iowa-Illinois would own 25 percent; Edison would operate the plant. For Commonwealth Edison, the Quad-Cities plant would stand advantageously close to the western part of the service territory, including the Dixon, Sterling, and Freeport areas. The station itself would actually operate from Iowa-Illinois territory. For that utility, the plant would conveniently serve the major population center of the Quad Cities—Moline, East Moline, and Rock Island, Illinois, and Davenport, Iowa.

The two units would cost $160 million. No one mentioned a $100-per-kw turnkey contract. Edison now estimated that plant would save 10 percent over the cost of generating electricity with a large coal-fired station. "(T)he arrival of competitive nuclear power has certainly been hastened by the advent of the very large generating unit," Ward declared. "Big unit economies and improved fuel technology add up to attractive power costs from nuclear power plants. . .(N)uclear fuel costs have come down and appear to be headed for further reductions."

Edison had become a true believer in the nuclear cause. All four of the new 800 megawatt units would start up by 1972, bringing nuclear's share of total generation to 25 percent and making Edison the largest generator of nuclear energy in the Western Hemisphere. Still, some, including engineers within the company, believed that Edison and the industry moved too quickly, that they should have installed units in the 400–600 megawatt range instead of leaping from 200 mw to 800 mw.

Dr. A. David Rossin, who has observed Edison from within and without since the early atomic days, strongly disagreed.

"Utilities didn't rush headlong into anything," said Rossin, Edison's onetime research director and later head of the Nuclear Safety Analysis Center (NSAC). "In fact, they were very conservative. In those days we were going too slow because we knew enough to be doing more things. The idea that the large plants were somehow brought on too fast doesn't wash very well because there was a logical upgrade of size over a period of time. The economics of the large plant looked awfully good, and it *was* awfully good for the few that were finished on schedule.

"I never saw the flamboyant spending that the utility industry has been accused of. I found that Commonwealth Edison was a very tough negotiator on contracts, and that they didn't tolerate any kind of padding."

The argument that Edison moved too fast, too soon with the Dresden and Quad-Cities units would become moot for at least a couple of reasons: the plants would prove to be safe, dependable performers, and the company, in response to the continuing postwar pattern, would need every bit of the capacity. The 1966 summer peak load soared 12.4 percent higher than that of the previous year, with overall annual sales up nearly 10 percent. In the past five years, sales had grown faster than in the previous ten. The company had now upped its estimated future sales growth to seven percent a year. If the prediction held true, sales would double in another ten years. However, Ward took nothing for granted. "We must help nature along with resourceful and persistent salesmanship," he advised. "Despite severe competition (from the gas companies), our customers must be convinced that electricity has more to offer in comfort, service, and efficiency than other forms of energy." Plugging the new Dresden and Quad-Cities units into the construction budget, along with the two Kincaid units, gave Edison its first billion-dollar building program, a plan that called for outlays of $1.02 billion for the five-year period 1967–71. The revised construction budget also included funds for the addition of 300,000 kw of peaking capacity at Fisk in 1968 and the construction of more than 850 miles of new 345,000-volt transmission lines over the five-year period.

The name "Public Service" was phased out. It was sanded off a truck in Maywood in the summer of 1965— more than 12 years after the Public Service Company of Northern Illinois merged with Commonwealth Edison.

"The Bright New Ideas Are Electric" proclaimed the newest promotional campaign to help human nature along. In the fall of 1966 bright new ideas popped up in newspapers, magazines, radio, and television, not only promoting consumer products, but also describing the company's progress and promoting the service territory as a good place to live and do business. A print ad explained that Dresden 1 had performed so efficiently and economically that the company would build four more nuclear units. A TV commercial promoting electric heat stated that "dust cloths have gone the way of the dinosaurs." The messages reached the public via radio and TV: on the news with Fahey Flynn, on the weather with Harry Volkman, on the Wally Phillips, Howard Miller, and Mal Bellairs radio programs, on Chicago Blackhawks hockey games, and on the pages of *Time*, *Life*, *Look*, *Family Circle*, *Newsweek*, and the Chicago metropolitan newspapers.

As always, the public face of Commonwealth Edison was inexorably changing. At the December 1965 Management Conference a young man with Edison only a little more than two years received the chance to speak at a major company function attended by some 1,200 persons. He spoke on "Keeping the Customer Happy." He was Morgan Murphy's bright administrative assistant, James J. O'Connor. Meanwhile, another member of the old guard departed. Cancer took Willis Gale in June 1966 at the age of 66. He had continued as a director of the company from the time of his retirement in August 1964 until the end. A symbol, too, went its way. In mid-1965, the name Public Service was officially retired. It had lingered on since the 1953 merger, mainly because of its longstanding identification with suburban customers.

The face of the service territory changed as well. Nearly 100,000 electricity users in the Rockford area became Edison customers in late 1966, when Central Illinois Electric and Gas Co. became an Edison division. Central Illinois also served customers in the downstate Albion and Lincoln areas. In unanimously approving the merger, the Federal Power Commission found that "(f)rom both a cost and reliability standpoint" the public would benefit from an integration of the electricity supply facilities in the Rockford vicinity with an Edison system that bordered them on three sides. In the Rockford area, Edison gained 677 former Central employes as well as two generating stations, the Sabrooke and Fordam plants. From a marketing standpoint, Rockford held the plum of 600 manufacturing industries.

The halcyon days of the 1920s had ended with a bang— the stock market crash. Edison's days of wine and roses of the 1960s also ended, not with a whimper, but with a roar—the roar of protest. A roar that built up gradually, over several years, concerned with something hovering since the first coal-fired generating station began operating. Edison's initial reaction to the mounting concern over air pollution invokes the famed poem by Hughes Mearns (1875–1965):

"As I was going up the stair
I met a man who wasn't there.
He wasn't there again today
I wish I wish he'd stay away."

Fourteen

The
Times
They
Are
A-Changin'

I

To a youngster growing up on Chicago's Southeast Side during the 1940s and '50s, the sharp aromas wafting from the Sherwin-Williams paint factory on a warm summer's evening, the rouge plumes rising from the steel mills, the black smoke from the two- and three-flats in the wintertime and the strange, brilliant hues in parts of Lake Calumet formed as much a part of the natural order of things as the neighborhood schoolyard or the Red Rockets and the Green Hornets on Cottage Grove Avenue. From time to time someone might complain about a particularly offensive odor, but no one ever suggested the possibility of alleviating the irritant. The terms air pollution and water pollution didn't find their way into the lexicon of most Chicagoans until about the mid-1960s, even though humanity had noticed them at least vaguely since the Industrial Revolution, if not before.

Outside the scientific community, few remembered or even knew that a killer smog which hung over London for five days in December 1952 took an estimated 4,000 lives. A similar incident in London in 1962 killed some 340 persons. But that was long ago and in another country, one could argue. Besides, everyone knew fog and smog were commonplace in London. Two Chicago physicians, however, began to wonder whether deadly smogs had infused their city, on a smaller scale, without anyone knowing it. With a $100,000 federal research grant, they began a lengthy study for an advisory group of the city's department of air pollution control. Hardly publicity-shy, the doctors talked often to the media about the progress of their work. In late 1966 one of the doctors was quoted in a newspaper as saying all of his chronic lung patients had been sick at the same time, even though they lived in different parts of the Chicago area and had different occupations. He suspected air pollution as the primary cause. An official of the city's air pollution control department confirmed that a weather inversion had kept pollutants trapped under a virtual lid for three days during the period in question. Chicago experienced several such episodes a year, he said.

At least conditions had not become as bad as in New York—to Chicagoans, *everything* is worse in New York—where a stagnant mass of air hung overhead for 10 days in 1963, causing an estimated 170 to 200 deaths. On Thanksgiving Day 1966 a massive weather inversion along the Eastern seaboard sent air pollution levels soaring in New York and rising to a lesser degree in other cities. Even non-respiratory sufferers felt their eyes burn and throats scratch. Chicago news people began to ask the inevitable question, "Could it happen here?". The city's air pollution control department answered "yes"; the same ingredients, including sulphur dioxide from coal burning, could come together and cause major problems here. Headlines such as "Air Pollution Here Reaches Dangerous High" and "Could Smog Hold Chicago in Death Grip?" became more and more common. John W. Gardner, U.S. Secretary of Health, Education and Welfare, called for a multi-faceted attack on air pollution, with Chicago, New York, and Philadelphia singled out for special attention. Gardner called a national conference on air pollution in December 1966 at which Vice President Hubert Humphrey declared, "More people are dying from emphysema than on the field of battle in Viet Nam," adding that the lung disease is "directly associated with air pollution." Shortly afterward, an officer of the U.S. Public Health Service said that if the air Chicagoans breathe were a packaged item, the Food and Drug Administration would ban it.

Commonwealth Edison never denied that its coal-fired generating stations put smoke into the air, but the company—Ward in particular—believed that no one gave the electric utility industry credit for its long-established pollution control program. Ward reminded employes in the company magazine that Edison had installed its first precipitator in 1929, long before the public became generally concerned about the issue. He went on to say that in 1966 the company had 56 of the stack cleaning devices at

326

its generating stations, representing the bulk of a $50 million investment to keep the environment clean. Edison also improved furnace combustion efficiency and expanded nuclear capability as two additional steps to combat air pollution, according to Ward. William Stanley, Chicago's chief of air pollution control, did not disagree. "Commonwealth Edison is giving us excellent cooperation by agreeing to not expand coal-burning power plants in the city," he said. "Rather, these capacity expansions are taking place at plant sites far removed from the city or through nuclear power generating stations. . ."

In January 1967 Stanley joined Mayor Daley in announcing that Edison and the city had mutually agreed on a five-year plan to reduce emissions at six generating stations in the Chicago area. Using 1965 as a base year, Edison agreed to cut the coal it burned by 2.6 million tons—from 6.5 million to 3.9 million—by 1970, causing sulfur dioxide emissions to decrease by 184,000 tons. The company pledged to retire 12 older coal-burning units by 1972 in addition to the 14 it had retired since 1956. Increased use of nuclear generation and, to a lesser degree, natural gas in existing coal-fired plants would take up the slack as well as meet anticipated new demand. "I doubt that any other electric power company in the country can point to a more positive program for fighting air pollution," Daley maintained.

At the very moment Daley announced the agreement with Edison, pollution levels had already begun to drop sharply. The mayor wielded enormous power in his heyday, but surely even he could not command the air to clear at a moment's notice. In fact, given the reason for the drop in pollution, Daley and just about everyone else would have opted for dirtier air for a few days, had they a choice. Pollution fell because its primary source, the automobile, was immobilized by a 24-inch snowfall that left drifts up to 20 feet deep. For several days, the metropolitan area stood still, creating special problems for Edison. For instance, for the first time, the company airlifted a lineman to the scene of a service interruption. When no other means of transportation would do, lineman Donald Peters traveled by helicopter to 79th Street and Harlem Avenue to replace a fuse shorted out by snow on top of a transformer. Milan Peinovich set the unofficial distance record by tromping 14 miles from his home in Hickory Hills to Ridgeland Station. Howard Green laid claim to the endurance mark, remaining on the job at Ridgeland for nearly 100 hours. Also at Ridgeland, Harvey Purtee spent hours digging his car out of the snow. When he finally turned on the ignition, nothing happened. Someone had stolen his battery. Most generating station hands worked 16-hour shifts for three days. Phil Gershon, office supervisor at State Line, said the plant was "like a wayside boarding house. Men were catnapping on the floor, dozing on locker room benches, on desks." At Fisk, employes marooned by the storm ate food from a nearby Chinese restaurant. The second day, they reported that they had grown a bit tired of Chinese cuisine.

The storm hit hardest in the downstate section of the newly-acquired Central Illinois Electric & Gas Company. More than 100 poles and miles of lines had fallen. Because of impassable highways, Edison airlifted crews from Rockford to Springfield, where vehicles waited to take them to trouble spots in the surrounding area. Summing up the Blizzard of '67, Operating Manager Harold Otto said it proved that "in the face of a superstorm, we can snap back with a super-recovery."

The reduced pollution levels underscored the fact that transportation, primarily the passenger car, caused the most air problems. A study conducted by the Illinois and Indiana public health departments indicated that 36 percent of air pollution in metropolitan Chicago came from motor vehicles, followed by commercial/industrial, residential, and other sources. Electrical generation fell in the lowest category, accounting for 11 percent of the problem.

In May 1967 Mayor Daley complained to a U.S. Senate subcommittee that unregulated companies undercut efforts by Chicago companies to clean up the skies. He targeted the steel mills in northwest Indiana, which continued to pollute Chicago's air. "This is obviously unfair to the Chicago companies—and unfair and hazardous to all of the people in the area," the mayor testified. "They all share the same air and the same economies." Daley urged controls on a regional rather than local basis.

On the positive side, "the scientific plum of the century," as the *Chicago Tribune* termed it, landed in Edison's service territory with the announcement that the little town of Weston, near Batavia, would become the site of the Atomic Energy Commission's (AEC's) $375-million proton accelerator, built to explore the mysteries of the atom. Weston won over more than 200 other locations throughout the country, and Edison played no small part in helping to land the prize. Company representatives worked on a task force that sold the site to the AEC on the strength of its accessibility, nearness to Argonne National Laboratory, desirable educational environment, and, by no means least, ample electrical power at reasonable rates. The accelerator, which would become known as Fermilab in honor of atomic pioneer Enrico Fermi, would have a demand of 200,000 kw, or the equivalent of Dresden Unit 1's total capacity.

Elsewhere in research and development, Edison joined General Electric and Westinghouse in two separate research projects to explore the fast breeder reactor, which acquired its name from its ability to make more fuel than it consumes by converting non-fissionable Uranium-238 into plutonium. Edison emphasized that it had no commitment to build a breeder but that the research could lead to a commercially adaptable breeder reactor in the future. The company formed an advanced reactor study group, headed by Wallace Behnke, to work with GE and Westinghouse as well as with the AEC.

In the meantime, plans to build additional conventional nuclear plants forged ahead. In February 1967 the company stated that it would build its sixth nuclear generating unit for service in 1972. Edison formally announced in July that the 2.2 million-kilowatt nuclear station would stand on the shoreline of Lake Michigan at Zion. Actually, two units of 1.1 million kw each were scheduled for service in 1972 and 1973. The company would thus exercise an option with Westinghouse to purchase a second pressurized water reactor unit. The cost of the two units came to $250 million and included the initial fuel loadings and two replacement cores. Operating the new Zion plant would increase the company's nuclear capacity to 5.2 million kw, which would account for about 35 percent of the anticipated net generating capacity. Zion, like all of the other nuclear units, would "generate a large amount of power without emitting one wisp of smoke," Ward told a press conference.

Local residents greeted the announcement enthusiastically. Zion Mayor Bruce Dunbar called the plant "a tremendous boon" to his community and said he looked forward to a bright new future, enhanced by fresh tax revenues for schools and civic improvements. Waukegan Mayor Robert Sabonjian said the plant would be "a wonderful thing for the whole area—Zion, Waukegan, and North Chicago. It will put more money into our economy and assure industrial stability." The Waukegan *News-Sun* praised it even more effusively, stating that Zion Station "will add stupendously to the area's property tax base," unlike Weston's tax-exempt government installation. "Edison is to be commended for boldly leading the field in the transition to safe, silent, smoke-free nuclear power."

As usual, Edison would need every bit of new capacity, as summer peak loads continued to build due to the ever-increasing use of air conditioning. The 1966 peak rose 12.3 percent over the previous year, kwh sales up 9.9 percent. With completion of the massive generating station construction program several years off, the company planned to have 664,000 kw of fast-start peaking units or turbines in place at various locations to help meet peak loads by the summer of 1968.

Less than a year after New York's Thanksgiving week bout with air pollution, Chicago discovered that the smog which produces watering eyes and hacking coughs did not plague just the East and West coasts. A mass of stagnant air pressed down on the city, causing it, as the *Tribune* graphically noted, to breathe its own bad breath. Many underwent the most painful experience with air pollution in their lives. The amount of pollution reached 2.5 times the danger level. Edison helped to ease conditions by switching from coal to gas at Chicago-area generating stations. If nothing else, the newspaper noted, the episode served as a reminder that air pollution was every bit as dangerous as water pollution.

But polluted water still grabbed most of the attention in the summer of 1967. The Metropolitan Sanitary District accused Fisk Station of discharging more than 700 million gallons of untreated wastewater into the Chicago River each day—the most of any industrial plant on the District's waterways. A cynic might have responded that it didn't make much difference; before talk of suburban stadiums arose, the three absolute truths about Chicago were that the Sox play on the South Side, the Cubs play on the North Side, and the Chicago River is polluted. Edison, however, was not cynical, and reminded the public that

330

it planned to spend $275,000 for a recirculating system to eliminate pollution of the river.

That summer Mayor Daley issued an urgent appeal to save Lake Michigan from death by pollution and, as with his approach to air pollution, called for uniform regional controls. Daley promised that the City of Chicago would take the lead by introducing an ordinance mandating that all boats using Chicago waters have retention or recirculation sanitary facilities on board. Next, the Mayor countermanded a recommendation by a panel of local anti-pollution administrators to extend, by two years, a deadline for industry on the lake to comply with clean water standards set in 1965. The panel had originally voted three to one in favor of the new deadline. The president of the Sanitary District, who owed his position to Daley, and a federal official who would later get a top job in the Daley Administration had voted with the majority. After the Mayor wired Interior Secretary Stewart Udall, however, denouncing extension, the two local officials recognized His Honor's wisdom and the error of their own ways, and promptly reversed their positions.

Edison did some reversing of its own late that year when it withdrew its application to the U.S. Army Corps of Engineers for a permit to fill 79 acres of Lake Michigan adjacent to State Line Station. After pledging not to expand coal-burning generation in or near the city and further promising to reduce the amount of coal burned, the company realized it no longer needed the landfill for coal storage and barge unloading facilities. A spokesman for the Save the Dunes Council, an environmental group which had fought the landfill plan, congratulated Edison for taking a "constructive" step.

State Line had made the news during the summer of 1966, the time of Chicago's infamous alewife invasion. Millions of the pesky, herring-like fish, averaging six inches, washed up on Chicago area beaches—and crashed through the intake screens at State Line. Tons of fish clogged all ten intakes. Workers alternately took generating units out of service and reduced their capability for about two hours each in order to clean the alewives out of the condensers. The alewives also plagued Waukegan. Oddly, more than three-fourths of them developed a preference for the seventh of 22 intakes. The following spring, the two stations strung 1,200-feet long nets around the perimeter of the intakes and diverted the fish, preventing a recurrence of the problem.

Everyone was pleased there were fish in Lake Kincaid in the summer of 1967. The company opened the lake, used to cool Kincaid Station near downstate Taylorville, to the public for fishing, hiking, and picnicking under the supervision of the Illinois Department of Conservation. The Edison-made lake, with 100 miles of shoreline, later became Sangchris Lake, combining the names of Sangamon and Christian counties.

As Chicagoans prepared to celebrate New Year's Eve 1967, air pollution levels in the Loop reached record highs for the year. News accounts of the episode again stated that during periods when experts foresee a prolonged pollution buildup, Commonwealth Edison cuts back on its use of coal at generating stations in and near the city. The stories further mentioned that sulfur dioxide injures health and property. As usual, the media named only Edison, among the companies responsible, by name. The company wondered whether it was being blamed for more than its 11 percent share of the area's air pollution problem, not only because of the continuing media exposure, but also because of the emission figures that Edison regularly submitted to pollution control officials. Edison's scrupulously accurate numbers often looked worse than the apparently less-accurate figures submitted by other industries.

Ever the master of timing, Mayor Daley in January 1968 introduced a series of tough new air pollution curbs in the City Council. The most controversial proposal required that a sulfur limitation of 2.5 percent, by weight, apply to all fuels burned within the city, beginning six months after adoption of the regulation. Two years later the limit would slide to two percent, and a year after that it would reach the final goal of 1.5 percent.

After studying the proposal, Edison announced that it could not comply with such a regulation at the present time. Assistant Vice President O'Connor explained at a public hearing low-sulfur coal's general unreliability and Edison's inability to easily switch its boilers from other grades of the fuel, primarily the higher-sulfur Illinois variety. O'Connor suggested that the five-year plan Edison and the city had agreed upon would have the same effect as the amendment. If the City Council passed the amendment, he said, Edison would request a variance from the city's air pollution appeals board. Another Edison spokesman, Assistant to the President Behnke, put it more bluntly: "If we don't get the variance, we'll either have to operate illegally or else turn out the lights."

Edison made it plain that it did not oppose the whole amendment, only that it would undoubtedly have to seek a variance. "Where Commonwealth Edison differs from many of those opposing the amendment is that it has its own long-range plan to reduce the total amount of coal burned in the city," the *Daily News* editorialized. "Others simply want to continue contaminating the air as they please, with little thought to improvements at some future date."

When the City Council met in June, however, aldermen approved somewhat less stringent amendments. They extended the deadlines for incremental reductions in coal sulfur content six months across the board. Additionally, the revised regulations allowed the continued burning of high-sulfur coal if the user could cut its use by 50 percent over a four-year period. And the limits on sulfur content would not apply to fuel contracted for or bought before each limit went into effect.

"I do not think this will offend the public, and it is something the industry can live with," said Alderman William Harvey, chairman of the council's Health Committee.

About the time public hearings on the air pollution ordinance were being held, Senator Edmund Muskie of Maine came to Chicago and introduced a relatively new term to the average person's environmental vocabulary—thermal pollution. Muskie, nominated as the Democratic candidate for vice president in Chicago later that year, warned that the increasing number of nuclear generating stations along Lake Michigan posed a threat because they discharged 50 percent more waste heat into the water than other types of power plants. Muskie complained to members of the Union League Club that the Atomic Energy Commission had issued construction licenses to nuclear plants without adequate research into the effects of thermal pollution on the ecological balance of the waterways. The senator said nuclear generating stations should be required to install cooling towers to diminish waste heat before it goes into the water. Muskie also announced that the Senate subcommittee on air and water pollution, of which he was chairman, would open hearings on thermal pollution the next day in Washington.

Zion Station, where excavation work had just begun, would hear plenty about thermal pollution in the years immediately ahead. Meanwhile, construction of Dresden 2 and 3 and Quad-Cities 1 and 2 started to bog down. Ward blamed much of the delay on a slowdown in the manufacturers' fabrication of reactor vessels but regarded the problem as temporary, something normal in a new technology. For the first time, he mentioned the turnkey contracts in a company publication, describing how they insulated the company against inflationary pressures in the construction market. However, the turnkey pacts could not alleviate the delays, so in order to meet faster-than-expected load growth, the company ordered a new 800,000-kilowatt unit for Powerton.

"With more base-load capacity needed by 1972 and longer lead times required for nuclear units, there was no alternative to a coal-fired unit," Ward explained, pointing out that Powerton lent itself to expansion because of a competent workforce already in place, proximity to Illinois coal fields, and right-of-way access to the company transmission system.

Meanwhile, Edison and American Electric Power readied a transmission line that would operate at the highest AC voltage in the country. The 765,000-volt "power expressway" would extend 90 miles from Lakeville, Indiana, to Joliet, Illinois. Planned for service in mid-1971, the "765" could transport large blocks of power between Edison and its eastern neighbor, particularly to meet periods of high demand and compensate for any sudden loss of generation. Technology also advanced in the operating divisions with the arrival of the computerized Customer Information System (CIS), which enabled service representatives to tap the company's storehouse of data at their own desks, using a keyboard and screen monitor. Among other things, the CIS enabled the service rep to instantly call up a customer's account record on the screen and provide quick and correct answers to the customer's questions. An IBM Model 65–360 computer was installed in the General Office and connected by telephone lines to more than 200 sending and receiving terminals in the divisions. This computer gave access to the bank of electronically-filed facts and figures, including accounting, addressing, and meter records for 2.5-million customers. From desks in Chicago

North, Joliet, Dixon, or wherever, employes could reach into the G.O. computer file and obtain the facts they needed almost as easily and quickly as tuning in their favorite television program.

More and more Edison women found their way into the booming world of computers. Ann Smilanic served as one of the company's first female methods analysts in what later became the Data Processing department. With her math degree in hand, Margaret Schultz came to Edison for a job interview and soon found herself the only woman in a three-month computer programming training session. Four others joined her shortly afterward on the Computer Systems staff—Susan Flank, Patricia McKeirnan, Janice Streit, and Cathy Deam.

As in the early '40s, an increasing number of photos of Edison employes in uniform appeared in the *Service News*. Like the earlier depictions, the welcome sight of ruddy, young faces masked the unwelcome reason for their being there: the war in Viet Nam had rapidly escalated. In early 1969 the *Service News* brought word that Marine Corporal Bill Weimer, formerly of Stores-Chicago North and Correspondence G.O., had been killed when his unit of the Third Marine Division came under enemy attack in Quan Tri province.

In 1969, the war was always there and so was The Man Who Wasn't There. In fact, he not only refused to go away, but several of his brothers joined him, named Thermal Pollution, Nuclear Delays, The Need for Rate Relief, and More Vocal Environmental Protest. Edison found itself engaged in defensive action on many sides.

In January the *Daily News* ran a story in the sports section under the headline, "Nuclear plants could foul up lake fishing." The story went on to state that Chicago could get its first taste of thermal pollution in Lake Michigan when Zion began operating. "Fish biologists . . . point to what they call 'the real danger of thermal pollution.' Coho salmon prefer temperatures near 55°F, but they can survive temperatures up to 77°F." The news that warm lake water could harm fishing came as a surprise to anglers who had reeled in big ones for years near the warm-water discharge of coal-fired Waukegan Station. On a more scientific if not necessarily more practical basis, Edison pointed to studies by a Northwestern University biologist with the apt name of Dr. Wesley Pipes. Dr. Pipes maintained that discharging cooling water at or below 85°F should not have an adverse effect on the lake ecology around Zion. He took a close look at Waukegan Station, the largest generating station then operating on the lake, which had run for more than 45 years. The doctor concluded that he would find any long-term effects on lake ecology caused by the Waukegan outfall around the discharge channel. He found that cooling water temperatures from Waukegan dissipated to within two to three degrees Fahrenheit of surrounding water temperature only 1,500 feet from the point of discharge and completely dissipated within 3,200 feet of the outfall. Edison noted that although a nuclear plant requires about 50 percent more cooling water than a coal-fired facility, they have about the same discharge temperatures.

Dr. Pipes' findings did little or nothing to assuage certain politicians, environmentalists, and members of the press who continued to sound strident warnings about the alleged hazards of thermal pollution and demand that cooling towers be erected. O'Connor referred to a visit he and Tom Ayers had received from two members of an environmental group. "One individual talked about boiling the lake," O'Connor said, "and when I asked her what she meant, she said it would be like a cauldron. When I explained that the hottest temperature around the outlet would be somewhere around 85 degrees, she said, 'that doesn't make any difference; that's boiling.' I pointed out to her that her version of boiling and what I learned in the textbooks were really two quite different things.

"But it showed the depth of emotionalism attached to this subject. People had it in their minds that we were doing something very damaging to the lake, and to try to dissuade them from this view was very tough."

Ironically, the most prophetic commentary on the subject came from, of all places, a small newspaper in Michigan, the Alma *Daily Record-Leader*. "From Britain, however, comes a report that fish that were raised in warm sea water discharged from a nuclear station in Ayrshire grew much faster than normally," an editorial stated. "Dover sole reached marketable size in 18 months compared to the three years required by fish living in cold water.

"According to one authority, a new industry may be in the making and every British power station may someday have a fish farm." Edison's LaSalle County Station's fish farm would one day confirm that vision, but in August 1969 who was the Alma *Daily Record-Leader* to question the wisdom of eminent politicians and environmentalists?

In June of that year Edison won a pyrrhic victory in the battle over air pollution control which set the stage for a renewed outcry and additional public relations problems. The Chicago City Council, at the request of Mayor Daley, approved a one-year postponement in the deadline for limiting the sulfur content of coal burned in Chicago. The first cutback, to 2.5 percent, would have taken effect within less than two weeks. The council's action pushed back the entire three-year reduction schedule by one year.

Anti-Daley aldermen and environmental leaders became incensed by the move, branding it "an outrage," "a tragedy," "unparalleled audacity," and an action that would cause people to die of lung disease. Newspaper editorials criticized the mayor for caving in to coal-burning industries, including Commonwealth Edison. Daley explained that he advocated delay partly because of an insufficient supply of low-sulfur coal in Illinois, adding that he didn't want to close down plants and put workers out of jobs. Critics replied that industry could ship low-sulfur coal from other areas.

At least one prominent newspaper columnist suggested that Edison's Morgan Murphy had spoken to his good friend and former high school classmate, Dick Daley, about getting a pass for Edison. To this day, the suggestion draws a strong denial from Murphy's former right-hand man.

"I can tell you from my own personal experience that never did the two of them confer," Jim O'Connor asserts. "Never did they strike an agreement as to what the program for Edison would or should be. The action taken by the city was the result of a number of appearances by company witnesses in lengthy hearings before the pollution board of the City of Chicago."

Harris Ward entered the debate by declaring that the council's action would not affect Edison's program to cut in half the amount of coal it burned in the Chicago generating stations over the next four years. "Two-and-a-half years ago we made a pledge to the city of Chicago and to its citizens to pursue a program for reducing our stack emissions," Ward emphasized. "We are keeping our promise and will continue to do so."

Ward's assurances didn't placate the critics. A South Side community organization ran a newspaper ad bearing the headline, "Caution: Commonwealth Edison is hazardous to your health." The copy claimed that the company consumed 3.9 million tons of coal a year which emitted more than 230,000 tons of "deadly sulfur dioxide." Edison replied that the actual figures stood at 2.3 million and 150,000 tons, respectively. The company also reiterated that it had spent $50 million on pollution control and that more would come. Finally, Edison cited its efforts, in turning to nuclear and gas-fired generation, to avoid the future use of coal as much as possible. A spokesman for the community group said that it didn't claim that Edison was doing nothing, just not enough.

"I think we may have been slow in assessing the degree of public concern and the rapid buildup," O'Connor admitted later. "The issue of air quality came from nowhere."

In this adversarial climate, the company did something that, however necessary, would further alienate public opinion. For the first time in 11 years, it filed for a rate increase. In August 1969, Edison went before the Illinois Commerce Commission (ICC) seeking an increase in revenues of 6.1 percent, or $45.8 million annually. Ward termed the request "modest" and said the company needed it because the cost of money to carry out the five-year, $1.7 billion construction program had increased by 50 percent in the past three years. The construction program required the raising of $850 million through public financing. Another major factor, taxes, had risen 86 percent in 10 years. A newer, more startling ingredient was the cost of plant construction. The estimated per-kilowatt cost of the new Powerton unit rose 60 percent higher than that of the recently completed Kincaid units.

Edison's request was challenged before the ICC by Illinois' telegenic Attorney General, William J. Scott, on the grounds that the company polluted the air. He said his action marked the first time in his knowledge that a state attorney general had intervened in a public utility rate case for this reason. Scott, later convicted and imprisoned for the illegal use of campaign funds, said that a utility that wants a rate increase

"must come to the commission and courts with clean hands. . ."
Ironically, Edison sought the increase to continue its program of
phasing out polluting coal-fired plants and replacing them with
non-polluting nuclear facilities.

But the nuclear program itself began to receive stronger
attacks. The same day that Scott intervened in the rate case, the
regional director of the United Auto Workers (UAW) and owners of property on or near Lake Michigan filed suit in Lake
County Circuit Court, seeking an injunction to restrain Zion
Station from thermally polluting the lake. The suit contended
that beaches in the area would become useless and that the lake
would become uninhabitable for game fish. Calling such fears
unfounded, Edison's Waukegan District Manager, John Hughes,
said the plant would warm the water only slightly, and even that
effect would stay confined to an area within 3,200 feet of the
cooling water discharge pipe. Four days after the UAW action,
the Metropolitan Sanitary District (MSD) also filed for an injunction against Zion but went a step further and asked that construction stop until the company could prove that the plant
would not dump radioactive materials or return heated water to
the lake.

The press only briefly mentioned the announcement that
Edison had taken three coal-fired units out of service—two units
at Calumet and one at Fisk. More would retire the following
year. In another positive environmental move, the company
presented 1,250 acres of land near Lake Kincaid to the state of
Illinois for recreational purposes. The Department of Conservation would develop the land for fishing, camping and picknicking. Governor Richard Ogilvie presented a certificate of achievement to Tom Ayers and said the gift showed how superbly
private industry and state government can work together to
expand recreational opportunities.

II

The governor's kind words provided only brief respite
from the escalating environmental protests. From Washington
came word that organizers of the Vietnam Moratorium Day,
along with other student activists and former aides of the late
Senator Robert Kennedy, had scheduled a nationwide day of

protest against pollution for next spring. "The kids are looking for a new issue after Vietnam, and this is it," according to one participant. At home, Edison got its first taste of street demonstrations. Company officials had to make their way through a line of pickets, some wearing gas masks, when they arrived at the State of Illinois Building to present Edison's case for rate relief. The pickets belonged to a newly-formed organization called Citizens Revolt Against Pollution (CRAP) whose stated purpose was to promote activity against the Edison request.

Mayor Daley kicked off Cleaner Air Week by reporting a slight decrease in the sulfur dioxide content of Chicago's air during the first six months of 1969. The Mayor's air pollution control aides confirmed that the sulfur dioxide level had dropped over several years, but that 1969 had brought a more significant decrease. In a speech to a civic luncheon, Daley noted that Edison had shuttered the three units at Calumet and Fisk and planned to close more.

Before the year was over, though, the air pollution graph would have rises as well as drops. In November, another of those infamous high pressure systems hung over the city for five days, trapping pollutants and driving sulfur dioxide levels above the danger level. Edison reduced coal burning at its Chicago generating stations so it generated only 10 percent of the power needs of the city in the city itself, with half of the city generation gas-fired. As the company took action, another newly-formed anti-utility group, Businessmen for the Public Interest (BPI), filed a petition with the ICC saying Edison should not receive a rate increase because it failed to utilize "more effective" devices to curb air pollution. William Stanley said Edison's equipment met the demands of the city's ordinance. In the City Council an anti-administration alderman introduced a resolution directing the mayor to declare "power dimouts" during times of air pollution alerts in which business, industrial and residential electricity users would reduce their consumption to the lowest possible minimum. The resolution, shunted to the council's Health Committee, met the fate of all proposals by Daley opponents.

This does not imply that Daley never considered the ideas of his adversaries or public opinion in general; he just never wanted to *appear* that they had any effect on him. He had to

340

initiate, not respond. In the immediate aftermath of Dr. Martin Luther King Jr.'s assassination, a Black independent alderman proposed that 47th Street be renamed in honor of the civil rights leader. Daley brushed the suggestion aside. A little later the mayor proposed to rename South Parkway in honor of Dr. King. And so it happened. For all of his power to bend city government to his will, he remained super-sensitive to what the public would or would not stand for. In one of his more grandiose public works ideas, he proposed an airport built in Lake Michigan and connected by causeway to downtown Chicago. Not only the environmentalists, but many others also thought this a most ill-advised idea and rallied behind the slogan, "Don't do it in the lake." Daley persisted for some time, but when he realized the breadth of opposition, he carefully backed away from the proposal. Now, in December 1969, with the press and public clamoring for officials to "do something" about pollution, the mayor revealed that he would establish a new city department to design and enforce programs to control air, water and noise pollution. Daley did not say who he would name as environmental control commissioner, but the public received the impression that Bill Stanley was on the way out. The mayor promised details shortly.

A few weeks earlier Edison had announced that it could not meet the extended deadline of July 5, 1970, for reducing the sulfur content of coal burned in the city to 2.5 percent or lower. "Even with a complete shutdown of Edison's six Chicago area plants, 98 percent of the (city's total) air contamination would remain," O'Connor told a news conference. "The company is already dealing with its responsibility in emergencies by switching to other fuels and to generating plants remote from the city. This present company plan goes beyond what could be achieved with a dimout."

Edison's experiments with low-sulfur coal, though, had not progressed well. Byron Lee Jr. reported at the time that tests using coal from three separate western areas in boilers at Crawford and Ridgeland had been "disappointing." In one test at Ridgeland, according to Lee, workers had to shut down the boiler because the slag runoff from the low-sulfur coal formed a rock-hard residue that only jackhammers could chip out. He said that the dust output at each station more than doubled. Nevertheless Lee said the experiments would continue, adding that coal from

Montana and Wyoming offered the best prospects of supply in significant quantities.

Soon afterward, the company decided to convert Ridgeland from coal to oil with a sulfur content of less than 1.5 percent. The cost of converting the furnace and fuel handling facilities reached $7 million, with another $5 million a year to go for higher fuel bills. Edison expected to finish the conversion, which would eliminate the burning of 1.3 million tons of coal a year, by the following July, or about the time the Chicago restrictions were to go into effect.

The new step did nothing to deter an estimated 250 anti-pollution demonstrators from descending on the State of Illinois Building to protest Edison's rate request and to demand that the company spend more money on pollution control. The noisy demonstrators presented petitions, supposedly bearing 10,000 signatures, to the rate case hearing examiner.

"In Chicago, Commonwealth Edison Company has become the symbol of the sulfur dioxide gas air pollution problem," a reporter concluded in a decade's-end column, and no one could argue with him.

To make matters worse, the company's nuclear construction program, cornerstone of the ongoing efforts to reduce emissions, continued to lag. Dresden 2, slated for operation in the immediate future, lagged nearly two years behind schedule. Edison anticipated similar delays for the other units under construction, mainly because of the late delivery of reactor vessels. Although the vessel represented no more than five percent of the total cost of the plant, it had welding and metallurgical requirements more rigorous than those of coal-fired units. Suppliers had to add manpower and machinery and subcontract various vessel components. Still, turnkey contracts sheltered Edison against big cost overruns for Dresden 2 and 3 and Quad-Cities 1 and 2. According to *Forbes* magazine, "That leaves (Edison) about $200 million ahead (per unit), and explains why GE and Westinghouse no longer make turnkey contracts." Additionally, the company had purchased, at reasonable prices, a 10-year supply of nuclear fuel for all six reactors under construction. Coal prices would not go any place but up, the company believed, while nuclear fuel stood a good chance of becoming cheaper through technological improvement.

342

In fact, Ward looked forward to new opportunities. "Somebody has to mine the uranium," he noted. "Somebody has to take it through the processing stages ... If you go into the nuclear power business, there are all sorts of opportunities available to you in the nuclear fuel cycle.

"I have the same faith in nuclear power as the first flyer had in the airplane. Of course, when the airplane was being developed, some people wanted to build dirigibles, and some people wanted to keep on walking."

Two men who would play important roles in Edison's nuclear program in the 1970s and beyond received promotions as the 1960s ended. Wallace Behnke became a vice president, and Byron Lee became assistant to the president.

Many other Edison employes also found new homes at this time. Approximately 700 General Office employes moved into the 60-story First National Bank Building at Madison and Clark Streets, the world's tallest bank building. As the largest tenant, Edison occupied five floors of the all-electric, heat-with-light structure. In addition to the executive offices, Advertising, Public Relations, Rate, Purchasing, Statistical Research, and other departments filled the five floors. Western Division got a new, all-electric headquarters in Glenbard. More than 100 employes moved into the building adjacent to the expanded structure that housed Glenbard Area personnel. The new headquarters featured heat-with-light, as well as the very latest in communications and computer equipment. Elsewhere in Western Division, company employes began to work in the new Des Plaines Valley Area (DVA) headquarters in Maywood. DVA's offices also featured heat-with-light. Located immediately west of Edison's Technical Center, DVA headquarters housed some 100 employes. Edison and Westinghouse announced plans to build a $5 million nuclear training center located near the company's newest nuclear generating station under construction at Zion. With the ability to train more than 200 people a year, employes of other organizations as well as Edison, the center stood as the largest and most versatile of its kind. The centerpiece of the new facility, a computerized simulator exactly reproducing the Zion control room, could duplicate any event that might occur in the operation of a pressurized water reactor generating station. Edison would supply the land and the 30,000-square-foot building. Westinghouse

343

would equip, staff, and operate the facility. Edison and General Electric had successfully maintained a similar operation near Dresden since 1968.

No sooner had the calendar uncovered a new decade than did events in the environmental arena, as if on cue, begin to accelerate. As expected, Mayor Daley dumped Bill Stanley as director of air pollution control and replaced him with H. Wallace Poston, a federal water pollution control administrator, who would preside over a new department of environmental control with a $2 million annual budget. "The mayor indicated he wanted the best program in the country and the best people," Poston commented. "The public is demanding cleaner air, cleaner water, and less noise." Three days later, Poston encountered the highest levels of air pollution since the "supersmog" of the previous November.

The environmental control department wasn't the only organization born in early 1970 with which Edison would have to contend. Founded on the same day as the smog alert, the Campaign Against Pollution (CAP) adopted a program calling for utility customers to pay their bills into a trust fund, rather than to Edison, and for customers to buy a single share of Edison stock so they could attend the annual meeting and protest against pollution. CAP also planned to urge present Edison stockholders to speak out on the issue or to turn over their proxies to the protest group.

The architect of the stock strategy, veteran social organizer Saul Alinsky, served as the behind-the-scenes organizer of CAP. One of the founders of the radical Students for a Democratic Society publicly headed the organization. According to the *Tribune*, a Chicago police officer had told a Senate subcommittee earlier that the CAP leader once dominated a meeting of still another group with his tirades against Mayor Daley. "He suggested to the group of 40 persons to go to Mayor Daley's home and demonstrate, to throw paint at the mayor, to harass his children, and even suggested the bombing of the Picasso statue in the Civic Center."

Soon after its inception, CAP urged Edison customers to delay paying their bills and to pay in pennies. Some customers made out their payment checks to the "Department of Pollution." In February, CAP picketed the company's First National

Bank offices. "We had a lot of marchers and shouters at the time, and I think that nobody wanted to listen," Ayers remembered. The company reported that it felt no slowdown in payments and added that pledges to send electricity payments to CAP's trust fund had not been kept. At the same time, Edison warned the public not to believe CAP's claim that the company wouldn't disconnect electricity for non-payment if "thousands of individuals stood together."

In the meantime the leader of a neighborhood clean air group, active long before CAP, lashed out at CAP's ongoing attacks against Edison, calling them "a radical attempt to tear down our form of government." He told a rally that CAP members were "the panic peddlers of pollution," rapped Alinsky as "a radical leader who is against our system of private enterprise," and said he had learned that Alinsky and his forces planned to disrupt Edison's April 27 annual meeting.

Edison responded to the increasing criticism in two ways. First it mounted a massive effort to communicate the company's story to the media, the public, and its own employes. The *Service News* ran features titled "Setting the Record Straight" and "Telling It Like It Is." An eight-page report, "Air Pollution in the Chicago Area," reached opinion leaders and other constituencies. Subtitled "What Commonwealth Edison is doing to help reduce (air pollution), what we will do, and when," the report explained just that—through plain language and easy-to-understand graphics. The company also increased the flow of news releases and official public statements.

Edison made a second, much more dramatic move which took just about everyone by surprise.

"I remember driving to work one morning," Gordon Corey recalled, "and saying to myself, 'OK, we've fought it long enough. We will stop trying to get permission to burn the cheapest coal. We will comply and do whatever is necessary.' I asked Glen (Beeman) and George (Rifakes) to make their deals for western coal, and we went ahead and did it." Corey added that the decision was agreed upon by Ayers and other members of the hierarchy.

The surprise announcement, on March 3, 1970, that Edison would fully comply with the city's upcoming restrictions on the use of high-sulfur coal rated major headlines in the newspapers.

"Public pressure and the desires expressed for cleaner air throughout the nation have accelerated our program," Ayers declared.

The company would purchase 4.5 million tons of low-sulfur coal, most of it from new mines in Wyoming and Montana. Ayers cautioned that problems in burning the new coal, including furnace clogging and difficulties with ash discharges, would persist. But he said that the company's production and fuel people had come up with an apparently workable mixture of Western and Illinois coal.

Low sulfur coal fills a unit train in Colstrip, Montana, in 1971. That was the year after Edison switched to Western coal to comply with clean air regulations.

The new program also featured the purchase of 300 rail cars at a cost of $4.75 million to carry the low sulfur coal from more than 1,000 miles away, the installation of demonstration sulfur removal devices at State Line and Will County, the displacement in 1970 of five million tons of coal with almost one billion therms of gas—a 50 percent increase over the amount of gas used in 1969—a new $22 million order for 228,000 kw of gas and oil-fired peaking capacity, and an additional $150 million outlay for pollution control facilities. Later in the month Edison announced that six more generating stations, outside the city of Chicago, would use low-sulfur coal.

Newspaper editorial writers and some environmentalists, but not CAP, expressed general satisfaction with Edison's moves. Two public relations hurdles, however, loomed in Edison's immediate future—"Earth Day" on April 22 and the stockholders' meeting five days after that.

The protest reached a boil at a noon rally in the Civic Center Plaza attended by some 10,000 persons. The protesters waved signs, wore gas masks, released black balloons symbolizing air pollution, and listened to speeches by Attorney General Scott, CAP leader Paul Booth, and others. Another activist, David Dinsmore Comey of BPI, did not participate in the demonstration but welcomed a television news crew to his office overlooking the plaza so they could film from a bird's-eye perspective. One hundred fifty Edison speakers, organized and coached by George Travers, fanned out across the service territory in an effort to make sure that the company's side of the environmental story didn't get drowned out in the chorus of protests. Most speakers appeared at high school and college teach-ins.*

On the eve of Earth Day, Edison scored a minor coup by announcing the formation of a 12-member, blue-ribbon environmental advisory council to help the company carry out programs to combat pollution while operating independently of Edison management. The panel included doctors, educators, and scientists, including Dr. John T. Rettaliata, President of the Illinois Institute of Technology (IIT); The Very Reverend John R. Cortelyou, President of DePaul University; The Very Reverend James McGuire, Chancellor and President of Loyola University; and Dr. Albert V. Crewe, physics professor at the University of Chicago's Enrico Fermi Institute. "I have no doubt the company is sincere in asking our assistance in solving pollution problems," Dr. Crewe said. CAP, on the other hand, blasted the panel, although its chagrin seemed to stem mainly from the fact that none of the five universities represented which owned Edison stock would turn their proxies over to CAP.

The annual meeting turned out to be the circus CAP had hoped it would be. A fist fight between a protestor and a security officer broke out in the lobby as a contingent of CAP members

---

*The Earth Day undertaking marked the beginning of Edison's Speakers Bureau.

tried to force their way into the 1,100-seat auditorium of the Prudential Building, already filled to capacity. Police subdued the protestor as about 150 demonstrators succeeded in getting into the meeting. Another 500 stood blocked at the door, where they spent the meeting chanting and singing. Thwarted in their efforts to pack the meeting, CAP's organizers led about 60 supporters down the center aisle as Ward attempted to convene the meeting. One of the leaders, a young Catholic priest, shouted demands for pollution controls at the Edison chairman against a background of boos, catcalls, and cautious applause. Then the CAP contingent left, promising to return for an answer. An hour later, the priest and several others did return to shout again at Ward, who replied, "I can't hear you." More shouts of "shut up" and "sit down" rose from stockholders, more cheers from protestors. After failing to be recognized, the group rejoined their companions in the lobby. CAP members passed around plastic bags for contributions, then dispersed, promising to hold a demonstration the next day at the City Council.

The Edison annual meeting hardly stood apart that year. Rowdy demonstrators also disrupted a number of other annual meetings, including those of AT&T, Honeywell, and Gulf Oil. The *Tribune* said in an editorial that the protest movement "was billed originally as anti-pollution but has degenerated into anti-war, anti-capitalist and anti-just-about-everything. Instead of fighting pollution, the demonstrators have contributed to it with stink bombs, leaflets, litter, noise, rudeness and unruly behavior."

The media themselves came under fire from one of their own in an article in *Quill*, a magazine for journalists, which charged that ecologists now manipulated reporters the way anti-Communist crusaders manipulated the press in the 1950s. Writer Dennis J. Chase maintained that certain ecologists tactically presented everything in terms of crisis: "(The) refrain is always the same: imminent danger, immediate action." Chase criticized news people for not casting a critical eye at the various reports, conclusions or opinions on which ecologists based the "crisis". He called this style of reporting "eco-journalism, the journalistic practice of reporting ecological crises by ignoring, treating as unimportant, or mishandling the evidence on which the crises are based." As an example, he

348

pointed to a *New York Times* story which stated that the air in New York City was seven percent dirtier in 1971 than in 1969. In the 14th of 17 paragraphs sat the basis for the claim: average particulate concentration had increased from 98 to 104 micrograms per cubic meter. But Chase showed that a closer reading of the statistics demonstrated quite a different trend: the particulate concentration in New York had steadily declined—from 520 micrograms per cubic meter in 1931–32, to 114 in 1957, to 98 in 1969, to 88 for the first four months of 1972. Under the rules of eco-journalism, Chase proclaimed, "Evidence is nice, but not necessary to make 'news'."

The next challenge to Commonwealth Edison came from a group of people about as far removed, culturally as well as geographically, from the unbarbered types who disrupted the annual meeting as the corn and soybean fields of rural Illinois from the steel and concrete of Chicago's Loop. Approximately 150 of the people who tilled those fields and the business people who served them gathered on the lawn of a farm home south of Seneca as Independence Day approached. They had no celebration in mind, however. The residents planned to block construction of Edison's proposed new LaSalle County Nuclear Generating Station, slated for construction about three miles south of Seneca. The twin-unit, boiling water reactor plant would require nearly 7,000 acres, mostly for a 4,480-acre cooling lake. Harris Ward assured the people of LaSalle County that the 2.2-million-kilowatt station, scheduled for service in 1975 and 1976, would be a good neighbor.

The farmers did not believe him. Edison planned to take good farmland, they complained, land too productive for the likes of a power plant and a cooling lake. One of the families had farmed the land since 1837, another since 1854. Fifty-six families would have to move if Edison built the plant, the farmers claimed. Most, ironically, were tenant farmers. They urged Edison to build the station on abandoned strip mine land in the area, a suggestion Edison declared unfeasible because of the need to build generating stations on flat land. The farmers planned to file a complaint with the newly-created Illinois Pollution Control Board, asking the panel to decide whether the public interest was best served by construction of an electric generating station or by the preservation of valuable farm land.

"It was a touchy issue to confront, being the big city utility against the poor struggling farmer," O'Connor remembered. "It made the public relations job very, very difficult for us."

In another corner of the state Edison and its partner in the Quad-Cities Nuclear Generating Station, Iowa-Illinois Gas & Electric, were about to be whacked with a federal lawsuit seeking to prevent the alleged thermal pollution of the Mississippi River. The local chapter of the Izaak Walton League demanded a closed-cycle cooling system for the plant under construction. The cooling system would tack an estimated $30 million onto the cost of the plant. A League spokesman said that the group was "very sympathetic" toward Edison and Iowa-Illinois. "They have increasing demands for more energy, but we feel they can meet those needs without downgrading the environment."

The only nuclear station unassailed for one reason or another was Dresden. Unit 2 quietly went into commercial service in the late spring of 1970, adding 809,000 kw to the system and joining historic Unit 1, which had produced more than nine billion kwh of electricity since 1960.

With demand for nuclear fuel growing, Edison announced plans to form a wholly-owned subsidiary corporation to specialize in the procurement and management of such fuels. The company filed a petition with the ICC, seeking authority to incorporate the new company with a capitalization of $10 million.

Such action by the ICC was considered a formality. What the Commission did on July 10 was not. The panel granted Edison a rate increase of 4.8 percent or $36 million but at the same time entered an unprecedented order that the company spend an estimated $200 million on pollution control over the next six years. The company would have to retire existing coal-burning generating stations, install and improve precipitators, install closed-cycle cooling at Zion, and take a number of other steps. If Edison failed to comply, the ICC could rescind up to 50 percent of the increase. As officials noted, Edison had already planned most of the steps ordered by the commission, but the ICC decision established ironclad deadlines. Ward said the company was "extremely disappointed" that it did not receive the 6.1

percent increase it had requested the previous August. He said the amount allowed could not meet rising costs.

ICC order or not, the company continued to raze smoke stacks at four generating stations where it had phased out coal-fired units. Down came three stacks at Northwest, five at Calumet, two at Waukegan, and two at Crawford. Northwest itself passed into history in September after 58 years of service in which it supplied 25 million kwh of electricity to Edison customers. Retirement of the plant, at 3400 N. California Ave. on Chicago's Northwest Side, eliminated the burning of 25 million tons of coal annually. Soon after its retirement, the station was razed.

The dean of public relations, Morgan Murphy, retired as chairman of the executive committee on September 1, wrapping up a career that had begun with Public Service Company in 1924. His protege, Jim O'Connor, had risen to vice president a few months earlier only seven years after his starting with Edison in 1963. Another relative newcomer, Preston Kavanagh, who had also started with Edison in '63, became secretary of the company. He succeeded William Colwell, who retired after 30 years of service.

The battle over thermal pollution seemed to turn against Edison and Zion Station with word that federal authorities had decided to impose a virtual ban on hot water discharges from generating stations along Lake Michigan. The decision set the stage for what newspapers called a "scientific confrontation" between Edison and the federal government before the Illinois Pollution Control Board. But a funny thing happened on the way to the "confrontation."

Attorney General Scott testified that no hot water should enter the lake—period. A state representative said the water temperature should not rise more than one degree. Members of CAP testified in favor of a zero limit and directed jeers and insults at the director of the Illinois Environmental Protection Agency when he declined to give his view. Testifying for Edison, Byron Lee proposed that only generating stations operating or planned along the lake be allowed to discharge heated water, subject to existing heat limits and proper design. Lee further advocated the careful monitoring of these discharges.

Edison rolled out its heaviest artillery on the second day of hearings. Six prominent scientists, including Dr. Donald W. Pritchard, an oceanographer from Johns Hopkins University, testified that little or no harmful effects should result from thermal discharges. Dr. Pritchard stated that no scientific evidence supported a federal recommendation that water released into the lake should not be one degree warmer than the natural temperature at the discharge point. What did the federal people say to that? Nobody knew for sure because, without giving any explanation, they failed to appear at the hearings. The "confrontation" never materialized. The government no-show drew a sharp retort from Pollution Control Board Chairman David Currie, who complained that all of the scientific testimony in the proceedings had come from Edison with nothing from the company's opponents.

In the months immediately following, three more developments strengthened Edison's position. The company warned that residential electricity bills could rise sharply with the installment of cooling towers at Zion. Edison's blue-ribbon advisory panel weighed in with a 57-page study that rejected closed-cycle cooling in favor of once-through or "open" cooling, given extensive monitoring to make certain there were no adverse effects. Finally, federal and state officials together proposed that utilities be allowed to discharge warm water into the lake through 1975, at which time they would have to prove that the discharges posed no threat to the lake.

Even though it now appeared that the company could avoid building costly cooling towers at Zion, the public began to realize that the era of cheap power was over. A new catch phrase crept into everyday language—"energy crisis." Continuing heavy demands for power, combined with strict new environmental laws and a shortage of fuels to meet the new requirements, contributed to the problem. Fuel prices skyrocketed. Utilities sought bigger and more frequent rate increases. In Edison's service territory, Illinois coal, a plentiful and cheap source of fuel, faded due to its high sulfur content. Low-sulfur coal, now rolling in at the rate of 80,000 tons a week from mines in Wyoming, Montana, Utah and eastern Kentucky, helped to clear the air but at much greater cost. Natural gas offered a clean-burning alternative to other boiler fuels, but the gas companies,

352

claiming a shortage of supplies, threatened to cut off Edison's allocation. Nuclear power, under assault for alleged thermal pollution, would come under additional criticism for alleged radiological and safety shortcomings. Edison used low-sulfur oil at Ridgeland but only after bringing it some 1,400 miles from the Bahamas under an import dispensation granted by the Interior Department. Furthermore, Edison's Fuel Manager, George Rifakes, sent up early warnings of the possible hazards of overdependence on Middle Eastern or South American oil. A hydroelectric dam would have escaped criticism. The ideal solution, but for the fact that northern Illinois is as flat as the proverbial table top.

III

Edison's relationship with its customers—its dealings with the "new consumerism"—came under scrutiny at the annual Management Conference as the tumultuous first year of the new decade drew to a close. "Organized action, militant expression, political response, and growing confidence gaps between buyer and seller are the character of the day," Behnke lamented. "(F)rom here on out we will live in an environmental fish bowl," Lee noted. "Our actions will be questioned and our plans will be probed. There will be hearings, investigations, and long questionnaires. There will be frustrations and large expenditures."

But the company had already begun counter-measures with a Speakers Bureau of 175 Edison people. Briefed on environmental matters and armed with a prototype speech, they addressed service clubs, church groups, schools, and most anyone else who would listen, usually on their own time. In its first 14 weeks, the group spoke to nearly 1,500 audiences representing 150,000 people.

Edison also revamped its advertising program. "Little Bill," Edison hero, retired. "Concern For Your Total Environment" became the new corporate slogan. In print and on television, the company explained the many ways it preserved the environment. A new, sharp logo came to represent the company. A lower case "e" circled by a larger lower case "c" symbolized Commonwealth Edison's concern for the environment. A TV spot focusing on Sangchris Lake served two purposes: it related that the company had deeded the power plant cooling pond to the state for public recreation while mentioning that no thermal pollution existed—the fish "bite like crazy."

The famous CE logo symbolizes two things: Commonwealth Edison and its "Concern For Your Total Environment."

In January 1971 Edison filed for its first double-digit rate increase—10.4 percent, or $95.2 million. Ward said that the company urgently needed the boost, particularly to help finance the construction budget which had now grown to $2.5 billion for the period of 1971–75. He pointed out that Edison's interest on debt in 1970 amounted to $85 million—nearly $37 million more than it had two years before. He also mentioned that the company's expenditures for environmental improvement would total at least $285 million by the end of 1975. If approved by the ICC, the request would have added $1.20 to the typical monthly residential electricity bill.

The rate filing seemed a fitting prelude for another go-around with protestors at the annual meeting, so Edison fortified its stance with tight security. Oddly enough, no demonstrators appeared. Instead, the meeting proceeded in an orderly fashion with discussion centering on the environment and the need for rate relief. Shareholders elected a Black executive, George Johnson, president of a cosmetics company that bore his name, to the board of directors. Meanwhile, Edison again became an all-electric company with the merger of Mid-Illinois Gas Company and Northern Illinois Gas. Mid-Illinois, formed as a wholly-owned Edison subsidiary in 1968, furnished gas to more than 100,000 customers in the areas of Rockford, Lincoln, and Tuscola. Edison had acquired the gas operation in the 1966 merger with Central Illinois Electric and Gas Company.

Dresden Station, which heretofore had avoided regulatory problems, now came in for its share. In March 1971 the

Pollution Control Board ruled that Unit 3 could not operate until the cooling lake under construction was ready, by about the beginning of October. The ruling set off alarm signals at Edison: could it meet the coming summer peak load? The Pollution Board said that rather than have Dresden 3 discharge heated water directly into the Illinois River, Edison must reduce voltage to customers. In other words, it must effect brownouts, cut off power to some industrial customers under the interruptible service clause, and buy more power from other utilities around the country.

At the end of April, after the company had testified to a summer reserve margin of approximately two percent, the Board softened its stand. Dresden 3 could operate without a cooling lake, but only with several strings attached. For one thing, Edison would have to spend $3 million for a spray cooling system to operate until the $24 million lake was ready. For another, the ruling would not allow the plant to operate at full capacity until the company had reduced voltage to all customers and had cut it off altogether to certain industrial customers. The board even suggested a future ban on all new electrical hookups. Without those conditions, Edison would have to keep 600,000 combined kw of Units 1 and 2 idle. Edison reluctantly agreed to the proposal which, according to Ward, was based on "a very questionable assumption that thermal effects of Dresden's full operation might harm an already dirty river." "It isn't as though the power company were dumping poisons into the river," a *Daily News* editorial added.

With 98 spray modules in operation, Dresden 3 generated its first power in July. The kwh arrived too late, however, for the 1971 peak load reached on June 28, an increase of 9.1 percent over the previous year. For three straight days temperatures hovered at or near 100 degrees. The absence of Dresden 3, along with a Kincaid unit down for repairs, made it a tight fit, but MAIN came to the rescue. At considerable expense, Edison brought in blocks of power from elsewhere in the Midwest and beyond to avert voltage reductions and industrial curtailments.

Quad-Cities Station was next on the thermal pollution hit list. Even though the company had announced plans to install a $9 million jet diffusing system to facilitate the mixing of discharged water with the Mississippi, Attorney General Scott filed suit in federal court to block the Atomic Energy Commission from issuing an operating license for the plant. Scott claimed that the cooling water discharge would raise the temperature of large sections of the river, causing a "significant impact on the quality of the human environment." A day earlier the Iowa Water Pollution Control Commission had denied the diffuser proposal. The double blow notwithstanding, the Illinois Pollution Control Board issued an operating permit to Quad-Cities with the restriction that it operate at only half power through April 1972. But that victory quickly evaporated a month later, in December 1971, when a federal judge in Washington granted Scott's request and issued a temporary injunction, barring the plant's operation until the AEC issued a detailed study on its environmental impact.

While the spotlight focused on Zion, Dresden, and Quad-Cities, Edison's low-key campaign to win approval of LaSalle County Station began to show results. After finding overwhelming opposition to the plant early on, a local newspaper discovered in a followup poll that a majority favored construction. Events outside the control of Commonwealth Edison helped. For instance, unemployment rose due to layoffs and strikes. The prospect of a plant employing thousands of construction workers and hundreds of permanent employes, with both groups pumping big dollars into the local economy, looked more attractive than ever. Most importantly, that scenario brought the skilled trade unions over to Edison's side. The argument that lack of an adequate supply of power would discourage industrial expansion didn't hurt, either. Edison finally revealed that much of the land was not quite as fertile as the opposing farmers claimed. Farmers had placed additional acreage in soil banks, the company noted.

In August 1971 the Illinois Commerce Commission voted unanimously to allow Edison to build LaSalle County Station as proposed. Commission Chairman David Armstrong said that the panel reached the decision after it weighed all public interest factors, incuding the electric power needs of two million homes, businesses and industries. "The location was chosen because it has the least ecological impact of any site proposed," Armstrong asserted.

The battle over the site pushed the service date of the plant back 18 months—from the end of 1975 to mid-1977. Then in November 1971 the farmers asked the Federal District Court in Chicago to enjoin Edison from taking condemnation action against reluctant landowners until the Atomic Energy Commission had determined the best use of the acreage.

The ICC decided the rate case just before the year concluded, granting the company an increase of 7.1 percent, or $65.9 million, which Edison called inadequate to carry out the construction program. However, the ICC left the door open for further increases effective in 1973 if the company could confirm the actual inadequacy of the increase. The commission did, in fact, approve an extra 2.9 percent, or $32.5 million, that year.

Over the winter, Edison repeatedly warned of impending brownouts and blackouts from the delay of its nuclear power program. In testimony before the Joint Committee on Atomic Energy and the Pollution Control Board, as well as in the annual report, officials stressed the importance of operating the Zion and Quad-Cities plants in the following summer. "We will make every effort to avert outages in our service area," Ward stated in the annual report, "but if our power sources and those of others are needlessly idled, we may be faced with an impossible task." On Capitol Hill Ayers went further, warning of selective or rolling blackouts affecting hundreds of thousands of customers.

The Calvert Cliffs Decision compounded the problem of existing legal, regulatory, and environmental challenges. In a case involving a nuclear station under construction at Calvert Cliffs, Maryland, the U.S. District Court of Appeals for the District of Columbia held that the AEC had erred by not conducting environmental impact reviews and cost-benefit analyses during the licensing process. The AEC promptly issued new regulations to implement the court decision, a turn of events that caused nuclear plant licensing activity practically to come to a halt and jeopardized the construction and operation of some 90 units around the country.

With the first breezes of spring came a compromise at Quad-Cities. In what appeared as the only chance to get the plant into operation for the summer, Edison and Iowa-Illinois agreed to install a $30 million closed-cycle spray canal cooling system. Installation would take more than two years to complete, so Edison had to go ahead with the $9 million diffuser, which would operate until the other system came on line. Attorney

General Scott and the Izaak Walton League, in turn, dropped their lawsuits, and the Iowa pollution board dropped its objections to the diffuser. Quad-Cities Unit 1, ready to go since the previous November, generated its first electricity in April. Edison estimated that it had lost more than $1 million a week as a result of the plant's idleness.

"When people can force you into very difficult litigating circumstances, while the interest is running on these huge projects, it becomes more economic to bow to the pressure and do things that you don't really feel are the right things to do," said O'Connor, reflecting on the agreement. "The bottom line becomes the final cost to the customer. If you don't do it (install closed-cycle cooling), the cost to the customer, long term, is going to be far greater."

A massive selective blackout did occur in the summer of 1972, but it did not occur in Edison's service territory; it happened in New York. "Where else?" said most Chicagoans. Consolidated Edison deliberately blacked out a section of Brooklyn inhabited by up to 300,000 persons after six of ten cables feeding the area failed during the thirteenth day of a heat wave. An overload on the remaining 27,000-volt cables would have caused the entire system to collapse, as it did in 1965.

"I don't care what they say about Chicago and Mayor Daley," a Chicago woman visiting Brooklyn said. "At least we always get our electricity."

The Chicago area also struggled in the throes of a July heat wave, but Edison averted a voltage reduction, not to mention a selective blackout, by invoking its interruptible service agreements with two steel mills and by purchasing power from other utilities. A *Daily News* editorial correctly pointed out that the area would have been in "a desperate fix" if the AEC hadn't issued a temporary permit for Quad-Cities to operate. "The output from that plant has provided the margin of difference in the last few days between normal living (which in these times includes the massive use of air conditioning) and an electrical breakdown, with all that implies in the way of discomfort and business shutdowns."

Environmentalists, including Businessmen for the Public Interest, now trained their sights on Zion, asking the AEC for permission to intervene in the licensing hearings. The intervenors contended that Edison should have to install closed-cycle cooling. Their announcement brought shudders to company officials, who foresaw more delay, more unnecessary costs, and more close calls with power shortages. Then late in the year, within a little more than a week, Edison received a double shot of good news: the AEC recommended that Zion operate without cooling towers and a federal judge in Chicago dismissed the suit by the farmers which sought to block condemnation proceedings for LaSalle County Station. The AEC said that only after Zion operated and harmful effects of thermal pollution appeared, would they order the addition of cooling towers or other appropriate devices. The judge ruled that the farmers were premature: Edison had only asked the AEC for authority to build the plant. If a construction permit were granted, the farmers could file suit again.

This wasn't the last that Edison would hear from the small, determined group from LaSalle County, but it effectively marked the end of the thermal pollution controversy. BPI would continue to make noise for awhile, but the non-issue was collapsing of its own weight. Put another way, it became obvious that the emperor wasn't wearing any clothes. No damage to the lake would occur. In a few years, people would forget the very term "thermal pollution," a curiosity from a period in which emotions sometimes got the better of judgments. One cannot easily forget the warm water discharge plume at Zion: all of those fishing boats cluster around it as a reminder.

Since the spring of 1972 fishermen without boats have enjoyed good luck from a bridge that Edison built across Waukegan Station's discharge canal. Constructed at a cost of $125,000, the bridge links a city park to the station's breakwater pier on Lake Michigan. The company presented the bridge to the city of Waukegan. After Tom Ayers and Mayor Sabonjian made the first "official" casts, the company held a contest for the largest catch of the day. A 12-year-old Zion boy pulled in a six-pound, two-ounce brown trout, winning the event. However, another local youth who had jumped the gun reeled in a 14-pounder. About the same time, Edison also opened the shoreline of State Line Station to public fishing, making nearly a half mile of casting room available.

359

In the summer of 1972 Edison hinted that it would build its fifth nuclear generating station in the Rockford area. The company had been buying land near the small town of Byron, in Ogle County, about 18 miles southwest of Rockford, causing several dozen farmers to band together and express concerns over land prices and the possible construction of a large cooling lake. A rumor surfaced that the total site would exceed 5,000 acres. Late in the year, when the company officially announced the plant location, the farmers heaved a sigh of relief heard all the way to Edison's corporate headquarters. The site would take up only 1,500 acres, and the plant would utilize cooling towers, not a man-made lake. With the LaSalle controversy still unresolved, the last thing Edison needed was another battle over land acquisition that would delay the startup of a needed generating station. According to news accounts, virtually all of the landowners who sold property to Edison thought they had made fine deals. Some farmers said they planned to retire, while others said they would buy other farms. One man even said he probably would have sold his land, but he hadn't been asked.

The Byron announcement overshadowed the simultaneous disclosure that Edison planned to build an identical pressurized water reactor plant in unincorporated Will County, about 20 miles southwest of Joliet. Named Braidwood Station, after a nearby town, the plant would occupy 7,700 acres, 4,900 of them for a cooling lake. Land acquisition would not pose a problem. Much of the land on which the lake would stand bore the deep, ugly scars of former strip mine operations. Both Byron and Braidwood would have two 1.1 million-kilowatt units supplied by Westinghouse. The Byron units were scheduled for operation in 1979 and 1980, Braidwood's units in 1980 and 1981.

As the nuclear program moved ahead, so, too, did the program to shut down obsolete coal-fired plants and make envionmental improvements in others. The 75-year-old Fordam Generating Station, once Rockford's only source of central station electric service, closed down in the fall of 1971. State Line and Will County Stations each obtained wet scrubbers, costing $4 million and $7 million, respectively, to test the ability of the process to eliminate sulfur dioxide and fly ash. To further reduce emissions at State Line, the company arranged to purchase an additional 22 million tons of low-sulfur coal from Montana over a six-year period starting in 1972.

Even as construction continued on Powerton Station Unit 5, Edison unveiled plans to build a second 840,000-kilowatt unit at a cost of more than $100 million, excluding major expenditures for environmental controls. The company said that plans to build Powerton 6 accelerated because of the delays at LaSalle County. The new unit, slated for service in 1976, would burn either low-sulfur western coal or Illinois coal with scrubbers, depending on how the scrubber systems at State Line and Will County performed.

Edison's gas turbine capacity increased to 228,000 kw with the addition of fast-start peaking units at Electric Junction in the far western suburbs and in Bloom Township in the south suburbs. Built at a total cost of $23 million, the peakers would help meet the sharply rising demand for electricity in the summer months. Although the peakers required only about one year for completion, the mounting costs of the oil and natural gas they burned would offset this advantage in the coming years.

Generating electricity with machines that approximate jet aircraft engines was Engineering 101 compared to a joint government-industry research and development project in which Edison took a lead role. Edison and the Tennessee Valley Authority (TVA) arranged to pool their management and engineering resources to design, construct, and operate the nation's first large fast breeder reactor demonstration plant. Edison pledged $11.4 million to help finance the $500 million project and agreed to supply another $2 million in services. A task force of Edison personnel went to work with Project Management Corporation (PMC), the group organized to bring the breeder to reality on a 1,360-acre site along the Clinch River, outside Oak Ridge, Tennessee. Edison's Wallace Behnke became chairman of the PMC board.

Government and industry counted on the breeder to play an important role in conserving energy resources by stretching the availability of uranium reserves from half a century to thousands of years. Given its ability to produce more fuel than it would consume, a commercial breeder introduced in the mid-1980s could save more than $200 billion in gross electric energy costs through the year 2020, government economists predicted.

President Nixon called the program "our best hope today for meeting the nation's growing demand for economical, clean energy."

Eclipsing even the new Dresden and Quad-Cities units in size, Powerton Unit 5 was up and running for the summer of '72. The 840,000-kilowatt unit cost $150 million over a three-and-one-half-year period. Powerton 5 also received its own cooling lake, costing $15 million, as well as electrostatic precipitators designed for 99.5 percent efficiency in the removal of particulate matter.

Also that summer, Edison revealed plans to build its first and only oil-fired steam generating station from scratch. Ridgeland had originally burned coal, though it later used oil. Named Collins Station, the plant would have five 500,000-kilowatt units located in Grundy County, about a mile-and-a-half west of Dresden. Collins' total capacity of 2.5 million kw would make it the company's biggest generating station. The plant, which would stand on 3,600 acres, would cost $500 million, including $20 million for a cooling lake. Collins would provide Edison's first cycling units, designed for rapid increases to full load and operated primarily during the weekday heavy demand period. The company tabbed the five units for service between 1976 and 1978 to help it overcome capacity deficits resulting from two years of regulatory delays at LaSalle.

Its regulatory delays behind it, Quad-Cities Station not only helped to meet summer peak loads but opened a Nuclear Information Center to the public consisting of a reception room, an exhibit area and a small theatre where visitors can learn about the history, safety, and operation of nuclear generating stations from guided tours as well as from various displays, many of them visitor-operated.

The last section of an Edison relic, Quarry Street Station, met the wrecker's ball after six decades of service. Power generation had ended in 1931, but some of the electrical equipment remained and the plant became a distribution center. The company would expand a 1959 transmission substation which would occupy the space taken up by the remnants of the old plant. The new TSS had four 25,000-kw transformers fed by four 69-kilovolt cables running under the south branch of the Chicago River from nearby Fisk Station.

The early 1970s saw Edison construct four new headquarters buildings to serve expanding areas to the north, south, and west. A new Crestwood Area which Edison marked off took some of the load off the Harvey office. Serving the growing southwest suburbs, Crestwood Area had a population of nearly 80,000 customers in a territory bounded by Oak Lawn, Hickory Hills, Tinley Park, and Interstate 57. Some 225 employes moved to the contemporarily-designed, all-electric headquarters building at 135th Street and Kostner Avenue. Three existing districts, Aurora, Elgin, and Waukegan, received new headquarters buildings.

At the general office, D. Robert Bower retired as treasurer after a 43-year career, succeeded by former Assistant Vice President Raymond Bachert. Later Bachert added the post of secretary to his resume, as Preston Kavanagh moved to Chicago North as division vice president. Byron Lee and Lawrence Cullen became vice presidents, while another executive on the move, Bide Thomas, became general division manager of the seven operating divisions.

Gordon Corey became the company's vice chairman in 1973.

The most significant personnel shift of the 1970s occurred on April 1, 1973, when Thomas Ayers was elected chairman of the board, succeeding the retiring J. Harris Ward. Ayers retained the title of president, as well. Gordon Corey, the other front-runner, was named to the re-created post of vice chairman. Was Corey disappointed? "I think a little bit," he recalled, "but basically I've always felt it was kind of nice to be number two because you never get called up in the middle of the night. Who ever calls the vice chairman?"

Ayers later related how he had been employed by Sears, Roebuck for "about two hours" before signing on with Public Service Company in 1938. Engaged to his "best girl, now my wife, Mary," on a Saturday night, laid off at the Packard auto plant in Detroit the following Monday, he had come to Chicago for a job interview with Sears. After accepting the offer, Ayers had about four hours until the next bus back to Detroit.

"I was wandering around the Loop, and I went by the 79 West Monroe Building where the Public Service Company had their offices. I went up to see if a fellow named Wayne Saggers was in. He was in charge of employment. I didn't know anyone in Chicago, and I had heard he was a nice fellow, so I thought I'd like to know him. Well, he decided that I should come to work for Public Service, and he twisted my arm. So having had a job with Sears, Roebuck for less than two hours, I called them up to quit and signed on with the Public Service Company." The story came full circle years later when Ayers became a member of Sears' board of directors.

Thirty-five years later, almost to the day, the man from Detroit became chairman of Public Service Company's successor. Ward, meanwhile, closed the book on a 35-year career, the last 11 as chairman. In the Ward years, sales and revenues more than doubled, costs to residential customers remained tightly reined, and the company led the way into the commercial nuclear age.

"Under his leadership, Edison has enjoyed unprecedented growth and earned industry-wide recognition for imaginative, constructive management," Ayers declared.

Sixteen months later J. Harris Ward lay dead in Chicago's Billings Hospital at age 66. The *Daily News* declared, "When Mr. Ward retired, Commonwealth had—and still has—a greater nuclear plant capacity than any other power company, and less dependence on oil or coal. His foresight helped to spare the Chicago area the threat of imminent power shortages."

Perhaps the most significant decision early in the Ayers administration was to compromise with the LaSalle County farmers in order to get LaSalle County Station under construction.

"We recognized that we would be tied up for years in getting that plant started and agreed to go to a two-unit lake to support the facility," O'Connor recollected. "LaSalle was originally planned to be a four-unit facility."

On the eve of Atomic Energy Commission hearings on the construction permits, Edison agreed to reduce the size of the site from nearly 7,000 acres to just under 3,000 acres. Nearly all of the reduction involved the cooling lake. The compromise took the anticipated fireworks out of the hearings. The permits and the start of construction swiftly followed.

About the same time, but away from the spotlight of LaSalle's well-publicized protest, the company also said it would reduce the size of Braidwood's cooling lake—from 4,800 acres to 2,000 acres. As in the case of LaSalle, Edison scaled the plant back from four to two units. In a statement submitted to the ICC, Lee explained that the company could reduce its current investment by $25 million and save $3 million annually in interest charges. Edison was also running into unexpected land acquisition problems.

"In every instance we struck a compromise that attempted to balance the long-term costs of getting hung up in court on sensitive issues against what the ultimate costs to our customers would be," O'Connor stated.

How could Edison scale back a total of four generating units and not find itself short of capacity? One answer lay in the far northwest corner of the state, outside Edison's service territory in Carroll County, where the company considered the construction of a twin-unit plant, probably nuclear, in the range of 2.2 million kw. Interstate Power Company and Iowa-Illinois Gas and Electric, Edison's partner in the Quad-Cities plant, also participated in the feasibility study. By the summer of 1973 they had obtained options on approximately 80 percent of the land needed for the site, but the companies stressed that they had made no final decision yet.

As a second answer to the possible problem of a capacity shortfall, they proposed the construction of two more coal-fired units at Will County Station. Both sets of units were to be added in the early to mid-1980s. However, a slackening of demand later in the decade caused the cancellation of the Will County capacity and the deferral of the Carroll County units.

In mid-1973 Edison began receiving power from an unconventional source—a $317 million pumped-storage hydroelectric plant near Ludington, Michigan. The company purchased a share of the plant's capacity from its owners, Consumers Power and Detroit Edison. Under the arrangement Edison fed power to the Ludington site during the night, primarily using low-cost nuclear generation, to help pump water into an elevated reservoir with a capacity of 27 billion gallons. The next day the water flowed down from the reservoir to turn generators located at the base of a bluff overlooking Lake Michigan. The arrangement gave Edison added flexibility to meet swings in demand and eliminated the need to install 600,000 kw of oil-fired peaking capacity.

Utilities had generated electricity with hydropower, albeit not pumped hydropower, for years, but now the City of Chicago proposed to generate power by burning garbage. Garbage? At the urging of Mayor Daley, who was fascinated by the idea, Edison agreed to burn refuse collected by the city at Crawford Station. City plans called for construction of a solid waste processing plant near Crawford which eventually would supply the plant with 250,000 tons of solid waste annually. Despite the mayor's enthusiasm and hefty publicity, the plant did not succeed, chiefly because large objects continued to slip through the waste processing and clog the station's boilers. After several years of fits and starts (mostly fits), city officials quietly shelved the project.

Linking system load dispatchers with 70 remote locations and eight neighboring utilities was the new System Power Supply Office in Glenbard, a fortress-like, hurricane-proof building soon nicknamed "The Blockhouse." The building housed the latest computer and technological equipment designed to upgrade the integrity of Edison's bulk power system. Two XDS Sigma 5 digital computers, one on standby, oversaw the entire data acquisition and control system, where fast-breaking information on load flow, voltages, load estimates, and generating reserves aided the load dispatchers in making quick decisions on buying or selling power or taking a unit out of service. The dispatchers now received instant computer information on the status of the system when determining, for example, whether or not to take a line out of service. Previously, they had to make such a decision on studies that bore only an approximate comparison to the real situation. Dispatchers monitored the generation and security of

366

the system 24 hours a day from consoles and charts that displayed system frequency, interchange power and control requirements, as well as the output of each generating station.

Edison estimated that it would spend $575 million for environmental control facilities by the end of 1977, including $160 million for water control systems at six generating stations. These mounting expenses, along with higher costs in general and the fact that generating stations cost two to three times as much to build as they had a few years earlier, prompted Edison to file for a 12.6 percent rate increase totaling $154 million annually in May 1973. The company pointed out that the average residential customer spent 1.7 percent of his or her annual earnings for electricity—the same as ten years earlier.

With another October came another nuclear first for Commonwealth Edison. In October 1960 it had been Dresden 1, the world's first. Now, in October 1973, the time arrived to dedicate Zion Station, with 2.2 million kw of capacity, the world's largest. The two reactor containment buildings that stood on the Lake Michigan shoreline towered nearly 14 stories, with

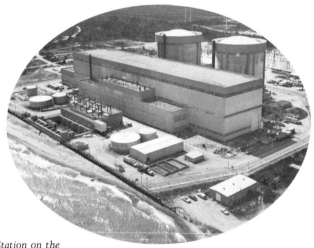

Zion Nuclear Generating Station on the shore of Lake Michigan.

walls two to five feet thick, each housing a 450-ton steel reactor vessel. Some 200 dignitaries gathered under an open tent next to the plant to hear Ayers explain that they had built Zion in a shorter time—about five-and-a-half years—and at a significantly lower cost—approximately $450 million—than any comparable facility in the country.

The principal speaker, Congressman John B. Anderson of Rockford, a member of the Joint Committee on Atomic Energy, warned that the nation would face "a very serious energy problem" and said Americans would have to cut back on their "wasteful and profligate" use of energy. Even as he declared that, in the short term, only nuclear energy could prevent an energy disaster, damp, chill winds blustered through the tent.

Fifteen

OPEC
Plugs
The
Pipe

A strange thing was happening all across America. People who had grown up believing in American superiority in the production of almost everything now were being told that the country was running out of almost everything. There were meat shortages, cement shortages, aluminum shortages, natural gas shortages, gasoline shortages, home heating oil shortages, and in some parts of the country, shortages of oil and natural gas to produce electricity. Northern Illinois Gas Company prepared to cut off supplies to Commonwealth Edison to make additional fuel available to residential customers, an action which would deprive Edison of one of its pollution-fighting weapons. At the same time the prospect of gasoline and oil rationing was being discussed seriously for the first time since World War II. The American psyche was traumatized. Who or what was responsible for this mess, anyway?

As in any crisis or perceived crisis, scapegoats were not difficult to find. More often than not, people singled out the big oil companies, then federal bureaucrats. The so-called "energy crisis" was a hoax, many Americans believed, perpetrated by the oil companies to justify higher prices. The government was either in league, inept, or indifferent, the theory went. Unknown to a sizeable segment of the public, the problem had been building for many years. In 1973 the United States, with six percent of the world's population, consumed 33 percent of the planet's energy. The average American, who used the energy equivalent of 42 barrels of oil in 1955, was using more than 61 barrels a year in the early 1970s. By this time U.S. wells were pumping at full capacity, so supplies to meet rising demands could come from only one source—abroad. In 1970 the country imported 25 percent of its total oil needs. By 1973 the amount had jumped to 35 percent, and forecasters predicted the dizzying climb would continue.

The supply/demand equation started to get out of balance in the spring and summer of 1972, the busiest driving months, when gasoline demands surged. Refineries were forced to maintain peak gasoline production longer than usual, postponing the refining of home heating oil. Government energy experts and the oil industry agreed that the demand for more gasoline was the result of more cars traveling more miles and the growing number of cars equipped with federally-required anti-pollution devices which reduced gas mileage. The smog devices alone increased daily gasoline demand by 300,000 barrels, the experts estimated.

Winter in the Chicago area came early that year. The gas companies cut off deliveries to their big customers to make more gas available to residential users. Industrial customers, in turn, switched to oil, which aggravated the shortages that had already resulted from the late start in heating oil refining. Major oil distributors initiated rationing programs to prevent the depletion of supplies by spring.

The inconveniences of the winter of '72–'73 were only a dress rehearsal for what was to come the following winter. But first, northern Illinois had to swelter through the late spring and summer of 1973. In early June, almost two weeks before the official start of summer, and again in late August Edison was forced to reduce voltage, curtail service to its largest customers, seek voluntary conservation, and purchase power from other utilities in order to meet heavy demands. Company employes did their usual admirable job of keeping everyone supplied with electricity, but their efforts might have been futile had it not been for a federal judge in Washington named John H. Pratt. Unknown in northern Illinois and mentioned only in passing by the newspapers, Judge Pratt prevented a potential massive power shortage in Edison territory and other parts of the country as well when he threw out a lawsuit, by Ralph Nader and a group called Friends of the Earth, aimed at shutting down 20 of the 31 nuclear generating stations operating in the U.S. On the last day of May 1973, as the nation headed into the peak electricity demand season, Nader and friends demanded that the plants be shuttered because they allegedly did not contain adequate safety precautions against an accidental loss of cooling water, which they claimed would threaten the health and safety of the public. Judge Pratt ruled in June that Nader and friends had failed to make a convincing case. Four of the units targeted by Nader were Dresden 2 and 3 and Quad-Cities 1 and 2. The absence of those four units, along with the others around the country, during a summer heat wave would have made the New York blackout of 1965 look like a minor inconvenience.

By the fall of 1973, home heating oil and propane gas were in short supply again, so President Nixon ordered the first peacetime allocation of these or any other fuels. The Administration acknowledged that the program would not increase supplies, but, in the words of Interior Secretary Rogers Morton, "spread the discomfort" during the coming cold weather season. Another Administration official, John Love, Director of the Energy Policy Office, warned that fuel shortages over the next several years were probably inevitable. The energy planners didn't mention it at the time, but they also were preparing to control the distribution of gasoline the following summer, at prices—horrors—that might reach the 50-cents-a-gallon mark.

Four days after the imposition of fuel allocations, on Yom Kippur, the most solemn day of the Jewish calendar, Egyptian forces attacked Israel, and the fourth Middle Eastern conflict since the end of World War II began. The renewed fighting set off a chain of events that would upend the world financial order, radically alter United States energy policy, wallop the average American right in his or her lifestyle, and cause Commonwealth Edison to reconsider its future plans and change the way it marketed its product. Eight Arab countries, including Saudi Arabia, the largest Middle Eastern supplier of oil to the United States, announced that they would cut back or cut off their oil supplies to this country in retaliation for American military support of Israel. Government energy experts admitted that they had underestimated the size and impact of the impending shortage, and said that the cutoff could mean a deficit of as much as 18 percent of the 18 million barrels of oil the nation's businesses and consumers used each day. Gasoline and fuel oil prices, recently freed of government price controls to stimulate domestic production, began to climb sharply.

Predicting the worst energy crisis since World War II, President Nixon went on nationwide radio and television and invoked a word that Americans were unaccustomed to hearing from their political leaders—sacrifice. The President outlined a series of mandatory and voluntary actions to reduce energy use and increase oil supplies. Among other steps, he ordered reductions in the allocation of home heating oil and airline jet fuel, called upon the AEC to speed up the licensing of nuclear power plants, and in a move that Edison found particularly ironic, prohibited utilities from converting coal-fired generating stations to oil and either required or encouraged oil-fired plants to convert to coal. Under threats of lawsuits and fines from the EPA, the company had already begun converting its Sabrooke generating station in Rockford from coal to oil, not to mention the earlier conversion of four Ridgeland Station units from coal to oil. "We're going to have to study this," was the best a company spokesman could muster.

Except for this dilemma Edison was in a strong position to face the heightened energy crisis, which, after all, was primarily a petroleum and natural gas crisis. About 90 percent of Edison's power was generated from uranium and low sulfur coal, unlike other parts of the country which were heavily dependent on foreign oil. In fact, the federal government asked the company, if possible, to send electricity to the hard-pressed Eastern Seaboard. "We think we are in pretty good shape, and that the homeowners in Illinois will not feel any electricity pinch," Bryon Lee stated. Strangely, that position created a public relations problem for Edison. President Nixon, in a followup address to the nation in late November, called for a ban on the Sunday sale of gasoline, a 50-mile-an-hour speed limit for passenger cars*, and a host of other measures—including a ban on outdoor Christmas lighting. The latter meant no little lights in the trees along North Michigan Avenue, no lights on the evergreens outside the home, no seasonal displays at the shopping centers. It would be a bleak Christmas, indeed.

Wait a minute, said Edison. If all homes and businesses in northern Illinois obeyed the ban, it would reduce the company's peak load by only two or three percent, and besides, most of the load is met with plentiful coal and uranium. The President's conservation message dealt solely with petroleum, and didn't say

*The limit became 55 M.P.H.

372

anything about saving coal or nuclear power, company spokesmen declared, but the disclaimers did little good. The country was gripped by near-hysteria over the energy crisis, and people were not about to distinguish between which forms of energy were in crisis and which were not. The prevailing mood was gloom. The crisis had to be made real and vivid to the public, according to a common argument, and it is difficult to remember that there are shortages of anything when the country is awash in ornamental lighting. Turning off lights became a patriotic gesture, and everyone jumped on the bandwagon. Edison gracefully withdrew from the debate by issuing a statement in support of the President's energy-saving program and urging customers to restrict the use of ornamental and non-essential lighting.

However, Chicago Alderman Roman Pucinski had the final word. A former newspaper reporter and congressman, Pucinski knew a PR opportunity when he saw one. He strung outside Christmas lights at his home, turned them on, and dared the government to arrest him. He urged all Chicagoans to do the same. "This talk of saving power by turning off outside lights is plain nonsense," Pucinski asserted. "What do they want us to do, reduce the Christmas and Hanukkah season to a degree of darkness and despair not equalled even in Russia? I say, 'Bah, humbug,' to Washington." The alderman called federal energy chief William Simon "a Grinch who is trying to steal our Christmas. If we ever needed to lift our spirits, it's this time of Christmas and Hanukkah, after the depressing year our nation has suffered."

As the energy crisis dimmed the lights in most other corners of the globe, many practitioners of the so-called dismal science—economics—made a dark and chilling economic forecast: world-wide recession. Forecasters wound down their predictions for economic growth and scaled up their estimates of inflation. "The Arab oil squeeze," the *Wall Street Journal* reported, "caught the economies of the major industrial nations in a precarious position: poised together at the top of an unusual synchronized business cycle like so many roller-coaster cars linked together for a downhill run." Exactly how steep or deep a run remained to be seen.

Edison's annual Marketing Conference acknowledged that the rules of the game had changed. With the cost of new generating capacity rapidly escalating, "economies of scale" had become a thing of the past. No longer was it to a utility's advantage to promote all electrical load and bring about the addition of larger generating units. The cost of serving new on-peak load had simply become too great. Now Edison had to expand sales in a way that did not require a corresponding increase in new plant investment. In other words, the company had to concentrate on selling "profitable" kilowatthours. The goal of the Marketing department became off-peak sales—those that would help fill the "valleys" in the load cycle, the non-summer months and the nighttime hours. Henceforth marketers emphasized electric heat sales and deemphasized the sale of air conditioners.

Zion Unit 2, the last generating unit built before construction costs skyrocketed, went into service the week before Christmas 1973, increasing the company's nuclear generation to 35 percent of the total. For once, Edison could predict no difficulty in meeting the next summer's peak demand, and considered selling power to oil-dependent utilities in the east. Zion 2 was also the last of the company's first generation of nuclear units to come on line, joining its sister unit as well as Dresden 1, 2, and 3 and Quad-Cities 1 and 2. The problems the last six experienced with regulators, intervenors, and politicians were only a preview of what was in store for the next generation, the twin units at LaSalle, Byron, and Braidwood. Nevertheless the AEC's pre-hearing conference on Byron began with only mild opposition to the plant. Mr. and Mrs. Fred Bushnell, who owned a farm near the station site, expressed concerns that the plant's cooling towers would change weather conditions and also about the presence of high voltage transmission lines across their property. The Bushnells later withdrew their petition to intervene, saying Edison and the AEC had cooperated in answering safety questions.

Early in 1974, Edison, Iowa-Illinois Gas & Electric, and Interstate Power made it official: they would build a $600 million nuclear generating station near Savanna, Illinois. Edison would build, operate, and own two-thirds of the plant, which would be known as Carroll County Station. The first of the two 1,100-megawatt pressurized water reactor units was scheduled for service in 1983, the second in 1984. On the fossil side of the company, Edison announced plans to construct a large scale test facility at Powerton Station to convert coal to natural gas. The Electric Power Research Institute (EPRI), the research and development arm of the industry, agreed to help fund the project. Slated for test operation by the end of 1976, the Powerton coal gasification project was designed to remove nine-tenths of the coal's sulfur content and convert about 60 tons of coal an hour into clean, low-BTU gas suitable as a boiler fuel for a 70,000 kw generating unit.

Edison continued to break new ground in personnel management as well as technology. Toward the end of 1973 the company appointed its first woman officer. Genevieve Dooner, formerly an administrative assistant, was elected assistant secretary of the company. In early 1974 women addressed the monthly Engineering Conference for the first time in the activity's 63-year history. Engineers Kathy Leitzell of Mechanical & Structural Engineering and Barbara Brunka of Environmental Affairs presented a program on generating station siting.

In April 1974 Edison obtained a rate order from the ICC which enabled it to keep pace with escalating inflation, interest charges, taxes, and operating expenses. The 10.7 percent, $134 million increase added $1.26 to the typical monthly residential electricity bill and incorporated two new features. First, the same rate for the first 100 kwh was maintained, ensuring that the smallest users would not get an increase, provided their consumption stayed below that level. Second, the commission made its first attempt to curb air conditioning use by increasing the rate that customers with all-electric homes must pay if they used more than 325 kwh a month from June through September. "Recent problems of energy supply have increased the public's awareness of the need for conservation and the fact that prices of all forms of energy are going to be higher than they have been in the past," Ayers stated. "Our product is no exception." Before the ICC decision, Edison attorney Hubert Nexon had said the company was not considering a rate increase to compensate for cutbacks by energy conscious customers. Several other electric utilities, including Consolidated Edison in New York, had recently applied for so-called "conservation adjustments"—rate increases to make up for sagging demand. Con Ed's request for an additional 6.7

percent was on top of a standard rate hike request of 22.6 percent. Before the New York Commission ruled on the double filing, Con Ed did something that sent shock waves through Wall Street and the electric utility industry: the company omitted its common stock dividend for the second quarter, breaking a chain of 343 consecutive payments since 1885. Con Ed said the step was necessary to protect its cash resources which had been adversely affected by conservation measures and rising fuel costs. The company also reported sharply lower first quarter earnings. One analyst said the drastic measure "raises questions in investors' minds about the viability of the industry as a whole."

The viability of Commonwealth Edison was not in question, *Forbes* magazine and *Chicago Today* assured their readers. Based on interviews with Ayers, each publication concluded that Edison's early commitment to nuclear power, the success of the nuclear program, the experience of its engineers and operators, the use of coal and uranium instead of imported oil, and a conservative budgeting approach explained, as the *Forbes* headline stated, "Why Commonwealth Edison Isn't Consolidated Edison."

In recognition of the company leadership role in developing nuclear technology, Commonwealth Edison received the electric utility's highest honor, the Edison Award, at the Edison Electric Institute's (EEI) annual convention in New York. Accepting the industry's 1973 award, Ayers thanked EEI for its recognition of the company's efforts to maintain high standards of electric service reliability.

Not standing still, the company bought a uranium company and sold its downstate service territories. With the nuclear program expected to generate half of all output by the early 1980s, Edison purchased Cotter Corporation, operator of a uranium mine and mill near Lakewood, Colorado, for $18 million in common stock. Cotter, which also owned uranium and other mineral rights in several western states, became an Edison subsidiary. The company could produce up to 1.5 million pounds of uranium a year. On the other side of the ledger, Edison sold its properties in the area of Lincoln, Homer, and Bement to Central Illinois Light Company (CILCO) for approximately $25 million. Edison had acquired the properties, containing about 22,000 customers, in the 1966 merger with Central Illinois Electric & Gas Co.

When the company acquired the Braidwood Station site, it also acquired Tully monsters, naked mollusks, jellyfish, and a dozen species of shrimp. These were among more than 140 previously undescribed animal fossils that were found in Peabody Coal Company's Pit 11, a 3,000 acre, one-time strip mine area about half of which would be occupied by the nuclear plant. In cooperation with the Field Museum of Natural History, Edison established a program to enable collectors to search for fossils during construction of the station. Once construction got underway, collectors were allowed to hunt for fossils only under the direct supervision of the museum. After the cooling lake was filled, museum personnel and affiliated amateur collectors were given access to the "spoil islands" of the former mine.

Back in downtown Chicago, in a mini-reenactment of World War II's end, the Wrigley Building turned on its famed floodlights for the first time in nine months. The floodlamps of the Chicago landmark had been turned off in compliance with President Nixon's energy-saving request to the nation. Wrigley Company officials acted only after getting approval from Mayor Daley and Governor Walker and assurances from Commonwealth Edison that nighttime lighting had no effect on the use of gas or oil to generate electricity. Did the illumination of the Wrigley Building symbolize the end of the energy crisis? By the summer of 1974 the hoarding of gasoline, the long lines of cars at the gas pumps, the run on firewood, the fear of going without were over, and the nation looked forward to improved fuel supplies for the coming winter.

But energy experts cautioned that the problem was only easing temporarily and would be around, in one guise or another, for a long time. Though fuel was plentiful again, the oil embargo had spawned the twin devils of recession and an alarming rate of inflation, along with high interest rates, unemployment, and general uncertainty. Additionally, a four-fold increase in crude oil prices, tight money, and continuing huge investments in non-productive pollution control equipment combined to put many utilities in their sorriest financial position in recent memory.

At the same time, electricity conservation efforts trimmed annual growth rates. Edison's kwh sales in 1974 slipped 1.8 percent from 1973. Citing cost increases that far outpaced advances in revenues, Edison asked the ICC for a 15.6 percent, or $241 million, rate increase to be granted in two steps. The company requested an immediate emergency increase of 7.3 percent and asked that the second part of 8.3 percent take effect following the commission hearings. Ayers said the increases were urgently needed to meet higher construction costs and 10 percent interest charges on new loans. The Edison chairman could point to the fact that the company's rates had gone up only 19.1 percent over the past two years, the third smallest climb among 35 major electric utilities. The national average was 52 percent, with four utilities exceeding 90 percent in increases. Edison's extensive use of nuclear power was the principal reason for its comparatively small price increases.

The ICC found that deferral of partial rate relief would result in an unreasonable and harmful loss of revenue. Thus in February 1975 the commission granted the company a 5.8 percent, $90-million interim rate hike which Ayers said would leave Edison far short of handling prevailing market conditions.

Edison suffered a series of setbacks during the winter of 1974–75. In December the AEC fined the company $25,500 for 18 alleged violations at Dresden, including the accidental release of low-level radioactive laundry water into the Illinois River and incomplete implementation of the station's security plan. It marked the first time the AEC had imposed a cash penalty on Edison. Lee described the incidents as "largely procedural matters which did not endanger the public." In subsequent years, the AEC and its successor, the NRC, would frequently use fines as a regulatory enforcement tool against Edison and other nuclear utilities.

"The 1970s witnessed an erosion of trust between the builders of nuclear power and the agencies governing nuclear activities," O'Connor said later. "The development by the NRC in the mid-'70s of an enforcement policy that was very punitive produced an adversarial, rather than a cooperative kind of relationship between utilities and the NRC. We were presented with a stick—no carrot. I'm aware of very few instances where the NRC has applauded the performance of a utility on a successful record. Generally, the only time utilities and the public hear from the NRC is when there is a problem or an alleged problem," O'Connor concluded.

The drop-off in business activity in northern Illinois caused Edison to slow its construction program, delaying the scheduled operation of various units from six months to two years. The construction budget was trimmed from $4.6 billion to $4.3 billion. "Right now, we're in the middle of a slump," Corey explained. "Housing is way down. We're projecting lower business for next year, but we think it will turn around." Edison, which traditionally experienced a 7.5 percent annual increase in peak load, expected growth to slump to four percent in 1975. The increase turned out to be only .3 percent, rebounding to 4.9 percent the following year.

Edison lost the argument with federal officials whether or not Sabrooke Station could be totally converted from coal to oil and decided to shut down two of the four units. The other two units, which were already undergoing conversion to comply with Illinois air pollution standards, were allowed to burn oil. In a related move, the company said it would close down a Calumet Station unit because of a shortage of natural gas. And downstate, Edison abandoned plans to build the coal gasification plant at Powerton because the price tag had jumped $1.2 billion in one year.

At the 1975 annual meeting, Edison shareholders elected a woman to the board of directors for the first time in the company's 88-year history. She was Jean Allard, prominent corporate attorney and a vice president of the University of Chicago.

It was a quiet meeting. In fact, the country was quiet, at least outwardly. Unrest on the campuses had subsided. Viet Nam, Watergate, and Richard Nixon were now in the past. The CIA and FBI had been taken to the woodshed. The shock of the oil embargo had demonstrated that the nation's best route to energy independence was through abundant coal and nuclear power. Or had it? Thirty-two of the country's leading scientists, 11 of them Nobel laureates, thought so. Ralph Nader did not. The Great Nuclear Debate revved up for a long run. "The U.S. choice is not coal or uranium; we need both," said the scientists. "We can see no reasonable alternative to an increased use of nuclear power to satisfy our energy needs." The scientists warned that the energy crisis had created the

379

most serious situation the country had faced since World War II. The expression of their views at a Washington news conference was largely ignored by the media. Instead, the headlines were going to Nader and his newly-formed anti-nuclear organization, Critical Mass. One of the group's foremost goals was to force abandonment of the Ford Administration's plan to have 200 nuclear power plants in operation by 1985. Nader convened almost 1,000 of his supporters in Washington in the summer of 1975 to map plans for achieving that goal. The session was reminiscent of a political convention, with delegates massed under state signs, getting progress reports on state-by-state petition drives to force a referendum prohibiting further nuclear plant construction in each area.

The central question in the Great Nuclear Debate became "How safe is safe?" In late 1974 Dr. Norman Rasmussen, a Massachusetts Institute of Technology (MIT) scientist hired by the AEC to do an exhaustive study of nuclear safety, concluded that the risk of death from a major accident at a nuclear power plant was several billion to one. Statistically speaking, Rasmussen and a team of 60 experts determined that a nuclear power plant presented less risk to an individual than walking into a kitchen or crossing a street, and infinitely less risk than smoking cigarettes or driving an automobile. However, the critics were hardly convinced. The Sierra Club, for instance, predicted that a major plant accident was a real possibility that could result in tens of thousands of deaths or serious illnesses. "While emotional jargon and statistical games and scary suppositions might have popular appeal," Ayers declared, "the evidence is on the side of nuclear power." So, too, he could have added, were a majority of the American people. A Harris poll taken in the late summer of 1975 showed that 63 percent of the public favored the building of more nuclear plants, while only 19 percent were opposed and the remainder undecided.

With Edison's kwh sales and peak load off sharply due to the recession and with an ambitious long-range plant construction program in progress, Chicago area utility critics, including Citizens for a Better Environment (CBE), first raised a charge that would be repeated to the present time: Edison was building too much capacity. It was an odd turnabout, considering that the company had struggled year-in, year-out till only recently to keep capacity ahead of demand, barely carrying the load on a number of occasions. A *Tribune* editorial in June 1975 succinctly stated Edison's position: "It is easy for critics of the power companies to say there is excess capacity and that conservation is a better solution than trying to keep up with future demand. If they are wrong, no one will remember. But if the utilities fail to plan for the future and the country is handicapped by a shortage of electric energy, it will be the utilities, not the critics, who get the blame. What it all boils down to is how much confidence we have in the future of our country. We think the future is bright."

If anyone doubted that the days of cheap energy were gone forever, they got another reminder in August 1975 when the ICC granted Edison a 6.8 percent rate increase, the second step of the two-stage request. The action increased the company's annual revenues by $116 million. "Quite simply, a $300 million generating unit, armor-plated with environmental facilities, cannot turn out kwh for the same price as an older unit of similar size that cost one-third as much," Ayers stated bluntly. "Multi-billion dollar utility system expansions financed at today's high money costs can't be maintained on investment returns held down to pre-inflation levels." The company would be back before the ICC the following year, seeking a 14.5 percent hike. But there was good news for consumers as well. In 1975 customers saved 10 percent on their electricity bills through Edison's nuclear generation rather than oil or low sulfur coal.

From the fall of 1975 through fall 1976, the generating system bustled with activity:

- Quad-Cities discontinued use of the diffuser cooling system and switched over to the spray canal;
- The NRC issued construction permits for Byron and Braidwood after the Atomic Safety and Licensing Board (ASLB) found that both met health and safety requirements;
- The company increased its five-year construction budget by $300 million—to $4.6 billion;
- Edison formed a Project Management System group to ensure value and exercise better expenditure control over the growing nuclear construction program;

- Dresden Unit 1 was scheduled to become the first nuclear plant in the country to undergo chemical cleaning to remove radioactive deposits in its pipes;
- A newly-completed Dresden Visitor Center, featuring films, displays, and other information, opened to the public;
- Powerton Unit 6 came on line, adding 850,000 kw to the grid;
- Calumet and Sabrooke Stations were retired, while the last remnants of Fordam Station were razed;
- And the company began buying land near the Illinois towns of Henry, Gladstone, Erie, Seneca, and Sheridan for possible generating station sites.

While much of the nation's attention in the summer and fall of 1976 was focused on the presidential campaigns, voters in several states had an opportunity for the first time ever to pass judgment on the future of nuclear power development. The first —and most critical—referendum was in the June primary in California, where the ballot's Proposition 15 would effectively hobble nuclear power with a dizzying array of impossible restrictions. Nuclear proponents embarked on a massive and ultimately successful campaign to convince Californians of the safety of nuclear energy. Voters trounced Proposition 15 by a margin of two to one, and as the *Daily News* editorialized, "injected some maturity and common sense into a debate too often typified by fear-mongering and rhetoric." In November the nuclear industry scored another major victory when voters in six more states— Washington, Oregon, Colorado, Ohio, Arizona, and Montana— indicated that they strongly favored the expanded use of nuclear power.

Less than three weeks later any lingering euphoria at Commonwealth Edison over the outcome of the balloting was quickly forgotten as the company was hit by a disaster that rivaled the Ridgeland explosion. About 8:45 Sunday evening, November 21, a construction crew at Fisk Station spotted flames shooting from a conveyor that carried coal to the plant. The fire had broken out at a point where the conveyor emerged from an underground passage below Throop Street and raced—in the words of an eyewitness—"like a fuse" up the 1,400-foot conveyor chute. Flames roared along the steel conveyor to a fly ash warehouse. Then the conveyor collapsed on a building where resistors were stored, toppling power poles and cables as it fell. The burning conveyor next set fire to the roof of a switch house, collapsed on the roof of a control room, and set fire to the roofs of the buildings housing boilers and turbine generators. The special-alarm blaze knocked out power to about 2,000 customers on Chicago's West Side, including sections of three hospitals, as the odor of burning coal drifted over the area. Damage was later estimated at more than $8 million.

Fisk Station's coal conveyor chute lies crumpled after a devastating fire on November 21, 1976. More than $8 million in damages resulted, and one Chicago firefighter lost his life.

About 300 firemen battled the flames. One did not return. Forty-one-year-old Walter Watroba and three other firemen from Engine Company 13 had climbed atop a roof 135 feet high to pump water on the conveyor in an effort to keep the flames from spreading. Watroba was leaning over the edge of the building, feeding hose to the others, when a huge section of the chute above their heads collapsed and buried him. Both of Watroba's legs were pinned against the inside wall of the building by a heavy steel beam. For seven-and-a-half hours, in high winds and swirling snow, specially trained firemen used air hammers, crowbars, jacks, and sheer muscle in a frantic effort to save their comrade, aware that additional tons of concrete and steel beams overhead could come crashing down on them if they were not extremely careful.

383

About two o'clock in the morning, Dr. Joseph Cari, a fire department physician, reported that Watroba's left leg had been freed, and it appeared that soon they would have the right leg free. The hope proved false. The right leg had been crushed between the steel chute and the concrete roof. There was no way. "Doctor, do what you have to do, but please get me out," Watroba pleaded. Dr. Cari, who had been administering morphine to the firefighter, realized what had to be done. The doctor went below and reported the situation to Fire Commissioner Robert Quinn. Then Cari returned to the roof with surgical equipment that had been flown in by helicopter. The amputation took only two minutes. A stretcher was raised to the roof, Watroba was strapped in, and lowered to a waiting ambulance. But the trauma had been too much. He showed no vital signs as he was placed in the ambulance and was dead on arrival at Mercy Hospital. Not once during the more than seven-hour ordeal, according to Dr. Cari, had he complained or cried out.

Walter Watroba left a wife and three daughters, ages 15, 12, and 5. Mrs. Janice Watroba, a former Edison employe, had worked for six years in the Fuel department. The company organized a collection for the family and raised approximately $10,000 from employes. Ayers and O'Connor presented the check to Mrs. Watroba.

Also that autumn, Edison mourned the death of Herbert Sedwick, president of Public Service Company when it merged with Edison in 1953. Sedwick died in Chicago at the age of 83.

Two years after Edison chose its first woman director, the company elected its first Black vice president—John Viera—head of the company's seven operating divisions. After joining the company in 1957, Viera held several engineering and administrative positions, including both commercial manager and Northern Division vice president. Holder of a degree in electrical engineering from Marquette University and an MBA from the Illinois Institute of Technology, Viera had also spent three years as an engineering officer aboard a U.S. Navy transport.

Another Navy veteran, who had bent the truth a bit by claiming to have been a nuclear engineer in the Navy, now occupied the White House. If the nuclear industry had expected friendly treatment from a kindred spirit, it was badly mistaken. After he had been in office for less than three months, President

Jimmy Carter indefinitely deferred commercial reprocessing and recycling of plutonium produced from nuclear reactors in a move to stop the spread of nuclear weapons capability to other nations. As part of this initiative, Carter said the U.S. would halt commercial development of the breeder reactor. Several nuclear and electric power organizations criticized the President for shutting off an energy source potentially as large as the nation's coal reserves or the oil reserves of the Middle East. Commonwealth Edison, the utility with the biggest financial stake in the breeder, called Carter's decision a mistake. Noting that France, West Germany, and the Soviet Union were going forward with breeder programs of their own, Lee said he believed the President was deluding himself in hoping that other nations would follow the U.S. lead in curtailing the use of plutonium as reactor fuel. "We think the breeder is still an important and viable energy alternative for the future," Lee maintained.

Closer to home, the company continued to find innovative ways to deliver electricity. The Chicago freight tunnel system, built at the turn of the century to haul freight and coal and remove trash and cinders from downtown buildings, was transformed into an underground pathway for electricity. Abandoned in 1959, the tunnel network underwent two years of partial construction and repairs to accommodate cable running from the Taylor Transmission Substation to downtown buildings. Use of the tunnel, granted to Edison by a special city ordinance, saved the company $10 million in new construction.

Groundbreaking in Southern Division marked the beginning of another Edison innovation, construction of joint division and area headquarters. Joliet Area joined the division in sharing an all-electric building with attached warehouse. Nearby, the first 500,000-kw unit of Collins Station went into service a few months later. The plant's five units, all of similar size, were oil-fired cycling power generators which were designed to be brought up to full load rapidly and targeted for use primarily on weekdays, during heavy load periods, to supplement power provided by the company's base load units. At about the same time Edison cut its estimate of annual peak load growth from 7.5 to 6.1 percent, reflecting customer conservation practices and slower population and industrial growth. The company's 12-member Load Estimates Committee concluded in a report that "the 1973 energy crisis was more than a temporary aberration," and that "historic trends probably won't recur in the future." That proved to be an accurate assessment and long-range forecast, but the near-term marked by a hotter-than-average summer of 1977, saw the summer peak increase by nearly eight percent over the previous year.

Edison carried the load by "squeezing every kilowatt possible from our stations," Ayers noted, but once again, New York was not as fortunate. Gripped by the same heat wave as Chicago, Gotham was paralyzed by a massive blackout that began upstate and spread a web of darkness across the city. Some 10 million persons were affected. This year's New York blackout was not as peaceful as its predecessors. Police were swamped with emergency calls from worried New Yorkers who found the long night more violent than amusing or romantic. More than 2,000 persons were arrested for looting, and 78 police officers were injured. For New Yorkers concerned about getting to work the next morning in the face of stalled subway trains, inoperable traffic signals and blocked river tunnels, Mayor Abraham Beame had two words: stay home.

In October the ICC granted Edison approximately half of its rate increase request, 7.6 of 14.5 percent, or $152.6 million on an annualized basis. The boost added about $2 a month to the average residential electricity bill. Ayers expressed 'extreme disappointment' with the decision, saying the increase left the company's return on plant investment far below the level necessary to make Edison's securities attractive to investors. Carrying out a multi-billion-dollar construction in times of inflation, high interest charges, higher costs in general, and tightening federal regulation would not get any easier. Edison would be forced to seek rate relief five times over the next six years.

"Unfortunately, our customers think that the company can raise its rates whenever it wants," Don Petkus, director of Marketing Development, lamented at the 1977 Management Conference. "Also, nearly half do not realize we are regulated. And even fewer understand our expenses." Petkus referred to a comprehensive customer attitude survey undertaken by the company which revealed a downward shift in the public's opinion of Commonwealth Edison. "Considering today's rising costs, it was not surprising to find that our customers consider our rates to be too high," Petkus said. The survey contained at least one bright spot: only eight percent of the respondents said Edison should not use nuclear power to generate electricity.

Chairman and President James J. O'Connor dons one of his many civic hats as the Chairman of the 1985-86 U.S. Savings Bonds Campaign in Illinois.

Jim O'Connor undoubtedly would have gotten to the Edison presidency anyway, but a solid understanding of public affairs certainly didn't handicap him in his climb there. The 40-year-old executive, who learned the public/governmental affairs trade from the master, Morgan Murphy, assumed the presidency in December 1977 from Ayers, who continued as chairman and chief executive officer. O'Connor thus emerged as the likely successor to Ayers, then 62. "O'Connor's rise to the top has been meteoric," said the *Tribune*, "especially for the tradition-bound public utility industry where the top rungs of the corporate ladder historically have been occupied by older executives approaching retirement." A native of Chicago's South Side, O'Connor was graduated from St. Ignatius High School, a venerable Near West Side institution which is arguably the metropolitan area's best college prep school. He has often said he would not trade his St. Ignatius diploma for all three of the college degrees he obtained later—a BS in economics from Holy Cross in 1958, an MBA from Harvard in 1960, and a law degree from Georgetown in 1963, earned at night while doing a three-year hitch in the Air Force. O'Connor was personally recruited by J. Harris Ward. While the young man mulled several promising offers, Ward, never one to waste words, sent O'Connor a letter that read: "Dear Jim, What's cooking? Sincerely yours..." O'Connor said that clinched his decision. Like Ayers and countless other recent graduates, O'Connor's first experience as an Edison employe was performing hard physical labor. The first thing he did on his first day was to dig a hole for a utility pole on Dempster Street in Skokie. Soon after the job was finished, a supervisor came along and told O'Connor that because of an error the hole had to be relocated. "I've never figured that one out," he said. "I've always thought someone must have been trying to teach me some humility."

O'Connor's promotion came at a time when the United Mine Workers were on strike once again. Coal inventories at utilities in many Eastern and Midwestern areas became dangerously low. Thousands of workers were laid off in Indiana, where state officials ordered residential customers, business, and industry and schools to scale back electricity use. State officials also ordered the discontinuance of all unnecessary outdoor floodlighting and display lighting. Officials in Virginia, Maryland, and West Virginia ordered cutbacks in electricity use by commercial and industrial customers. The Carter Administration, meanwhile, warned that as many as four million workers would be laid off by mid-March 1978 if the strike were not settled. Northern Illinois, which got its power primarily from the atom and low-sulfur Western coal not affected by the strike, did not suffer any consequences. In fact, Edison, which generated almost half of its electricity from nuclear power in January, went to the aid of its stricken neighbors. In mid-February the company ordered an all-out effort to increase its generating capability. A retired unit at Fisk was placed back in service, adding 75,000 kw of capacity. Emergency repairs were made to peaking units, normally used only in the summer, adding another 300,000 kw. Refuelings at Zion and Quad-Cities were accelerated and units brought back ahead of schedule. Likewise, Ridgeland 3 came back one week earlier than planned, adding another 143,000 kw. Kilowatthours flowed east, helping to ease the crisis. Were it not for Edison's decision to move heavily into nuclear power, the Rockford *Register-Star* editorialized, "we too would be suffering the direct impact of closed plants, homes only partially heated and strict limits on the use of electricity."

388

Once the strike was settled and warmer temperatures returned, nuclear energy's beneficial role in the crisis was quickly forgotten by many. The question now being debated in the media and by the public, in addition to "Is the energy crisis real?," became "Is nuclear power dying or even dead?" Petkus once answered the latter inquiry in a speech by relating a story that President Truman used to tell about a man who passed out at a party. His friends decided to play a morbid joke on him. They carried him to the local funeral parlor, laid him out in a casket, and lighted candles all around. When the man awoke, he was terrified. Then he thought, "Wait a minute. If I'm alive, what am I doing here? And if I'm dead, how come I have to go to the bathroom?"

Nuclear power, as a headline in *Forbes* accurately observed, was very much "alive and well and living in Chicago." However, there was no doubt that the U.S. industry as a whole was navigating through rough seas. Ironically, the industry's troubles began with the oil embargo. While the quadrupled cost of oil made nuclear seem more appealing to utilities, the turbulent new economics of energy in the post-embargo period worked against the new technology. Confronted with a new conservation ethic, utilities found revenues falling and construction costs soaring because of runaway inflation, high interest rates, and over-zealous regulation. Reactor orders plunged from a high of 30 in 1974 to only three in 1976.

"The economics fell apart when the delays, the backfits, and the regulatory changes in the middle of a construction project began to take their toll," Dr. David Rossin explained. "The regulatory process congealed to the point where there was a penalty for innovation. It became very risky to make changes because if you did there was a chance that the operating license hearings could be extended or construction permit hearings reopened. That effectively froze the technology at the stage it was in when the construction permit was issued and made it impossible to take advantage of new developments."

Enactment of the National Environmental Policy Act also had a chilling effect on the development of nuclear energy, according to Rossin. "We needed something like that in this country," he continued, "but the way the courts interpreted the Act was not what thoughtful people in Congress had intended. It became accepted that you could delay anything, regardless of what it would do to the project, in order to complete all of the environmental reviews, all of the paper work, all of the data gathering about wildlife and everything else. A lot of that was good, but when it was evident that a project was needed and that any environmental impacts would be minor, you still had to go through this whole process. The price was delay, very heavy delay." Time, as the saying goes, is money. The prospect of borrowing money at double-digit interest to construct multi-billion dollar plants under regulations that were changing with the blink of an eye gave pause to many a utility.

Then, too, the safety question was being re-examined. The Rasmussen study, often quoted by nuclear supporters to back up their conviction that the technology is safe, was criticized by a committee formed by the NRC to review the safety analysis. While the panel, headed by Dr. Harold Lewis of the University of California at Santa Barbara, concluded that the study's estimates of accident probability could have been too low or too high, it faulted the methodology of the Rasmussen group. "We just found too many things that were either done poorly or with an inadequate data base," Lewis said. Rasmussen maintained that his findings were largely valid and that "reactor accident risks are small compared to other societal risks." Nevertheless, the NRC withdrew much of its support of the Rasmussen study and nuclear critics had fresh ammunition.

Anti-nuclear demonstrations swept the country in the summer and fall of 1978. One of the largest, at the construction site of the Seabrook nuclear power plant in New Hampshire, drew a crowd estimated variously between 12,000 and 18,000 persons. Folk singers Pete Seeger and Arlo Guthrie entertained while comedian Dick Gregory warned that nuclear power was causing 30,000 cases of cancer and leukemia among plant workers and people living near nuclear generating stations. Mentioned far down in most news accounts was a rally in Manchester by 3,000 people who favored construction of Seabrook.

At Edison's Byron Station construction site, about 200 demonstrators held a rally to coincide with the one at Seabrook. The company provided the protesters with a designated demonstration area. Later in the summer, the first arrests at an anti-nuclear demonstration in Illinois occurred at General Electric's spent-fuel storage facility near Morris. Fifteen protesters were arrested when they climbed a fence and trespassed on GE property. A *Tribune* article suggested that the confrontation may have been a historic event and alluded to the "minutemen at Concord bridge and the cavalrymen at the Battle of Little Big Horn." On a chilly October day, 24 demonstrators were arrested when they attempted to block access to Edison's Zion Station by sitting down in the three roads that lead to the plant. The protesters initially blocked only the main road but eventually realized they had made a tactical error. "Commonwealth Edison was willing to let them sit there until hell froze over," the Chicago *Reader* noted. "With a chilly northeast wind blowing off the lake, that moment didn't seem too far. A television reporter, glancing at his watch, said he thought he could get them on that night's news if they could get themselves arrested in the next 10 minutes. The protesters decided to split up and block all three roads. Once that was accomplished, the Zion Police moved in. Paddy wagons roared down the road, followed by an endless string of police cars. The policemen tossed them one by one into the wagons. This act of civil disobedience achieved two things: it made both the newspapers and that night's TV news." None of the 24 was from Lake County where the plant is located.

Edison, which had authorized the arrests, learned a lesson: don't play into the hands of demonstrators by providing dramatic scenes for cameras. Henceforth, company officials would do everything possible to avoid confrontation, in effect heeding an observation by author Gay Talese: "When the press is absent, politicians have been known to cancel their speeches, civil rights marchers to postpone their parades, alarmists to withhold their dire predictions." Over the ensuing years, there would be only a few, equally small demonstrations at Edison's nuclear facilities.

Demonstrations and other industry-wide problems notwithstanding, Edison passed a milestone in 1978: nuclear exceeded coal-fired generation for the first time ever. Quad-Cities Unit 1 broke one world record for continuous operation and another for availability. Dresden 2 ranked third in world-wide availability, while all of the base-load nuclear stations set a new company mark for availability. During the year, Edison also scaled down its forecast of peak load growth from 6.1 to 5.1

percent. The reduction was a major reason why Dixon Station, a 60-year-old coal-fired facility acquired in the merger with Northern Illinois Utility Co., was retired one year earlier than previously announced. Fisk, meanwhile, marked its 75th anniversary with a civic luncheon on the spruced-up floor of the turbine room. Just when it looked as if 1978 would pass with no domestic nuclear reactor sales, Edison ordered two 1,150,000-kw nuclear steam supply systems and initial fuel loads from Westinghouse for Carroll County Station. The contracts, containing cancellation clauses to be used at Edison's discretion, were the last in the United States into 1986.

In the final days of 1978 the ICC, which had authorized construction of Byron and Braidwood, ordered an investigation into whether the projects were still necessary. The commission wanted to determine the feasibility and potential cost of stopping construction at each plant and directed Edison to investigate the possibility of selling any excess power. Several days before the start of the unprecedented hearings Edison again scaled down its forecast of annual peak load growth, to 4.5 percent. Attorney Hubert Nexon, the company's senior vice president, said a combination of factors, including slower population growth, fewer housing starts, poor economic conditions, saturation of the air conditioning market, and higher electricity prices appeared to be depressing growth more than Edison had thought a year earlier. Edison faced a crucial decision—one that would chart the course for years to come.

"At the time we had about $765 million invested in Braidwood," Ayers remembered. "We determined that it was cheaper to finish it and produce low-cost power, even though it would be kind of painful in the rate area for a time. We decided to go ahead because the customer would be better off. The decision to proceed was based on very careful studies over a long period of time. I was right up front, looking at the projections. Everybody felt this was what we had to do.

"If anything, we've been burned by having less capacity than we needed," Ayers related. "We also had a lot of units approaching the time when they ought to be retiring. You can keep fixing up these old dogs and spend ungodly amounts of money, but it doesn't show quite the same. You get a big maintenance bill and unreliability. You're never sure whether or not the damn thing is going to work."

No one in the top command demurred. The construction of LaSalle, Byron, and Braidwood proceeded, continuing to draw criticism from opponents.

As the State of Illinois and the nation pondered the future of nuclear power, a development overseas again reminded Americans that they were not fully in control of their own energy destiny. In the vacuum that developed between the overthrow of the Shah and the Ayatollah Khomeini's consolidation of power, oil exports from Iran fell to near zero. The country that was once the world's second largest oil exporter after Saudi Arabia now produced barely enough oil to meet its domestic needs. Across the United States, there were cries of "Here we go again." The country witnessed a rerun of Sunday gas station closings, calls for rationing, and general hand-wringing. At least a popular new movie came along to take the public's mind off the latest oil crisis. The thrilling but factually flawed picture starring Jane Fonda dealt with a major accident at a nuclear power plant that nearly resulted in a "meltdown" and the "China syndrome." These were eerie new expressions to many Americans, but terms they soon would be hearing in frightening TV news reports and newspaper stories. It would be as if "The China Syndrome" and Three Mile Island were running as a double feature, confusing some as to where fantasy ended and fact began. Never in recent memory had life performed such an uncanny imitation of art.

Sixteen

Beyond
Three
Mile
Island

I

Nineteen seventy-nine was to have been such a bright year for the electric utility industry. In late 1978, an international committee, comprised of utility leaders such as Tom Ayers along with those of allied industries, launched the Centennial of Light, a 15-month celebration commemorating the 100th anniversary of Thomas Edison's invention of the incandescent electric light bulb. Throughout the world, scientific exhibits, science fairs, scholarship presentations, films, radio and television programs, lectures, parades, and the issuance of commemorative coins and stamps highlighted the centennial. But 1979 would not be remembered, even within the industry itself, for the Centennial of Light. It would be remembered forever as the Year of Three Mile Island.

The year had gotten off to a bad start for Commonwealth Edison even before the accident. On Wednesday, March 28, the day the drama began to unfold in Pennsylvania, Ayers, O'Connor, and Behnke were in New York, presenting one of the company's regular briefings to that city's Society of Security Analysts. Ayers reported a number of problems. Extremely cold temperatures, accompanied by one of the worst blizzards on record, had caused coal and coal-handling equipment to freeze, and slowed or stopped coal and oil deliveries by barge and rail. Non-weather-related equipment failures had kept three large generating units out of service for almost the entire first quarter. The bad weather and the equipment failures forced Edison to sharply increase its use of costly oil and purchased power, deflating earnings for January and February by 27 cents a share compared to the same two months in 1978. The first news of

Three Mile Island that reached the Edison leaders told of a serious mishap but did not suggest the near-panic that would develop later. Behnke told the analysts that Metropolitan Edison, operator of the plant, appeared to have the situation in hand. Unfortunately, the opposite proved true.

The accident began at 4 a.m. when Three Mile Island Unit 2 was operating at 97 percent power. The reactor developed a leak of coolant. Unknown to the reactor operators, someone had left two valves in the auxiliary feedwater system closed following servicing two days earlier. While dealing with a separate problem which had already existed for 11 hours, the operators inadvertently caused a condensate pump to trip. The main feedwater pumps stopped, as designed, causing a total loss of feedwater to the generators and a trip of the main turbine. Since the valves in the auxiliary feedwater system had been left closed in error, there was no flow of auxiliary feedwater. With no water entering the generator and no steam leaving it, no heat was removed from the reactor coolant system following the loss of feedwater. Within less than two minutes, the steam generators boiled dry.

During the first few minutes of the accident, "more than 100 alarms went off, and there was no system for suppressing the unimportant signals so that operators could concentrate on the significant alarms," according to the presidential commission that investigated the accident. When the operators were confronted with a situation they had never faced before—conflicting readings apparently showing adequate cooling water in the reactor and high temperatures—they decided to cut off an emergency core cooling system to the reactor core. As a result, the highly radioactive core became uncovered. The operators did not understand that the water was being flashed into steam in the reactor system, the commission's report stated. Because they did not realize that a loss-of-coolant accident was transpiring, the operators expected the natural circulation of coolant to protect the core in the absence of forced pumping.

Exposure of the core damaged the fuel elements, released radioactive core fission products, and created a hydrogen bubble that formed at the top of the reactor vessel. The bubble resulted from a chemical reaction between the overheated metal tubes containing the fuel rods and the steam. While hydrogen is flammable and can form explosive mixtures with air, the hydrogen in the bubble could not have exploded because of the absence of oxygen. According to the investigation, NRC Chairman Joseph Hendrie, unaware that oxygen wouldn't form in the reactor in the presence of all that hydrogen, became concerned that the hydrogen bubble could explode.

Revelation of this concern by an unnamed NRC source to a wire service reporter triggered a round of sensational, confusing media coverage by many of the nearly 600 newspersons who had descended on the Middletown, Pennsylvania, area. One Commonwealth Edison news staffer termed the coverage a "media riot." Earlier, another false report, that radiation levels 100 times above normal had been detected in a nearby town, caused the NRC to recommend to the state of Pennsylvania that a precautionary evacuation be undertaken. Governor Thornburgh recommended that pregnant women and small children leave the area, but altogether some 144,000 people, roughly 39 percent of the population within 15 miles of the plant, took it upon themselves to flee. The actual radiation levels near the plant proved to be only slightly above normal background levels.

"The overreaction of the NRC's personnel contributed more to the panic atmosphere at Three Mile Island than any other single factor," Jim O'Connor stated. Another President named James, watching the events unfold on television at the White House, reportedly blamed the media, particularly television, for the widespread public anxiety. According to syndicated columnists Evans and Novak, President Carter told his advisers that the coverage of Three Mile Island was "exaggerated, irresponsible and outrageous." The President never said that publicly, but he did do something that greatly calmed an anxious public: he and his wife, Rosalynn, toured the Three Mile Island plant site the Sunday following the accident, standing only 1,000 feet from the disabled reactor core but receiving less radiation than a person receives from a medical x-ray. That the Carters appeared on television screens and in newspapers around the world wearing only street clothes was additionally reassuring.

"It doesn't make much difference that no one was killed or harmed as a result of that accident," O'Connor said. "The fact is that it put an indelible mark in the public's mind about nuclear power. It scared them. Nuclear power went into the doghouse."

Commonwealth Edison was bombarded with hundreds of calls from the media, including many from other parts of the country which sought the company's views because it was the nation's largest nuclear utility. Almost invariably the key question was, "Could it happen to Edison?" The company's answer was, "extremely unlikely, although nothing is impossible." Edison spokespersons added that the two units at Zion were the company's only operating pressurized water reactors, the type of units at Three Mile Island. Edison engineers did a quick but thorough comparison of the two plants and found that the Zion design was much more conservative in a number of critical aspects. Unlike the steam generators at Three Mile Island, which boiled dry within less than two minutes, Zion's steam generators had adequate water for about 30 minutes, giving the operators considerably more time to take action in the event of feedwater loss. Edison people further explained that the Zion containment building was engineered to isolate itself on any number of signals, preventing radioactive water from being pumped from the containment to the auxiliary building. At Three Mile Island, isolation did not occur until some 15,000 gallons of radioactive water had been pumped from the containment to the auxiliary building. The company's more general message to the press and public stated that Edison has been in the nuclear electricity business longer than any other utility; the safety of the public and its employes has always been Edison's foremost concern; and that everything possible was being done to make sure nuclear power continued to work safely, locally as well as nationally.

Edison's leaders understood that much more than statements to the media were needed to cope with the reverberations of Three Mile Island.

"Was I concerned? Yes. Did I think it meant the end of nuclear power? No," said O'Connor.

On the Saturday following the start of the accident, calls went out to the company's officers and other principals associated with the nuclear program to attend an emergency meeting the next morning in the board room at Edison's First National Bank headquarters. The weather mirrored the mood. A dark, bleak day punctuated by drizzle, Sunday, April 1, marked Ayers' sixth anniversary as Edison chairman. He convened the meeting, then asked O'Connor to chair a task force that would develop a comprehensive response plan. In keeping with his deferential style, O'Connor began by apologizing for calling the managers out on Sunday but quickly explained that the enormity of the situation presented no other choice.

"We wanted first to determine precisely what had happened at Three Mile Island and what adjustments, if any, we should make in our own plants," O'Connor related. "We outlined a host of assignments for all of the various disciplines in the company—technical and non-technical. Also, we wanted to provide resources to GPU" (General Public Utilities, parent corporation of Metropolitan Edison).

What GPU could have used as much, if not more, than technical help was public relations assistance. The media response overwhelmed the small PR staff at Three Mile Island. Complicating matters were the often contradictory statements of the NRC, the state, and the utility along with those of self-appointed experts such as the Union of Concerned Scientists, Jane Fonda, Tom Hayden, and various anti-nuclear politicians. It was one thing that the person watching television didn't understand what was happening, but the impression that the experts themselves couldn't agree upon, much less correct, the problem terrified a considerable number of people.

"I think that GPU did a poor job on public relations," Ayers maintained. "I think they were too interested in saying nothing to the public, which, of course, is a terrible mistake when you have a news story that big. They were pretty much stonewalling it."

Altogether, Ayers and O'Connor implemented a 15-point action program. One of the first actions taken at the Sunday meeting was the dispatch of Vice President Byron Lee, Nuclear Stations Division Manager Frank Palmer, and Health Physicist Robert Pavlik to assist in the recovery effort. At home, O'Connor appointed Edison representatives to promptly call on public officials and agencies, neighboring utilities, the financial community, and the company's legal advisors to let them know of the company's efforts to review the entire accident. O'Connor himself briefed members of the Illinois congressional delegation.

Edison also formed an independent panel of scientists, headed by Dr. Thomas Martin, president of the Illinois Institute of Technology (IIT), to determine which additional safety measures the company should adopt. Internally, Edison set up two task forces —one for pressurized water reactors and one for boiling water reactors—to review safety systems, procedures, equipment and the emergency response plan. Taking note of the public information fiasco at Three Mile Island, the company established another task force to review Edison's ability to respond swiftly and accurately in the event of a major accident.

On Monday, April 2 the size of the infamous hydrogen bubble shrank dramatically, relieving the crisis atmosphere in the Middleton region and clearing the way for a cold shutdown of the unit.* Once the accident was over, President Carter appointed his blue-ribbon investigating committee, chaired by Dartmouth College President John Kemeny. Still later came two ironic footnotes: in early May, Roger Mattson, director of the NRC's Division of Systems Safety, admitted that, "We fouled up. There never was any danger of a hydrogen explosion in that bubble. It was a regrettable error." By July, tourists from all over the world flocked to Three Mile Island. A wire service photo in newspapers around the country showed a family picknicking in the shadow of the cooling towers which had now become the international symbol of nuclear energy.

The long-awaited report by the 12-member Kemeny Commission came out in late October, blaming the accident on inadequate and misguided regulation, poorly designed equipment and equipment failures, poor training of operators, and human error. Despite fears of health effects, the commission, bolstered by a staff of 85, concluded that the amount of radiation released into the atmosphere was so small it was entirely possible that not a single extra cancer death would occur within 50 miles of the plant. The most serious health effect, the panel stated, was severe but short-lived mental stress. Of critical importance to Commonwealth Edison, with its ambitious, multi-billion dollar nuclear construction program, was the commission's recommendation that there be no moratorium on building new plants.

---

*Unit 1, unaffected by the accident, remained shutdown by NRC order until 1985.

400

Ayers hailed the report's "spirit of reform" which "provides the nuclear industry with constructive criticism on which to build an even more reliable energy source." Ayers said Edison would incorporate suggestions not only by the Kemeny Commission but by the NRC, industry trade organizations and a nuclear safety committee established by Illinois Governor James Thompson.

Even though Edison's construction program continued, the government's massive reappraisal of nuclear safety exacted a heavy toll from the company. The NRC shifted staff members from licensing new generating stations to investigating the Three Mile Island accident, forcing Edison to delay the start up of Byron and Braidwood stations by one year each and Carroll County station by two years. LaSalle County Station, a boiling water reactor plant, unlike the other three, was delayed by nine months so the company could voluntarily reinforce the containment structures. All told, the delays represented the biggest setback in Edison's nuclear construction program. "We agree with the NRC that learning all we can about the Three Mile Island incident should be given top priority," O'Connor stated. "If this means a temporary slowdown in the licensing process for other plants, that's the price we'll have to pay."

In September an action by the Illinois Commerce Commission (ICC) compelled Edison to stop construction of Braidwood altogether, triggering another emergency meeting in the Board Room. The ICC had intended to grant a $45 million interim rate increase, enough to improve the company's bond coverage so it could go forward with a desperately needed $200 million offering. But it committed a mathematical error in computing the increase and granted only $9 million, or 1.65 percent. Edison promptly laid off more than 1,500 construction workers at the Braidwood site and began mothballing the twin units. Ayers assailed the ICC decision as "totally irresponsible," adding that "it seems the commission has determined that Illinois citizens should be forced to accept second-rate utility service in the years ahead." The company's earnings per share had already fallen 23 percent in the first half of 1979, Standard & Poor's rating service had dropped Edison's bond rating one notch, and the prospect of additional de-ratings seemed likely, further hampering the company's ability to raise funds for its construction program. Ayers described the financial squeeze as the worst he had seen in his 41 years with Edison.

Conditions would not improve quickly. It was as if Three Mile Island had set off a chain reaction of hammer blows that would strike the company periodically for years to come. Criminal prosecution, a pseudo-drug scandal, and an unprecedented nuclear license denial would account for just three of the reversals. Before the year ended, the company and the industry launched a counter-offensive. Edison, along with other nuclear utilities, established three major self-improvement organizations —the Institute of Nuclear Power Operations (INPO), the Nuclear Safety Analysis Center (NSAC) and a self-insurance program later dubbed Nuclear Electric Insurance Limited (NEIL). Functioning independently of its sponsors, INPO's sole purpose is to elevate performance standards of nuclear plants across the country, primarily through evaluations by veteran nuclear station operators on loan from member utilities. "It's a great success story," according to O'Connor. "INPO has appealed to the industry's pride. There's a lot of peer pressure to perform better." He also noted that a key objective of the evaluations is to find good practices at nuclear stations and to share them with other member utilities. "This is a refreshing difference from our experience with the NRC."

The industry created NSAC to perform detailed technical analyses of Three Mile Island and to evaluate the lessons learned. "NSAC can communicate immediately with the industry about hardware problems or experiences of other utilities," O'Connor continued. "We didn't have that before. After Three Mile Island, we all became far more aware that the industry's reputation would be held hostage to the performance of each individual plant." Something else the industry didn't have prior to the accident was a way to provide a utility with financial assistance to help cover the cost of replacement power during a prolonged outage. NEIL was formed from the unhappy experience of General Public Utilities, which wound up paying more than $20 million a month to replace the power of the shuttered Three Mile Island plant.

Edison also embarked on a counter-offensive of its own— an aggressive, issue-oriented advertising campaign to gain support for higher rates and continued development of nuclear energy. The first ad pictured an open grave with the stark headline, "Will burying nuclear waste bury us all?" The text chided the federal government for delays that prevented the establishment of a safe waste repository, explained that disposal is not a technical problem, and concluded that, "The only problem we haven't solved yet is how to get the show back on the road." Another ad used the company's current slogan to grab reader attention: "We're working for you. And we need a raise." The text described the steep cost increases in generating station construction and cited the need for a "realistic" rate increase "before it's too late." Three years later the nuclear industry formed the U.S. Committee for Energy Awareness (USCEA) to tell the pro-nuclear story through print, video, and in-person messages. USCEA constituted a broadening of industry PR efforts begun after Three Mile Island.

Not all of Edison's innovations during this period came in reaction to Three Mile Island. Two months before the accident, the company began the Spotlight on the Pro program to publicly recognize generating station employes who perform beyond the normal requirements of their jobs. Each quarter, candidates are nominated by their supervisors, and at year's end a Pro of the Year is selected. The first Pro of the Year, 35-year veteran James W. Conner of Ridgeland Station, joked at the presentation ceremony that the similarity of his name to that of James J. O'Connor might have had something to do with the award. Rising to the bait, O'Connor replied, "Jim, there's something I've been meaning to tell you all day—congratulations, Dad!" The performance that earned Conner Pro of the Year honors was no joke: he averted a potentially long, large-scale power outage when he corrected an overloaded transmission line at Ridgeland.

II

The events at Three Mile Island overshadowed implementation of a new seasonal rate structure for Edison's residential customers which was accompanied by a switch from bimonthly to monthly billing. The new rate lowered kilowatthour charges in the eight non-summer months but increased them in the four summer months in an attempt to curb peak electricity

From left: Vice President George Rifakes talks with Vice President Preston Kavanagh and Vice Chairman Wallace Behnke at a company financial conference.

demands when generating costs are higher. The ICC, which mandated the change over Edison's misgivings, said it hoped to improve the company's annual load factor by reducing summer peak loads. The ICC did not intend to increase Edison's annual revenues nor the average customer's annual electricity costs. Unfortunately, the change created a stubborn public relations problem for Edison because many customers perceived only a summertime increase with no corresponding relief in the non-summer months.

Death took retired public relations chief Morgan Murphy in April 1979 after a lengthy illness. Later that year, Corey and Vice President Glen Beeman retired, following Edison careers that spanned more than four decades. As an outgrowth of Three Mile Island, Edison consolidated all of its nuclear operations under the direction of one executive—19-year veteran engineer Cordell Reed, who was elected a vice president soon afterward, when James W. Johnson became vice president for fossil operations.

404

On January 31, 1980 O'Connor completed his meteoric rise when the company's directors elected him chairman of the board and chief executive officer, effective March 1, to succeed Ayers who reached the company's mandatory retirement age for officers of 65. O'Connor retained the title of president. His promotion ended any remaining speculation about whether he or Wallace Behnke would be appointed to the top job. Behnke was elected vice chairman, replacing Corey. Ayers and Corey continued as Edison directors. At the same meeting, the board also elected Byron Lee and Bide Thomas executive vice presidents.

O'Connor, at 42 the youngest electric utility CEO in the country, set his first goal as improving earnings. "We're going to do everything possible to be as productive as possible," he vowed. How did he go from digging post holes on Dempster Street to chief executive officer in 17 years? "I worked hard," he told an interviewer. "But there were people who helped pull me along the way, people like Tom Ayers and Morgan Murphy Sr." Ayers would be remembered as the man who made Edison the country's foremost nuclear utility, but O'Connor reminded the interviewer of his predecessor's long involvement in civil rights, including equal opportunity employment and housing and the city's social progress in general. "One of Tom Ayers' greatest accomplishments is that he has raised the social consciousness of many businessmen in this town," O'Connor delcared. "And he wasn't just doing it for business reasons." After four decades of service to Edison, years filled with turmoil as well as growth, Ayers said he was set to pass the torch to O'Connor. "Jim is ready to run the company," he observed. "He's young of age, but he's a wise administrator. I think he'll do a good job." As for himself, Ayers said, "I'm not retiring. I'm just not going to be chairman and chief executive officer of Edison any longer. It's time to give the younger fellows a chance."

No sooner had O'Connor been installed than he had to face an unprecedented problem—the indictment of the company and two management employes by a federal grand jury on charges of fraud and conspiracy to evade security regulations at Quad-Cities Station. Edison thus became the first utility in the nation to be indicted by the government. The industry buzzed with rumors that the Carter Administration, stung by criticism of the way it had policed nuclear power before and during the Three Mile Island accident, had decided to demonstrate just how tough a cop it could be and had singled out the biggest nuclear utility for arrest.

Edison had waited a long time for the shoe to drop. The case began in 1977 when a disgruntled member of the security force that Edison employed at Quad-Cities went to the FBI with allegations of lax security. The company maintained that the issues should have been resolved with the NRC through normal administrative channels. The Justice Department charged that the defendants failed in their obligation to record security doors found open, to make certain that visitors were provided with company escorts at all times and that they further failed to report the infractions to the NRC. The government argued that the employes, in fact, changed security practices in early 1976 to avoid criticism by the NRC for finding open doors and unescorted visitors, and that these incidents constituted a serious threat to the plant, possibly allowing a terrorist or saboteur to gain entry to vital areas. Edison and the two employes, station superintendent Nicholas Kalivianakis and station security director Walter Meehan, denied any wrongdoing.

The trial occurred during the steamy first week of August at the aging federal courthouse in Rock Island, Illinois, 20 miles downriver from the Quad-Cities plant. "The nuclear power industry goes on trial today," the *Wall Street Journal* proclaimed, quoting an unnamed attorney as saying that if the Justice Department won a conviction, other utilities might also be indicted. The local press described the trial as the biggest news event in town since Dwight Eisenhower made a presidential campaign appearance there in 1952.

As the trial unfolded, Edison did not dispute that doors had been left open at the plant or that visitors had been without escorts for short periods, but the company vigorously denied that it had attempted to conceal information from the NRC. Defense testimony painted a much different scenario from that of potential terrorists running through the plant. For example, one unescorted visitor proved to be a Commonwealth Edison delivery driver who made regular runs between a company warehouse and the generating station. In every incident, the company showed, visitors were either company or contractor employes

406

who were unescorted only during their last few steps to the security building as they left the premises.

The government did not present any evidence to show that a visitor was left unescorted inside the plant or near any security door. Dan Webb, Kalivianakis' lawyer and later the U.S. Attorney for the Northern District of Illinois, ridiculed the government's suggestion that visitors could have wandered into vital areas of the plant and become exposed to high levels of radiation. Webb continually asked witnesses whether or not any visitor had been "eradicated," seeming to deliberately mispronounce "irradiated," to the amusement of spectators and at least a few jurors. Edison further maintained that the NRC regulation that certain doors be locked or guarded was adopted after the plant had been designed and constructed, forcing the company to consider nearly every door into the plant as leading to a vital area. Expecting employes who had to move from room to room, dozens of times a day, to lock doors each time was unrealistic, the defense stated. In one instance an employe who worked in a stuffy area regularly opened a door that faced the river to get a breeze. In any case, Edison maintained, the security plan in effect at the time of the alleged infractions did not obligate the company to report unlocked doors or unescorted visitors to the NRC.

After five days of proceedings and seven hours of deliberations, the jury of six men and six women found Edison, Kalivianakis, and Meehan not guilty on all counts. Relatives and colleagues of the two men shouted with joy as the pair embraced their attorneys with tear-filled eyes. The judge banged his gavel and demanded order. Outside, Byron Lee told a gaggle of reporters, "We're overwhelmed and tremendously relieved for Nick and Wally and our people. They always did the best they could. We had two people's lives at stake."

On the other side of the state construction of Braidwood Station gradually regained momentum, following a six-month delay. Improved financial conditions, brought about by the Commerce Commission's approval of a 12.8 percent or $344 million rate increase, allowed the company to begin calling back tradesmen who had been laid off. Meanwhile, company shareholders flashed their own green light to the nuclear program, voting 14 to 1 at the annual meeting against a proposal by a handful of dissident holders to halt nuclear plant construction.

Conservation efforts by customers, set in motion by the OPEC embargo and encouraged by Commonwealth Edison, continued to influence the company's annual load growth estimates, now trimmed to three percent, less than half of the level which had been the norm for decades before 1973. The company named Klaus Wisiol, former Chicago Central Division Vice President, to the newly created position of Manager of Load Management and Conservation. His task: coordinate Edison's myriad conservation, load management, and related research and development programs. New efforts included participation in the Illinois Energy Audits Association, a non-profit organization of electric and gas utilities which for a nominal fee inspected homes and made recommendations for saving energy costs. In cooperation with home builders, Edison promoted the Energy Smart House—a dwelling loaded with conservation features such as thick insulation, airtight windows, and an electric heat pump. Edison also established the Peak Alert program, which asked customers to voluntarily reduce their use of electricity on the hottest summer days. Finally, under a different definition of conservation, Edison opened Collins Station's cooling lake to public fishing and provided the state Department of Conservation with a grant to improve parking and boat launching facilities.

Jim O'Connor didn't have much time for fishing or other recreation in the summer of 1980. Four months into the top job, he undertook a grueling schedule of visits to 40 work locations throughout the company, delivering nearly 60 briefings and answering hundreds of questions from employes. His message of belt-tightening was made necessary by continuing inflation and a deepening recession in which kilowatthour output had dropped 3.7 percent below the pace of 1979, itself a poor year. Conditions deteriorated further when Powerton Station was ripped by a multi-million dollar explosion, and some of the worst thunderstorms on record swept through the service territory.

July 1980 went into the record books as easily the worst July for storms in the company's history. Three devastating storms, packing winds up to 90 miles an hour, lashed northern Illinois, cutting power to hundreds of thousands of customers.

The total cost of the cleanup amounted to approximately $4 million—twice as much as the company had expended on restoring electricity after storms in the entire year of 1978.

Powerton Station's coal crusher house as it still smouldered following an explosion and fire in October, 1980.

Powerton erupted early October 14 with a blast of fire and smoke that knocked the plant out of service and injured eight employes. The explosion marked the second time in less than three years that Powerton had been hit by a serious accident. Two construction workers had been killed and 40 other workers injured in December 1977 when a silo containing 1,000 tons of fly ash collapsed. Damage from the 1980 accident was eventually placed at $20 million, five times less than initially estimated. The fire started in the coal crusher house, where chunks of coal are broken into quarter-inch pieces which are fed into the boilers. Flames spread up the conveyor to the main power house. The explosion's force knocked out sections of the roof and walls, igniting a series of fresh fires. Seven local fire departments responded to the alarm, and several employes, evacuated earlier, volunteered to return and help fight the blaze. O'Connor and Petkus flew to the scene immediately upon hearing the news at 5 a.m. They were among the first persons to reenter the plant. Powerton officials expected Units 5 and 6 to be out of service for three and five months respectively, their 1,400 megawatts of power to be replaced by rescheduling maintenance outages at other plants and by purchasing power from other utilities. Edison installed several new fire control devices, including a deluge system that helped minimize damage nearly three years later, in July 1983, when fire, accompanied by a series of explosions, again struck Powerton. No one was injured this time, and the force of the blast was confined to the tripper room, where coal arrives from the crusher house for distribution to bunkers. Station hands took each of the twin 750 mw units out of service until repairs could be completed. Insurance covered most of the plant loss.

While Powerton literally still smouldered in 1980, the nuclear side of the company got a welcome directive from the Illinois Commerce Commission: proceed "in as timely and economic a manner possible" to complete the construction of Byron and Braidwood. The ICC had undertaken an investigation of Edison's construction program in December 1978 after critics charged that the company was overestimating its future needs. But the ICC found that delays in completing the plants would add significantly to their costs—by more than $600 million if construction required an additional four years. Therefore, the commission concluded that "it is in the economic interest of ratepayers and shareholders alike that. . .construction of the Braidwood and Byron nuclear generating plants be completed at the earliest possible date." Two weeks later came more good nuclear news. Edison, the State of Illinois, and local governments received high marks from federal officials for the way they performed in the first major test of their ability to protect the public in the event of a nuclear accident. The mock disaster exercise at Dresden included the evacuation of 180 schoolchildren from their classrooms. The youngsters thus became the first volunteers in the Midwest to go through such a drill. Edison would participate in dozens more emergency exercises in subsequent years at all of its nuclear generating stations, in keeping with one of the maze of new requirements mandated by the government after Three Mile Island.

The year ended with the death of John Evers, who rose from clerk to president of Commonwealth Edison during a 46-year career. He died in Boca Raton, Florida, at age 86. Evers was followed in death the following July by nuclear pioneer Murray Joslin, who succumbed in Chicago's Northwestern Memorial Hospital at age 79.

By the summer of 1981 plans moved rapidly forward for a 1992 Chicago World's Fair to mark the 500th anniversary of Columbus' discovery of America. With Ayers as chairman and Petkus as treasurer, the not-for-profit Chicago World's Fair-1992 Corporation selected a lakefront site that ran from Balbo Drive on the north to 31st Street on the south, and the Illinois Central Gulf Railroad tracks on the west. On the east, 200 acres of landfill were to be added to Lake Michigan. The blue-ribbon group then set out to win the necessary approvals, including those of city, state and Park District officials, the U.S. Department of Commerce, and the all-important Bureau of International Expositions (BIE), the Paris-based international organization that officially sanctions world's fairs. Plans for the fair enjoyed the enthusiastic support of Chicago Mayor Jane Byrne, but noting the city's ever-shifting political sands the *Christian Science Monitor* advised readers to mark the Chicago 1992 reservation in pencil rather than ink.

Earl Moore (front left), Superintendent of Division Services and coordinator of Chicago Central Division's Adopt-A-School program, discusses a class project with 8th graders in 1983 at Michelle Clark Middle School on the city's West Side.

As Chicago's schoolchildren headed back to class for the 1981–82 term, many boasted an adoptive corporate parent. Under the Chicago Board of Education's Adopt-A-School program,

Edison's Chicago Central Division adopted the Michelle Clark Middle School on the city's West Side, providing guest instructors, classroom materials, and field trips. Later, Chicago North adopted Lane Technical High School and Chicago South a pair of elementary schools, Dawes and Dyett.

Since the earliest days of nuclear power—and particularly after Three Mile Island—scientists have grappled with the question, "How safe is safe?" A team of Edison scientists, engineers and independent consultants provided an answer in September 1981—a 6,000-page study, 18 months in preparation, which concluded that Zion Station poses no unique public risk. The Edison team used new methods of statistical and engineering analysis to discount the likelihood of a catastrophic meltdown of the nuclear fuel. The study showed that the emergency core cooling system, which would prevent the fuel from melting, could be made inoperable only by unimaginable events such as an earthquake in northern Illinois as powerful as the one that struck San Francisco in 1906, or by the "very unlikely simultaneous failures of multiple items of plant equipment." The study, which the company presented to the NRC, maintained that there is "a 99 percent probability" that even a meltdown would not release radioactivity.

Critics of nuclear energy themselves have frequently raised "what if" questions in their efforts to discredit the technology, piling one unlikely hypothesis on top of another until they construct a frightening, though implausible, scenario. In December 1981 the NBC television outlet in Chicago, Channel 5, raised a new question: What if nuclear plant operators worked under the influence of drugs or alcohol? A serious matter, to say the least. Edison had begun beefing up its substance abuse program 10 months earlier after two Zion Station employes were arrested on their lunch break, near the plant, and charged with selling narcotics to an undercover police officer. The company fired one of the employes, but reinstated the other after an investigation determined that he had been a bystander to the transaction. Chicago and Lake County media reported the arrests in detail.

As far as the media apparently were concerned, the question of drugs in nuclear generating stations lay dormant until a number of disgruntled present and former employes of

Edison's security contractor, Burns International Security Services, Inc., contacted a Channel 5 reporter. The guards, most of whom had been fired for cause, told a lurid tale of wisespread drug and alcohol abuse, sexual misconduct, and inadequate security at Dresden and Zion Stations. They first tried to place the story with another Chicago television station and a daily newspaper outside metropolitan Chicago. Each rejected the overture because the charges could not be substantiated and because the accusers demanded total anonymity. Such scruples did not deter Channel 5, which aired videotape of the unidentified accusers, their faces obscured by shadows, their voices electronically garbled. The guards and ex-guards provided no specifics of misconduct.

Branding the charges incredible and insulting to generating station workers, Edison officially notified the NRC, which began its own investigation. Other guards telephoned Chicago newspapers and television stations to voice their outrage over what they considered an attack on their professionalism. Security personnel interviewed by the newspapers maintained that the overriding problem at Dresden was a struggle between two unions seeking to represent the guards and speculated that the accusations to Channel 5 constituted an attempt to discredit Burns. Edison reiterated its drug abuse policy to employes and the public alike. "We have a long record of being tough on drugs," Petkus declared. "If we find someone using drugs during company hours, we dismiss them."

The charges might have fallen of their own weight at that point had it not been for a young woman who had worked at Zion as an undercover agent assigned to investigate drug abuse. As part of its stepped-up campaign to prevent drug abuse following the arrest of the two Zion employes, Edison hired a detective agency which, in turn, placed the woman agent in the plant under the guise of being a new employe. Knowledge of the company's action was limited to a handful of officials, for obvious reasons. For about three months the agent submitted regular reports that produced indirect allegations, but no substantive evidence about the activities of Edison employes. She did purchase two small packages of marijuana from contractor employes, one in the plant's parking lot, the other at a private residence. Edison terminated her assignment after learning that she had publicly discussed her role with a Zion employe's wife.

After watching the first installment in the Channel 5 series, the former private detective contacted Channel 5, which then broadcast her charges that Edison had failed to follow up on her information. In Joseph McCarthy fashion, Channel 5 showed a list of job titles, minus names, of alleged drug or alcohol abusers at Zion. The broadcast inferred that the list was the product of the agent's undercover work, when in reality it had been provided to her at the outset of the investigation for possible leads. The names had been furnished by one of the two Zion employes arrested the previous February, possibly in the hope of getting the charges against him dropped or reduced. Not mentioned in the Channel 5 telecast was the fact that the agent's subsequent investigation failed to turn up any proof of wrongdoing by any employe on the list.

In a letter to Zion employes two days before Christmas 1981, Vice President Reed said, "It is unfortunate that the media can do this by using hearsay and innuendo. . .It is unfortunate that the employes of the station, who are hard-working, who are members of the community and family people, have been accused of these activities. . .We are hurt by these allegations and know that you must be hurt, too."

Early in the new year Edison hired Peter Bensinger, former Administrator of the U.S. Drug Enforcement Administration, to conduct an in-depth study of company policies and procedures concerning drug abuse, and to make recommendations for strengthening them. The NRC had the final word on the allegations the following November, when it issued a 57-page report that concluded that some unidentified workers had smoked marijuana at Zion, but that drug use at the plant was not widespread and did not affect safe operations. The report also stated that the NRC could not confirm "allegations pertaining to sexual activities, inadequate firearms training, inadequate response training to site threats, improper functioning of access control equipment, and intoxicated guards being issued weapons."

Channel 5's drug series had barely run its course when the station trumpeted new allegations against Edison—that two contractors had overcharged the company by as much as $2

414

million for drilling work at the LaSalle County Station construction site. This series suggested that a careless Edison and its ratepayers had been cheated out of the money. Left unreported was the fact that Edison had been aware of the overbilling for months, had turned the discrepancies over to its auditors and attorneys, and was energetically pursuing its claims. The contractor ultimately reimbursed the company. While investigating these charges, Illinois Attorney General Tyrone Fahner claimed that LaSalle's twin containment buildings might be unsafe because workers had drilled thousands of holes through the steel reinforcing bars during construction. Fahner, appointed to the post by Governor Thompson after incumbent William Scott had been dispatched to a federal penetentiary, petitioned the NRC to block Edison's request to load fuel and begin low power testing later that week. Instead, he urged the NRC to hold public hearings on LaSalle's safety. Edison's first notification of Fahner's action came when a *Tribune* reporter called to get the company's reaction.

Fahner, facing a tough election campaign against popular Democrat Neil Hartigan, based his request to the NRC on two affidavits: one by a former driller employed by a construction contractor, the other by a widely known anti-nuclear consulting engineer from California. The ex-driller stated that it was common for workers to drill through the reinforcing bars. The Attorney General's office then forwarded that affidavit to the consultant in California, bypassing the state's own top nuclear expert, Dr. Philip Gustafson, respected head of the Illinois Department of Nuclear Safety. Predictably, the consultant, who did not visit the LaSalle site, concluded that because of potential safety significance the drilling practices should be thoroughly investigated before the plant began operation. Edison explained that extra bars are routinely imbedded in the concrete of containment structures in the knowledge that many of them will be hit by drillers. Regulations require contractors to keep records of how many bars are hit by drills. Inspectors then review the number and location of the hits, to determine their effect on the integrity of the structure and to assure that an adequate safety margin exists.

Following an 11-week investigation, the NRC reported that any construction defects at LaSalle did not pose a threat to the public health and safety. In dismissing Fahner's charges, the report concluded that "adequate procedures to control concrete drilling and coring are and have been in place at LaSalle; these procedures are being successfully implemented; the engineering disposition of damaged reinforcing steel. . .was proper and complete; and the completed drilling and coring represents no compromise to the structural integrity of the LaSalle plant structures." Edison estimated that each day of delay in placing LaSalle Unit 1 in commercial service cost customers $600,000 in fuel savings.

No sooner had the NRC dismissed the drilling allegations than Channel 5, in cooperation with anti-nuclear groups, criticized the heating, ventilating and air conditioning work at the plant. Reed acknowledged that Edison had had problems in 1979 with the contractor who performed the job, but in the meantime had ordered some work redone and all of it reinspected. In early August the NRC voted unanimously to grant Edison a full power license to operate LaSalle 1. The Chicago *Sun-Times* called the decision "a corporate triumph in the face of intense controversy." Reed expressed elation; anti-nuclear intervenors expressed denunciation; and in the November election, Hartigan easily outdistanced Fahner. The following month, the ICC reaffirmed its endorsement of the company's total construction program, stating that "neither delay nor cancelation will benefit ratepayers."

The "intense controversy" over LaSalle overlapped several significant developments, including the retirement of Ridgeland Station, an historic power outage on Chicago's West Side, and political jockeying over proposals to elect members of the ICC and create a Citizens Utility Board (CUB). Under the elected ICC scheme, a commission appointed by the governor would be replaced with one elected by the voters. The idea raised the specter of impartial professional regulators replaced by politicians running on a promise not to raise utility rates. At the other extreme, critics of the proposal suggested the utilities might pool their financial resources to run their own candidates who would posture as consumer advocates but support their backers once elected. Governor Thompson vowed to veto any legislation to elect the ICC, but such action never came close to necessary. Democrat Michael Madigan, speaker of the Illinois

House, did not like the legislation any more than Thompson, so the bill met swift death in the Democratic-controlled House Public Utilities Committee.

The proposal to create CUB was another matter. Roundly criticized by some editorial voices—the Copley newspaper chain branded it "a hare-brained idea"—CUB was viewed by Madigan and other political leaders as a compromise of the more radical elected-ICC proposal. The legislation compelled the utilities to include CUB's recruiting and other literature in their bill mailings. Membership would be open to any utility ratepayer for a minimum $5.00 fee, and members would elect a steering committee consisting of one representative from each of Illinois' 22 congressional districts. The purpose of the organization would be to hire a staff of lawyers and accountants to challenge utility rate requests before the ICC. Protests by the utilities, other businesses, and some members of the media—that consumers were already represented by units in the offices of the governor, attorney general, Cook County States Attorney, and various private groups—went to no avail. The legislature approved the legislation creating CUB, and Governor Thompson signed it into law. Not surprisingly, CUB members elected an anti-utility activist as their president.

III

Ridgeland's four units generated their last kilowatthours in April and May of 1981, ending 32 years of service. Edison retired the station because of higher costs associated with oil-fired generation, the high expenditures that would be required to extend its life span, and because of slower peak load growth, now pegged at two percent a year. One-time home of the historic Edison clock and site of the tragic 1954 explosion, Ridgeland boasted a list of "firsts" that included the first centralized control of all steam and electrical equipment, the first exclusive use of cyclone furnaces on the system, and the first Edison station designated for wholesale power production.

Beginning Nov. 30 Edison grappled with an unprecedented operating problem—the failure of three transformers at the same substation, two of them at almost the same time. The failure knocked out power to approximately 20,000 customers in a heavily industrialized eight-square-mile area of Chicago's West Side. The ordeal began at the Humboldt Park Transmission Substation, 2413 W. Thomas St., which houses four transformers, each weighing 75 tons and standing 20 feet tall. The transformers convert electricity from 138,000 to 12,000 volts. Transformer #72 shut down at 8:21 a.m., joining #71, which had failed two weeks earlier. A manufacturer's expert, called upon to investigate the problem, planned to arrive the next day, but just two hours after the second failure, transformer #74 went down, leaving only #73. Within seconds, Chicago Central division placed its Restoration of Major Service (RMS) plan into operation.

The division set a primary goal of restoring as much load as possible without overheating the one operating transformer. At the same time, Chicago Central faced the task of bringing in a portable transformer, repairing the one that had been out of service, and removing and replacing the other two. The division sent 20 teams, each consisting of a marketing representative and an engineer, to call on commercial and industrial customers within the stricken area and ask them to cut their electricity use by 50 percent. Most complied, some even closing down completely. Nevertheless, the company had to shut off several feeder lines periodically to preserve even limited service to the area. Only essential installations such as hospitals, police and fire stations, and persons on life-support systems received full power around the clock. During the lower load nighttime periods, all customers got service.

Meanwhile, Chicago Central arranged to ship an Edison portable transformer to Humboldt from the company's Technical Center in Maywood, while Chicago South Substation Construction forces prepared a spare transformer for a trip from Crawford Station. The company also asked Wisconsin Power and Light to ship in another portable transformer in case Edison's portable failed. Central's Substation Construction crews erected a scaffolding 30 feet above ground on which the portable would be placed for linkup to the 138,000-volt primary connection in the substation. But the crews ran into a brick wall—literally. To gain access to the 138,000-volt cable, a 12-inch diameter hole needed to be drilled through the building's 16-inch steel-reinforced concrete walls. Workers burned out several core drill bits when they hit steel, but after 16 hours, they finally completed the job. As far as the public realized, the worst was over at 7:01 p.m. on Wednesday, December 2, when the portable transformer began to carry load. However, customers in the area were still urged to conserve electricity until more capacity became available. The arrival of one of the failed transformers following repairs and a fourth transformer from Fisk Station several days later returned conditions to near normal.

"We were forging into new territory—connecting an overhead portable transformer to an underground system," said Bob Manning, Chicago Central division vice president. "But we worked around the clock and installed it in two days. Emergencies bring out the best in people. The cooperation and teamwork of Edison employes was tremendous."

Shifting from Edison's smallest to its largest operating division, the news in Rock River was much less dramatic, but equally encouraging. Following years of operations in an antiquated office building in downtown Rockford, the division put the finishing touches on a new headquarters complex, appropriately located at 123 Energy Avenue in that city.

In late 1982 O'Connor executed his highest-level personnel move since becoming chairman when he exchanged the responsibilities of Executive Vice Presidents Byron Lee and Bide Thomas, an action not unprecedented within the company. Lee became responsible for the seven operating divisions, industrial relations, purchasing, and marketing groups that previously were overseen by Thomas. Thomas, on the other hand, assumed Lee's earlier responsibilities for engineering, construction, and operation of the company's bulk power system. The following June, five additional members of Edison's top command moved into new positions. Raymond Bachert, formerly secretary and treasurer, became comptroller; Ernest Roth took over as treasurer; Klaus Wisiol as secretary. Roth had been manager of investments, Wisiol manager of load management and conservation.

Death came in January 1983 for the man who once seemed a step away from the Edison chairmanship. Samuel Insull Jr., who estimated his own worth in the early 1930s at more than $13 million, died in a Batavia nursing home at age 82. According to friends, Insull remained unspoiled by the sharp turns in his life, retaining a gentle manner and keen sense of humor. Following active duty in the Navy during World War II and a few other business ventures, he returned to selling insurance. It took many years, but Insull prided himself in the fact that he finally settled all of the civil claims against his father's estate. In 1958 he filed a suit of his own—a $4 million libel action against three writers and their publishers who stated that the Insulls had bribed public officials and ended up in jail. He claimed the family name had been blackened. Besides, he added, he "could use the money." The case was dismissed on a technicality. Survivors included his second wife, Margaret, who died in October 1985, and a son, Samuel III.

Death stalked a number of nuclear—not to mention fossil-fueled—power plants under construction in 1983, once again raising the question, "Is the nuclear option dead?" The long overdue and over-budget plants, the *Wall Street Journal* observed, "threaten to overwhelm the utilities that are building them. Several companies face an excruciating choice: either abandon the problem plants, some of which already have cost billions of dollars, or continue to pour money into them with no assurance that they will ever operate. Either way, grave consequences loom for the companies, their investors and consumers," the *Journal* warned, raising the prospect of utility bankruptcies. The plants in trouble included Zimmer in Ohio, where the NRC had halted construction due to alleged faulty workmanship one year earlier with the station 97 percent complete; Seabrook in New Hampshire, where the lead utility and its 15 partners on the project were running out of money; Shoreham on Long Island, plagued by some of the highest costs in the nation and a running battle with local officials over adoption of the mandatory emergency plan for the public; and Marble Hill in Indiana, nearly identical to Byron and Braidwood, but estimated to cost $7 billion, twice as much as either Edison plant.

Nevertheless, these woes did not represent the status of the entire industry, O'Connor wrote in the 1983 Electric Utility Executives' Forum conducted by *Public Utilities Fortnightly* magazine. Acknowledging "a few highly publicized construction and operating problems," O'Connor maintained that two facts remained clear: that nuclear would continue to generate an increasing share of the country's electricity, and that "there are simply no alternatives to coal and uranium as the basic fuels the industry must rely on over the next few decades." Then he ticked off five reasons for optimism: congressional passage of nuclear waste disposal legislation, NRC recognition of the need for regulatory reform, the increased availability of property damage insurance covering a nuclear accident, the continuing economic advantage of nuclear over coal or oil-fired generation, and a multi-million-dollar television campaign by the U.S. Committee for Energy Awareness (USCEA) to convince Americans of the necessity and safety of nuclear power. O'Connor could have added that Edison itself had raised its advertising budget for the first time in 13 years—from approximately $3.2 million to $5.4 million—to explain the advantages of nuclear energy, illustrate the company's reliability, and discuss electricity rates factually, rather than emotionally.

While the industry itself continued to resemble Harry Truman's partygoer-in-the-casket, the U.S. Senate left no doubt about the fate of the Clinch River breeder reactor. Voting 56 to 40 on October 26, 1983, the Senate turned down a 1984 budget appropriation for the breeder, effectively killing the project one year after preliminary work had begun, concluding years of licensing delays. After 11 years and the expenditure of $1.6 billion in federal funds, however, even many of the project's earlier supporters had concluded that enough was enough. Increased supplies of oil and uranium and slackening demand for electricity in the years since the breeder first had been proposed helped to seal its doom. "One of these days, I think we will regret not having an entry in this field," Sen. Howard Baker of Tennessee, the project's principal supporter, sadly noted.

Back in northern Illinois, Edison again demonstrated its faith in the future of nuclear power by opening the state-of-the-art Production Training Center (PTC) near Braidwood. Completed on time and on budget for $21 million, the PTC trains both fossil and nuclear plant workers in maintenance and operations. A pair of nuclear control room simulators—one replicating Braidwood Unit 1, the other LaSalle County 1—function as the heart of the facility. Instructors use the simulators to train plant operators how to anticipate and react to emergencies as well as how to operate the plants under normal conditions. Additionally, the PTC is equipped with a chemistry laboratory, a mechanical maintenance laboratory, two electrical maintenance labs, a pair of instrumentation and control labs, and a welding facility, each allowing students to gain "hands-on" experience.

The summer of 1983 again provided a tale of two cities. In mid-August, New York struggled through its fourth major blackout, a three-day outage in the city's garment district that cost nearly $9 million in lost retail sales and another $750,000 in sales taxes. Three-fourths of New York's 5,500 clothing manufacturers attempted to carry on without power—some setting up shop in the street—during the district's busiest week of the year, when buyers from around the country arrive to stock up for the fall and Christmas seasons. Less than one week later, Edison established a new record peak load—14,517 mw on August 19—the ninth time during that season of record heat and humidity that the figure had topped the company's estimated peak load.

Another month later, Edison had to cope with another serious operating problem of its own, right at the doorstep of its corporate headquarters. Fire in a transformer, three floors below sidewalk level outside One First National Plaza at Clark and Monroe Streets, darkened sections of the complex, cut some elevator and escalator service, and caused the evacuation of occupants. However, the principal concern of Edison and firefighters stemmed from the presence in the transformer of toxic polychlorinated biphenyls (PCBs), a man-made chemical used as an insulating and cooling fluid. When PCBs burn they create the toxic substance dioxin, so, logically, fears mounted that the building might become contaminated. Firefighters wearing breathing masks and protective clothing used dry chemicals to put out the fire within five minutes, then noticed liquid on the floor of the transformer vault. About 15 of the 200 gallons of the insulating liquid containing PCBs had spilled out of the transformer, but did not appear to have been touched by the flames. Still, Edison took no chances. O'Connor, Manning (now general division manager), and other company officials marched down 37 flights of stairs from their offices to establish a corporate command post in a section of the bank near the transformer. By now the downtown streets were filled with firefighters and equipment under the personal command of Fire Commissioner Louis Galante. Edison spokespersons conducted periodic sidewalk briefings for swarms of newspeople.

Further checking by underground crews from Chicago Central Division showed that the vault contained no air ducts which could have channeled smoke into the building's heating and air conditioning system. Nevertheless, members of Edison's Environmental Affairs department and the Illinois Environmental Protection Agency combed the 60-story building, taking soot and air samples which were rushed to Edison's Technical Center as well as to an independent laboratory for analysis. Positive results could force the building to remain closed. Edison, bank, and public officials waited anxiously through the night. Then came the results from Tech Center: no evidence of toxic contamination anywhere in the complex. The building opened for business as usual the next morning. The following day, the independent lab confirmed Tech Center's conclusion. Edison, which had routed power to the building through other transformers, replaced the damaged transformer with one that did not contain PCBs. Ironically, the company had been phasing out all capacitors containing PCBs as well as inspecting transformers containing the substance for possible phase-out. The bank transformer had not been replaced because it was new and did not appear to require changes.

Concerns over PCBs, financial health, criticism of nuclear power, and other issues stood aside the night of Sept. 17, 1983, as approximately 7,900 Edison employes, family members and friends contributed to a standing-room-only crowd at Comiskey Park that watched the White Sox attempt to clinch the American League's Western Division championship. The ball game marked the largest employe gathering away from the workplace in decades, easily topping the Edison Club dinner dances and approaching the combined day-night total of the annual Christmas parties of the 1920s. Of course, the occasion, Edison Family Night, had been arranged well before anyone realized the Sox would be shooting for the title in that particular game. Dick Thorsen, director of Employment Programs, led the singing of the national anthem from home plate, while Arlene Grochowski, of Northwest Area Operating Clerical, threw out the first pitch. Raffle winners received box seats or autographed baseballs. Countless employes who consider themselves hard workers, frequently attacked unfairly by critics, mentioned how the evening revived their corporate spirit. The Sox made the

423

celebration complete by beating Seattle in the bottom of the ninth, 4–3.

With the onset of winter, Edison began a financial assistance program to help needy customers. The company contributed $250,000 to a Consumer Participation Fund—more money later—then asked customers to check a box on their monthly bill if they wanted the company to add an additional dollar from its general revenues. The Fund ultimately raised $780,000 which the Salvation Army distributed to qualified customers. Edison noted, however, that the long-range problems of the needy are best solved by elected officials and urged the Illinois General Assembly to earmark a portion of state taxes paid by utilities as a fund to help those who are unable to pay their utility bills. The plea fell on deaf ears, so the following year, Edison again conducted a financial assistance program. In 1985, the legislature did craft a so-called Affordable Budget Plan under which qualifying customers were required to pay no more than 12 percent of their total income for home energy costs during the heating season. The law did not establish any mechanism for utilities to collect the unpaid amounts. Edison opposed the program because it was funded not with taxes, but ultimately by the remaining customers. Edison pegged its bad debt losses as a result of the legislation at $19.1 million, nearly equal to the company's total annual bad debt amount.

In early 1984 Edison wondered whether it should add an astrologer to its nuclear planning team, because an event that would cause the most damage to the construction program since the ICC's short-sighted 1979 rate decision carried almost mystic overtones. The setback occurred on Friday, long known as hangman's day, according to *Webster's Unabridged Dictionary*, because it was the customary day for hangings. Not just any Friday, but Friday the 13th. Friday, Jan. 13, 1984—the year that served as the title of George Orwell's chilling novel of life in a future totalitarian society.

O'Connor had wound up an industry meeting in Phoenix and was at the airport, awaiting a flight home, when he made the last of his customary four daily calls to his office when out of town. What he heard was "an absolute shock, not just to me, but to everyone else who had been following the proceedings." For the first time ever, the NRC's Atomic Safety and Licensing

Board (ASLB) had refused to recommend an operating license to a nearly-completed nuclear generating station—Byron. The three-member board did not cite any structural or equipment deficiencies, but questioned the adequacy of quality assurance inspections performed by company contractors. Once over its initial incredulity, Edison vowed to challenge the ruling, which prevented the plant from starting up, and expressed confidence that Byron would obtain a license, load fuel, and generate power that year.

"There had been some last minute questions raised by the intervenors dealing with the quality of work done by contractors and the documentation of this work," O'Connor stated. "But no one felt that anything in the record would have suggested a denial. The worst we might have expected was a conditional approval, where the board would say, 'We give you the license subject to your proof of certain things.' "

O'Connor readily acknowledged a point made on Wall Street and in the newspapers: if a problem of this magnitude could strike Commonwealth Edison, then every nuclear utility faced potential trouble. "Because we have traditionally been considered among the premier operators of nuclear plants in the country, getting the denial really gave us a black eye," O'Connor observed. He did not acknowledge the truth of another story making the rounds: that somebody in the federal bureaucracy had decided to cut Edison down to size. "I've not found any credence in that," the chairman asserted. "Now, that doesn't mean that we haven't been aggressive where we felt certain situations warranted it. Where we felt that we had a strong case on certain actions that involved the NRC, we would do our very best to present our case. That posture could be interpreted as being arrogant in some people's minds."

The company faced a long, difficult process to reverse the denial. Taking a page from the post-Three Mile Island period, O'Connor summoned the high command downtown for a day-long Sunday meeting to chart the counterattack. Officials quickly decided to continue work at Byron, where Unit 1 was almost complete and Unit 2 was 65 percent complete, while awaiting the outcome of an appeal. Edison was particularly disturbed because the ASLB rendered its decision before the company had completed a sweeping reinspection of work reviewed by electrical contractor inspectors whose credentials the board had called into question. Had the ASLB waited for the results of the nearly-complete reinspection, the company strongly believed, the outcome would have been different. Ten days after the denial, Edison filed an application for an expedited hearing before the ASLB's three-member appeal board which would consider, among other evidence, the reinspection results.

The ASLB decision occurred only days before the company had planned to announce some bad news on its own: cost increases for Byron and Braidwood and six-month construction delays for Byron 2 and the two Braidwood units, primarily to meet design and regulatory changes. Edison now pegged the total cost of Byron at $3.77 billion, up from $3.35 billion, and Braidwood at $3.58 billion, up from $3.09 billion. The company estimated that the licensing imbroglio would delay the start of Byron 1 by four months and add $97 million to its cost. Even with the increases, the cost of the two plants remained approximately one-half the average of those being built elsewhere in the country.

Edison's licensing problem, which caused its common stock to dip four dollars a share and a credit rating agency to lower the company's rating, combined with ongoing problems at other nuclear utilities to touch off a new round of stories in the national press that again wondered whether or not Harry Truman's partygoer had finally expired. In a newspaper interview, O'Connor admitted that investors were reeling from the "uncertainty that clouds the entire nuclear industry." He referred to the recent cancellation of the Marble Hill plant and equally recent announcement that the Zimmer plant would be converted to coal. Yet the Edison chairman took pains to distance his company from the others, reminding the newspaper and anyone else within earshot that Edison should not be lumped with the other companies because its problem at Byron resulted from a misjudgment concerning paperwork, not construction errors or inordinate cost overruns.

In what one industry official described as "one hell of a stroke," Edison nominated highly regarded nuclear expert Eugene Wilkinson to its board of directors one month after the Byron denial. Personally recruited by O'Connor, the retired Navy vice-admiral and first commander of the nuclear subma-

in 1984. Byron is Edison's only nuclear
plant with cooling towers.

*Byron Station as it neared completion
in 1984. Byron is Edison's only nuclear
plant with cooling towers.*

rine *U.S.S. Nautilus* had announced his retirement as president
of the Institute of Nuclear Power Operations (INPO), where he
had worked closely with the Edison chairman. "Wilkinson has
clearly made a mark that has caught the NRC's eye," the
unidentified industry official said in the *Tribune*. "What they've
(Edison) done is found someone with a tremendous amount of
technical credibility to put on the board."

Although coincidental, the Wilkinson appointment began a string of favorable developments:

- In late March, the NRC approved a full power license
  for LaSalle County Unit 2;
- About the same time, a report by NRC staff investiga-
  tors declared that the ASLB made "a clear error of
  judgment" in denying an operating license to Byron;
- In August, the NRC's Midwest regional director,
  James Keppler, testified before the ASLB Appeal Board
  that he and his staff had confidence in the quality of

427

Byron's construction, but "we did not do a very good job of articulating that confidence to the (first) board." Keppler said he and his people had been preoccupied with the problems at Zimmer and the Midland plant in Michigan;

- Another NRC official, reactor inspector Kavin Ward, testified that Byron is "probably the safest plant there is because of all the reinspection they've gone through;"
- A *Tribune* editorial concluded that "what the NRC needs to do at this point is to establish some clearly articulated rules and procedures that utilities can follow to build plants. The present system is costing the government, the utilities and the public billions of dollars with no apparent return on the investment."

Finally, in mid-October, the ASLB reversed its earlier ruling and recommended that Byron 1 be granted a license, an action the NRC took two weeks later. Station employes immediately began loading fuel into the reactor in preparation for startup testing. O'Connor pointed out that even with the additional costs due to the delay, Byron would be among the least expensive nuclear plants being built anywhere in the country and that Unit 1 alone would return $185 million in fuel savings to customers every year.

"We were vindicated, but you're never totally vindicated," the chairman said in retrospect. "You still live with it. Your reputation is like a piece of china; once cracked it's never completely mended."

The startup of Byron, in turn, began another string of good news stories:

- A credit rating agency raised its debt rating on Edison's bonds by two notches, reversing 11 years of consecutive downgradings. The agency explained that it based its action on Edison's progress toward completing its nuclear construction program;
- A highly favorable article in *Forbes* magazine contrasted Edison's "nuclear power success story" with "all those nuclear power horror stories," and concluded that "Edison's nuclear power stations will generate some of the lowest-cost new power in the U.S.;

- Edison signed a 30-year contract for nuclear fuel enrichment services with the U.S. Department of Energy which company officials estimated would save customers more than $1 billion over the life of the agreement.

IV

In late summer Edison began the pioneering effort to flush radioactive sediments from Dresden Unit 1's water and steam system. The $50 million project, the first full-scale reactor decontamination in the world, utilized 9,500 gallons of special solvent to dissolve a contaminated residue the thickness of cellophane. The chemical cleaning served as Dresden 1's swan song. Edison decided to retire the veteran, which had not generated power since 1978, rather than spend an estimated $300 million to bring it into compliance with present NRC regulations. O'Connor provided the epitaph: "Unit 1 began life as a pioneer, and it's closing out its years of service as a pioneer."

The continuing construction of Byron 2 and Braidwood 1 and 2 further demonstrated just how much nuclear regulation had changed over the years. Edison delayed the completion dates of Byron 2 and Braidwood 1 by six months and Braidwood 2 by eight months, raising the cost of each twin-unit facility to $4.18 billion and $4.11 billion, respectively. The company explained that time and manpower had to be diverted from Byron Unit 2 to help resolve the license controversy over Unit 1, and that it would conduct a top-to-bottom reassessment of Braidwood to make certain that it did not suffer the same indignity as Byron 1.

Not content with the ICC's rulings in 1980 and 1982 that Braidwood should be completed, the company's longtime antagonist, BPI, succeeded in having the Commission reopen the issue. BPI again argued that it would be cheaper for Edison to cancel the plant than complete it; Edison continued to maintain the opposite. "It is quite simply too late to stop the Braidwood plant," the *Tribune* editorialized. "The ICC has twice authorized Edison to complete the facility and was fooled into reopening the issue again this year.

"It should put its foot down now or it may still be listening to lawyers argue about cost-benefit analyses when the power lines from Braidwood begin to hum." The commission did no such thing, and Round Three began as the units approached the 90 and 60 percent complete marks.

Another ongoing debate that threatened to last longer than the Broadway run of "Hello, Dolly" concerned the proposed World's Fair. After gaining approval for a lakefront fair from the Bureau of International Expositions (BIE), the project's organizers encountered opposition from neighborhood groups which claimed they were being excluded from the planning process. Additionally, Harold Washington, a lukewarm supporter of the fair at best, had replaced Jane Byrne as Mayor of Chicago. In March 1984 Washington, in a letter to Governor Thompson, all but ruled out any city contribution to the project's cost. Thompson replied that he could not possibly convince the state legislature to approve funding for the fair if Washington persisted in saying the city would not help. "You can't ask for and receive designation as a World's Fair city and then say, well, we'll take all the benefits but we won't pay one penny of expense," Thompson declared. Later that spring, a poll conducted by the *Sun-Times* and Channel 5 showed that two-thirds of Chicagoans favored the fair.

Edison also mapped plans for a celebration of its own, marking the company's 100th anniversary in 1987. A Centennial Committee, chaired by George Travers, began preparations that included leasing space for an Edison centennial museum. The committee also held a contest for employes to pick the centennial theme. LaSalle County Station instrument maintenance foreman David Welsh won the competition with "A Bright Past. A Brilliant Future." The committee chose Welsh's entry from nearly 1,500 suggestions submitted by more than 700 employes.

The year which had started so dismally with the denial of Byron's license looked quite good upon reflection. Not only had Byron won its license and LaSalle 2 begun operating, but Edison's nuclear units set a new company record by accounting for 54 percent of the company's total generation. The previous high, 45 percent had been recorded in 1981. Edison estimated that it would have cost an extra $885.2 million to generate the same amount of kilowatthours using low-sulfur coal, the next lowest cost alternative. In March, an independent audit ordered by the ICC found that Byron was being built at less cost and in shorter time than comparable nuclear generating stations by a company that "has made a strong corporate commitment to assuring quality in its nuclear construction and operations." Edison officials were delighted with the two-volume study by the management consulting firm of Arthur D. Little, Inc., which found that Byron 1 was built at 27 percent less cost per kilowatt ($1,682 vs. $2,297) and in 15 percent less time (9.17 vs 10.73 years) than comparable plants. Edison had been concerned about the outcome of the audit, because similar studies at other plants elsewhere in the country had resulted in sharp criticism of construction practices and recommendations that certain expenditures be disallowed from the utility's rate base. The report also challenged a practice by nuclear critics and some members of the media of comparing current cost figures with original estimates. "Comparing the actual cost and schedule of Byron to its original estimates is not a meaningful way to gauge the effectiveness of management," the report concluded. "The extent of regulatory changes (and the stage of the project when they occurred) and the resulting schedule extensions, inflationary cost increases, and the like render such original/final evaluations virtually meaningless for such purposes."

Edison, the ICC, and intervenors, including BPI, had mutually agreed upon A.D. Little to perform the audit. The ICC directed that the cost of the evaluation, approximately $630,000, be paid by Edison.

Two of the principal architects of Edison's nuclear program, Ayers and Corey, officially ended nearly a half-century with the company at the April 19 annual meeting when they stepped down as directors after reaching the mandatory retirement age of 70. Ayers continued to serve as chairman of the Chicago World's Fair-1992 Authority and to pursue other civic activities, while Corey, in addition to his ongoing civic and charitable endeavors, went to work as an independent utility consultant. Byron Lee and Bide Thomas replaced them on the board.

That spring and summer Edison faced new challenges from two different directions—restless municipal and industrial customers and restless members of the General Assembly. In the dawning of what O'Connor called "the new age of competition," the far west suburban city of Geneva, population less than 10,000, announced that it would disconnect from the Edison system in May 1986 and begin buying electricity from Wisconsin Electric Power Company. Geneva, along with Batavia, Naperville, St. Charles, and Rock Falls, had operated their own municipal distribution system for years, purchasing all of their power wholesale from Edison. Two other communities, Winnetka and Rochelle, generate their own electricity and rely on Edison for partial or backup power. For years, the so-called River Towns had contended that Edison overcharged them. Geneva ultimately elected to break away after Edison had agreed, as part of a legal settlement, to let the River Towns use its lines for a fee to import power, provided the towns gave the company one year's notice of their intention to leave. Spurred on by Geneva's announcement, Edison negotiated new two-year contracts with Batavia, Naperville, and St. Charles, which the communities said would save millions of dollars in electricity costs. "We'd like to keep them all as customers," said Edison vice president George Rifakes. "It's in everyone's best interest."

In the industrial sector, some customers went out of business or departed for other parts of the country, while still others explored the feasibility of generating their own power through co-generation, a long-understood process of using heat from a manufacturing function to produce electricity. In an effort to retain industrial customers and jobs and to stimulate investment growth in the service territory, Edison in September proposed a Jobs Preservation Rate which provided discounts ranging from 20 to 100 percent of demand charges to qualifying industrial customers. The rate, approved by the ICC, applied only to increased electricity use, so it would not constitute a subsidy of some customers by others. "When more kilowatt-hours are spread among our customers, it means everyone pays less toward the fixed costs of supplying electricity," O'Connor explained. Edison patterned the rate after a similar one that its largest customer, Northwestern Steel and Wire Co. of Sterling, had accepted the previous month. The steel company, with 2,200 employes, a $60 million a year payroll, and energy bills totaling nearly $3 million a month, had not shown a profit for nearly four years, a trend reversed in September. Northwestern increased its electricity usage by about 50 percent after receiving the discount rate.

Recommendations to revise the Illinois Public Utilities Act for the first time since 1922 set the stage for one of Edison's fiercest legislative battles in many years. With the Act set to expire at the end of the year, a Joint Committee on Public Utility Regulation recommended several changes which would punish utilities and their shareholders. The recommendations became Senate Bill 1021 whose most onerous provision, in the eyes of Edison, other utilities, and business organizations, called for a 25 percent cap on reserve generating capacity, with stockholders penalized for any reserve above that amount.

"Senate Bill 1021 was marketed to legislators and utility customers as a vehicle that would reduce electricity rates, while the opposite was true," O'Connor maintained. He explained that any savings would be wiped out by additional costs because the financial community would react negatively to legislation clearly designed to punish investors. Edison's position was particularly precarious because the addition of Byron and Braidwood figured to temporarily push the company above the 25 percent mark.

Edison argued that passage of S.B. 1021 would increase its financing costs. "Using a modest one percent increase as a benchmark," O'Connor continued, "we calculated that higher equity costs would raise rates by $110 million to $150 million in 1986 and by $4 billion over the lifetime of the generating stations now being completed.

"The state of Illinois told Edison in 1980 and 1982 to complete the generating stations under construction. Then came proponents of Senate Bill 1021 saying we should be penalized for completing them. The message . . . is that whatever the state of Illinois promises or authorizes one year it may take away in another. This is hardly a foundation for confidence."

Many groups around the state agreed. As hearings on the bill got underway, representatives of 45 organizations, including business, labor, and community groups, joined Edison in opposing the legislation, with only the City of Chicago, a charitable group, and two anti-utility organizations appearing in favor of the measure. Most of the state's leading newspapers also expressed opposition. In an unprecedented action, Edison urged its employes and shareholders to take a stand against S.B. 1021 in letters to their state legislators. The response surprised even the most optimistic company officials. Lawmakers received more than 250,000 pieces of mail urging the defeat of S.B. 1021. The blitz, along with lobbying by the company and the state's principal business organizations, partially succeeded. The House amended the bill to allow the ICC to decide on a case-by-case basis whether a utility has imprudent excess generating capacity. Other provisions opposed by the business community, including creation of an office of public counsel to join the platoon of intervenors already participating in rate proceedings, and the granting of sweeping new regulatory powers to the Appellate Court, remained intact. The bill, as amended, cleared both houses. Governor Thompson signed it into law amid predictions from all quarters that anti-utility forces would try again to impose a reserve margin cap.

Another legislative effort supported by Edison and its allies ended in defeat late in the session when House Speaker Michael Madigan declared his strong opposition to state funding of the World's Fair. Governor Thompson, the fair's chief political sponsor, promptly declared that without Madigan's support, "the fair is dead." The exposition's apparent demise touched off a round of finger-pointing by officials and post-mortems in the media.

"Using the 20–20 vision that hindsight provides," Petkus observed, "it became obvious that our strategy of creating a governmental authority in late 1983 to help finance the fair was a mistake. The authority moved several steps away from the position originally put forward by the 1992 Corporation—that the private sector and investors would finance the exposition—to a position that at least a portion of the financial risk would have to be borne by Illinois taxpayers."

Petkus also blamed the failure of the "smaller, ill-conceived" New Orleans Exposition of 1984 for the collapse of Chicago's plans. "The poor publicity surrounding the financial troubles of the New Orleans Exposition, coupled with its disappointing attendance, created a very low confidence level in the ability of the Chicago World's Fair to deliver on the benefits being forecasted."

434

Supporters of the fair did not fold up their tents after the defeat in Springfield; they merely retrenched. In December 1985 Petkus reported to a BIE meeting in Paris that the original corporation remained intact, working quietly to find other financing alternatives.

"Our first task has been to reconfirm the endorsements of all key elected officials for the exposition," Petkus told the BIE. "The only resistance we have received is from (Mayor) Harold Washington ... It is admittedly difficult to plan an exposition that will attract world-wide participation, without the full cooperation of the government of the host city." With that caveat in mind, fair planners began discussions with suburban officials and developers. Initial plans for financing the fair had failed, Petkus concluded, but the exposition itself had not. "We continue to believe that a means can be found to return our efforts to full speed ahead."

Meanwhile, Edison redoubled its community relations efforts. Under the banner "Look for the E-Team," Edison and members of the International Brotherhood of Electrical Workers (IBEW) began a program in the spring to assist lost or threatened children. The company and union introduced an information program in schools throughout the service territory, alerting teachers, parents, and the children themselves that Edison employes stand ready to help a youngster in trouble, especially if a police officer is not available. Edison reminded parents and children that it maintains 1,800 radio-equipped trucks, 1,650 service representative cars, and 22 office buildings to which a child can turn in an emergency. The Illinois Association of School Boards along with numerous educators and community leaders enthusiastically endorsed the E-Team concept.

For the first time ever, the ranks of the line crews that made up an integral part of the E-Team included a woman. In June 1985, Laurie Teska of Bolingbrook District became Edison's first female lineman after completing a rigorous training course that qualified her to handle lines of up to 600 volts. Teska enjoyed the team concept and physical challenge of the work; her male counterparts found her to be an excellent worker, someone who can be counted on.

The contribution of Edison land for recreational activities represents a community program of longstanding duration.

435

After the longtime sparkplug of that effort, assistant real estate director Al Heidecke, died in December 1984, his friends and colleagues at the Illinois Department of Conservation (IDOC) sought a way to honor their trusted partner in the quest for more outdoor recreational space. The following June, at the request of IDOC, Edison renamed Collins Lake "Heidecke State Fish and Wildlife Area," the first time an Illinois state park had been named for an employe of a private company and the first time Edison had allowed the use of an employe's name for one of its facilities. Heidecke had been instrumental in opening Collins Lake to public fishing in 1980 and in negotiating a long-term management and operation lease with IDOC.

Later that summer the mainland Chinese came calling. A high level delegation of about 20 officials, led by Vice-Premier Li Peng, toured Braidwood as part of a nuclear technology shopping trip which they hoped would enable them to build eight nuclear generating stations by the year 2000. The visit to Braidwood, the only American nuclear station on their itinerary, followed the signing of agreements with the United States including one that would permit American firms to build peaceful nuclear energy facilities in China. Members of the delegation received hardhats with Braidwood logos, and Li told reporters that the American people can be secure with the level of safety he observed at the plant.

General Public Utilities (GPU) and the NRC issued similar assurances in early October as the utility restarted the undamaged Three Mile Island reactor, six-and-one-half years after the accident to its sister unit. Rulings by the U.S. Supreme Court and a federal appeals court in Philadelphia removed the last legal roadblocks by nuclear opponents. People on the streets of Middletown, Pennsylvania conducted business as usual as the 800-megawatt Unit 1 underwent a testing process at gradually escalating power levels. Nuclear industry spokesmen hailed the restart as a significant victory and a turning point toward better times.

The restlessness in the River Towns spread to the biggest river town in the territory in October when the city of Chicago delcared that it would investigate means of removing some or all customer demand from the Edison system. Complaining of rising energy costs, Mayor Washington directed a task force to look into four options: creating a municipal utility, leasing Edison lines to transmit electricity purchased from other utilities, building refuse-fueled power plants to serve municipal properties, and buying Edison's two coal-fired plants in the city, Fisk and Crawford Stations. The company reacted coolly. Petkus pointed out that the cost of Edison's distribution facilities alone would be at least $5 billion and the two plants another $226 million. He questioned whether the city, which chronically encounters trouble making ends meet, could raise the needed amounts. Petkus added that Edison was not legally required to wheel power to municipalities which did not own their own distribution systems. He cited the option of burning city refuse in a municipal power plant as the most promising. Although city officials stated that their annual electricity bill had reached $32 million, Petkus countered with the fact that Chicago in 1984 received $140 million in corporate taxes from Edison, tax revenue that obviously would vanish if the city totally disconnected from the utility. The Edison vice president suggested that the company's corporate headquarters might vanish as well. "If, in fact, we didn't serve Chicago—well, it wouldn't really make much sense to be a member of a community you don't serve," he observed.

The city's announcement received a good news, bad news judgment from the *Tribune*: "Mayor Washington's administration has some good ideas for creating competition for Commonwealth Edison in order to cut electrical costs," an editorial stated. "But the proposal to form a new power company run by the city is so dimwitted that it casts the others into the shadows." Somewhere, Sam Insull was chuckling over *deja vu*.

The possible defection of municipal and industrial customers—together with reduced revenues owing to one of the coolest summers on record, the passage of costly or potentially costly state legislation, anticipated changes in the federal tax laws that would increase the company's liability by hundreds of millions of dollars, and the desire to reduce or postpone future rate increases needed to complete the construction program—caused Edison to embark on its most intensive austerity progam since the depression. The company set an ultimate goal of zero growth in operating expense budgets from 1986 through 1988. To help accomplish the goal, Edison declared a freeze on upper and middle management salaries, a freeze on all hiring, restrictions on overtime work, and established a task force under Vice President Kavanagh to investigate and recommend all feasible cost-cutting measures. It further cancelled company-wide conferences and dropped most plans for the centennial celebration, including those for an Edison museum. Edison emphasized that the austerity program would not affect stock dividends, but the company did not rule out the possibility of layoffs, an action not taken even during the depression.

O'Connor went before the video camera to explain to employes that the company did not face a financial crisis but did need to make some basic corrections in response to the rapidly changing business environment. He said Edison would re-examine the economics of continuing to operate some fossil-fueled generating stations and all options concerning the construction program, ranging from acceleration to delay or stoppage of work on some units. Also under review: the possibility of consolidating some division and district operations.

"We felt that to be intellectually honest in our approach, we had to look at every possibility," O'Connor told a newspaper reporter, who in turn wrote that opponents of Edison's construction program were "jubilant" over the austerity program. Any jubilation ended three weeks later when the ICC granted Edison a $494.8 million rate increase, approximately 90 percent of the amount requested. Nearly all of the increase constituted the cost of placing Byron 1 in service. Two-thirds of the boost was to go into effect almost immediately, the remaining one-third on January 1, 1987. The commission vote, 4–3, represented the narrowest margin ever in an Edison rate case. Under the ICC order, overall revenue would increase by 11 percent, residential by 14.7 percent, with most of the latter applied to summer rates. Beginning in 1987, summer rates would stand about twice as high as non-summer rates, a fact that displeased customers and Edison alike. On the one hand, company surveys had continually found higher summer rates to be extremely unpopular with consumers. On the other, Edison's annual revenues now would become far more dependent on weather than ever before. The four summer months would represent, in effect, a make-or-break period. Within days of the decision, Edison announced that it would file a request with the ICC to narrow the gap between summer and non-summer rates.

Almost overlooked in the ensuing publicity over the decision was the minimal increase in non-summer rates—4.2 percent initially, a figure trimmed even further by current fuel adjustment credits. More than six months would elapse before customers would begin seeing the heavier end of the increase. Nevertheless, headlines proclaimed "Electric Bills to Soar...," "Com Ed gets whopping rate hike," and "Electric bills will leap." Many customers cringed as they opened their next bills—only to find them comparatively modest.

Although the ICC staff and the rate case hearing examiner had recommended separately that Edison receive increases similar to the final amount—recommendations that were well publicized—the commission's decision drew cries of surprise and anguish from politicians and the public.

For several frantic days following the decision, the three major candidates for governor—Republican incumbent Thompson, Democratic Attorney General Hartigan, and former Democratic U.S. Senator Adlai Stevenson—engaged in a contest of one-upmanship in denouncing the increase. Hartigan blamed Thompson for the increase because the governor had appointed the ICC members. Stevenson blamed both of the others—Thompson because of the appointments and Hartigan for allegedly not fighting hard enough when the request was before the Commission. The governor said *he* spoke out first against the decision and stressed the independence of the ICC. Thompson and Hartigan, whose offices had been parties to the case, appealed to the commission to overturn its decision. The ICC rejected the overtures by the same 4–3 vote. The two officials then appealed to the Cook County Circuit Court, which had never reversed an electric rate decision by the ICC.

Edison's new five-year construction budget, unveiled in mid-November, told of new delays in starting up Byron 2 and Braidwood 1 and 2. The company rescheduled Byron 2 and Braidwood 1 for service in May 1987, a postponement of seven months, and Braidwood 2 for September 1988, a nine-month delay. At the same time, Edison raised the cost estimate of Braidwood to $5.05 billion from $4.107 billion, and Byron by $281 million, to $4.65 billion. The company attributed much of the extension and cost increases at Byron to time and effort diverted from Unit 2 construction to efforts to obtain Unit 1's operating license in the wake of the ASLB denial. At Braidwood, where BPI and other anti-nuclear activists contested the operating license, the ASLB had admitted a string of quality assurance contentions—six years after the filing deadline, assuring lengthy hearings.

"It became clear to me," said Braidwood Project Manager Mike Wallace, "that the time and attention of senior Commonwealth Edison project managers could not be effectively allocated between the competing demands of completing project construction and supporting the litigation of the QA contention. It was therefore necessary to make significant revisions to overall project priorities."

Simultaneously—some might say duplicitously—BPI argued before the ICC that Edison should scrap the plant because it had become too costly and was taking too long to build.

Following the Byron denial, Edison had resolved to do everything in its power to avoid a recurrence at Braidwood. There evolved a massive assessment of construction practices, the Braidwood Construction Assessment Program (BCAP), whose results, made public two days before Thanksgiving, showed no safety deficiencies. The assessment, monitored continuously by the NRC staff and a team of independent technical experts, lasted 17 months and considered more than 650,000 plant attributes to make certain that hardware conformed to safety-related design requirements. Less than two percent of the plant attributes covered in BCAP revealed any discrepancies, and none of those was design-significant. "Stated differently," the report noted, "even if any or all of these discrepancies remained undetected and uncorrected, the plant could be operated without undue risk to the health and safety of the public."

Preliminary results of another Edison study, begun in conjunction with the austerity program, showed that Braidwood and Byron 2 still should be completed as soon as possible, reaffirming the ICC's decisions of 1980 and 1982. Even with the recent increases, the per-kilowatt costs of Byron 2 and Braidwood remained lower than those of nearly all other nuclear plants under construction in the nation. Updated studies, reflecting the latest changes in Braidwood's cost and completion dates, showed that completing the plant would ultimately save ratepayers an estimated $2.7 billion.

V

As 1985 drew to a close, Edison savored two additional items of good news: for the second consecutive year, nuclear power production exceeded one-half of total generation, and for the fifth year in a row, the market price of the company's common stock closed higher than at the end of the previous year. Yet as many uncertainties as ever, particularly in the regulatory arena, loomed on the horizon:

- Braidwood's future remained firmly in the hands of the ICC and the NRC;
- The chairman of the ICC, Philip O'Connor (no relation to James), who supported Edison's October rate order, resigned effective Dec. 15 and was replaced by Commissioner Mary Bushnell, one of three members who voted against the increase and an early opponent of Byron Station;
- The ICC, in turn, chose its first executive director who would exercise broad powers under the rewritten Public Utilities Act;
- Edison recognized that additional rate relief would be required to complete the construction program and sought non-traditional formulas to lessen the burden on customers;
- Utility rates and regulation again promised to become an issue in the 1986 election campaigns;
- The chairman of the NRC, Nunzio Palladino, announced his retirement, effective in the spring of 1986, with no successor named immediately;*
- Revision of the federal tax laws, with adverse effects for capital intensive industries such as electric utilities, remained a strong possibility;
- Less regulation and more competition among utilities appeared certain as Edison considered diversification into related fields on a limited basis;
- And the consolidation of Chicago Central and Chicago North divisions, as part of the ongoing austerity pro-

---

*President Reagan subsequently appointed NRC Commissioner Lando Zech, a retired Navy vice admiral, to the chairmanship.

gram, promised savings of $14.5 million annually but raised understandable concerns among some employes.

Edison, of course, exercises only limited ability to shape developments outside its control. The company understood that one of its best opportunities to manage its future lay with the austerity program, whose direction—and ultimate success or failure—would set the tone of the last months of the first 100 years and the beginning of the second century.

The ability to prevail over adversity has been the hallmark of Commonwealth Edison throughout its existence—from Sam Insull and an initially skeptical Fred Sargent, challenging the conventional engineering wisdom that said Fisk Unit 1 couldn't be built, to an injured Bill Nicholl and his co-workers, displaying personal courage to bring Edison's worst generating station accident under control—from Willis Gale, resurrecting the company from the Insull Crash and bringing it into the Nuclear Age, to Murray Joslin and his cadre of young engineers, showing the world that the most horrible weapon ever devised could foster a technology to supply economical electric power—from Bob Manning's Chicago Central team and their colleagues at Fisk, Crawford, Tech Center, and the other divisions, improvising to overcome a one-in-a-million outage, to Tom Ayers, Jim O'Connor, and the Project Management team, demonstrating not only that Edison could recover from Three Mile Island, but still could build the best and among the least expensive nuclear generating stations in the country.

As always, people hold the key to the future, O'Connor declared:

"Over time we have attracted extremely able people who find Edison a very challenging and exciting place to work, people who have a high degree of confidence in themselves and in the abilities of their colleagues. A brilliant future won't happen by itself. People will have to make it happen. Working together, we can have the best utility system in the world, provide reliable energy at a very competitive price, remain in a strong position for a lot of years to come, and continue to be the proud successors of previous generations of Edison employes who have entrusted such a rich legacy to us."

442

Bibliography

Commonwealth Edison Company *History of Commonwealth Edison Company and predecessor companies: 1887-1934.* I.C.C. Rate Hearings, 1934.

Costello, John *Marketing History of Commonwealth Edison.* Commonwealth Edison Co., 1975.

Dedmon, Emmett *Fabulous Chicago.* Expanded Edition. Atheneum, 1981.

Farr, Finis *Chicago.* Arlington House, 1973.

Forbes, B. C. *Men Who Made America Great.* Forbes Publishing Co., 1917.

Galbraith, John Kenneth *The New Industrial State.* Houghton Mifflin, 1967.

Hertsgaard, Mark *Nuclear, Inc.: The men and money behind the nuclear power industry.* Pantheon Books, 1983.

Hughes, Thomas P. *Networks of Power: Electrification in Western Society, 1880-1930.* Johns Hopkins University Press, 1983.

Hyman, Leonard S. *America's Electric Utilities: Past, Present & Future.* Public Utilities Reports, Inc., 1983.

Insull, Samuel *Central-station electric service: Its commercial development and economic significance as set forth in the public addresses (1897-1914).* Ed. with an introduction by William Eugene Keily. Private printing, 1915.

Kolflat, Alf *The Sargent & Lundy Story.* Private printing, n.d.

Lohr, Lenox *Fair Management: The story of a Century of Progress Exposition.* Cuneo Press, 1952.

Manchester, William *The Glory and the Dream.* Little, Brown and Company, 1973.

McCullough, David *The Great Bridge.* Simon & Schuster, 1972.

McDonald, Forrest *Insull.* The University of Chicago Press, 1962.

National Electric Light Association *How Commonwealth Edison Company Works.* N.E.L.A., 1914.

Rice, J. F. "History of Commonwealth Edison Company." Photocopy, 1952.

Seaborg, Glenn T., Corliss, William R. *Man and Atom: Building a New World Through Nuclear Technology.* E. P. Dutton, 1971.

Seymour, H. A. "History of the Commonwealth Edison Company." Typescript, 1934.

Talese, Gay *The Kingdom and the Power.* The New American Library, Inc., 1969.

Wade, Richard C. & Mayer, Harold M. *Chicago: Growth of a Metropolis.* University of Chicago Press, 1973.

Whetstone, Imogene E. *Historical factors in the development of Northern Illinois and its utilities.* Public Service Company of Northern Illinois, 1928.

443

Index

449

450